THE ART
OF PHILOSOPHY

THE ART
OF PHILOSOPHY

An Introductory Reader

Edited by

FRED A. WESTPHAL
University of Miami (Florida)

PRENTICE-HALL, INC., Englewood Cliffs, New Jersey

Printed in the United States of America

ISBN: 0-13-048025-8

Library of Congress Catalog Card No.: 78-38042

10   9   8   7   6   5   4   3   2   1

Prentice-Hall International, Inc. (*London*)
Prentice-Hall of Australia, Pty. Ltd. (*Sydney*)
Prentice-Hall of Canada, Ltd.(*Toronto*)
Prentice-Hall of India Private Limited (*New Delhi*)
Prentice-Hall of Japan, Inc. (*Tokyo*)

For Grace and Morris
and in memory of my father and mother

CONTENTS

Preface   page xi

WHAT IS PHILOSOPHY? I
page 1

1. The Opportunity of Philosophy
   Brand Blanshard   3

2. Philosophy As Conceptual Analysis
   Alan R. White   16

THE PROBLEM OF GOD: II
Does a Perfect Person Exist? page 25

3. Theology and Falsification
   Antony Flew/R. M. Hare/Basil Mitchell   27

4. Anselm's Ontological Arguments
   Norman Malcolm   34

5. Aquinas' Proof from Necessary Being
   Etienne Gilson   41

6. The Argument from Apparent Design
   David Hume   44

7. A Contemporary Form of the Design Argument
   Richard Taylor   51

8. The Problem of Evil
   J. L. Mackie   57

9. The Meaning of Life
   Kurt Baier   68

THE PROBLEM
OF MIND AND IMMORTALITY: III
Can I Survive the Death of My Body? page 75

10. Can a Man Witness His Own Funeral?
    Antony Flew   77

11. Man As Two Different Substances
    René Descartes   85

12. Persons and Their Bodies
    Jerome Shaffer   95

13. The Privacy of the Mental
    C. J. Ducasse   99

14. Mind As Dispositions to Behave
    Gilbert Ryle   102

15. Language and Mind: Wittgenstein's Critique of Dualism
    A. M. Quinton   110

16. The Mental and the Physical As Identical
    J. J. C. Smart   114

17. A Critique of the Identity Theory
    Norman Malcolm   120

THE PROBLEM OF FREE ACTION:
Am I Ever Justly Held Responsible for Any of My Actions? page 129

IV

18. The Range of Human Freedom
    John Hospers   131

19. Avoidability and Responsibility
    Roderick Chisholm   135

20. All Choices Are Predetermined
    P. H. D. d'Holbach   138

21. Some Choices Are Not Predetermined
    C. A. Campbell   147

22. A Pragmatic Argument Against Determinism
    William James   157

23. The Unpredictability of Choices
    D. M. MacKay   162

24. An Attempt to Reconcile Determinism
    and Moral Responsibility   *P. H. Nowell-Smith* 168

25. Reasons for Actions Distinguished from
    Causes of Actions   *S. I. Benn/R. S. Peters*   175

THE PROBLEM OF MORALITY:
Can I Know What Is Morally Right? page 181

V

26. Ethical Relativism
    Paul Taylor   183

27. Egoism in Ethics
    Kai Nielsen   195

28. Right Acts As Those Which Produce the
    Most Happiness   *John Stuart Mill*   204

29. Right Acts As Those Which Conform to
    Optimific Rules   *John Rawls*   214

30. Right Acts As Those Which Are Universalizable
    Immanuel Kant   223

31. What If Everyone Did That?   234
     Colin Strang

32. Moral Obligations As Self-Evident
     W. D. Ross   241

33. A Critique of Ethical Intuitionism
     P. F. Strawson   252

34. Why Be Moral?
     Kurt Baier   258

35. Can the Moral Point of View Be Justified?
     J. C. Thornton   263

36. Racism
     R. M. Hare   265

37. War
     Richard Wasserstrom   272

38. Civil Disobedience
     John Rawls   282

THE PROBLEM OF KNOWLEDGE:
When Am I Justified in Claiming to Know? page 295

VI

39. Knowledge As the Right to Be Sure
     A. J. Ayer   297

40. Some Problems with Defining Knowledge As
     "Justified True Belief" *Edmund Gettier*   301

41. The *A Priori* and the Empirical
     A. C. Ewing   304

42. Knowledge As Indubitable Belief
     René Descartes   314

43. Can the Principle of Induction Be Justified?
     Bertrand Russell   318

44. Attempts to Justify Induction Are Mistaken
     P. F. Strawson   324

45. Physical Objects As Nothing but Perceptions
     George Berkeley   327

46. Physical Objects As Not Reducible to Perceptions
     C. H. Whiteley   336

47. The Objects of Perception Are Not Sense-Data
     J. L. Austin   344

PREFACE

I take it that an introductory philosophy course is designed to accomplish at least three goals: (1) Clarify the nature of philosophical problems, their importance, and their roots in human experience. (2) Provide the beginning student-philosopher with some comprehensible, representative forms of philosophical reasoning. He should have before him examples of how more experienced and seasoned thinkers have responded to the challenge of philosophical issues. (3) Stimulate and encourage the student-philosopher to exercise his own critical and creative powers in the activity of philosophy.

One of the most frustrating tasks facing the introductory philosophy teacher is deciding what he should have his students read so that maximum progress can be made in realizing these goals. Unless wise choices are made here, the result will be more confusion than clarification, and interest in doing philosophy may well be stifled. If the student is served only "primary source" readings, that is, the writings of the philosophers themselves without accompanying commentary or explanatory guides, bewilderment and confusion are likely to result for all but a handful of beginning students. On the other hand, a diet which consists solely of "secondary source" reading, that is, commentary and explanation by a single author, runs the risk

xi

of not only distorting the arguments of philosophers but, more importantly, of failing to provide the student with first-hand knowledge of how philosophy is actually done.

It is the conviction of many introductory philosophy teachers that a mixed diet of "primary" and "secondary" material stands the best chance of preventing what could be called "intellectual indigestion." In one's first encounter with philosophy one's portions should be not only small enough to chew and digest, but also reasonably palatable to the understanding.

In order to provide the student-philosopher with some guidance before and as he reads the philosophers for himself, several years ago I wrote *The Activity of Philosophy*. That book, however, was never intended as a substitute for the real article—the writings of thoughtful and seasoned minds which have grappled with the incredibly complex and difficult questions of philosophy. This collection of essays and selections will hopefully be a useful and versatile companion not only to *The Activity of Philosophy* but to other single author introductory texts as well.

THE ART
OF PHILOSOPHY

WHAT IS PHILOSOPHY?

I

1. THE OPPORTUNITY OF PHILOSOPHY

Brand Blanshard

Brand Blanshard (1892–   ) is Professor Emeritus at Yale. He is a past president of the American Philosophical Association and a Fellow of the British Academy. Blanshard's major work is The Nature of Thought *(1939).* Reason and Analysis *(1962) and* Reason and Goodness *(1961) are his most recent works. Blanshard is a philosopher with an uncommonly lucid writing style, to which the following essay will attest.*

One of the main agenda of philosophers in all times and places has been the disclosure of unity in diversity. For example, philosophers have been convinced immemorially that certain principles of evidence and proof are valid equally for every subject and every mind, and they have formulated and systematized these principles in the science of logic. It has been one of their cherished ends to perform a like service for artistic and literary criticism. They have held that to assert responsibly of anything that it is beautiful is covertly to "assert the possibility and goodness of our own experience for every rational imagination," [1] and thus to set ourselves, if we reflect, upon the search for common standards.

More pertinent, perhaps, to the special needs of the present is the search of philosophy for common standards of behavior. To the present-day student, with countless and curious anthropological findings spread out before him, it seems as if, on the major issues of conduct, every conceivable practice had been somewhere or other approved; and the inference is tempting that there is nothing right or wrong but thinking makes it so. When he finds this conclusion accepted by sociologists like Sumner and Westermarck, whose learning was perhaps in advance of their philosophic discernment, his first feeling is one of liberation. He likes the tolerance of the new view, its sophistication, and its freedom from conceit and dogmatism. At the same time he believes with all his

From "The Opportunity of Philosophy" by Brand Blanshard in Philosophy in America, *Edited by Charles W. Hendel, Brand Blanshard et al., Copyright, 1945 by Harper & Row, Publishers, Inc., pp. 101–117. Reprinted by permission of the publishers.*

[1] E. F. Carritt, *The Theory of Beauty*, III, 2nd ed., revised. London: Methuen Company, Ltd., 1923. (New York: Macmillan Company, 1914.)

heart that democracy is superior to nazism, not in his own prejudices alone but really, that in the disputes of peoples there is a right and just course to be found, and that the hope of the world lies in some impartial body which shall undertake to find it. Thus his thought on ultimate matters of conduct is muddled. Now, the cure for such muddled thought is more thought, not in the form of collecting more cases, but rather of that sensitive self-scrutiny which looks into one's own meanings. When we seem to differ about ultimate goods, do we really have the same goods in mind? And if we do have the same goods in mind, do we not always value them in the same way? Socrates, confronting a confusion and relativism strikingly like our own, believed that we did. He believed that the nearer we came to understanding what we meant by the true and the good, the nearer we came to understanding each other, since in the end we all meant the same. What was deepest in each was common to all. And philosophy was the midwife which brought the hidden meanings to light. So teaching, he set the course of Western thought.

That thought in turn gives us our conclusion regarding the demand we are now considering, the demand that philosophy should supply some set of common standards and principles, some intellectual idiom that will make discussion, understanding, and a measure of common judgment possible among educated men. For such an office philosophy is the inevitable nominee, by reason both of its nature and of its inveterate bent. Whether it can do the job in practice depends, of course, on far more than this ideal fitness. It depends partly on the hearing philosophers are allowed to receive, partly also on their own attitude toward their work. Are they really interested in the fields—politics, taste, religion, morals—where common convictions on ultimate matters are important and needed? Or are they more interested in grinding their weapons to razor sharpness and making impressive play with them?

PHILOSOPHER, HEAL THYSELF

Here we come upon a criticism of philosophers which we saw to be one of those most frequently offered: they never agree. They seem to differ on everything. Jacques Maritain accepts an extensive religious creed of which Bertrand Russell accepts no single article. John Dewey holds views on the nature of knowledge, mind, and truth which differ radically from W. P. Montague's, who on all these points differs radically from W. E. Hocking, while Morris Cohen again differs from all of them on each several point. Is there not something absurd in asking philosophers to supply common standards and principles when they cannot agree among themselves? Such widespread difference of opinion on cardinal points, it is said, would bring any of the sciences into discredit; should it not discredit philosophy too?

The answer here is not simple, so we may well set it out somewhat formally. (1) Philosophers do differ on fundamental issues more often and more conspicuously than scientists do. (2) This does not spring chiefly from incompetence or contentiousness, but from the character of their inquiry. (a) Scientists often differ about what is *true* and what is *proved*; philosophers also differ about what is *truth* and what is *proof*. Science lives within a great framework of assumptions regarding logic and the theory of knowledge, which by an old and sound convention it takes for granted. It is a prime function of philosophy to *refuse* to take these assumptions for granted; and in investigating them it develops many differences which science avoids. Such differences are inevitable, and philosophers are not to be blamed for divisions that others escape only by avoiding the problems which give rise to them. (b) The problems of philosophy, if handled with professional seriousness, are of inordinate difficulty. (i) They are so linked up with each other that in order to solve one it may be necessary to solve half a dozen others along with it. The truth about the existence of God, for example, is bound up in the most intimate way with the truth about causality, freedom, infinity, evil, and the nature and status of values. (ii) The ideas dealt with by the technical philosopher call for a high degree of abstraction. No one has any trouble in thinking of an event, but let him try to think of time as such or in the abstract, and he will find it a different story. (iii) Nor does the difficulty lie only in the abstractness of such ideas. It lies also in the fact that empirical check by observation and instrument is commonly out of the question. When we differ about the properties of sodium, we can settle the matter by experiment, on whose visible results all agree. When we differ about the nature of justice, our ultimate test is our own meaning, which, as anyone who has tried it will testify, is inordinately hard to capture. (3) Because we lack empirical tests, the same word may mean different things in different mouths, in which case Smith's assertion that X is A and Jones's assertion that it is B may not be a difference of opinion at all, but a mere difference in their use of "X." Countless philosophical disputes have in this fashion been verbal merely. (4) Many of the philosopher's problems are such as to engage deeply his desires and fears. No one is stirred by a secret passion to think that the triangle inscribed in a semicircle is other than a right angle; but it would be a cold or stupid man who was *not* tempted by desire to think one way rather than the other about materialism or the survival of death. Though philosophers are more aware than most others of the dangers here, it is idle to suppose that they either do or can escape them wholly. Indeed there is one irrational tendency which may be said to form their special occupational risk. Since independent and rigorous thinking is their profession, they take a natural satisfaction in anything that gives evidence to themselves or others that they are proficient in this high calling. Now there is nothing suggestive of such proficiency in merely saying "ditto" to someone else. But to show that some other philosopher, preferably one of great name, has been shockingly loose in his use of terms, has lumped together what are really distinct, and has made references worse than dubious, does carry the implication that one is a pretty formidable fellow oneself. One is challenging a redoubtable adversary at his own difficult game. This "pride of the instrument," which has led philosophers to make much of their points of difference and little of their points of agreement, would seem to be not uncommon, but it is clearly something to be deprecated both as abetting disunity and as creating an impression of even more disunity than there is.

PHILOSOPHY IS NOT ALL DISAGREEMENT

Our appraisal of the charge of disunity has so far combined admission with palliation. We must now go on to point out that there is far more agreement among philosophers than the critics insinuate. (5) Agreement as to what is false is often as important as agreement regarding truth, and all sorts of religious superstitions, political fallacies, and ethical monstrosities that have at one time or another prevailed upon the public have not only been rejected with one voice by the philosophers, but have largely disappeared in consequence of that rejection. *Si monumentum requiris, circumspice.* The very world of the modern mind, with the freedom it carries with it from irrational fanaticisms and fears is due, in the main, to the rise and influence of that rationalism, that insistence on reasonableness in belief and conduct, of which philosophy is the purest exemplar. That at any particular time philosophers have been less than unanimous in their rejection of charlatanism and folly may well be true; rationality is always a matter of degree. But it remains true that the very spirit of rational inquiry which has made them so ready to differ among themselves has tended in every age to draw them together into a united and formidable front against the darker varieties of contemporary unreason.

(6) The fact is—and this is our final point in appraising the charge—that however widely philosophers differ in their individual convictions they are pretty largely at one as to method. They would all, or nearly all, insist alike on proportioning belief to evidence, distinguish relevant from irrelevant evidence in the same way, form and develop their hypotheses in the same way, and test them in the same way. Of course they argue with each other vehemently about

method, as they do about everything else. But it would be a mistake to take their differences here at face value. For if their division over method were really fundamental, they could not even argue with profit; argument implies a common logic and a common court of appeal. What were fallacies for Aristotle remain fallacies for John Dewey. Indeed if, in Elysium, Aristotle and Dewey ever meet over their ambrosia with St. Thomas, Hegel, and Bertrand Russell, the complaint of the attendant spirits is not likely to be that, finding each other unintelligible, they sat in silence and parted early, but rather that they found an understanding so long awaited that talk and laughter went on incontinently till after dusk fell over Olympus.

THE DEMAND FOR A SUBSTITUTE FOR FAITH

We turn now to another demand upon philosophy, and since space is limited, we may appraise along with it a frequent and cognate criticism. Philosophy, the criticism runs, is too negative, too destructive, too infertile of positive and generous beliefs. Philosophy, according to the demand, must be looked to as the main resource for filling the vacant place left by vanishing religious belief. These attitudes are less inconsistent than they seem, since in many cases the criticism is only a preliminary bit of chiding designed to prepare for the exhortation that follows. Together they constitute what is perhaps the most deeply felt appeal that philosophers are receiving.

The ground for this appeal is usually the belief that American youth are lacking in basic convictions and larger loyalties. The evidence offered for this belief is sometimes the contrast between the ardent willingness of fascist and communist youth to do and suffer for their principles and the apathy and bickering that were so widespread before the war on the democratic side. More frequently, however, the evidence used is drawn from the waning of religious conviction. The complaint is continually made that our young men and women "do not believe anything." What this means is really twofold. It is partly that the great mass of religious beliefs which form so important a part of the Christian tradition is in process of disintegration, but partly—and this is for many the chief matter for concern—that the ethical attitudes associated with these beliefs—the high sense of duty, the reverence for persons, the placing of moral above material goods—are bound to be undermined as their religious foundations crumble away.

Now that moral idealism logically rests on religious beliefs and that it is in point of fact declining in this country are both propositions which there might be some difficulty in making out. But there can be little doubt that the framework of religious belief within which Americans have traditionally lived is losing its distinctness and influence. The reason may be put in a phrase: the overwhelming prestige of science. This does not imply that the individual man has gone over the older beliefs in the light of science and one by one found them refuted. It means that the mental atmosphere created by modern science, with its preoccupation with natural processes, its penchant for the measurable, and its insistence on empirical evidence, is an atmosphere in which the traditional beliefs tend to wither away; they lose their interest, begin to seem unreal, and are then merely forgotten until one notices with surprise and a pang that they are no longer there. The slowness of the process does not mean, however, that their disappearance makes no difference. It makes an immense difference. For what has disappeared is a whole congenial world, a world in which confidence, fearlessness, and hope were natural and easy to justify. Their justification is now less obvious.

Those who deplore the waning of traditional religious belief are aware that it is not to be restored by any crusade against science. Science is entrenched immovably. But they are not without hope. They know that what gives science its power is the employment of a clear, precise, and impersonal reason. They think that if the older belief is true, it should admit of defense by that reason, and that if science will not undertake the defense, there is another reputable wielder of the same potent instrument that may be called on instead. This of course is philosophy. So they turn to the philosophers with an eager and urgent expectancy.

Can philosophy accept this assignment? No, it clearly cannot. For one thing, it would be stultified if its results were prescribed in advance; it is a process of inquiry, not of advocacy; if it is honest, it knows its own mind only at the end. Furthermore, philosophers are deeply divided about the measure of support that may be accorded to traditional belief, so that even if a philosopher here and there could subscribe to it entirely, he could speak only for himself and not for his subject. Hence if the appeal to philosophers to help youth "believe something" is an appeal to throw the weight of their discipline behind traditional faith, it is asking a kind of aid that philosophy cannot possibly render.

PHILOSOPHY AND CONSTRUCTIVE BELIEF

Does it follow that when faced by the need of youth for significant beliefs and high loyalties, philosophy has nothing to offer? Quite the contrary. The truth is . . . that philosophy has something to offer of far more value than any set of beliefs, namely, an interest and a standard from which reliable beliefs may spring.

Since we are making a large claim here, it may be well to be a little clearer what the claim is made for. When we say that philosophy, taken seriously, can confer upon youth autonomy and integrity of mind, we do not mean that one is likely to gain these from what goes on in any classroom, from Professor X's clever performances in logic, or Professor Y's well-rehearsed lectures on Descartes-to-Kant. The true philosophic spirit may be exemplified in such places, and of course the teacher is in duty bound to exemplify it so far as he can; but there is no certainty that it will strike fire. Philosophy is not a body of communicable facts, nor a set of agreed-upon doctrines, nor something that can be said or written, nor anything that can be passively received. And the person who comes to it for a compact list of finalities will go away disappointed. The philosopher, to be sure, has a set of conclusions which he tentatively holds and hopes that further reflection will allow him to go on holding. But these are not *philosophy*. Philosophy means philosophizing. It is not truth but the search for truth, a constantly baffled but passionately and stubbornly renewed pursuit of understanding. Socrates declared himself the lover, the wooer, the pursuer of truth, not the bridegroom in complacent possession. So the philosopher remains today.

Now, this interest and activity of his, though they cannot be communicated, may through tact and example be awakened in another mind; they may even take hold and persist as permanent, shaping forces of a life. And we should insist that, if they do, the student has something of far more value than any set of beliefs that could be given him, for the priceless key has been placed in his hands of the method by which all ultimate beliefs must be attained and validated. It is important, Edward Caird used to say, that a belief should be true, and it is important that it should be reasoned, but it is *more* important that it be reasoned than that it be true. A belief that is true but unreasoned is at the mercy of the sophistries of the day. A belief that is false, if it is also reflective, carries the means of its amendment with it. Thus to touch into life the student's own philosophic interest, though it provides him no ready-made beliefs, sets his feet on the road to attaining beliefs on his own, which, because they are his authentic achievements, have a vitality far greater than any that could be handed out to him. Indeed such awakening does much more. In stirring him to autonomy of mind, it helps him to maturity of mind. And it reveals to him as nothing else can the meaning of intellectual integrity.

To be sure, philosophy makes him skeptical, not in the sense of being averse to believing anything, since his passion is to know,

9

but of being suspicious of first appearances. In the presence of the countless beliefs urged by naïveté, or inertia, or fanaticism, or authority, or desire, it speaks through what W. K. Clifford called "the still small voice that murmurs 'fiddlesticks.'" And when the young man comes to apply his reflection to problems that engage men's passions, his coolness may be hard to bear. He knows that such issues as whether there is a God, whether we shall live again, whether might makes right, are not issues on which feeling is neutral; and precisely because they are so difficult to appraise dispassionately, he feels when he comes to deal with them a peculiarly stern sense of his judicial mission. If such an attitude toward belief is charged with indifference, the reply is surely easy: it is this attitude above all others that takes belief most seriously; it is this precisely whose final judgments are most deeply respected and most eagerly sought.

PHILOSOPHY AND MORAL COMMITMENT

We may be reminded that the concern of many is not so much over what is happening to traditional beliefs as over an apparent waning of ethical loyalties. Is there to be found in philosophy any bolster or substitute for these? To which the reply must be that the experience of value or the delight in it—the interest in love or beauty or goodness or power—is not for philosophy to give or withhold. Such goods spring from impulse and feeling. But here again, reason, though it cannot generate, may usefully serve as arbiter. It is part of the ancient mission of the philosopher to enter in imagination into the goods that impulse and feeling spread out, to reflect on their significance, and to appraise them as best he can in the light of experience as a whole. Indeed it is in his grasp of relative value that his wisdom is commonly thought to be best exemplified. This wisdom is not practical judgment in the narrower sense; one might appeal to it with no profit about one's plumbing or one's investments; if the story of Thales falling into the well while walking with his head in the clouds is perennially retold, it is because it is perennially in point. "We come to the philosopher," says Hume, "to be instructed how we shall choose our ends, more than the means for attaining the ends." *"How we shall choose our ends."* After all, what in the moral life is more important than that? If, in the face of impulses from within and voices from without that would make money, sex, power, comfort, "glamour," life according to nature, life according to Scripture, life according to Freud, the chief or the only good, philosophic reflection is the sanest and most reliable guide. If it alone can recognize ethical bigotry, caprice, and perverseness for what they are and responsibly mark out the ends that bring "the enduring satisfactions of life," then we have our answer to those who ask about its ethical relevance. We have seen that in the realm of theory philosophy, with its instrument of self-critical reason, supplies the only adequate test. Similarly in the realm of practice it supplies the only compass known whose needle follows the pole of the rational good.

THE IVORY TOWER AGAIN

Here, however, we must face what is perhaps the most often repeated of the current criticisms of philosophers. Philosophy may be ever so potent an instrument in the good life, but what is the use of it, we are asked, if those who master it only retreat into ivory towers, and neither acquaint nor concern themselves with the issues of their time and community? So far as the philosopher admits the detachment charged, his defense must be in principle that which was offered in the last chapter: his best contribution is a ripe and impartial judgment; detachment is the condition of such judgment. And if the sacrifices his detachment and the largeness of view made possible by it for the sake of immediate influence, he is abandoning the only thing which in the long run can maintain that influence. He is discarding the substance for the shadow.

But the critics persist. Their charge is a double one: the philosophers have left undone those things they ought to have done, and have done a great many unprofitable things they ought not to have done. They have been silent when their words would have been golden, and they have busied themselves with trifles. Is there any force in these charges?

The first of them takes its immediate point from the war, and it gives us reason for self-examination. The issues before the public mind in recent years have been fundamental issues—the priority of national or of international allegiance, the existence of general standards of right and wrong, the nature of justice, the very continuance of the conditions under which a rational life can be lived. It is precisely issues of this kind—difficult, but profound and central—on which philosophic judgment is most weighty and most needed. Detachment of spirit is admittedly necessary if the philosopher is to fulfill his primary calling. But it is also true that in the degree to which the problems confronting the public are problems about first principles, the duties of detachment and participation tend to coincide, and the judgment of the philosopher on the issues of the day becomes pertinent and even imperative. A speaker at one of our conferences quoted an eminent German scholar to the effect that a chief factor in the rise of social fanaticism in his country had been the habit among his colleagues of washing their hands of responsibility, even when the foundations of free scholarship itself were endangered. Can it be said with truth that in our own country the voice of the philosophers has been raised with a clearness or an authority proportioned to the weight of their judgment on the great issues that have been at stake?

The truth seems to be that the philosophers have emerged from the crisis neither with glory nor with discredit. They have swayed no tribunals at critical moments; they have not appeared conspicuously in the press or on the radio. There is no recorded recent instance in which the public has hung on their words. It would be satisfactory to know that philosophers here and there could perform such feats. But to criticize them generally for not doing so is inept. It assumes that a philosopher should be a spellbinder, whereas the whole tenor of his temper and discipline, with their stress on precision, qualified statement, and judicial moderation, unfits him for such an office. He must be content to speak to the many through the comparatively few, the few who are accessible to the reflective statement of a case. And if it is asked whether philosophers have done their part in their own undramatic fashion, it appears that they must receive at least a passing grade. They have been in advance of public opinion in a direction which that opinion eventually followed; they have argued the larger issues in many books, and in many of the more thoughtful journals. They have taken an important part in organizing college and university discussion of these issues; some clear and firm voices among them, without sacrificing moderation of statement, have achieved large carrying power. It is perhaps not fanciful to say that the very existence of their order, with its dedication to the method of reason as the solution of all problems and disputes, has been a continual quiet witness on one side in the great debate. There are some, including the present writer, who think that philosophers might well have done more. But it would be unfair to mistake that determined objectivity, that almost passionate dispassionateness which forms part of their professional conscience and which in the end gives them their hearing, for indifference to human need.

THE CHARGE OF TRIVIALITY

Let us turn to the second count in this indictment: philosophers are preoccupied with the unimportant. While problems of the first moment in ethics, value theory, the philosophy of religion, metaphysics, remain to be solved, they talk about the characteristics of sense data and the distinguishing properties of formal, material, and strict implication. And having lost their perspective as to what is important, they are forfeiting the respect that was formerly paid to thinkers engaged on problems of significance. To this criticism, too, the answer in principle has been given. Persons who speak from the outside are not in a good position to see which issues in the philosophical realm are central and which trivial. Impatient laymen, hot for certainty and eager to get the great seal of philosophy affixed to their private creeds, are really not entitled to tell philosophers to stand and deliver. The philosophers should deal with important problems; granted. But among these important problems is the problem what *is* important. And why should they accept dictation on that more than on their other problems?

The criticism becomes more formidable, however, when it is repeated from within the fold, as it was in a conference at Boston, where distinguished philosophers joined those from other fields in taking the philosophers to task for their concern with trivialities. And it will hardly serve to protest that other subjects—in mathematics, for example, or physics—scholars would not tolerate meddling and prescription from without. For the fact must be admitted that the philosopher is not as independent of the public as the mathematician or the physicist. These scientists have purchased exemption from public pressure by a degree of specialization which has cost them much in the way of public interest and influence, though of course with their own consent. The philosopher can, if he wishes, become a still more technical specialist. But then he, too, must pay the price. He must be ready to abandon the preferred position of his subject, an ancient and honorable position which it holds in virtue of many services rendered to the general human cause of pushing back the dark. Whether he can speak directly to the many or not, his problems have always been the plain man's problems in a way in which those of the physicist and mathematician have not, and the public ear and heart are therefore peculiarly open to him if he does know how to speak to them. He may well think twice before he gives up this birthright of general interest in order to become an unhampered technician. But then there is the other side too. Much as he may appreciate the privilege of being guide, philosopher, and friend to the mass of men, he can scarcely allow them to dictate to him, for he clearly knows better than they what is important in his own field. What can he do?

He can do two things: first, he can clear his own mind as to how to judge the importance of problems; second, when he is forced into extreme technicality, as he often is and must be, he can take some pains to put this in perspective.

HOW MEASURE IMPORTANCE?

First, as to the criterion of importance. A distinguished philosopher from abroad recently spent some years in this country at various leading universities, and at each of these he gave a course in which, to the casual eye, he seemed to be discoursing endlessly about the matchbox he held in his hand. The sort of problem that fascinated him was whether, when he looked at the matchbox, what he saw was or was not a part of the physical matchbox, and to these problems he devoted the resources of an extraordinarily acute and indefatigable mind. Are such questions important? If their importance is to be measured by the difference that would be made in human conduct or experience by one solution or another, the verdict about them is clear: they are a waste of time. But that is not the verdict that most philosophers would pass upon them, nor probably the plain man either if he saw all that was involved. What is the criterion that would be implicit in a well-informed judgment here?

It is *theoretic* importance. And what does that mean? Put in the simplest fashion, it means general illuminating power, the capacity of a particular solution to help us forward in the larger business of understanding the world. In this enterprise some problems are clearly central, some peripheral, and a technical question may fall in either class. There are many technical problems not worth solving, and there are many others, which at first glance look like these, whose solution is of the highest moment, since, if it could be gained, it would carry with it the solution of whole ranges of other problems. The problems of the matchbox would seem to fall in this latter group. If the philosopher could find the answer to his questions about its color and shape, that answer would throw light forward on the problem of our knowledge of nature generally; and this is one of the key problems for understanding man's place in the world. On the other hand, an application of the same standard would dismiss some current problems as trivial puzzles. Of course, in using such terms as "general illuminating power" and "help in understanding the world," one is not speaking with all desirable definiteness. But perhaps it is well, in order to avoid controversy, to leave them a little vague. They are not useless as they stand; let readers interpret them in their own way—adding a pinch of good will—and it is to be suspected that the standard will yield surprisingly similar results.

Besides reflecting on his standard of importance, there is another thing which the writer on philosophy may do to meet the charge of triviality. When called on to write technically, he can make clear to himself and to his reader what the larger bearing of his problem is. We are not intimating that he fails to do this more often or more flagrantly than the scientist; he may have an even better record; neither of them is sinless. Perhaps one illustration will serve for both. Anthropologists and moral philosophers alike are in the habit of stressing the diversity of custom. The anthropologist documents this diversity

14

in great detail. The moralist takes various lines; if he happens to be a positivist, for example, he submits the moral judgment to a careful psychological analysis, exhibiting it as the expression of the feelings or attitudes of the person judging. Now, great numbers of students and others listen to these statements and analyses, or read them in books, without any conception of their larger bearing and without any help in discerning that bearing. In many cases the writers give no evidence of having seen the bearing themselves. It is a curious fact that, during the years when mankind has been divided over the view that moral law rested on the desire or will of particular peoples, one found in the technical journals elaborate analyses of moral judgment which made this view inevitable, and yet with no indication that the author had so much as tried to place his analysis in its larger reflective setting. It is not suggested, of course, that his conclusions should be swayed by their practical results. What is suggested is that the writer who presents his analyses with some sense of their ulterior bearings gains a manifold advantage: he conveys a philosophically truer picture; he conveys a more reassuring sense of his own responsibility. He avoids the charge of misleading his reader, and he adds greatly to the reader's interest and understanding. It is absurd to object to technicality as such, for in thorough work it is inevitable. But for the technicality that is myopic, irresponsible, and without perspective, it is perhaps harder to find a defense in philosophy than anywhere else. Is not intellectual perspective the gift above all others that philosophy is supposed to confer?

LAST IMPRESSIONS

The space allotted to the review of these criticisms and demands is exhausted. A great variety of criticisms are being hurled at the philosophers. But none go deeper than those we have here considered—of disunity, of destructiveness, of irresponsible detachment. We have seen that these charges are not groundless. Philosophers do love unduly to differ; they *are* more adept at demolition than construction; perhaps more of them than one realizes, if they could have their secret wish, would make off to their cells and gloat there over puzzles, "the world forgotten, by the world forgot." Still, what strikes at least one of the brotherhood after much note-taking of his kind is how often these and other criticisms have turned out to be mere misunderstandings, or at most of a merely local pertinence. The final impression carried away was of a body of men and women of high ability, deeply devoted to their subject and task, a little gray perhaps from carrying a load of teaching that is almost everywhere too heavy, a little lacking perhaps in those outstanding personalities which, if they appear, are heaven-sent, but still thoughtful, sensitive, sane in judgment and counsel, public-spirited, eager to maintain their contact with the intellectual currents of the world, extraordinarily responsible as teachers. They are doing an important job, if not everywhere with distinction, at least with devotion and competence.

But we have been considering in this chapter not only criticisms upon the philosophers, but also demands upon them, the demands of the present-day educated public. Here the picture is different. The dominant impression is of a great opportunity. In the colleges the defects of the elective system are revealing the need for philosophic integration and perspective. Among our graduates, trained in their various specialties, the sense of living on professional islands is leading to a general hunger for more means of intellectual intercourse, and for a body of standards and principles that will make life at once less insular and more humane. And in both groups the decay of traditional authority is calling for a new measure of individual and responsible thinking. Hence a widespread turning to philosophy of curious, expectant, even entreating eyes. The demands being made upon it betray a confidence both touching and inspiriting. Whether our college administrations will accord to philosophy a place commensurate with these demands, and whether, if they do, the graduate schools will give us men of sufficient light and leading to fulfill them, it is not now possible to say. One thing, however, we can say: the opportunity is immense.

2. PHILOSOPHY AS CONCEPTUAL ANALYSIS

Alan R. White

Alan R. White *(1922–   ) is Ferens Professor of Philosophy at the University of Hull in England. He is the author of* G. E. Moore: A Critical Exposition *(1958),* Attention *(1964), and* The Philosophy of Mind *(1969).*

THE MEANING OF "PHILOSOPHY"

The word "philosophy" is commonly used in two, not necessarily mutually exclusive, ways. In such phrases as "the Communist or

American philosophy," "my philosophy of life," or "a liberal philosophy," it refers to a general set of attitudes and views, especially on moral, social and political matters. It is here synonymous with what in German is called *Weltanschauung*, or "outlook on life." An uneducated man who expresses an interest in questions of value, or who makes generalizations on life, such as "Women are all the same," is sometimes called "a bit of philosopher." Perhaps because one of the earliest such philosophies—that preached by the Stoics—enjoined calmness and absence of emotion in time of trouble, we commend for his "philosophical" way of taking things someone who meets disaster with calm and balance.

The second common use of the world "philosophy" is to cover the type of inquiry pursued and the body of knowledge built up by those who in the past and the present are called "philosophers," in the same way that "history" and "chemistry" refer to the inquiries and findings that are associated with historians and chemists. Philosophy is a subject that may also be pursued and taught; it has its own history and its body of professionals. To find out what exactly philosophy is, as a subject, we would have to examine the writings of those who are generally called "philosophers."

Such an examination of the history of philosophy reveals, I think, that the subject has been something of a mixed bag, whose contents have been narrowed from the time of the Greeks—for whom philosophy (literally, "love of wisdom") covered every pursuit of knowledge—to contemporary analytic philosophers—for whom it is confined to conceptual analysis, that is, an examination of the logical features of the various concepts that we employ in our thinking. Historically, philosophers have studied sciences—such as mathematics, physics, biology, and psychology—evaluative systems and codes in morals, politics and aesthetics, and a heterogeneous group of subjects that includes theology, metaphysics, and logic. The contents of this mixed bag can, however, usefully be divided into three groups: (a) suggestions for a way of life, that is, a worked-out system of philosophy in what I called above the first use of "philosophy"; (b) contributions to the development of science; and (c) conceptual analysis. Sometimes groups (a) and (b) are combined as examples of first-order knowledge, concerned respectively with what ought to be and what is; group (c) is then contrasted with them, in a way to be explained shortly, as second-order knowledge of how we think about what ought to be and what is.

For reasons which we do not have space to go into now, I shall confine myself, as do most contemporary English-speaking philosophers, to group (c)—that is, to philosophy as the analysis of concepts and, particularly, of those concepts that we use in thinking about the mind and its functioning.

CONCEPTUAL ANALYSIS

We can distinguish between an interest in understanding the world and an interest in understanding our understanding of the world. If we give the title of "first-order" to the questions and answers, investigations and theories, ideas and methods that are involved in attempting to understand or think about the world—whether it be animate or inanimate, nature, the human or the divine, things scientific or things artistic, what is so or what ought to be so—then we can distinguish as "second-order" problems that have to do with these attempts to understand—that is, these questions and answers, investigations and theories, ideas and methods themselves. For instance, the question of what kind of causes and motives make or lead people to commit certain kinds of crimes is a first-order problem, whereas the question of whether explanation in terms of motive excludes explanation in terms of cause, and also the questions of whether and, if so, why people of different ages and cultures seek for one or the other kind of explanation are second-order problems. The questions of how we are to attain knowledge of the constitution of the center of the earth, or of the prime numbers greater than a given prime, or of how to play the piano, are first-order problems; on the other hand, the questions of whether these are three different kinds of knowledge and whether children attain one kind earlier than the others are second-order problems. What sorts of things are valuable is a first-order question, while inquiries—whether psychological, sociological or logical—into our thinking about values are second-order.

An important distinction can be made, however, between different features of our understanding or thoughts of the world and, consequently, between different kinds of second-order questions. If our attention is devoted to discovering whether and why people at different historical times and in different cultures have employed different ways of trying to understand the world—e.g., whether they have employed both motive and causal explanations—then we are engaged in the sociology of knowledge. If, like the Swiss psychologist Piaget, we investigate how and at what stages children come to think about mathematical and empirical problems in the way that adults normally do, we are engaged in the psychology of knowledge. Both these attempts to understand our understanding are, for that very reason, second-order. Yet they are essentially of the same nature as our first-order attempts to understand the world, and employ the same scientific method; they are part of psychology, sociology, anthropology, and history.

The feature of our understanding of the world that has interested philosophers from the earliest times is what we may call the "logical" relations among the various ideas, or ways of thinking, that we employ in our reflection upon and struggle with the problems of everyday life and of the arts and sciences. Practitioners of the various arts and sciences, as well as all of us in our everyday thinking, *employ* these ideas, or ways of thought; philosophers *examine* them. The latter wish to know, for example, how an explanation in terms of motives differs from an explanation in terms of causes; or how the knowledge we have of empirical matters, such as the core of the earth, differs from the knowledge we have of mathematical matters, such as the number of primes in a given range; or how knowledge of anything is related to belief about it and evidence for it. This distinction between philosophy as a second-order study and the sciences as, in general, first-order studies explains the traditional negative definition of philosophy as the subject that tackles those problems that are unanswerable by science.

In thinking about something in a particular way—that is, in using a particular idea, or concept, such as *motive, cause, knowledge, belief, mind* or *memory*—we take up a certain position with regard to what we are thinking about; we look at it in a certain way or put it into a particular category. To say that someone did not have a certain concept would be to say that he did not do this. In thinking of something in one way, we necessarily connect it with some of our other ways of thinking about things and disconnect it from still others, just as in taking up a physical position with regard to anything we erect a barrier against some parts of our surroundings while we leave a flank exposed to other parts, or in describing one point in space, we necessarily link it to, as well as separate it from, other points in space. For example, if we think, or say, that A *knows* that X is Y, we are logically committed to thinking, or saying, that X really is Y; on the other hand, if we think, or say, that A *believes* that X is Y, we are not thereby committed to thinking, or saying, that X really is Y. Thinking about something in a particular way—that is, using a particular concept—commits us in our further thinking to using certain other concepts about that same thing; to use the first concept is, partly or wholly, to use the second concept. What is *known* to be so is really so, whereas what is *believed* to be so need not be so. If I hold that X is totally included in Y and that Y is totally included in Z, then I am committed to holding that X is totally included in Z, because this is, under another guise or seen from another angle, at least part of what I held in the first place. A diagram of "X is totally included in Y and Y is totally included in Z," namely,

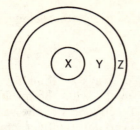

would contain the diagram of "X

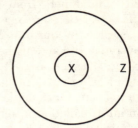

is totally included in Z," namely,

When we take up a physical position, examination of this position shows us what other spatial positions it is near to or distant from, included in or excluded from, which positions it overlooks or is hidden from, which it is open to or blocked by, where it can most easily be attacked or defended. When we take up a position in thought, examination shows what other positions are contained in or excluded from our position, what supports it or rebuts it, what is relevant or irrelevant to it. Very much as physical positions are spatially related, so positions in thought—that is, concepts—are "logically" related. While physical points include or exclude one another, the uses of concepts imply or contradict one another. The philosopher's task is to elucidate the network of inferences that one becomes committed to by making a particular categorization of things. He has to discover what the situations are in which we can use a certain concept, what concepts precede or follow it, of what set of concepts it is a part.

An examination of the logical features of the ways in which we think about things—that is, of the concepts we use—attempts to discover what is implied or excluded by a given way of thinking, whether it supports or rebuts or is merely irrelevant to something else we might think, and whether to combine one way of thinking with another is consistent or gives rise to contradictions. Further, we wish to know how a given way of thinking is related to what it is used to think about. Does it, for instance, describe it or evaluate it, or endorse it; does it relate it to other things? In discovering the relations of one way of thinking to other ways—that is, the relation of the use of one concept to that of other concepts—we are discovering the nature of the concepts under examination. For concepts are, in this respect, like mathematical points: they have no qualities other than their relations to other concepts. Just as a mathematical point has no size or any other quality, but only its position relative to other points, which is indicated by a set of coordinates, so a concept is defined by what its use implies, contradicts, supports, rebuts, etc. Naming a concept by mentioning the word that is used in a given language to express it merely identifies the concept, just as making a chalk mark on the blackboard merely provides a representation of a mathematical point. Concepts are, of course, in some respects unlike mathematical points. The uses of concepts are related not only to each other but also to the material in the world about which we use them. We not only think in various ways, we also think about various sorts of things. Further, whereas every point has some other point standing to it in every possible spatial relation, not every type of concept has every type of relation to one or another concept—for example, only relational concepts have converses.

Both the nature of a concept—that is, of a way of thinking—and a philosophical inquiry into it are best exemplified by considering briefly some of the ways in which we discover and test hypotheses about its logical features.

One way is to see what the use of the concept implies. The difference between thinking that something is beautiful and that it is colored is different in kind from the difference between thinking that something is colored and that it is old. For if A and B are identical in every other respect, then it follows that they are equal in beauty; but they could be identical in every other respect without being of the same color or of the same age.

A second way of discovering the logical features of a concept is to find out what questions may be appropriately asked about it. We can ask a man when he first realized that he had for years felt jealous of his sister and that she had felt jealous of him; but whereas we can ask him when he first realized that his sister had for years felt pains in her back, we cannot ask him when he first realized that he himself had for years felt pains in his back.

Similarly, we may look for the characteristics and qualifications that are relevant or irrelevant to the concept in question. If we *think about* a problem, we are doing something in which we may be engaged all morning, that we may be interrupted at, or may do to no avail; whereas, if we *think that* Hume was a greater philosopher than Locke, we are not doing something in which we can be engaged for a period, be interrupted at, or do with or without success. If a man believes that his wife has deceived him, his *belief* may be passionate and sincere enough, but too hasty and false; on the other hand, passion, sincerity, haste and falsity are not the sort of characteristics that we could either attribute to or deny of his friend's *knowledge* that the wife had been unfaithful.

Thirdly, we may put forward a hypothesis, or consider some hypothesis already put forward, about the logical features of a certain concept and see whether it leads us to contradictions, paradoxes or fantasies. For example, some philosophers have held that the *meaning* of a phrase is the object, or kind of object, to which the phrase refers, as "motor car" refers to a kind of vehicle. If this theory about the idea of *meaning* were true, then two phrases that referred to the same object, or to the same kind of object, would have the same meaning. But, although the phrases "the Prime Minister of Great Britain during most of the 1939–45 war" and "the famous descendant of Marlborough, known for his large cigars and his V-sign" both refer to Winston Churchill, they obviously do not have the same meaning. Further, one could understand either phrase without knowing to whom it referred. Again, William James' theory that to say a belief is *true* is to say that it works is refuted by the fact that we often find that lies work, even in the long run, just as well as the truth.

Fourthly, we may inquire how a concept is related to whatever our thinking is about. This is to inquire what are the kinds of situations and conditions in which it is used or not used. For instance, if my wife asks me to transplant the Masquerades, and I, not knowing much about roses, dig up Peace, then I may plead I disturbed Peace *by mistake;* whereas, if I trample on Peace in my attempts to dig up the Masquerades, my plea is that I disturbed Peace *accidentally.* If I am not certain about the concept of an *electron,* I may ask whether tracks in cloud chambers are related to scientists' assertions about electrons in the same way as vapor trails in the sky are related to our assertions about jet planes.

A philosophical examination of the concepts we use in either our everyday or our specialized thinking consists, therefore, in an attempt, by the methods mentioned, to discover how the uses of these concepts are logically related to each other and to their subject matter. It consists in revealing to us what is involved in the ways of thinking that we employ. Nor is there anything strange about the fact that a person may all his life employ quite correctly certain concepts—and in this sense understand what he is doing—and yet be unable to say correctly how he does it and, therefore, be puzzled about these concepts. Most of us can speak grammatically, argue logically, or make and appreciate jokes, without knowing exactly how we do it. Augustine observed that he knew what time was, so long as he was not asked to say what it was. To say that someone's views about a concept X are confused is not *per se* to deny that he uses the concept correctly. Philosophical analysts of ideas are related to the users of ideas somewhat as preachers are to practitioners, critics to poets, grammarians to the native speakers of a language, map-makers to explorers, or Molière's philosopher to M. Jourdain, who had spoken prose all his life without realizing until then that it was prose.

Because we ordinarily think with the help of language, our ways of thinking are embodied in our ways of talking. To employ a concept is ordinarily to use a verbal expression in a certain way; to indicate a concept is to mention a word or phrase. What we mean by a word "X," or by its synonyms "X_1" and "X_2," is our concept of X. Einstein's concept of relativity is what he meant by "relativity." If the word "X" has several meanings, it expresses several concepts. Hence, to discover the relations of one concept to another is to discover the relations of one meaning or use of a word both to other meanings or uses of the same word and to the meanings or uses of other words. An analysis of *interest* as an *inclination to pay attention* can take the linguistic form that to say that A is interested in Z is to say that he is inclined to pay attention to Z. Two people could use the same word differently, but they could not use the same concept differently; for the so-called "difference in the use of a concept" is really the use of a different concept, just as a difference in the spatial coordinates of a point makes it a different point. What concept a man is employing depends not on what word he uses, but on how he uses the word. If A and B use the same word differently, then they are not expressing the same concept by it. Furthermore, once we have plotted some of the relations of a given concept, as of a given point, to others, then other relations necessarily follow from that.

THE PROBLEM OF GOD

II

Does a Perfect Person Exist?

3. THEOLOGY AND FALSIFICATION

Antony Flew / R. M. Hare / Basil Mitchell

Antony Flew (1923–   ) is Professor of Philosophy at the University of Keele, England. Flew's major works are A New Approach to Psychical Research *(1953),* Hume's Philosophy of Belief *(1961), and* God and Philosophy *(1966). He also edited an influential collection of papers in analytic philosophy,* Logic and Language *(1951, 1953) as well as* New Essays in Philosophical Theology *in which the following discussion appeared. R. M. Hare (see essay 36 for biographical note). Basil Mitchell teaches at Oxford University.*

Antony Flew

Let us begin with a parable. It is a parable developed from a tale told by John Wisdom in his haunting and revelatory article "Gods." Once upon a time two explorers came upon a clearing in the jungle. In the clearing were growing many flowers and many weeds. One explorer says, "Some gardener must tend this plot." The other disagrees, "There is no gardener." So they pitch their tents and set a watch. No gardener is ever seen, "But perhaps he is an invisible gardener." So they set up a barbed-wire fence. They electrify it. They patrol with bloodhounds. (For they remember how H.G. Wells's *The Invisible Man* could be both smelt and touched though he could not be seen.) But no shrieks ever suggest that some intruder has received a shock. No movements of the wire ever betray an invisible climber. The bloodhounds never give cry. Yet still the Believer is not convinced. "But there is a gardener, invisible, intangible, insensible to electric shocks, a gardener who has no scent and makes no sound, a gardener who comes secretly to look after the garden which he loves." At last the Skeptic despairs, "But what remains of your original assertion? Just how does what you call an invisible, intangible, eternally elusive gardener differ from an imaginary gardener or even from no gardener at all?"

From New Essays in Philosophical Theology, *ed. Antony Flew and Alasdair MacIntyre, pp. 96–108, published by The Macmillan Company, New York, and Student Christian Movement Press, Ltd., London, in 1955, and reprinted with their permission.*

In this parable we can see how what starts as an assertion, that something exists or that there is some analogy between certain complexes of phenomena, may be reduced step by step to an altogether different status, to an expression perhaps of a "picture preference." [1] The Skeptic says there is no gardener. The Believer says there is a gardener (but invisible, etc.). One man talks about sexual behaviour. Another man prefers to talk of Aphrodite (but knows that there is not really a super-human person additional to, and somehow responsible for, all sexual phenomena). The process of qualification may be checked at any point before the original assertion is completely withdrawn and something of that first assertion will remain (tautology). Mr. Wells's invisible man could not, admittedly, be seen, but in all other respects he was a man like the rest of us. But though the process of qualification may be, and of course usually is, checked in time, it is not always judiciously so halted. Someone may dissipate his assertion completely without noticing that he has done so. A fine brash hypothesis may thus be killed by inches, the death by a thousand qualifications.

And in this, it seems to me, lies the peculiar danger, the endemic evil, of theological utterance. Take such utterances as "God has a plan," "God created the world," "God loves us as a father loves his children." They look at first sight very much like assertions, vast cosmological assertions. Of course, this is no sure sign that they either are, or are intended to be, assertions. But let us confine ourselves to the cases where those who utter such sentences intend them to express assertions. (Merely remarking parenthetically that those who intend or interpret such utterances as crypto-commands, expressions of wishes, disguised ejaculations, concealed ethics, or as anything else but assertions are unlikely to succeed in making them either properly orthodox or practically effective.)

Now to assert that such and such is the case is necessarily equivalent to denying that such and such is not the case. Suppose then that we are in doubt as to what someone who gives vent to an utterance is asserting, or suppose that, more radically, we are skeptical as to whether he is really asserting anything at all, one way of trying to understand (or perhaps it will be to expose) his utterance is to attempt to find what he would regard as counting against or as being incompatible with, its truth. For if the utterance is indeed an assertion, it will necessarily be equivalent to a denial of the negation of that assertion. And anything which would count against the assertion, or which would induce the speaker to withdraw it and to admit that it had been mistaken, must

---

[1] Cf. J. Wisdom, "Other Minds," *Mind* (1940), reprinted in his *Other Minds* (Oxford: Basil Blackwell, 1952).

be part of (or the whole of) the meaning of the negation of that assertion. And to know the meaning of the negation of an assertion is as near as makes no matter to know the meaning of that assertion. And if there is nothing which a putative assertion denies then there is nothing which it asserts either: and so it is not really an assertion. When the Skeptic in the parable asked the Believer, "Just how does what you call an invisible, intangible, eternally elusive gardener differ from an imaginary gardener or even from no gardener at all?" he was suggesting that the Believer's earlier statement had been so eroded by qualification that it was no longer an assertion at all.

Now it often seems to people who are not religious as if there was no conceivable event or series of events the occurrence of which would be admitted by sophisticated religious people to be a sufficient reason for conceding "There wasn't God after all" or "God does not really love us then." Someone tells us that God loves us as a father loves his children. We are reassured. But then we see a child dying of inoperable cancer of the throat. His earthly father is driven frantic in his efforts to help, but his Heavenly Father reveals no obvious sign of concern. Some qualification is made—God's love is "not a merely human love" or it is "an inscrutable love," perhaps—and we realize that such sufferings are quite compatible with the truth of the assertion that "God loves us as a father (but, of course, . . .)." We are reassured again. But then perhaps we ask: what is this assurance of God's (appropriately qualified) love worth, what is this apparent guarantee really a guarantee against? Just what would have to happen not merely (morally and wrongly) to tempt but also (logically and rightly) to entitle us to say "God does not love us" or even "God does not exist"? I therefore put to the succeeding symposiasts the simple central questions. "What would have to occur or to have occurred to constitute for you a disproof of the love of, or of the existence of, God?"

R. M. Hare

I wish to make it clear that I shall not try to defend Christianity in particular, but religion in general—not because I do not believe in Christianity, but because you cannot understand what Christianity is, until you have understood what religion is.

I must begin by confessing that, on the ground marked out by Flew, he seems to me to be completely victorious. I therefore shift my ground by relating another parable. A certain lunatic is convinced that all dons want to murder him. His friends introduce him to all the mildest and most respectable dons that they can find, and after each of them has retired, they say, "You see, he doesn't really want to murder you; he spoke to you in a most cordial manner; surely you are convinced now?" But the lunatic replies "Yes, but that was only his diabolical cunning; he's really plotting against me the whole time, like the rest of them; I know it I tell you." However many kindly dons are produced, the reaction is still the same.

Now we say that such a person is deluded. But what is he deluded about? About the truth or falsity of an assertion? Let us apply Flew's test to him. There is no behaviour of dons that can be enacted which he will accept as counting against his theory; and therefore his theory, on this test, asserts nothing. But it does not follow that there is no difference between what he thinks about dons and what most of us think about them—otherwise we should not call him a lunatic and ourselves sane, and dons would have no reason to feel uneasy about his presence in Oxford.

Let us call that in which we differ from this lunatic, our respective *bliks*. He has an insane *blik* about dons; we have a sane one. It is important to realize that we have a sane one, not no *blik* at all; for there must be two sides to any argument—if he has a wrong *blik*, then those who are right about dons must have a right one. Flew has shown that a *blik* does not consist in an assertion or system; but nevertheless it is very important to have the right *blik*.

Let us try to imagine what it would be like to have different *bliks* about other things than dons. When I am driving my car, it sometimes occurs to me to wonder whether my movements of the steering-wheel will always continue to be followed by corresponding alterations in the direction of the car. I have never had a steering failure, though I have had skids, which must be similar. Moreover, I know enough about how the steering of my car is made to know the sort of thing that would have to go wrong for the steering to fail—steel joints would have to part, or steel rods break, or something—but how do I know that this won't happen? The truth is, I don't know; I just have a *blik* about steel and its properties, so that normally I trust the steering of my car; but I find it not at all difficult to imagine what it would be like to lose this *blik* and acquire the opposite one. People would say I was silly about steel; but there would be no mistaking the reality of the difference between our respective *bliks*—for example, I should never go in a motor-car. Yet I should hesitate to say that the difference between us was the difference between contradictory assertions. No amount of safe arrivals or bench-tests will remove my *blik* and restore the normal one; for my *blik* is compatible with any finite number of such tests.

It was Hume who taught us that our whole commerce with the

world depends upon our *blik* about the world; and that differences be-tween *bliks* about the world cannot be settled by observation of what happens in the world. That was why, having performed the interesting experiment of doubting the ordinary man's *blik* about the world, and showing that no proof could be given to make us adopt one *blik* rather than another, he turned to back-gammon to take his mind off the prob-lem. It seems, indeed, to be impossible even to formulate as an assertion the normal *blik* about the world which makes me put my confidence in the future reliability of steel joints, in the continued ability of the road to support my car, and not gape beneath it revealing nothing below; in the general non-homicidal tendencies of dons; in my own continued well-being (in some sense of that word that I may not now fully understand) if I continue to do what is right according to my lights; in the general likelihood of people like Hitler coming to a bad end. But perhaps a formulation less inadequate than most is to be found in the Psalms: "The earth is weak and all the inhabiters thereof: I bear up the pillars of it."

The mistake of the position which Flew selects for attack is to regard this kind of talk as some sort of *explanation,* as scientists are ac-customed to use the word. As such, it would obviously be ludicrous. We no longer believe in God as an Atlas—*nous n'avons pas besoin de cette hypothèse.* But it is nevertheless true to say that, as Hume saw, without a *blik* there can be no explanation; for it is by our *bliks* that we decide what is and what is not an explanation. Suppose we believed that everything that happened, happened by pure chance. This would not of course be an assertion; for it is compatible with anything hap-pening or not happening, and so, incidentally, is its contradictory. But if we had this belief, we should not be able to explain or predict or plan anything. Thus, although we should not be *asserting* anything different from those of a more normal belief, there would be a great difference between us; and this is the sort of difference that there is between those who really believe in God and those who really disbelieve in him.

The word "really" is important, and may excite suspicion. I put it in, because when people have had a good Christian upbringing, as have most of those who now profess not to believe in any sort of reli-gion, it is very hard to discover what they really believe. The reason why they find it so easy to think that they are not religious is that they have never got into the frame of mind of one who suffers from the doubts to which religion is the answer. Not for them the terrors of the primitive jungle. Having abandoned some of the more picturesque fringes of religion, they think that they have abandoned the whole thing—whereas in fact they still have got, and could not live without, a religion of a comfortably substantial, albeit highly sophisticated, kind, which differs from that of many "religious people" in little more than this, that "religious people" like to sing Psalms about theirs—a very natural and proper thing to do. But nevertheless there may be a big difference lying behind—the difference between two people who, though side by side, are walking in different directions. I do not know in what direction Flew is walking; perhaps he does not know either. But we had some examples recently of various ways in which one can walk away from Christianity, and there are any number of possibilities. After all, man has not changed biologically since primitive times; it is religion that has changed, and it can easily change again. And if you do not think that such changes make a difference, get acquainted with some Sikhs and some Mussulmans of the same Punjabi stock, you will find them quite different sorts of people.

There is an important difference between Flew's parable and my own which we have not yet noticed. The explorers do not *mind* about their garden; they discuss it with interest, but not with concern. But my lunatic, poor fellow, minds about dons; and I mind about the steering of my car; it often has people in it that I care for. It is because I mind very much about what goes on in the garden in which I find myself, that I am unable to share the explorers' detachment.

Basil Mitchell

Flew's article is searching and perceptive, but there is, I think, something odd about his conduct of the theologian's case. The theologian surely would not deny that fact of pain counts against the assertion that God loves men. This very incompatibility generates the most intractable of theological problems—the problem of evil. So the theologian *does* recognize the fact of pain as counting against Christian doctrine. But it is true that he will not allow it—or anything—to count decisively against it; for he is committed by his faith to trust in God. His attitude is not that of the detached observer, but of the believer.

Perhaps this can be brought out by yet another parable. In time of war in an occupied country, a member of the resistance meets one night a stranger who deeply impresses him. They spend that night in conversation. The Stranger tells the partisan that he himself is on the side of the resistance—indeed that he is in command of it, and urges the partisan to have faith in him no matter what happens. The partisan is utterly convinced at that meeting of the Stranger's sincerity and constancy and undertakes to trust him.

They never meet in conditions of intimacy again. But sometimes the Stranger is seen helping members of the resistance, and the partisan is grateful and says to his friends, "He is on our side."

Sometimes he is seen in the uniform of the police handing over patriots to the occupying power. On these occasions his friends murmur against him: but the partisan still says, "He is on our side." He still believes that, in spite of appearances, the Stranger did not deceive him. Sometimes he asks the Stranger for help and receives it. He is then thankful. Sometimes he asks and does not receive it. Then he says. "The Stranger knows best." Sometimes his friends, in exasperation, say "Well, what *would* he have to do for you to admit that you were wrong and that he is not on our side?" But the partisan refuses to answer. He will not consent to put the Stranger to the test. And sometimes his friends complain, "Well, if *that's* what you mean by his being on our side, the sooner he goes over to the other side the better."

The partisan of the parable does not allow anything to count decisively against the proposition "The Stranger is on our side." This is because he has committed himself to trust the Stranger. But of course he recognizes that the Stranger's ambiguous behaviour *does* count against what he believes about him. It is precisely this situation which constitutes the trial of his faith.

When the partisan asks for help and doesn't get it, what can he do? He can (*a*) conclude that the stranger is not on our side; or (*b*) maintain that he is on our side, but that he has reasons for withholding help.

The first he will refuse to do. How long can he uphold the second position without its becoming just silly?

I don't think one can say in advance. It will depend on the nature of the impression created by the Stranger in the first place. It will depend, too, on the manner in which he takes the Stranger's behaviour. If he blandly dismisses it as of no consequence, as having no bearing upon his belief, it will be assumed that he is thoughtless or insane. And it quite obviously won't do for him to say easily, "Oh, when used of the Stranger the phrase 'is on our side' *means* ambiguous behaviour of this sort." In that case he would be like the religious man who says blandly of a terrible disaster "It is God's will." No, he will only be regarded as sane and reasonable in his belief, if he experiences in himself the full force of the conflict.

It is here that my parable differs from Hare's. The partisan admits that many things may and do count against his belief: whereas Hare's lunatic who has a *blik* about dons doesn't admit that anything counts against his *blik*. Nothing *can* count against *bliks*. Also the partisan has a reason for having in the first instance committed himself, viz., the character of the Stranger; whereas the lunatic has no reason for his *blik* about dons—because, of course, you can't have reasons for *bliks*.

This means that I agree with Flew that theological utterances must be assertions. The partisan is making an assertion when he says, "The Stranger is on our side."

Do I want to say that the partisan's belief about the Stranger is, in any sense, an explanation? I think I do. It explains and makes sense of the Stranger's behaviour: it helps to explain also the resistance movement in the context of which he appears. In each case it differs from the interpretation which the others put upon the same facts.

"God loves men" resembles "the Stranger is on our side" (and many other significant statements, e.g., historical ones) in not being conclusively falsifiable. They can both be treated in at least three different ways: (1) as provisional hypotheses to be discarded if experience tells against them, (2) as significant articles of faith, (3) as vacuous formulae (expressing, perhaps, a desire for reassurance) to which experience makes no difference and which make no difference to life.

The Christian, once he has committed himself, is precluded by his faith from taking up the first attitude. "Thou shalt not tempt the Lord thy God." He is in constant danger, as Flew has observed, of slipping into the third. But he need not; and, if he does, it is a failure in faith as well as in logic.

4. ANSELM'S ONTOLOGICAL ARGUMENTS
Norman Malcolm

Anselm (1033 (?) –1109), who served as Archbishop of Canterbury, wrote primarily in the area of theology but at least two of his works have received great philosophical attention. His monologion *(1076) and* Proslogion *(1077–78) are his major works in philosophy; his famous version of the ontological argument for the existence of God is found in the latter.* Norman Malcolm *(1911–   ) teaches philosophy at Cornell University. He received his graduate education at Harvard and studied at*

From "Anselm's Ontological Arguments," Philosophical Review, Vol. LXIX, 1960, pp. 42–50. Reprinted with permission of the author and The Philosophical Review.

Cambridge University under G. E. Moore, John Wisdom, and Ludwig Wittgenstein. His friendship and study with Wittgenstein provided the basis for his fascinating and widely read book Ludwig Wittgenstein: A Memoir *(1958). He has also written* Dreaming *(1959) and* Knowledge and Certainty *(1963), a collection of essays and lectures.*

When Anselm says "And certainly, that than which nothing greater can be conceived cannot exist merely in the understanding. For suppose it exists merely in the understanding, then it can be conceived to exist in reality, which is greater," [1] he is claiming that if I conceived of a being of great excellence, that being would be *greater* (more excellent, more perfect) if it existed than if it did not exist. His supposition that "it exists merely in the understanding" is the supposition that it is conceived of but does not exist. Anselm repeated this claim in his reply to the criticism of the monk Gaunilo. Speaking of the being a greater than which cannot be conceived, he says:

I have said that if it exists merely in the understanding it can be conceived to exist in reality, which is greater. Therefore, if it exists merely in the understanding obviously the very being a greater than which cannot be conceived, is one a greater than which can be conceived. What, I ask, can follow better than that? For if it exists merely in the understanding, can it not be conceived to exist in reality? And if it can be so conceived does not he who conceives of this conceive of a thing greater than it, if it does exist merely in the understanding? Can anything follow better than this: that if a being a greater than which cannot be conceived exists merely in the understanding, it is something a greater than which can be conceived? What could be plainer? [2]

He is implying, in the first sentence, that if I conceive of something which does not exist then it is possible for it to exist, and *it will be greater if it exists than if it does not exist.*

The doctrine that existence is a perfection is remarkably queer. It makes sense and is true to say that my future house will be a better one if it is insulated than if it is not insulated; but what could it mean to say that it will be a better house if it exists than if it does not? My future child will be a better man if he is honest than if he is not; but who would understand the saying that he will be a better man if he exists than if he does not? Or who understands the saying that if God exists He is more perfect than if He does not exist? One might say, with some intelligibility, that it would be better (for oneself or for

[1] *Proslogion* 2, Deane, *St. Anselm*, p. 8.
[2] *Responsio* 2, Deane, *St. Anselm*, pp. 157–158.

mankind) if God exists than if He does not—but that is a different matter.

A king might desire that his next chancellor should have knowledge, wit, and resolution; but it is ludicrous to add that the king's desire is to have a chancellor who exists. Suppose that two royal councilors, A and B, were asked to draw up separately descriptions of the most perfect chancellor they could conceive, and that the descriptions they produced were identical except that A included existence in his list of attributes of a perfect chancellor and B did not. (I do not mean that B put non-existence in his list.) One and the same person could satisfy both descriptions. More to the point, any person who satisfied A's description would *necessarily* satisfy B's description and *vice versa*! This is to say that A and B did not produce descriptions that differed in any way but rather one and the same description of necessary and desirable qualities in a chancellor. A only made a show of putting down a desirable quality that B had failed to include.

I believe I am merely restating an observation that Kant made in attacking the notion that "existence" or "being" is a "real predicate." He says:

By whatever and by however many predicates we may think a thing—even if we completely determine it—we do not make the least addition to the thing when we further declare that this thing *is*. Otherwise, it would not be exactly the same thing that exists, but something more than we had thought in the concept; and we could not, therefore, say that the exact object of my concept exists.[3]

Anselm's ontological proof of *Proslogion* 2 is fallacious because it rests on the false doctrine that existence is a perfection (and therefore that "existence" is a "real predicate"). It would be desirable to have a rigorous refutation of the doctrine but I have not been able to provide one. I am compelled to leave the matter at the more or less intuitive level of Kant's observation. In any case, I believe that the doctrine does not belong to Anselm's other formulation of the ontological argument. It is worth noting that Gassendi anticipated Kant's criticism when he said, against Descartes:

Existence is a perfection neither in God nor in anything else; it is rather that in the absence of which there is no perfection. . . . Hence neither is existence held to exist in a thing in the way that perfections do, nor if the thing lacks existence is it said to be imperfect (or deprived of a perfection), so much as to be nothing.[4]

---

[3] *The Critique of Pure Reason,* tr. by Norman Kemp Smith (New York: The Macmillan Company, 1929), p. 505.

[4] Haldane and Ross, *The Philosophical Works of Descartes,* II, 186.

II

I take up now the consideration of the second ontological proof, which Anselm presents in the very next chapter of the *Proslogion*. (There is no evidence that he thought of himself as offering two different proofs.) Speaking of the being a greater than which cannot be conceived, he says:

> And it so truly exists that it cannot be conceived not to exist. For it is possible to conceive of a being which cannot be conceived not to exist; and this is greater than one which can be conceived not to exist. Hence, if that, than which nothing greater can be conceived, can be conceived not to exist, it is not that than which nothing greater can be conceived. But this is a contradiction. So truly, therefore, is there something than which nothing greater can be conceived, that it cannot even be conceived not to exist.
> And this being thou art, O Lord, our God.[5]

Anselm is saying two things: first, that a being whose nonexistence is logically impossible is "greater" than a being whose nonexistence is logically possible (and therefore that a being a greater than which cannot be conceived must be one whose nonexistence is logically impossible); second, that *God* is a being than which a greater cannot be conceived.

In regard to the second of these assertions, there certainly is *a* use of the word "God," and I think far the more common use, in accordance with which the statements "God is the greatest of all beings," "God is the most perfect being," "God is the supreme being," are *logically* necessary truths, in the same sense that the statement "A square has four sides" is a logically necessary truth. If there is a man named "Jones" who is the tallest man in the world, the statement "Jones is the tallest man in the world" is merely true and is not a logically necessary truth. It is a virtue of Anselm's unusual phrase, "a being greater than which cannot be conceived," [6] to make it explicit that the sentence "God is the greatest of all beings" expresses a logically necessary truth and not a mere matter of fact such as the one we imagined about Jones.

With regard to Anselm's first assertion (namely, that a being whose nonexistence is logically impossible is greater than a being whose nonexistence is logically possible) perhaps the most puzzling thing about it is the use of the word "greater." It appears to mean exactly the same

---

[5] *Proslogion* 3, Deane, *St. Anselm*, pp. 8–9.

[6] Professor Robert Calhoun has pointed out to me that a similar location had been used by Augustine. In *De moribus Manichaeorum* (Bk. II, ch. 11, sec. 24), he says that God is a being *quo esse aut cogitari melius nihil possit* (*Patrologiae Patrum Latinorum*, J. P. Migne, ed. [Paris, 1841–1845], Vol. 32; *Augustinus*, Vol. 1).

as "superior," "more excellent," "more perfect." This equivalence by itself is of no help to us, however, since the latter expressions would be equally puzzling here. What is required is some explanation of their use.

We do think of *knowledge,* say, as an excellence, a good thing. If A has more knowledge of algebra than B we express this in common language by saying that A has a *better* knowledge of algebra than B, or that A's knowledge of algebra is *superior* to B's, whereas we should not say that B has a better or superior *ignorance* of algebra than A. We do say "greater ignorance," but here the word "greater" is used purely quantitatively.

Previously I rejected *existence* as a perfection. Anselm is maintaining in the remarks last quoted, not that existence is a perfection, but that *the logical impossibility of nonexistence is a perfection.* In other words, *necessary existence is a perfection.* His first ontological proof uses the principle that a thing is greater if it exists than if it does not exist. His second proof employs the different principle that a thing is greater if it necessarily exists than if it does not necessarily exist.

Some remarks about the notion of *dependence* may help to make this latter principle intelligible. Many things depend for their existence on other things and events. My house was built by a carpenter: its coming into existence was dependent on a certain creative activity. Its continued existence is dependent on many things: that a tree does not crush it, that it is not consumed by fire, and so on. If we reflect on the common meaning of the word "God" (no matter how vague and confused this is), we realize that it is incompatible with this meaning that God's existence should *depend* on anything. Whether we believe in Him or not we must admit that the "almighty and everlasting God" (as several ancient prayers begin), the "Maker of heaven and earth, and of all things visible and invisible" (as is said in the Nicene Creed), cannot be thought of as being brought into existence by anything or as depending for His continued existence on anything. To conceive of anything as dependent upon something else for its existence is to conceive of it as a lesser being than God.

If a housewife has a set of extremely fragile dishes, then as dishes they are *inferior* to those of another set like them in all respects except that they are *not* fragile. Those of the first set are *dependent* for their continued existence on gentle handling; those of the second set are not. There is a definite connection in common language between the notions of dependency and inferiority, and independence and superiority. To say that something which was dependent on nothing whatever was superior to ("greater than") anything that was dependent in any way upon anything is quite in keeping with the everyday use of the terms "superior" and "greater." Correlative with the notions of dependence and independence are the notions of *limited* and *unlimited*. An engine requires fuel and this is a limitation. It is the same thing to say that an engine's operation is *dependent* on as that it is *limited* by its fuel supply. An engine that could accomplish the same work in the same time and was in other respects satisfactory, but did not require fuel, would be a *superior* engine.

God is usually conceived of as an *unlimited* being. He is conceived of as a being who *could not* be limited, that is, as an absolutely unlimited being. This is no less than to conceive of Him as *something a greater than which cannot be conceived*. If God is conceived to be an absolutely unlimited being He must be conceived to be unlimited in regard to His existence as well as His operation. In this conception it will not make sense to say that He depends on anything for coming into or continuing in existence. Nor, as Spinoza observed, will it make sense to say that something could *prevent* Him from existing.[7] Lack of moisture can prevent trees from existing in a certain region of the earth. But it would be contrary to the concept of God as an unlimited being to suppose that anything other than God Himself could prevent Him from existing, and it would be self-contradictory to suppose that He Himself could do it.

Some may be inclined to object that although nothing could prevent God's existence, still it might just *happen* that He did not exist. And if He did exist that too would be by chance. I think, however, that from the supposition that it could happen that God did not exist it would follow that, if He existed, He would have mere duration and not eternity. It would make sense to ask, "How long has He existed?," "Will He still exist next week?," "He was in existence yesterday but how about today?," and so on. It seems absurd to make God the subject of such questions. According to our ordinary conception of Him, He is an eternal being. And eternity does not mean endless duration, as Spinoza noted. To ascribe eternity to something is to exclude as senseless all sentences that imply that it has duration. If a thing has duration then it would be merely a *contingent* fact, if it was a fact, that its duration was endless. The moon could have endless duration but not eternity. If something has endless duration it will *make sense* (although it will be false) to say that it will cease to exist, and it will make sense (although it will be false) to say that something will *cause* it to cease to exist. A being with endless duration is not, therefore, an absolutely unlimited being. That God is conceived to be eternal follows from the fact that He is conceived to be an absolutely unlimited being.

---

[7] *Ethics,* Part I, prop. 11.

I have been trying to expand the argument of *Proslogion* 3. In *Responsio* 1 Anselm adds the following acute point: if you can conceive of a certain thing and this thing does not exist then if it *were* to exist its nonexistence would be *possible*. It follows, I believe, that if the thing were to exist it would depend on other things both for coming into and continuing in existence, and also that it would have duration and not eternity. Therefore it would not be, either in reality or in conception, an unlimited being, *aliquid quo nihil maius cogitari possit*.

Anselm states his argument as follows:

> If it [the thing a greater than which cannot be conceived] can be conceived at all it must exist. For no one who denies or doubts the existence of a being a greater than which is inconceivable, denies or doubts that if it did exist its non-existence, either in reality or in the understanding, would be impossible. For otherwise it would not be a being a greater than which cannot be conceived. But as to whatever can be conceived but does not exist: if it were to exist its non-existence either in reality or in the understanding would be possible. Therefore, if a being a greater than which cannot be conceived, can even be conceived, it must exist.[8]

What Anselm has proved is that the notion of contingent existence or of contingent nonexistence cannot have any application to God. His existence must either be logically necessary or logically impossible. The only intelligible way of rejecting Anselm's claim that God's existence is necessary is to maintain that the concept of God, as a being a greater than which cannot be conceived, is self-contradictory or nonsensical.[9] Supposing that this is false, Anselm is right to deduce God's necessary existence from his characterization of Him as a being a greater than which cannot be conceived.

Let me summarize the proof. If God, a being a greater than which cannot be conceived, does not exist then He cannot *come* into existence. For if He did He would either have been *caused* to come into existence or have *happened* to come into existence, and in either case

---

[8] *Responsio* 1; Deane, *St. Anselm,* pp. 154–155.

[9] Gaunilo attacked Anselm's argument on this very point. He would not concede that a being greater than which cannot be conceived existed in his understanding (*Gaunilonis Pro Insipiente,* secs. 4 and 5; Deane, *St. Anselm,* pp. 148–150). Anselm's reply is: "I call on your faith and conscience to attest that this is most false" (*Responsio* 1; Deane, *St. Anselm,* p. 154). Gaunilo's faith and conscience will attest that it is false that "God is not a being a greater than which is inconceivable," and false that "He is not understood (*intelligitur*) or conceived (*cogitatur*)" (*ibid.*). Descartes remarks that one would go to "strange extremes" who denied that we understand the words *"that thing which is the most perfect that we can conceive;* for that is what all men call God" (Haldane and Ross, *The Philosophical Works of Descartes,* II, 129).

He would be a limited being, which by our conception of Him He is not. Since He cannot come into existence, if He does not exist His existence is impossible. If He does exist He cannot have come into existence (for the reasons given), nor can He cease to exist, for nothing could cause Him to cease to exist nor could it just happen that He ceased to exist. So if God exists His existence is necessary. Thus God's existence is either impossible or necessary. It can be the former only if the concept of such a being is self-contradictory or in some way logically absurd. Assuming that this is not so, it follows that He necessarily exists. . . .

5. AQUINAS' PROOF FROM NECESSARY BEING

Etienne Gilson

St. Thomas Aquinas (1225–1274) is generally acknowledged to be the greatest philosopher of the Middle Ages. His writings, which comprise over thirty volumes, reflect a sustained effort to reconcile religious faith and reason, specifically the doctrines of Christian theology and the philosophy of Aristotle. His most famous works are the Summa Theologica *and the* Summa Contra Gentiles. *Etienne Gilson (1884–   ) has taught at the Sorbonne, Harvard, and the University of Toronto where he was Director of the Institute for Medieval Studies. His many publications include* The Unity of Philosophical Experience *(1937),* Reason and Revelation in the Middle Ages *(1938),* God and Philosophy *(1941),* The Christian Philosophy of St. Thomas Aquinas *(1956).*

We find in nature things that are possible to be and not to be, since they are found to be generated and to be corrupted, and consequently it is possible for them to be and not to be. But it is impossible for them always to exist, for that which can not-be at some time is not. Therefore, if everything can not-be, then at one time nothing was in existence. Now, if this were true, even now there would be nothing in existence, because that which does not exist begins to exist only through something already existing. Therefore, if at one time nothing was in existence, it would have been impossible for anything to

From Elements of Christian Philosophy *by Etienne Gilson. Copyright © 1960 by Doubleday and Company, Inc. Reprinted by permission of Doubleday and Company, Inc.*

have begun to exist, and thus even now nothing would be in existence—which is absurd. Therefore, not all beings are merely possible, but there must exist something the existence of which is necessary. But every necessary thing either has its necessity caused by another, or not. Now it is impossible to go on to infinity in necessary things which have their existence caused by another, as has been already proved in regard to efficient causes. Therefore, we cannot but admit the existence of some being having of itself its own necessity, and not receiving it from another, but rather causing in others their necessity. This all men speak of as God.[1]

The beginning of this third way [2] can help us to understand what Thomas Aquinas considers an empirical starting point given in sense experience. For him, to start from possibility and necessity, two supremely abstract notions, really means to start from the visible fact that certain things are born and others die. In still other terms, it is to start from the fact that, for certain beings, it is possible to be and not to be. . . .

Starting from the fact that things come to be and pass away, which implies that it is possible for them to be and not to be, one can prove that the notion of a universe in which all things, without a single exception, would be merely possible is inconceivable without contradiction.

If the existence of a certain thing is merely possible, its non-existence likewise is possible, and we still are arguing on the premise that the world has always existed. Now, within a finite time, however long, a mere possibility may well not materialize. On the contrary, if it did not materialize during an infinite duration of time, it would not be a possibility at all. On the strength of these principles, one can say that if it has been merely possible from all eternity, there must have come a moment when a thing ceased to exist. But this applies to all merely possible things, singly and collectively. There should therefore have come a time when, given that all things ceased to exist, there was nothing in existence, and since what no longer is cannot bring itself back to existence, there still should be nothing in existence. Now this consequence is absurd, for there are things about which we are asking the question of their first cause; moreover, we ourselves must be existing in order to be able to ask the question. Consequently, the supposition that all beings are merely possible is an absurd one.

If not all beings are merely possible, some being must be necessary. Now, since it is impossible for one and the same thing to be and not to be at one and the same time, everything is necessary so long as

---

[1] *Summa Theologica*, I. q.2, a.3.

[2] [*Editor's note*: Aquinas advanced five arguments for the existence of God. He called them "ways" of demonstrating the existence of such a being.]

it is. It is necessary so long as its cause makes it to be. This is called "to be necessary by another." In discussing the notions of motion and of efficient casualty, we pointed out that one cannot go to infinity in the series of causes. For if all actually existing beings held their necessity from some other being, what there is of necessity in the world could not be accounted for. We must therefore admit the existence of a being that is necessary by itself; that is to say, a being which, having of itself its own necessity, is to others the cause of such necessity as they have. Whereupon, turning for the third time to "the meaning of the name," Thomas Aquinas observes that this being that is necessary by itself is "what all men speak of as God." Consequently, there is a God.

This third way has identically the same nature and structure as the previous two. It differs from them only in that it brings into play modalities of being that are, so to speak, practically identical with being *qua* being. The sense experience from which it starts is here translated into metaphysical terms nearly as abstract, and therefore as indefinable, as being itself. With good reason, Avicenna had observed that "thing," "being," and "the necessary" (*necesse*) are the very first notions formed by the human mind as soon as, through sense knowledge, it establishes contact with material things. And, indeed, being is necessary to the extent that it is. This is the philosophical point, too often overlooked by its readers, that confers upon the proof its true meaning. The third way does not consist in establishing that a necessary being is required in order to account for the possibility of the beings subject to generation and corruption, but rather in order to account for what they have of necessity (*i.e.*, of being) while they last. It will suffice to read again the end of the demonstration in order to place this point beyond doubt. The proof intends to show that one cannot go on to infinity in necessary things" which have "their necessity" caused by another. Again, in reaching the conclusion of the proof, Thomas affirms the existence of a first necessary being causing in others *their* necessity. This point should be kept in mind, not only in interpreting the third way to God, but also in view of the time when, describing the nature of the created universe, Thomas Aquinas will attribute to its being an astonishing necessity.

6. THE ARGUMENT FROM APPARENT DESIGN

David Hume

David Hume (1711–1776) is acknowledged by friend and foe alike to be one of the most important and influential philosophers in the Western world. Immanuel Kant claimed that Hume was the thinker who awakened him out of his "dogmatic slumber." Hume attacked the notion that a person could have knowledge beyond what was experienced through sense perception and this empiricist theme is carried out in his critiques of the arguments for the existence of God. Hume's most important works are Treatise of Human Nature (1739), An Inquiry Concerning Human Understanding (1748), An Inquiry Concerning the Principles of Morals (1751). *The following selection is reprinted from* Dialogues Concerning Natural Religion *which, along with other anti-religious writings, was published after his death. It is not clear which speaker represents Hume's own position but most interpreters concede that it is probably that of Philo. Cleanthes obviously represents the view of a theist who thinks that the existence of God can be proved by appealing to various facts garnered from experience. Demea's position is that theistic belief is purely a matter of faith, with evidence for it being neither possible nor required.*

Not to lose any time in circumlocutions, said *Cleanthes,* addressing himself to *Demea,* much less in replying to the pious declamations of *Philo;* I shall briefly explain how I conceive this matter. Look round the world: Contemplate the whole and every part of it: You will find it to be nothing but great machine, subdivided into an infinite number of lesser machines, which again admit of subdivisions, to a degree beyond what human senses and faculties can trace and explain. All these various machines, and even their most minute parts, are adjusted to each other with an accuracy, which ravishes into admiration all men, who have ever contemplated them. The curious adapting of means to ends, throughout all nature, resembles exactly, though it much exceeds the productions of human contrivance; of human design, thought, wisdom, and intelligence. Since therefore the effects resemble each other, we are led to infer, by all the rules of analogy, that the causes also resemble; and that the Author of nature is somewhat similar to the mind of man; though possessed of much larger faculties, proportioned to the grandeur of the work, which he has executed. By this argument *a posteriori,* and by this argument alone, do we prove at once the existence of a Deity, and his similarity to human mind and intelligence.

I shall be so free, *Cleanthes,* said *Demea,* as to tell you, that from the beginning, I could not approve of your conclusion concerning the similarity of the Deity to men; still less can I approve of the mediums, by which you endeavour to establish it. What! No demonstration of the being of a God! No abstract arguments! No proofs *a priori!* Are these, which have hitherto been so much insisted on by philosophers, all fallacy, all sophism? Can we reach no farther in this subject than experience and probability? I will not say, that this is betraying the cause of a Deity: But surely, by this affected candour, you give advantage to atheists, which they never could obtain, by the mere dint of argument and reasoning.

What I chiefly scruple in this subject, said *Philo,* is not so much, that all religious arguments are by *Cleanthes* reduced to experience, as that they appear not to be even the most certain and irrefragable of that inferior kind. That a stone will fall, that fire will burn, that the earth has solidity, we have observed a thousand and a thousand times; and when any new instance of this nature is presented, we draw without hesitation the accustomed inference. The exact similarity of the cases gives us a perfect assurance of a similar event; and a stronger evidence is never desired nor sought after. But wherever you depart, in the least, from the similarity of the cases, you diminish proportionably the evidence; and may at last bring it to a very weak *analogy,* which is confessedly liable to error and uncertainty. After having experienced the circulation of the blood in human creatures, we make no doubt that it takes place in men and other animals. The analogical reasoning is much weaker, when we infer the circulation of the sap in vegetables from our experience that the blood circulates in animals; and those, who hastily followed that imperfect analogy, are found, by more accurate experiments, to have been mistaken.

If we see a house, *Cleanthes,* we conclude, with the greatest certainty, that it had an architect or builder; because this is precisely that species of effect, which we have experienced to proceed from that species of cause. But surely you will not affirm, that the universe bears such a resemblance to a house, that we can with the same certainty infer a similar cause, or that the analogy is here entire and perfect. The dissimilitude is so striking, that the utmost you can here pretend to is a guess, a conjecture, a presumption concerning a similar cause; and how that pretension will be received in the world, I leave you to consider.

It would surely be very ill received, replied *Cleanthes;* and I should be deservedly blamed and detested, did I allow, that the proofs of a Deity amounted to no more than a guess or conjecture. But is the whole adjustment of means to ends in a house and in the universe so slight a resemblance? The economy of final causes? The order, proportion, and arrangement of every part? Steps of a stair are plainly contrived, that human legs may use them in the mounting; and this inference is certain and infallible. Human legs are also contrived for walking and mounting; and this inference, I allow, is not altogether so certain, because of the dissimilarity which you remark; but does it, therefore, deserve the name only of presumption or conjecture?

Good God! cried *Demea*, interrupting him, where are we? Zealous defenders of religion allow, that the proofs of a Deity fall short of perfect evidence! And you, *Philo*, on whose assistance I depended, in proving the adorable mysteriousness of the divine nature, do you assent to all these extravagant opinions of *Cleanthes?* For what other name can I give them? Or why spare my censure, when such principles are advanced, supported by such an authority, before so young a man as *Pamphilus?*

You seem not to apprehend, replied *Philo*, that I argue with Cleanthes in his own way; and by showing him the dangerous consequences of his tenets, hope at last to reduce him to our opinion. But what sticks most with you, I observe, is the representation which *Cleanthes* has made of the argument *a posteriori;* and finding that that argument is likely to escape your hold and vanish into air, you think it so disguised, that you can scarcely believe it to be set in its true light. Now, however much I may dissent, in other respects, from the dangerous principles of *Cleanthes,* I must allow, that he has fairly represented that argument; and I shall endeavour so to state the matter to you, that you will entertain no farther scruples with regard to it.

Were a man to abstract from everything which he knows or has seen, he would be altogether incapable, merely from his own ideas, to determine what kind of scene the universe must be, or to give the preference to one state or situation of things above another. For as nothing, which he clearly conceives, could be esteemed impossible or implying a contradiction, every chimera of his fancy would be upon equal footing; nor could he assign any just reason, why he adheres to one idea or system, and rejects the others, which are equally possible.

Again; after he opens his eyes, and contemplates the world, as it really is, it would be impossible for him, at first, to assign the cause of any one event; much less, of the whole of things or of the universe. He might set his Fancy a rambling; and she might bring him in an infinite variety of reports and representations. These would all be possible; but being all equally possible, he would never, of himself, give a satisfactory account of his preferring one of them to the rest. Experience alone can point out to him the true cause of any phenomenon.

Now according to this method of reasoning, *Demea*, it follows (and is, indeed, tacitly allowed by *Cleanthes* himself) that order, arrangements, or the adjustment of final causes is not, of itself, any proof of design; but only so far as it has been experienced to proceed from that principle. For aught we can know *a priori* matter may contain the source or spring of order originally, within itself, as well as mind does; and there is no more difficulty in conceiving, that the several elements, from an internal unknown cause, may fall into the most exquisite arrangement, than to conceive that their ideas, in the great, universal mind, from a like internal, unknown cause, fall into that arrangement. The equal possibility of both these suppositions is allowed. But by experience we find (according to *Cleanthes*), that there is a difference between them. Throw several pieces of steel together, without shape or form; they will never arrange themselves so as to compose a watch: Stone, and mortar, and wood, without an architect, never erect a house. But the ideas in a human mind, we see, by an unknown, inexplicable economy, arrange themselves so as to form the plan of a watch or house. Experience, therefore, proves, that there is an original principle of order in mind, not in matter. From similar effects we infer similar causes. The adjustment of means to ends is alike in the universe, as in a machine of human contrivance. The causes, therefore, must be resembling.

I was from the beginning scandalised, I must own, with this resemblance, which is asserted, between the Deity and human creatures; and must conceive it to imply such a degradation of the supreme Being as no sound theist could endure. With your assistance, therefore, *Demea,* I shall endeavour to defend what you justly call the adorable mysteriousness of the divine nature, and shall refute this reasoning of *Cleanthes;* provided he allows, that I have made a fair representation of it.

When *Cleanthes* had assented, *Philo,* after a short pause, proceeded in the following manner.

That all inferences, *Cleanthes,* concerning fact, are founded on experience, and that all experimental reasonings are founded on the supposition, that similar causes prove similar effects, and similar effects similar causes; I shall not, at present, much dispute with you. But observe, I entreat you, with what extreme caution all just reasoners proceed in the transferring of experiments to similar cases. Unless the cases be exactly similar, they repose no perfect confidence in applying their past observation to any particular phenomenon. Every alteration of circumstances occasions a doubt concerning the event; and it requires new experiments to prove certainly, that the new circumstances are of no moment or importance. A change in bulk, situation, arrangement, age, disposition of the air, or surrounding bodies; any of these particulars may be attended with the most unexpected consequences: And unless the objects be quite familiar to us, it is the highest temerity to expect with assurance, after any of these changes, an event similar to that which

before fell under our observation. The slow and deliberate steps of philosophers, here, if any where, are distinguished from the precipitate
march of the vulgar, who, hurried on by the smallest similitude, are incapable of all discernment or consideration.

But can you think, *Cleanthes,* that your usual phlegm and philosophy have been preserved in so wide a step as you have taken, when
you compared to the universe houses, ships, furniture, machines; and
from their similarity in some circumstances inferred a similarity in their
causes? Thought, design, intelligence, such as we discover in men and
other animals, is no more than one of the springs and principles of the
universe, as well as heat or cold, attraction or repulsion, and a hundred
others, which fall under daily observation. It is an active cause, by which
some particular parts of nature, we find, produce alterations on other
parts. But can a conclusion, with any propriety, be transferred from
parts to the whole? Does not the great disproportion bar all comparison
and inference? From observing the growth of a hair, can we learn any
thing concerning the generation of a man? Would the manner of a
leaf's blowing, even though perfectly known, afford us any instruction
concerning the vegetation of a tree?

But allowing that we were to take the *operations* of one part
of nature upon another for the foundation of our judgment concerning
the *origin* of the whole (which never can be admitted); yet why select
so minute, so weak, so bounded a principle as the reason and design
of animals is found to be upon this planet? What peculiar privilege
has this little agitation of the brain which we call *thought,* that we must
thus make it the model of the whole universe? Our partiality in our
own favour does indeed present it on all occasions: But sound philosophy
ought carefully to guard against so natural an illusion.

So far from admitting, continued *Philo,* that the operations of a
part can afford us any just conclusion concerning the origin of the whole,
I will not allow any one part to form a rule for another part, if the
latter be very remote from the former. Is there any reasonable ground
to conclude, that the inhabitants of other planets possess thought, intelligence, reason, or any thing similar to these faculties in men? When
nature has so extremely diversified her manner of operation in this small
globe; can we imagine, that she incessantly copies herself throughout
so immense a universe? And if thought as we may well suppose, be confined merely to this narrow corner, and has even there so limited a
sphere of action; with what propriety can we assign it for the original
cause of all things? The narrow views of a peasant, who makes his
domestic economy the rule for the government of kingdoms, is in comparison a pardonable sophism.

But were we ever so much assured, that a thought and reason, resembling the human, were to be found throughout the whole universe, and were its activity elsewhere vastly greater and more commanding than it appears in this globe: Yet I cannot see, why the operations of a world, constituted, arranged, adjusted, can with any propriety be extended to a world, which is in its embryo-state, and is advancing towards that constitution and arrangement. By observation, we know somewhat of the economy, action, and nourishment of a finished animal; but we must transfer with great caution that observation to the growth of a foetus in the womb, and still more, to the formation of an animalcule in the loins of its parent. Nature, we find, even from our limited experience, possesses an infinite number of springs and principles, which incessantly discover themselves on every change of her position and situation. And what new and unknown principles would actuate her in so new and unknown a situation as that of the formation of a universe, we cannot, without the utmost temerity, pretend to determine.

A very small part of this great system, during a very short time, is very imperfectly discovered to us: And do we thence pronounce decisively concerning the original of the whole?

Admirable conclusion! Stone, wood, brick, iron, brass, have not, at this time, in this minute globe of earth, an order or arrangement without human art and contrivance: Therefore the universe could not originally attain its order and arrangement, without something similar to human art. But is a part of nature a rule for another part very wide of the former? Is it a rule for the whole? Is a very small part a rule for the universe? Is nature in one situation, a certain rule for nature in another situation, vastly different from the former?

And can you blame me, *Cleanthes*, if I here imitate the prudent reserve of Simonides, who, according to the noted story, being asked by Hiero, *What God was?* desired a day to think of it, and then two days more; and after that manner continually prolonged the term, without ever bringing in his definition or description? Could you even blame me, if I had answered at first, *that I did not know*, and was sensible that this subject lay vastly beyond the reach of my faculties? You might cry out sceptic and rallier as much as you pleased: But having found, in so many other subjects, much more familiar, the imperfections and even contradictions of human reason, I never should expect any success from its feeble conjectures, in a subject, so sublime, and so remote from the sphere of our observation. When two species of objects have always been observed to be conjoined together, I can *infer*, by custom, the existence of one wherever I see the existence of the other: And this I call an argument from experience. But how this argument can have place, where the objects, as in the present case, are single, individual, without parallel, or specific resemblance, may be difficult to explain.

And will any man tell me with a serious countenance, that an orderly universe must arise from some thought and art, like the human, because we have experience of it? To ascertain this reasoning, it were requisite, that we had experience of the origin of worlds; and it is not sufficient surely, that we have seen ships and cities arise from human art and contrivance. . . .

Philo was proceeding in this vehement manner, somewhat between jest and earnest, as it appeared to me; when he observed some signs of impatience in *Cleanthes,* and then immediately stopped short. What I had to suggest, said *Cleanthes,* is only that you would not abuse terms, or make use of popular expressions to subvert philosophical reasonings. You know, that the vulgar often distinguish reason from experience, even where the question relates only to matter of fact and existence; though it is found, where that *reason* is properly analysed, that it is nothing but a species of experience. To prove by experience the origin of the universe from mind is not more contrary to common speech than to prove the motion of the earth from the same principle. And a caviller might raise all the same objections to the Copernican system, which you have urged against my reasonings. Have you other earths, might he say, which you have seen to move? Have. . . .

Yes! cried *Philo,* interrupting him, we have other earths. Is not the moon another earth, which we see to turn round its centre? Is not Venus another earth, where we observe the same phenomenon? Are not the revolutions of the sun also a confirmation, from analogy, of the same theory? All the planets, are they not earths, which revolve about the sun? Are not the satellites moons, which move round Jupiter and Saturn, and along with these primary planets, round the sun? These analogies and resemblances, with others, which I have not mentioned, are the sole proofs of the Copernican system: And to you it belongs to consider, whether you have any analogies of the same kind to support your theory.

In reality, *Cleanthes,* continued he, the modern system of astronomy is now so much received by all enquirers, and has become so essential a part even of our earliest education, that we are not commonly very scrupulous in examining the reasons upon which it is founded. It is now become a matter of mere curiosity to study the first writers on that subject, who had the full force of prejudice to encounter, and were obliged to turn their arguments on every side, in order to render them popular and convincing. But if we peruse Galileo's famous *Dialogues* concerning the system of the world, we shall find that that great genius, one of the sublimest that ever existed, first bent all his endeavours to prove, that there was no foundation for the distinction commonly made between elementary and celestial substances. The schools, proceeding from the illustrations of sense, had carried this distinction very far; and had established the latter substances to be ingenerable, incorruptible, unalterable, impassible; and had assigned all the opposite qualities to the former. But Galileo, beginning with the moon, proved its similarity in every particular to the earth; its convex figure, its natural darkness when not illuminated, its density, its distinction into solid and liquid, the variations of its phases, the mutual illuminations of the earth and moon, their mutual eclipses, the inequalities of the lunar surface, &c. After many instances of this kind, with regard to all the planets, men plainly saw, that these bodies became proper objects of experience; and that the similarity of their nature enabled us to extend the same arguments and phenomena from one to the other.

In this cautious proceeding of the astronomers, you may read your own condemnation, *Cleanthes;* or rather may see, that the subject in which you are engaged exceeds all human reason and enquiry. Can you pretend to show any such similarity between the fabric of a house, and the generation of a universe? Have you ever seen nature in any such situation as resembles the first arrangement of the elements? Have worlds ever been formed under your eye? and have you had leisure to observe the whole progress of the phenomenon, from the first appearance of order to its final consummation? If you have, then cite your experience, and deliver your theory.

7. A CONTEMPORARY FORM OF THE DESIGN ARGUMENT

Richard Taylor

Richard Taylor *(1919–   ) is Professor of Philosophy at the University of Rochester and has taught at Brown and Columbia Universities. He has written* Action and Purpose *(1968),* Good and Evil *(1970), and* Metaphysics *(1963).*

CHANCE AND EVIDENCE

The idea we want to develop here is not easy to grasp without misunderstanding, so it will be best to approach it stepwise by considering first an example or two that should make it quite obvious.

Richard Taylor, Metaphysics, © *1963. Reprinted by permission of Prentice-Hall, Inc., Englewood Cliffs, New Jersey.*

Suppose, then, that you are riding in a railway coach and glancing from the window at one of the stops, you see numerous white stones scattered about on a small hillside near the train in a pattern resembling these letters: THE BRITISH RAILWAYS WELCOMES YOU TO WALES. Now you could scarcely doubt that these stones do not just accidentally happen to exhibit that pattern. You would, in fact, feel quite certain that they were purposefully *arranged* that way to convey an intelligible message. At the same time, however, you could not prove, just from a consideration of their arrangement alone, that they were arranged by a purposeful being. It is possible—at least logically so—that there was no guiding hand at all in back of this pattern, that it is simply the result of the operations of inanimate nature. It is possible that the stones, one by one, rolled down the hill and, over the course of centuries, finally ended up in that interesting arrangement, or that they came in some other accidental way to be so related to each other. For surely the mere fact that something has an interesting or striking shape or pattern, and thus *seems* purposefully arranged, is no proof that it is. There might always be some other explanation. Snowflakes, viewed under magnification, exhibit symmetrical, interesting and often beautiful shapes, and yet we know that these are not designed but can be explained simply in terms of the physics of crystallization. We find *apparently* purposeful arrangements and contrivances around us all the time, but we cannot always conclude that these are in fact the expressions of any purpose. Our own bodies and their organs seem purposeful not only in their individual structures but in their relationships to each other, and yet there are well known theories, resting on such nonpurposeful concepts as chance variation, natural selection, and so on, which are able, at least in the opinion of many learned men, to explain these structures without introducing any ideas of purpose and design at all.

Here, however, is the important point which it is easy to overlook; namely, that *if,* upon seeing from the train window a group of stones arranged as described, you were to conclude that you were entering Wales, and *if* your sole reason for thinking this, whether it was in fact good evidence or not, was that the stones were so arranged, *then* you could not, consistently with that, suppose that the arrangement of the stones was accidental. You would, in fact, be presupposing that they were arranged that way by an intelligent and purposeful being or beings, for the purpose of conveying a certain message having nothing to do with the stones themselves. Another way of expressing the same point is, that it would be *irrational* for you to regard the arrangement of the stones as evidence that you were entering Wales, and at the same time to suppose that they might have come to have that arrangement accidentally, that is, as the result of the ordinary interactions of natural or physical forces. If, for instance, they came to be so arranged over the course of time, simply by rolling down the hill, one by one, and finally just happening to end up that way, or if they were strewn upon the ground that way by the forces of an earthquake or storm or whatnot, then their arrangement would in no sense constitute evidence that you were entering Wales, or for anything whatever unconnected with themselves.

Consider another example. Suppose a stone were dug up and found to be covered with interesting marks, all more or less the same size and more or less in rows. Now there is nothing very remarkable about that. Glaciers and volcanoes have produced stones no less interesting in abundance. They may at first sight seem purposefully fabricated, but a geologist who knows how they came to be there can usually explain their interesting shapes and properties. Suppose further, however, that the marks on this stone are found to resemble the characters of an ancient alphabet. This, too, does not prove that they were purposefully inscribed, for natural forces can leave such marks as these on stones, and over the course of millions of years it is entirely possible that this should occasionally happen. There are places where one can, at will, pick up stones that are almost perfect rectangles and look exactly as though they were hewn by stonecutters, though in fact they resulted from glaciation. But now suppose that these marks are recognized by a scholar having a knowledge of that alphabet, and that with considerable uncertainty due to the obscurity of some of the marks and the obliteration of others, he renders a translation of them as follows: HERE KIMON FELL LEADING A BAND OF ATHENIANS AGAINST THE FORCES OF XERXES. Now one can, to be sure, still maintain that the marks are accidental, that they are only scratches left by volcanic activity, and that it is only a singular coincidence that they resemble, more or less, some intelligible message. Nature sometimes produces effects hardly less interesting and arresting than this. The point to make again, however, is this: if anyone having a knowledge of this stone concludes, solely on the basis of it, that there was someone named Kimon who died in battle near where this stone was found, then he cannot, rationally, suppose that the marks on the stone are the result of the chance or purposeless operations of the forces of nature. He must, on the contrary, assume that they were inscribed there by someone whose purpose was to record an historical fact. If the marks had a purposeless origin, as from volcanic activity or whatnot, then they cannot reveal any fact whatever except, perhaps, certain facts about themselves or their origin. It would, accordingly, be irrational for anyone to suppose *both* that what is seemingly expressed by the marks is true, and *also* that they appeared as the result of non-purposeful forces, provided the marks are his *sole* evidence for believing that what they seem to say is true.

SENSATION AND EVIDENCE

Our own organs of sense, to say nothing of our brains and nervous systems, are things of the most amazing and bewildering complexity and delicacy. No matter how far and minutely psychologists and physiologists press their studies of these organs, they seem hardly any closer to a real understanding of them, and how they enable us to *perceive* the world around us. At best they discover only how they convey stimuli and impress physical changes upon the brain. Theories of perception, drawing upon all the scientific and physiological knowledge accumulated to date, are hardly less crude than the speculations of the Greeks.

Some of these organs, moreover, strikingly resemble things purposefully designed and fabricated by men, though they greatly exceed in their delicacy and versatility anything men have invented. The parts and structure of the eye, for example, closely resemble those of a camera. Yet the comparison of these, however striking, is superficial, for the eye does not take pictures. Unlike a camera, it somehow enables its possessor to perceive and thereby to understand. Things like this can be more or less imitated by men, but they are usually crude and makeshift in comparison. It is sometimes almost irresistible, when considering such a thing as the eye, to suppose that, however it may have originated, it is constructed in that manner *in order* to enable its possessor to see. Many persons quite naturally think in these terms, without at all realizing the implications of such purposeful or teleological conceptions.

It must be noted, however, that just as it is possible for a collection of stones to present a novel and interesting arrangement on the side of a hill, and for marks to appear on a stone in a manner closely resembling some human artifact, and for these things still to be the accidental results of natural, nonpurposeful forces, so also it is possible for such things as our own organs of sense to be the accidental and unintended results, over ages of time, of perfectly impersonal, nonpurposeful forces. In fact, ever so many biologists believe that this is precisely what has happened, that our organs of sense are in no real sense purposeful things, but only appear so because of our failure to consider how they might have arisen through the normal workings of nature. It is supposed, for example, that if we apply the conceptions of chance mutations and variations, natural selection, and so on, then we can see how it is at least possible—perhaps even almost inevitable—that things of this sort should finally emerge, without any purpose behind them at all.

It would be astonishing indeed if a quantity of stones were hurled into the air and fell to earth in a pattern spelling out some intelligible message. Any man would feel, quite irresistibly, that it had been somehow *arranged* that they should fall that way. It would be less astonishing, however, if those stones were thrown a million times, and sooner or later fell to earth in such a pattern. Our astonishment would be still less if we found some perfectly natural, nonpurposeful explanation why they might sooner or later fall in that manner and, having so fallen, be thus preserved. If, for instance, we found that the stones were of slightly different weights, sizes and shapes, that these influenced how they were thrown and how they rolled upon landing, that these slight differences tended to favor the likelihood that certain ones would come to rest in the striking maner in which they do come to rest, and that certain obstructions on the ground would tend to preserve them in this arrangement, and so on, then we might find it entirely plausible how they might fall as they do without the intervention of any purposeful being at all. If our explanation were of this kind, however, then, as noted before, their arrangement would constitute no evidence whatever for anything not causally connected with themselves.

The mere complexity, refinement and seemingly purposeful arrangement of our sense organs do not, accordingly, constitute any conclusive reason for supposing that they are the outcome of any purposeful activity. A natural, nonpurposeful explanation of them is possible, and has been attempted—successfully, in the opinion of many.

The important point, however, and one that is rarely considered is that we do not simply *marvel* at these structures, and wonder how they came to be that way. We do not simply view them as amazing and striking things, and speculate upon their origins. We, in fact, whether justifiably or not, *rely* on them for the discovery of things that we suppose to be true and which we suppose to exist quite independently of those organs themselves. We suppose, without even thinking about it, that they reveal to us things that have nothing to do with themselves, their structures, or their origins. Just as we supposed that the stones on the hill told us that we were entering Wales—a fact having nothing to do with stones themselves—so also we suppose that our senses in some manner "tell us" what is true, at least sometimes. The stones on the hill could, to be sure, have been an accident, in which case we cannot suppose that they really tell us anything at all. So also, our senses and all our faculties could be accidental in their origins, and in that case they do not really tell us anything either. But the fact remains, that we do trust them, without the slightest reflection on the matter. Our seeing something is often thought to be, quite by itself, a good reason for believing that the thing exists, and it would be absurd to suggest that we *infer* this from the structure of our eyes or speculations upon their evolutionary origins. And so it is with our other faculties. Our remembering something is often considered to be, quite by itself, a good reason for believing that the thing remembered did happen. Our hearing a sound is often considered, quite by itself, a good reason for believing that a sound exists; and so on.

We are not here suggesting that our senses are infallible, nor even, that we ought to rely upon their testimony. The point is that we do rely upon them. We do not believe merely that our senses are remarkably interesting things. We do not believe merely that they produce interesting effects within us, nor merely that they produce beliefs in us. We assume, rightly or wrongly, that they are *trustworthy* guides with respect to what is true, and what exists independently of our senses and their origins; and we still assume this, even when they are our only guides.

We saw that it would be irrational for anyone to say *both* that the marks he found on a stone had a natural, nonpurposeful origin and *also* that they reveal some truth with respect to something other than themselves, something that is not merely inferred from them. One cannot rationally believe both of these things. So also, it is now suggested, it would be irrational for one to say *both* that his sensory and cognitive faculties had a natural, nonpurposeful origin and *also* that they reveal some truth with respect to something other than themselves, something that is not merely inferred from them. *If* their origin can be entirely accounted for in terms of chance variations, natural selection, and so on, without supposing that they somehow embody and express the purposes of some creative being, then the most we can say of them is that they exist, that they are complex and wondrous in their construction, and are perhaps in other respects interesting and remarkable. We cannot say that they are, entirely by themselves, reliable guides to any truth whatever, save only what can be inferred from their own structure and arrangement. If, on the other hand, we do assume that they are guides to some truths having nothing to do with themselves, then it is difficult to see how we can, consistently with that supposition, believe them to have arisen by accident, or by the ordinary workings of purposeless forces, even over ages of time.

At this point persons who have a deep suspicion of all such arguments as this, and particularly persons who are hostile to any of the claims of religion, are likely to seize upon numberless objections of a sort that it would hardly occur to anyone to apply to our first two examples, involving the stones. Thus, it is apt to be said that our cognitive faculties are not so reliable as some would suppose, which is irrelevant;

or that arguments from analogy prove nothing, which is also irrelevant, since none of the foregoing is an argument from analogy. Or it is claimed that we rely on our cognitive faculties only because we have found them reliable in the past, and thus have a sound inductive basis for our trust, which is absurd, if not question-begging. The reason I believe there is a world around me is, quite simply, that I see it, feel it, hear it, and am in fact perpetually in cognitive contact with it, or at least assume myself to be, without even considering the matter. To suggest that I *infer* its existence from the effects that it has within me, and that I find the inference justified on the ground that such inner effects have, in the past, been accompanied by external causes, is not only a ridiculous caricature, but begs the question of how, without relying upon my faculties, I could even confirm such an idea in the first place. Again, it is sometimes said that the capacity to grasp truths has a decided value to the survival of an organism, and that our cognitive faculties have evolved, quite naturally, through the operation of this principle. This appears farfetched, however, even if for no other reason than that man's capacity to understand what is true, through reliance upon his senses and cognitive faculties, far exceeds what is needed for survival. One might as well say that the sign on the hill welcoming tourists to Wales originated over the course of ages purely by accident, and has been preserved by the utility it was then found to possess. This is of course possible, but also immensely implausible.

8. THE PROBLEM OF EVIL

J. L. Mackie

J. L. Mackie (1917–   ) is Professor of Philosophy at the University of York, England. He has written a number of significant articles in the areas of ethics, philosophy of science, and philosophy of religion.

The traditional arguments for the existence of God have been fairly thoroughly criticised by philosophers. But the theologian can, if he wishes, accept this criticism. He can admit that no rational proof of God's

From Mind, *Vol. LXIV, 1955, pp. 200–212. Reprinted by permission of the author and the editor.*

existence is possible. And he can still retain all that is essential to his position, by holding that God's existence is known in some other, non-rational way. I think, however, that a more telling criticism can be made by way of the traditional problem of evil. Here it can be shown, not that religious beliefs lack rational support, but that they are positively irrational, that the several parts of the essential theological doctrine are inconsistent with one another, so that the theologian can maintain his position as a whole only by a much more extreme rejection of reason than in the former case. He must now be prepared to believe, not merely what cannot be proved, but what can be *disproved* from other beliefs that he also holds.

The problem of evil, in the sense in which I shall be using the phrase, is a problem only for someone who believes that there is a God who is both omnipotent and wholly good. And it is a logical problem, the problem of clarifying and reconciling a number of beliefs: it is not a scientific problem that might be solved by further observations, or a practical problem that might be solved by a decision or an action. These points are obvious; I mention them only because they are sometimes ignored by theologians, who sometimes parry a statement of the problem with such remarks as "Well, can you solve the problem yourself?" or "This is a mystery which may be revealed to us later" or "Evil is something to be faced and overcome, not to be merely discussed."

In its simplest form the problem is this: God is omnipotent; God is wholly good; and yet evil exists. There seems to be some contradiction between these three propositions, so that if any two of them were true the third would be false. But at the same time all three are essential parts of most theological positions: the theologian, it seems, at once *must* adhere and *cannot consistently* adhere to all three. (The problem does not arise only for theists, but I shall discuss it in the form in which it presents itself for ordinary theism.)

However, the contradiction does not arise immediately; to show it we need some additional premises, or perhaps some quasi-logical rules connecting the terms 'good,' 'evil,' and 'omnipotent.' These additional principles are that good is opposed to evil, in such a way that a good thing always eliminates evil as far as it can, and that there are no limits to what an omnipotent thing can do. From these it follows that a good omnipotent thing eliminates evil completely, and then the propositions that a good omnipotent thing exists, and that evil exists, are incompatible. . . .

There are, in fact, many so-called solutions which purport to remove the contradiction without abandoning any of its constituent propositions. These must be fallacious, as we can see from the very statement of the problem, but it is not so easy to see in each case precisely where the fallacy lies. I suggest that in all cases the fallacy has the general form suggested above: in order to solve the problem one (or perhaps more) of its constituent propositions is given up, but in such a way that it appears to have been retained, and can therefore be asserted without qualification in other contexts. Sometimes there is a further complication: the supposed solution moves to and fro between, say, two of the constituent propositions, at one point asserting the first of these but covertly abandoning the second, at another point asserting the second but covertly abandoning the first. These fallacious solutions often turn upon some equivocation with the words 'good' and 'evil,' or upon some vagueness about the way in which good and evil are opposed to one another, or about how much is meant by 'omnipotence'. I propose to examine some of these so-called solutions, and to exhibit their fallacies in detail. Incidentally, I shall also be considering whether an adequate solution could be reached by a minor modification of one or more of the constituent propositions, which would, however, still satisfy all the essential requirements of ordinary theism.

1. "Good cannot exist without evil" or "Evil is necessary as a counterpart to good."

It is sometimes suggested that evil is necessary as a counterpart to good, that if there were no evil there could be no good either, and that this solves the problem of evil. It is true that it points to an answer to the question "Why should there be evil?" But it does so only by qualifying some of the propositions that constitute the problem.

First, it sets a limit to what God can do, saying that God *cannot* create good without simultaneously creating evil, and this means either that God is not omnipotent or that there are *some* limits to what an omnipotent thing can do. It may be replied that these limits are always presupposed, that omnipotence has never meant the power to do what is logically impossible, and on the present view the existence of good without evil would be a logical impossibility. This interpretation of omnipotence may, indeed, be accepted as a modification of our original account which does not reject anything that is essential to theism, and I shall in general assume it in the subsequent discussion. It is, perhaps, the most common theistic view, but I think that some theists at least have maintained that God can do what is logically impossible. Many theists, at any rate, have held that logic itself is created or laid down by God, that logic is the way in which God arbitrarily chooses to think. (This is, of course, parallel to the ethical view that morally right actions are those which God arbitrarily chooses to command, and the two views encounter similar difficulties.) And *this* account of logic is clearly inconsistent with the view that God is bound by logical necessities—unless it is possible for an omnipotent being to bind himself, an issue which we shall consider later, when we come to the Paradox of Omnipotence. This solution of the problem of evil cannot, therefore, be consistently adopted along with the view that logic is itself created by God.

But, secondly, this solution denies that evil is opposed to good in our original sense. If good and evil are counterparts, a good thing will not "eliminate evil as far as it can." Indeed, this view suggests that good and evil are not strictly qualities of things at all. Perhaps the suggestion is that good and evil are related in much the same way as great and small. Certainly, when the term 'great' is used relatively as a condensation of 'greater than so-and-so,' and 'small' is used correspondingly, greatness and smallness are counterparts and cannot exist without each other. But in this sense greatness is not a quality, not an intrinsic feature of anything; and it would be absurd to think of a movement in favour of greatness and against smallness in this sense. Such a movement would be self-defeating, since relative greatness can be promoted only by a simultaneous promotion of relative smallness. I feel sure that no theists would be content to regard God's goodness as analogous to this—as if what he supports were not the *good* but the *better*, and as if he had the paradoxical aim that all things should be better than other things.

This point is obscured by the fact that 'great' and 'small' seem to have an absolute as well as a relative sense. I cannot discuss here whether there is absolute magnitude or not, but if there is, there could be an absolute sense for 'great,' it could mean of at least a certain size, and it would make sense to speak of all things getting bigger, of a universe that was expanding all over, and therefore it would make sense to speak of promoting greatness. But in *this* sense great and small are not logically necessary counterparts: either quality could exist without the other. There would be no logical impossibility in everything's being small or in everything's being great.

Neither in the absolute nor in the relative sense, then, of 'great' and 'small' do these terms provide an analogy of the sort that would be needed to support this solution of the problem of evil. In neither case are greatness and smallness *both* necessary counterparts *and* mutually opposed forces or possible objects for support and attack.

It may be replied that good and evil are necessary counterparts in the same way as any quality and its logical opposite: redness can occur, it is suggested, only if non-redness also occurs. But unless evil is merely the privation of good, they are not logical opposites, and some further argument would be needed to show that they are counterparts in the same way as genuine logical opposites. Let us assume that this could be given. There is still doubt of the correctness of the metaphysical principle that a quality must have a real opposite: I suggest that it is not really impossible that everything should be, say, red, that the truth is merely that if everything were red we should not notice redness, and so we should have no word 'red'; we observe and give names to qualities only if they have real opposites. If so, the principle that a term must have an opposite would belong only to our language or to our thought, and would not be an ontological principle, and, correspondingly, the rule that good cannot exist without evil would not state a logical necessity of a sort that God would just have to put up with. God might have made everything good, though *we* should not have noticed it if he had.

But, finally, even if we concede that this *is* an ontological principle, it will provide a solution for the problem of evil only if one is prepared to say, "Evil exists, but only just enough evil to serve as the counterpart of good." I doubt whether any theist will accept this. After all, the *ontological* requirement that non-redness should occur would be satisfied even if all the universe, except for a minute speck, were red, and, if there were a corresponding requirement for evil as a counterpart to good, a minute dose of evil would presumably do. But theists are not usually willing to say, in all contexts, that all the evil that occurs is a minute and necessary dose.

2. "Evil is necessary as a means to good."

It is sometimes suggested that evil is necessary for good not as a counterpart but as a means. In its simple form this has little plausibility as a solution of the problem of evil, since it obviously implies a severe restriction of God's power. It would be a *causal* law that you cannot have a certain end without a certain means, so that if God has to introduce evil as a means to good, he must be subject to at least some causal laws. This certainly conflicts with what a theist normally means by omnipotence. This view of God as limited by causal laws also conflicts with the view that causal laws are themselves made by God, which is more widely held than the corresponding view about the laws of logic. This conflict would, indeed, be resolved if it were possible for an omnipotent being to bind himself, and this possibility has still to be considered. Unless a favourable answer can be given to this question, the suggestion that evil is necessary as a means to good solves the problem of evil only by denying one of its constituent propositions, either that God is omnipotent or that 'omnipotent' means what it says.

3. "The universe is better with some evil in it than it could be if there were no evil."

Much more important is a solution which at first seems to be a mere variant of the previous one, that evil may contribute to the goodness of a whole in which it is found, so that the universe as a whole is better as it is, with some evil in it, than it would be if there were no evil. This solution may be developed in either of two ways. It may be supported by an aesthetic analogy, by the fact that contrasts heighten beauty, that in a musical work, for example, there may occur discords which somehow add to the beauty of the work as a whole. Alternatively, it may be worked out in connexion with the notion of progress, that the best possible organisation of the universe will not be static, but progressive, that the gradual overcoming of evil by good is really a finer thing than would be the eternal unchallenged supremacy of good.

In either case, this solution usually starts from the assumption that the evil whose existence gives rise to the problem of evil is primarily what is called physical evil, that is to say, pain. In Hume's rather half-hearted presentation of the problem of evil, the evils that he stresses are pain and disease, and those who reply to him argue that the existence of pain and disease makes possible the existence of sympathy, benevolence, heroism, and the gradually successful struggle of doctors and reformers to overcome these evils. In fact, theists often seize the opportunity to accuse those who stress the problem of evil of taking a low, materialistic view of good and evil, equating these with pleasure and pain, and of ignoring the more spiritual goods which can arise in the struggle against evils.

But let us see exactly what is being done here. Let us call pain and misery 'first order evil' or 'evil (1).' What contrasts with this, namely, pleasure and happiness, will be called 'first order good' or 'good (1).' Distinct from this is 'second order good' or 'good (2)' which somehow emerges in a complex situation in which evil (1) is a necessary component—logically, not merely causally, necessary. (Exactly *how* it emerges does not matter: in the crudest version of this solution good (2) is simply the heightening of happiness by the contrast with misery, in other versions it includes sympathy with suffering, heroism in facing danger, and the gradual decrease of first order evil and increase of first order good.) It is also being assumed that second order good is more important than first order good or evil, in particular that it more than outweighs the first order evil it involves.

Now this is a particularly subtle attempt to solve the problem of evil. It defends God's goodness and omnipotence on the ground that (on a sufficiently long view) this is the best of all logically possible worlds, because it includes the important second order goods, and yet it admits that real evils, namely first order evils, exist. But does it still hold that good and evil are opposed? Not, clearly, in the sense that we set out originally: good does not tend to eliminate evil in general. Instead, we have a modified, a more complex pattern. First order good

62

(*e.g.* happiness) *contrasts with* first order evil (*e.g.* misery): these two are opposed in a fairly mechanical way; some second order goods (*e.g.* benevolence) try to maximise first order good and minimise first order evil; but God's goodness is not this, it is rather the will to maximise *second* order good. We might, therefore, call God's goodness an example of a third order goodness, or good (3). While this account is different from our original one, it might well be held to be an improvement on it, to give a more accurate description of the way in which good is opposed to evil, and to be consistent with the essential theist position.

There might, however, be several objections to this solution.

First, some might argue that such qualities as benevolence—and *a fortiori* the third order goodness which promotes benevolence—have a merely derivative value, that they are not higher sorts of good, but merely means to good (1), that is, to happiness, so that it would be absurd for God to keep misery in existence in order to make possible the virtues of benevolence, heroism, etc. The theist who adopts the present solution must, of course, deny this, but he can do so with some plausibility, so I should not press this objection.

Secondly, it follows from this solution that God is not in our sense benevolent or sympathetic: he is not concerned to minimise evil (1), but only to promote good (2); and this might be a disturbing conclusion for some theists.

But, thirdly, the fatal objection is this. Our analysis shows clearly the possibility of the existence of a *second* order evil, an evil (2) contrasting with good (2) as evil (1) contrasts with good (1). This would include malevolence, cruelty, callousness, cowardice, and states in which good (1) is decreasing and evil (1) increasing. And just as good (2) is held to be the important kind of good, the kind that God is concerned to promote, so evil (2) will, by analogy, be the important kind of evil, the kind which God, if he were wholly good and omnipotent, would eliminate. And yet evil (2) plainly exists, and indeed most theists (in other contexts) stress its existence more than that of evil (1). We should, therefore, state the problem of evil in terms of second order evil, and against this form of the problem the present solution is useless.

An attempt might be made to use this solution again, at a higher level, to explain the occurrence of evil (2): indeed the next main solution that we shall examine does just this, with the help of some new notions. Without any fresh notions, such a solution would have little plausibility: for example, we could hardly say that the really important good was a good (3), such as the increase of benevolence in proportion to cruelty, which logically required for its occurence the occurrence of some second order evil. But even if evil (2) could be explained in this way, it is fairly clear that there would be third order evils contrasting with this third order good: and we should be well on the way to an infinite regress, where the solution of a problem of evil, stated in terms of evil (n), indicated the existence of an evil $(n + 1)$, and a further problem to be solved.

4. "Evil is due to human freewill."

Perhaps the most important proposed solution of the problem of evil is that evil is not to be ascribed to God at all, but to the independent actions of human beings, supposed to have been endowed by God with freedom of the will. This solution may be combined with the preceding one: first order evil (*e.g.* pain) may be justified as a logically necessary component in second order good (*e.g.* sympathy) while second order evil (*e.g.* cruelty) is not *justified,* but is so ascribed to human beings that God cannot be held responsible for it. This combination evades my third criticism of the preceding solution.

The freewill solution also involves the preceding solution at a higher level. To explain why a wholly good God gave men freewill although it would lead to some important evils, it must be argued that it is better on the whole that men should act freely, and sometimes err, than that they should be innocent automata, acting rightly in a wholly determined way. Freedom, that is to say, is now treated as a third order good, and as being more valuable than second order goods (such as sympathy and heroism) would be if they were deterministically produced, and it is being assumed that second order evils, such as cruelty, are logically necessary accompaniments of freedom, just as pain is a logically necessary pre-condition of sympathy.

I think that this solution is unsatisfactory primarily because of the incoherence of the notion of freedom of the will: but I cannot discuss this topic adequately here, although some of my criticisms will touch upon it.

First I should query the assumption that second order evils are logically necessary accompaniments of freedom. I should ask this: if God has made men such that in their free choices they sometimes prefer what is good and sometimes what is evil, why could he not have made men such that they always freely choose the good? If there is no logical impossibility in a man's freely choosing the good on one, or on several, occasions, there cannot be a logical impossibility in his freely choosing the good on every occasion. God was not, then, faced with a choice between making innocent automata and making beings who, in acting freely, would sometimes go wrong: there was open to him the obviously better possibility of making beings who would act freely but always go right. Clearly, his failure to avail himself of this possibility is inconsistent with his being both omnipotent and wholly good.

If it is replied that this objection is absurd, that the making of some wrong choices is logically necessary for freedom, it would seem that 'freedom' must here mean complete randomness or indeterminacy, including randomness with regard to the alternatives good and evil, in other words that men's choices and consequent actions can be "free" only if they are not determined by their characters. Only on this assumption can God escape the responsibility for men's actions; for if he made them as they are, but did not determine their wrong choices, this can only be because the wrong choices are not determined by men as they are. But then if freedom is randomness, how can it be a characteristic of *will?* And, still more, how can it be the most important good? What value or merit would there be in free choices if these were random actions which were not determined by the nature of the agent?

I conclude that to make this solution plausible two different senses of 'freedom' must be confused, one sense which will justify the view that freedom is a third order good, more valuable than other goods would be without it, and another sense, sheer randomness, to prevent us from ascribing to God a decision to make men such that they sometimes go wrong when he might have made them such that they would always freely go right.

This criticism is sufficient to dispose of this solution. But besides this there is a fundamental difficulty in the notion of an omnipotent God creating men with free will, for if men's wills are really free this must mean that even God cannot control them, that is, that God is no longer omnipotent. It may be objected that God's gift of freedom to men does not mean that he *cannot* control their wills, but that he always *refrains* from controlling their wills. But why, we may ask, should God refrain from controlling evil wills? Why should he not leave men free to will rightly, but intervene when he sees them beginning to will wrongly? If God could do this, but does not, and if he is wholly good, the only explanation could be that even a wrong free act of will is not really evil, that its freedom is a value which outweighs its wrongness, so that there would be a loss of value if God took away the wrongness and the freedom together. But this is utterly opposed to what theists say about sin in other contexts. The present solution of the problem of evil, then, can be maintained only in the form that God has made men so free that he *cannot* control their wills.

This leads us to what I call the Paradox of Omnipotence: can an omnipotent being make things which he cannot subsequently control? Or, what is practically equivalent to this, can an omnipotent being make rules which then bind himself? (These are practically equivalent because any such rules could be regarded as setting certain things beyond his control, and *vice versa.*) The second of these formulations is relevant to the suggestions that we have already met, that an omnipotent God creates the rules of logic or causal laws, and is then bound by them.

It is clear that this is a paradox: the questions cannot be answered satisfactorily either in the affirmative or in the negative. If we answer "Yes," it follows that if God actually makes things which he cannot control, or makes rules which bind himself, he is not omnipotent once he has made them: there are *then* things which he cannot do. But if we answer "No," we are immediately asserting that there are things which he cannot do, that is to say that he is already not omnipotent.

It cannot be replied that the question which sets this paradox is not a proper question. It would make perfectly good sense to say that a human mechanic has made a machine which he cannot control: if there is any difficulty about the question it lies in the notion of omnipotence itself.

This, incidentally, shows that although we have approached this paradox from the free will theory, it is equally a problem for a theological determinist. No one thinks that machines have free will, yet they may well be beyond the control of their makers. The determinist might reply that anyone who makes anything determines its ways of acting, and so determines its subsequent behaviour: even the human mechanic does this by his *choice* of materials and structure for his machine, though he does not know all about either of these: the mechanic thus determines, though he may not foresee, his machine's actions. And since God is omniscient, and since his creation of things is total, he both determines and foresees the ways in which his creatures will act. We may grant this, but it is beside the point. The question is not whether God *originally* determined the future actions of his creatures, but whether he can *subsequently* control their actions, or whether he was able in his original creation to put things beyond his subsequent control. Even on determinist principles the answers "Yes" and "No" are equally irreconcilable with God's omnipotence.

Before suggesting a solution of this paradox, I would point out that there is a parallel Paradox of Sovereignty. Can a legal sovereign make a law restricting its own future legislative power? For example, could the British parliament make a law forbidding any future parliament to socialise banking, and also forbidding the future repeal of this law itself? Or could the British parliament, which was legally sovereign in Australia in, say, 1899, pass a valid law, or series of laws, which made it no longer sovereign in 1933? Again, neither the affirmative nor the negative answer is really satisfactory. If we were to answer "Yes," we should be admitting the validity of a law which, if it were actually made, would mean that parliament was no longer sovereign. If we were to answer "No," we should be admitting that there is a law, not logically absurd, which parliament cannot validly make, that is, that parliament is not now a legal sovereign. This paradox can be solved in the following way. We should distinguish between first order laws, that is laws governing the actions of individuals and bodies other than the legislature, and second order laws, that is laws about laws, laws governing the actions of the legislature itself. Correspondingly, we should distinguish two orders of sovereignty, first order sovereignty (sovereignty) (1)) which is unlimited authority to make first order laws, and second order sovereignty (sovereignty (2)) which is unlimited authority to make second order laws. If we say that parliament is sovereign we might mean that any parliament at any time has sovereignty (1), or we might mean that parliament has both sovereignty (1) and sovereignty (2) at present, but we cannot without contradiction mean both that the present parliament has sovereignty (2) and that every parliament at every time has sovereignty (1), for if the present parliament has sovereignty (2) it may use it to take away the sovereignty (1) of later parliaments. What the paradox shows is that we cannot ascribe to any continuing institution legal sovereignty in an inclusive sense.

The analogy between omnipotence and sovereignty shows that the paradox of omnipotence can be solved in a similar way. We must distinguish between first order omnipotence (omnipotence (1)), that is unlimited power to act, and second order omnipotence (omnipotence (2)), that is unlimited power to determine what powers to act things shall have. Then we could consistently say that God all the time has omnipotence (1), but if so no beings at any time have powers to act independently of God. Or we could say that God at one time had omnipotence (2), and used it to assign independent powers to act to certain things, so that God thereafter did not have omnipotence (1). But what the paradox shows is that we cannot consistently ascribe to any continuing being omnipotence in an inclusive sense.

An alternative solution of this paradox would be simply to deny that God is a continuing being, that any times can be assigned to his actions at all. But on this assumption (which also has difficulties of its own) no meaning can be given to the assertion that God made men with wills so free that he could not control them. The paradox of omnipotence can be avoided by putting God outside time, but the freewill solution of the problem of evil cannot be saved in this way, and equally it remains impossible to hold that an omnipotent God *binds himself* by causal or logical laws.

CONCLUSION

Of the proposed solutions of the problem of evil which we have examined, none has stood up to criticism. There may be other solutions which require examination, but this study strongly suggests that there is no valid solution of the problem which does not modify at least one of the constituent propositions in a way which would seriously affect the essential core of the theistic position.

Quite apart from the problem of evil, the paradox of omnipotence has shown that God's omnipotence must in any case be restricted in one way or another, that unqualified omnipotence cannot be ascribed to any being that continues through time. And if God and his actions are not in time, can omnipotence, or power of any sort, be meaningfully ascribed to him?

9.　THE MEANING OF LIFE

Kurt Baier

Kurt Baier *(1917–　　) is Professor of Philosophy at the University of Pittsburgh. His major work is* The Moral Point of View *(1958). The following selection is part of Baier's Inaugural Lecture at Canberra University College, 1957.*

How can there be any meaning in our life if it ends in death? What meaning can there be in it that our inevitable death does not destroy? How can our existence be meaningful if there is no after-life in which perfect justice is meted out? How can life have any meaning if all it holds out to us are a few miserable earthly pleasures and even these to be enjoyed only rarely and for such a piteously short time?

I believe this is the point which exercises most people most deeply. Kirilov, in Dostoevsky's novel, *The Possessed*, claims, just before committing suicide, that as soon as we realize that there is no God, we cannot live any longer, we must put an end to our lives. One of the reasons which he gives is that when we discover that there is no paradise, we have nothing to live for.

". . . there was a day on earth, and in the middle of the earth were three crosses. One on the cross had such faith that He said to another, 'To-day thou shalt be with me in paradise.' The day came to an end, both died, and they went, but they found neither paradise nor

From "The Meaning of Life," Inaugural Lecture at Canberra University College, 1957. Reprinted by permission of the author and the Registrar, The Australian National University.

resurrection. The saying did not come true. Listen: that man was the highest of all on earth . . . There has never been any one like Him before or since, and never will be . . . And if that is so, if the laws of Nature did not spare even *Him*, and made even Him live in the midst of lies and die for a lie, then the whole planet is a lie and is based on a lie and a stupid mockery. So the very laws of the planet are a lie and a farce of the devil. What, then, is there to live for?"[1] And Tolstoy, too, was nearly driven to suicide when he came to doubt the existence of God and an after-life.[2] And this is true of many.

What, then, is it that inclines us to think that if life is to have a meaning, there would have to be an after-life? It is this. The Christian world view contains the following three propositions. The first is that since the Fall, God's curse of Adam and Eve, and the expulsion from Paradise, life on earth for mankind has not been worth while, but a vale of tears, one long chain of misery, suffering, unhappiness, and injustice. The second is that a perfect after-life is awaiting us after the death of the body. The third is that we can enter this perfect life only on certain conditions, among which is also the condition of enduring our earthly existence to its bitter end. In this way, our earthly existence which, in itself, would not (at least for many people if not all) be worth living, acquires meaning and significance: only if we endure it, can we gain admission to the realm of the blessed.

It might be doubted whether this view is still held to-day. However, there can be no doubt that even to-day we all imbibe a good deal of this view with our earliest education. In sermons, the contrast between the perfect life of the blessed and our life of sorrow and drudgery is frequently driven home and we hear it again and again that Christianity has a message of hope and consolation for all those "who are weary and heavy laden".[3]

It is not surprising, then, that when the implications of the scientific world picture begin to sink in, when we come to have doubts about the existence of God and another life, we are bitterly disappointed. For if there is no afterlife, then all we are left is our earthly life which we have come to regard as a necessary evil, the painful fee of admission to the land of eternal bliss. But if there is no eternal bliss to come and if this hell on earth is all, why hang on till the horrible end?

---

[1] Fyodor Dostoyevsky, *The Devils* (London: The Penguin Classics, 1953), pp. 613–614.

[2] Leo Tolstoy, *A Confession, The Gospel in Brief, and What I Believe,* The World's Classics, p. 24.

[3] See for instance J. S. Whale, *Christian Doctrine*, pp. 171, 176–178, etc. See also Stephen Neill, *Christian Faith To-Day,* p. 241.

Our disappointment therefore arises out of these two propositions, that the earthy life is not worth living, and that there is another perfect life of eternal happiness and joy which we may enter upon if we satisfy certain conditions. We can regard our lives as meaningful, if we believe both. We cannot regard them as meaningful if we believe merely the first and not the second. It seems to me inevitable that people who are taught something of the history of science, will have serious doubts about the second. If they cannot overcome these, as many will be unable to do, then they must either accept the sad view that their life is meaningless or they must abandon the first proposition: that this earthly life is not worth living. They must find the meaning of their life in this earthly existence. But is this possible?

A moment's examination will show us that the Christian evaluation of our earthly life as worthless, which we accept in our moments of pessimism and dissatisfaction, is not one that we normally accept. Consider only the question of murder and suicide. On the Christian view, other things being equal, the most kindly thing to do would be for every one of us to kill as many of our friends and dear ones as still have the misfortune to be alive, and then to commit suicide without delay, for every moment spent in this life is wasted. On the Christian view, God has not made it that easy for us. He has forbidden us to hasten others or ourselves into the next life. Our bodies are his private property and must be allowed to wear themselves out in the way decided by Him, however painful and horrible that may be. We are, as it were, driving a burning car. There is only one way out, to jump clear and let it hurtle to destruction. But the owner of the car has forbidden it on pain of eternal tortures worse than burning. And so we do better to burn to death inside.

On this view, murder is a less serious wrong than suicide. For murder can always be confessed and repented and therefore forgiven, suicide cannot—unless we allow the ingenious way out chosen by the heroine of Graham Greene's play, The Living Room, who swallows a slow but deadly poison and, while awaiting its taking effect, repents having taken it. Murder, on the other hand, is not so serious because, in the first place, it need not rob the victim of anything but the last lap of his march in the vale of tears, and, in the second place, it can always be forgiven. Hamlet, it will be remembered, refrains from killing his uncle during the latter's prayers because, as a true Christian, he believes that killing his uncle at that point, when the latter has purified his soul by repentance, would merely be doing him a good turn, for murder at such a time would simply despatch him to undeserved and everlasting happiness.

These views strike us as odd, to say the least. They are the logical consequence of the official medieval evaluation of this our earthly existence. If this life is not worth living, then taking it is not robbing the person concerned of much. The only thing wrong with it is the damage to God's property, which is the same both in the case of murder and suicide. We do not take this view at all. Our view, on the contrary, is that murder is the most serious wrong because it consists in taking away from some one else against his will his most precious possession, his life. For this reason, when a person suffering from an incurable disease asks to be killed, the mercy killing of such a person is regarded as a much less serious crime than murder because, in such a case, the killer is not robbing the other of a good against his will. Suicide is not regarded as a real crime at all, for we take the view that a person can do with his own possessions what he likes.

However, from the fact that these are our normal opinions, we can infer nothing about their truth. After all, we could easily be mistaken. Whether life is or is not worthwhile, is a value judgment. Perhaps all this is merely a matter of opinion or taste. Perhaps no objective answer can be given. Fortunately, we need not enter deeply into these difficult and controversial questions. It is quite easy to show that the medieval evaluation of earthly life is based on a misguided procedure.

Let us remind ourselves briefly of how we arrive at our value judgments. When we determine the merits of students, meals, tennis players, bulls, or bathing belles, we do so on the basis of some criteria and some standard or norm. Criteria and standards notoriously vary from field to field and even from case to case. But that does not mean that we have *no* idea about what are the appropriate criteria or standards to use. It would not be fitting to apply the criteria for judging bulls to the judgment of students or bathing belles. They score on quite different points. And even where the same criteria are appropriate as in the judgment of students enrolled in different schools and universities, the standards will vary from one institution to another. Pupils who would only just pass in one, would perhaps obtain honours in another. The higher the standard applied, the lower the marks, that is, the merit conceded to the candidate.

The same procedure is applicable also in the evaluation of a life. We examine it on the basis of certain criteria and standards. The medieval Christian view uses the criteria of the ordinary man: a life is judged by what the person concerned can get out of it: the balance of happiness over unhappiness, pleasure over pain, bliss over suffering. Our earthly life is judged not worthwhile because it contains much unhappiness, pain, and suffering, little happiness, pleasure, and bliss. The next life is judged worth while because it provides eternal bliss and no suffering.

Armed with these criteria, we can compare the life of this man and that, and judge which is more worth while, which has a greater balance of bliss over suffering. But criteria alone enable us merely to make comparative judgments of value, not absolute ones. We can say which is more and which is less worth while, but we cannot say which is worth while and which is not. In order to determine the latter, we must introduce a standard. But what standard ought we to choose?

Ordinarily, the standard we employ is the average of the kind. We call a man and a tree tall if they are well above the average of their kind. We do not say that Jones is a short man because he is shorter than a tree. We do not judge a boy a bad student because his answer to a question in the Leaving Examination is much worse than that given in reply to the same question by a young man sitting for his finals for the Bachelor's degree.

The same principles must apply to judging lives. When we ask whether a given life was or was not worth while, then we must take into consideration the range of worthwhileness which ordinary lives normally cover. Our end poles of the scale must be the best possible and the worst possible life that one finds. A good and worthwhile life is one that is well above average. A bad one is one well below.

The Christian evaluation of earthly lives is misguided because it adopts a quite unjustifiably high standard. Christianity singles out the major shortcomings of our earthly existence: there is not enough happiness; there is too much suffering; the good and bad points are quite unequally and unfairly distributed; the underprivileged and underendowed do not get adequate compensation; it lasts only a short time. It then quite accurately depicts the perfect or ideal life as that which does not have any of these shortcomings. Its next step is to promise the believer that he will be able to enjoy this perfect life later on. And then it adopts as its standard of judgment the perfect life, dismissing as inadequate anything that falls short of it. Having dismissed earthly life as miserable, it further damns it by characterizing most of the pleasures of which earthly existence allows as bestial, gross, vile, and sinful, or alternatively as not really pleasurable.

This procedure is as illegitimate as if I were to refuse to call anything tall unless it is infinitely tall, or anything beautiful unless it is perfectly flawless, or any one strong unless he is omnipotent. Even if it were true that there is available to us an after-life which is flawless and perfect, it would still not be legitimate to judge earthly lives by this standard. We do not fail every candidate who is not an Einstein. And if we do not believe in an after-life, we must of course use ordinary earthly standards.

I have so far only spoken of the worthwhileness, only of what a person can get out of a life. There are other kinds of appraisal. Clearly, we evaluate people's lives not merely from the point of view of what they yield to the persons that lead them, but also from that of other men on whom these lives have impinged. We judge a life more significant if the person has contributed to the happiness of others, whether directly by what he did for others, or by the plans, discoveries, inventions, and work he performed. Many lives that hold little in the way of pleasure or happiness for its owner are highly significant and valuable, deserve admiration and respect on account of the contributions made.

It is now quite clear that death is simply irrelevant. If life can be worthwhile at all, then it can be so even though it be short. And if it is not worthwhile at all, then an eternity of it is simply a nightmare. It may be sad that we have to leave this beautiful world, but it is so only if and because it is beautiful. And it is no less beautiful for coming to an end. I rather suspect that an eternity of it might make us less appreciative, and in the end it would be tedious.

It will perhaps be objected now that I have not really demonstrated that life has a meaning, but merely that it can be worthwhile or have value. It must be admitted that there is a perfectly natural interpretation of the question, "What is the meaning of life?" on which my view actually proves that life has no meaning. I mean the interpretation discussed in section 2 of this lecture [omitted here, ed.], where I attempted to show that, if we accept the explanations of natural science, we cannot believe that living organisms have appeared on earth in accordance with the deliberate plan of some intelligent being. Hence, on this view, life cannot be said to have a purpose, in the sense in which man-made things have a purpose. Hence it cannot be said to have a meaning or significance in that sense.

However, this conclusion is innocuous. People are disconcerted by the thought that *life as such* has no meaning in that sense only because they very naturally think it entails that no individual life can have meaning either. They naturally assume that *this* life or *that* can have meaning only if *life as such* has meaning. But it should by now be clear that your life and mine may or may not have meaning (in one sense) even if life as such has none (in the other). Of course, it follows from this that your life may have meaning while mine has not. The Christian view guarantees a meaning (in one sense) to every life, the scientific view does not (in any sense). By relating the question of the meaningfulness of life to the particular circumstances of an individual's existence, the scientific view leaves it an open question whether an individual's life has meaning or not. It is, however, clear that the latter is the important sense of "having a meaning." Christians, too, must feel that their life is wasted and meaningless if they have not achieved salvation. To know that even such lost lives have a meaning in another sense is no consolation to them. What matters is not that life should have a guaranteed meaning, whatever happens here or here-after, but that, by luck (Grace) or the right temperament and attitude (Faith) or a judicious life (Works) a person should make the most of his life.

"But here lies the rub," it will be said. "Surely, it makes all the difference whether there is an after-life. This is where morality comes in." It would be a mistake to believe that. Morality is not the meting out of punishment and reward. To be moral is to refrain from doing to others what, if they followed reason, they would not do to themselves, and to do for others what, if they followed reason, they would want to have done. It is, roughly speaking, to recognize that others, too, have a right to a worthwhile life. Being moral does not make one's own life worthwhile, it helps others to make theirs so.

THE PROBLEM OF MIND AND IMMORTALITY

III

Can I Survive the Death of My Body?

10. CAN A MAN WITNESS HIS OWN FUNERAL?

Antony Flew

Antony Flew. *(See selection number 3 for biographical note.)*

"Whether we are to live in a future state, as it is the most important question which can possibly be asked, so it is the most intelligible one which can be expressed in language" (Bishop Butler in the dissertation *Of Personal Identity*).

I

The purposes of this paper are, *first*, to try to begin to raise what Butler called "strange perplexities" [1] about the meaningfulness of this question and, *second*, to attempt to dispose of the counter-thesis, maintained by Schlick, that it must be significant because the possibility being discussed is not merely conceivable but also imaginable. These are very strictly limited objectives. We shall not, and shall not pretend to, do more than attack these two of the vast complex of problems, both logical and empirical, compendiously described as the questions of Survival and Immortality.

II

Now suppose someone offers the gambit "We all of us survive death" or "We all of us live forever." Might we not reply "Whatever in the world do you mean? For, in the ordinary senses of the words you use, the former sentence is self-contradictory and the latter denies one of the most securely established of all empirical generalisations; for it is the contrary of that traditional darling of the logicians 'All men are mortal'." As the objections to the two sentences are different, let us deal with each of them separately.

From "Can A Man Witness His Own Funeral?," *Hibbert Journal*, Vol. 54, pp. 242–250. Reprinted by permission of the author and the Hibbert Trustees.

---

[1] *Op. cit.*

"We all of us survive death" is self-contradictory because we use the words "death" and "survival" and their derivatives in such a way that the classification of the crew of a torpedoed ship into "Dead" and "Survivors" is both exclusive and exhaustive. Every member of the crew must (logical "must") have either died or survived: and no member of the crew could (logical "could") have both died and survived. It is easy to overlook that "We all of us survive death" is self-contradictory because we all habitually and wisely give all utterances the benefit of the doubt. Generously assuming that other people usually have something intelligible to express even when they speak or write in unusual or incorrect ways, we attempt to attach sense even to expressions which are strictly self-contradictory. This tendency is frequently exploited by advertisers. Posters advertising the film *Bachelor Husband* catch the eye precisely because the expression "bachelor husband" is self-contradictory, and therefore paradoxical. We tend to puzzle over the title, to ponder—doubtless to the advertiser's eventual profit—over the non-linguistic improprieties suggested by this linguistically improper expression. If we see the headline "We survived death!" we do not just exclaim (in the tone of voice of rigid logical schoolmasters) "Nonsense: you either survive or you die!", but, curiosity aroused, we read on to learn how the death was only 'death' (in inverted commas), that the people in question had only pretended, been reported, appeared, to die; but had not of course in fact died. Sometimes, for instance, people show all the usual 'symptoms' of death, all the usually reliable signs that they will not walk, or talk, or joke again, but then, surprisingly, recover and do walk and talk and joke once more. This happened quite often in World War II: Russian doctors in particular reported many cases of patients who showed the usual indications of death—the heart not beating and so forth—but were brought back to life by shock treatments, blood transfusions, and suchlike. These patients thus survived 'death' (in inverted commas) to refer to the condition of the patients or at least the language of *Soviet War News* (London) was adapted— to meet the new situation: "We cannot survive death" was retained as the expression of a necessary truth; and the expression "clinical death" was introduced as a more precise and less awkward substitute for 'death' (in inverted commas) to refer to the condition of the patients who showed all the usual 'symptoms' but who nevertheless might or might not survive to tell the tale. "We survive death" thus was, and remains, self-contradictory. The paradox use of "survives death" in advertising and headlines, and the inverted-comma use of 'death' in which people can be said to return from the 'dead' (in inverted commas), do not in the least weigh against this contention. They positively reinforce it: it is precisely because "He survived death" is self-contradic-

The Problem of Mind and Immortality

tory that it is a good headline; it is precisely because "to survive death" is self-contradictory that the doctors put the word "death" between warning inverted commas when first they had to report that a patient survived 'death,' and later introduced the new expression "clinical death" to replace the makeshift 'death' (in inverted commas) when similar cases occurred repeatedly.

"We all of us live forever" is, on the other hand, not self-contradictory but just as a matter of fact false, being as it is the flat contrary of the massively confirmed generalisation "All men are mortal." (Though if you choose to use the latter expression to express not a factual generalisation but an artificial truth of logic, making it true by definition that all *men* are mortal, thus incurring the probably unwelcome consequence that on this definition neither the prophet Elijah nor—on the Roman view—the Virgin Mary can count as human beings; then, of course, "we all of us [men] live forever" will on your definition become self-contradictory, and not merely false as a matter of manifest empirical fact.) But, like "We all of us survive death," "We all of us live forever" has what we might call 'headline value.' Both are 'shockers' and thus catch the eye and arouse curiosity. They make us wonder what the writer is up to, what is the story which he is going to tell under these arresting headlines. For surely he cannot really be intending to say something so obviously nonsensical or so notoriously false as what at first glance he seems to be saying.

Now many stories have been and still more could be told under these headlines. People have claimed that "We all of us live forever, *because* the evil (and sometimes even the good) that men do lives after them." People have argued that "We survive death, *because* our descendants will live on after we are dead." And in the variety and irrelevance of their supporting reasons they have revealed the variety and irrelevance of the theses which they have been concerned to maintain when they used these and similar paradoxical expressions. The only use with which we are concerned here—and certainly the only use which would justify Butler's claim that here was "the most important question which can possibly be asked"—is that in which they are intended to support or express what Wisdom has called "the logically unique expectation," [2] the expectation that we shall see and feel, or at any rate and more noncommittally, that we shall 'have experiences' after we are dead. Therefore we shall take it that the person who has said "We all of us survive death" or "We all of us live forever" was making a move intended to justify such expectations.

---

[2] In 'Gods' PAS 44/5, reprinted in *Logic and Language* I, A. G. N. Flew, ed. (Blackwell, 1951).

And against this move the simple-minded counter-move is to attempt a sort of philosophical fools' mate. Clearly this expectation cannot (logical "cannot") be well grounded unless we are going to exist after our deaths. But we have been insisting that it is not merely false but actually self-contradictory to say that we survive death. So we cannot (logical "cannot") exist after our deaths. Therefore these logically unique expectations cannot be well founded. Indeed the suggestion on which they are based, the assumption which they presuppose (*viz.* that "We survive death") is self-contradictory and therefore senseless.

III

Well, of course there are several possible defences against this sort of attack; and the possible variations on these defences are innumerable. The traditional one depends on the distinction between body and mind, or body and soul (what Professor Ryle, unaccountably ignoring Plato, insists on calling the *Cartesian* Myth; a notion which—far from being a philosopher's fancy—is incapsulated in the idiom of innumerable languages and is a widespread, though not universal, element in folklore and religion). The first stage is to maintain that people consist of two elements, one, the body, visible, tangible and corporeal, the other, the mind or soul, invisible, intangible and incorporeal. The second stage is to maintain that we are our souls or minds. This stage is indispensable: unless we are our souls the survival of our souls will not be our survival; and the news that our souls were to be preserved after we died would be of no more importance or concern to us than the news that any other parts of us—our appendices, say—were to be preserved. Granted these two presuppositions (and "presuppositions" is surely the *mot juste*: for they are rarely either distinguished from one another or argued for) it is then significant and even plausible to say that we (our incorporeal souls, that is) survive death (which is "the mere death of the body"). The desire to allow doctrines of personal immortality to be significant and plausible is one of the main drives behind dualist conceptions, and one perhaps insufficiently stressed by Professor Ryle in *The Concept of Mind*. But this is a vast and another subject; here we propose to concentrate exclusively on one more modern defence, that which claims that "I shall survive my death" cannot be self-contradictory and therefore senseless, because it refers to a possibility which is not merely conceivable but imaginable.

This argument was used by Moritz Schlick [3] "I take it for granted that . . . we are concerned with the question of survival after 'death'."

---

[3] *Philosophical Review* (July, 1936), p. 356. Reprinted in Feigl and Sellars' *Readings in Philosophical Analysis,* pp. 159–160.

—[His inverted commas. These surely tacitly concede the claim that "to survive death" is a self-contradictory expression: compare the similar tacit admission made in the tombstone insistence "Not dead but sleeping". A.F.] I think we may agree with Professor Lewis when he says about this hypothesis: "Our understanding of what would verify it has no lack of clarity. In fact I can easily imagine, e.g. witnessing the funeral of my own body and continuing to exist without a body, for nothing is easier than to describe a world which differs from our ordinary world only in the complete absence of all data which I would call parts of my own body. We must conclude that immortality, in the sense defined, should not be regarded as a metaphysical 'problem,' but is an empirical hypothesis, because it possesses logical verifiability. It could be verified by following the prescription 'Wait until you die!'." A briefer and more puckish version of the same argument can be found in John Wisdom's unending saga *Other Minds*. "I know indeed what it would be like to witness my own funeral—the men in tall silk hats, the flowers, and the face beneath the glass-topped coffin" [4] and it is also deployed by Dr. Casimir Lewy in his 'Is the Notion of Disembodied Existence Self-contradictory?'

So far as I know this argument has never been challenged: presumably partly because we can most of us imagine (image) a scene such as Wisdom describes; and partly because no one wants to arrogate to himself the right to decide what Wisdom or Schlick or anyone other than he himself can or cannot imagine (image). But the argument can and should be challenged: and it can be done without arbitrarily prescribing any limit to Wisdom's obviously very considerable imaginative powers. For there is all the difference in the world between: imagining what it would be like to witness my own funeral (which requires only a minor effort); and imagining what it would be like to witness me witnessing *my own* funeral (which is logically impossible. Or at least, less dogmatically, is very far from being a logically straightforward matter). If it really is I who witness it then it is not my funeral but only 'my funeral' (in inverted commas): and if it really is my funeral then I cannot be a witness, for I shall be dead and in the coffin.

Of course I can imagine many situations which might be described as my watching 'my own funeral' (in inverted commas): I can remember Harry Lime in the film *The Third Man* watching 'his own funeral,' and of course I can imagine being in the same situation as Harry Lime; but it was not really Harry Lime's own funeral, and what I can imagine would not really be mine. Again I can imagine my own funeral—I shall not try to better Wisdom's whimsical description of such a scene—but

---

[4] *Mind* (1942), p. 2 and *Other Minds* (Blackwell, 1952), p. 36.

now what I am imagining is not *my* witnessing *my own* funeral but merely my own funeral. (Parenthetically, it should be pointed out that Wisdom is far too good a writer to have committed himself to the former—and improper—description of his imaginings (imagings). What he wrote was "I know indeed what it would be like to witness my own funeral." Unfortunately, this will not, under examination, support his thesis: which requires that he should be able to imagine his surviving his own death and his witnessing his own funeral: which seems to be impossible, since the latter supposition, like the former, is apparently self-contradictory).

But surely this is merely slick? Surely I can perfectly well imagine my own funeral, really my own funeral with my body in the coffin and not a substitute corpse or a weight of bricks; with me there watching it all, but invisible, intangible, a disembodied spirit? Well, yes, this seems all right: until someone asks the awkward question "Just how does all this differ from your imagining your own funeral without your being there at all (except as the corpse in the coffin)?"

Certainly Schlick could imagine, as he claimed, "the funeral of his own body": though it is perhaps a pity that he should describe what he imagined in this way and not, more naturally, as "his own funeral." But then he goes on to talk of imagining his "continuing to exist without a body": which he tries to justify by claiming that "nothing is easier than to describe a world which differs from our ordinary world only in the complete absence of all data which I would call parts of my own body." But the fact that we can all of us describe, or even imagine, a world which would differ from our ordinary world only in the complete absence of all data describable as parts of our respective bodies has not, by itself, the slightest tendency to show that anyone could imagine or describe a world in which, after his funeral, he continued to exist without a body. By itself it merely shows that we can each imagine what the world would be like if he were obliterated from it entirely, and no trace of his corpse remained. Schlick has misdescribed what he could imagine. Misled by the fact that a man can easly imagine what his funeral will be like, and hence what it would be like to watch it, it is tempting to insist he can imagine what it would be like *for him* to watch *his own* funeral. Schlick is thus able to "conclude that immortality, in the sense defined . . . is an empirical hypothesis. . . . It could be verified by following the prescription 'Wait until you die!'." But he has not defined a sense of "immortality" at all: apparently he has merely misdescribed some rather humdrum exercises of his imagination in an extremely exciting and misleading way. He has failed to say anything to prevent his opponent from objecting to his conclusion: "But, on the contrary, nothing whatever could be verified (by me) by (my) following the prescription 'Wait until you die!': (for me my) death is so final that it is logically impossible (for me) to survive it to verify any hypotheses at all."

IV

We have now fulfilled the two strictly limited purposes of this paper. But perhaps it is worth while to add comments on three other possible objections to the attempted philosophical fools' mate; emphasising that nothing we have said or shall say must be interpreted to mean that we ourselves consider it to be decisive. *First* it may be said that this is all too cut and dried, the logic of our ordinary language is not as sharp, clear, and uncomplicated as has been made out. This is true and important. To take only one example: any adequate treatment of the logic of survival and immortality (the enquiry initiated by Plato's *Phaedo*) would demand the use of the distinction between death and dissolution; just as any full discussion of the logic of metempsychosis and pre-existence (the enquiry initiated by Plato's *Meno*) would have to take account of the parallel distinction between birth and conception. But for our first purpose, the raising of "strange perplexities," soft shading and rich detail is confusing, while for the second, dealing with one counter-move crudely made, it is unnecessary.

Second, it may be suggested that, although Schlick and Wisdom as a matter of fact only succeeded in imagining their own funerals and the world going on without them (and then misdescribed and/or mistook the significance of what they did imagine), it would nevertheless be quite possible to imagine all sorts of bizarre phenomena which we should feel inclined to describe as "the activities of disembodied people" or even as "evidence of survival." This again is true and important. Anyone who has read at all widely in the literature of psychical research must often have felt inclined to apply such expressions to phenomena, or putative phenomena, recorded in this literature. But it is all too easy to misinterpret what we shall be doing if we do allow ourselves to describe such *outré* phenomena in these paradoxical ways. In fact we shall be attaching sense to an expression—"disembodied person"—for which previously no sense had been provided: either directly as an idiomatic expression; or indirectly through the uses given to its constituent words. We are thereby introducing a new sense of the word "person." Yet it may appear to us and to others as if we have discovered a new sort of person, or a new state in which a person can be. Whereas a disembodied person is no more a special sort of person than is an imaginary person: and (except in the Services—which have their peculiar sense of the word "disembodied") disembodiment is no more a possible state of a person than is non-existence.

Now it is perfectly possible to specify a sense for the expression "disembodied person": just as it is possible to attach sense to any expression, even one which on present usage would be self-contradictory. The difficulty is to attach a sense to it so that some expression incorporating it will, if true, provide a ground for the logically unique expectation. In their present use person words have logical liaisons of the very greatest importance: personal identity is the necessary condition of both accountability and expectation; which is only to say that it is unjust to reward or punish someone for something unless (as a minimum condition) he is the same person who did the deed; and also that it is absurd to expect experiences for Flew in 1984 unless (as a minimum condition) there is going to be a person in existence in 1984 who will be the same person as I. The difficulty, not necessarily insuperable, is to change the use of person words so radically that it becomes significant to talk of people surviving dissolution, without changing it to such an extent that these vital logical liaisons are lost.

The *third* obvious criticism returns us to the traditional foundation for what we might call a "logic of immortality." The objection might be made that it has been assumed throughout that people are merely bodies, that people are bodies and nothing more. Even though we have excluded discussion of the traditional dualisms from this paper, this criticism has to be met. It is met by pointing out that no one has either argued or assumed anything of the sort. What has been done is merely to take for granted the ordinary meaning and use of person words, and to use them—we hope—in the conventional and proper way: a very different matter. People are what you meet. Person words refer to men and women like you and me and the other fellow. They are taught by pointing at people: indeed how else could they or should they be taught? They do not refer to anything invisible and elusive, to any mysterious incorporeal substances. Even children can be taught them, can and do know what is meant by "Father," "I," "man," "person," or "butcher." But that is not to say that they refer merely or at all to bodies. "Person" is no synonym for "body": though "body" is used peculiarly in the Services as a slightly pejorative substitute for "person," the degrading point of the substitution would be lost if the words were really synonymous; there is a difference, a difference of life and death, between "We brought a person down from the foot of the Z'mutt ridge" and "We brought a body down from the foot of the Z'mutt ridge." Person words do not mean either bodies or souls nor yet any combination of the two: "I" is no synonym for "my body" nor yet for "my mind" or "my soul" nor yet for any combination of these (as anyone who tries a few substitutions must soon discover). If we are indeed compound of two such disparate elements, that is a contingent fact about people and not part of what is meant by "person" and other person words. To suggest that it has been assumed that people are merely bodies is surely to reveal that you yourself assume that everyone must be a dualist—or at least a dualist with one component missing—a sort of one-legged dualist. And this is a mistake. But though this third criticism is mistaken, it does go straight to the heart of the matter. For the whole position does depend on the fact that people are what you meet: we do not just meet the sinewy containers in which other people are kept; they do not just encounter the fleshy houses which we ourselves inhabit. The whole position depends on the obvious, crucial, but constantly neglected fact that person words mean what they do mean. This paper has consisted in insistent and obstinate underlining of this fact; and in pointing out two implications of it, important but limited in scope: that Butler was wrong to deny that there were logical difficulties about the notion of a future life; and that Schlick's short way with these difficulties will not do. Perhaps attention to it can transform discussion of the problems of Survival and Immortality in a way very similar to that in which Moore's insistence that we do know that some material things exist has transformed discussions of Idealism and of the problems of Epistemology. As Berkeley, with his usual insight, remarked, "the grand mistake is that we know not what we mean by 'we,' 'selves' or 'mind,' etc."

11. MAN AS TWO DIFFERENT SUBSTANCES

René Descartes

René Descartes (1596–1650) is generally considered to be the father of modern philosophy because of his adoption of a philosophical method different from those used in ancient and medieval thought. His emphasis upon theory of knowledge and philosophy of mind set the course of philosophical enquiry for several centuries. His chief works were: Rules for the Direction of the Mind *(1628),* Discourse on the Method of Rightly Conducting the Reason and Seeking for Truth in the Sciences *(1637), and* Meditations on the First Philosophy *(1641).*

MEDITATION II

Of the nature of the human mind, and that it is more easily known than the body.

From Meditations, *translated by E. S. Haldone and G. R. T. Ross and included in* The Philosophical Works of Descartes, *published by The Cambridge University Press and reprinted with their permission.*

The Meditation of yesterday filled my mind with so many doubts that it is no longer in my power to forget them. And yet I do not see in what manner I can resolve them; and, just as if I had all of a sudden fallen into very deep water, I am so disconcerted that I can neither make certain of setting my feet on the bottom, nor can I swim and so support myself on the surface. I shall nevertheless make an effort and follow anew the same path as that on which I yesterday entered, i.e. I shall proceed by setting aside all that in which the least doubt could be supposed to exist, just as if I had discovered that it was absolutely false; and I shall ever follow in this road until I have met with something which is certain, or at least, if I can do nothing else, until I have learned for certain that there is nothing in the world that is certain. Archimedes, in order that he might draw the terrestrial globe out of its place, and transport it elsewhere, demanded only that one point should be fixed and immoveable; in the same way I shall have the right to conceive high hopes if I am happy enough to discover one thing only which is certain and indubitable.

I suppose, then, that all the things that I see are false; I persuade myself that nothing has ever existed of all that my fallacious memory represents to me. I consider that I possess no senses; I imagine that body, figure, extension, movement and place are but the fiction of my mind. What, then, can be esteemed as true? Perhaps nothing at all, unless that there is nothing in the world that is certain.

But how can I know there is not something different from those things that I have just considered, of which one cannot have the slightest doubt? Is there not some God, or some other being by whatever name we call it, who puts these reflections into my mind? That is not necessary, for is it not possible that I am capable of producing them myself? I myself, am I not at least something? But I have already denied that I had senses and body. Yet I hesitate, for what follows from that? Am I so dependent on body and senses that I cannot exist without these? But I was persuaded that there was nothing in all the world, and there was no heaven, no earth, that there were no minds, nor any bodies: was I not then likewise persuaded that I did not exist? Not at all; of a surety I myself did exist since I persuaded myself of something [or merely because I thought of something]. But there is some deceiver or other, very powerful and very cunning, who employs his ingenuity in deceiving me. Then without doubt I exist also if he deceives me, and let him deceive me as much as he will, he can never cause me to be nothing so long as I think that I am something. So that after having reflected well and carefully examined all things, we must come to the definite conclusion that this proposition: I am, I exist, is necessarily true each time that I pronounce it, or that I mentally conceive it.

But I do not yet know clearly enough what I am, I who am certain that I am; and hence I must be careful to see that I do not imprudently take some other object in place of myself, and thus that I do not go astray in respect of this knowledge that I hold to be the most certain and most evident of all that I have formerly learned. That is why I shall now consider anew what I believed myself to be before I embarked upon these last reflections; and of my former opinions I shall withdraw all that might even in a small degree be invalidated by the reasons which I have just brought forward, in order that there may be nothing at all left beyond what is absolutely certain and indubitable.

What then did I formerly believe myself to be? Undoubtedly I believed myself to be a man. But what is a man? Shall I say a reasonable animal? Certainly not; for then I should have to inquire what an animal is, and what is reasonable; and thus from a single question I should insensibly fall into an infinitude of others more difficult; and I should not wish to waste the little time and leisure remaining to me in trying to unravel subtleties like these. But I shall rather stop here to consider the thoughts which of themselves spring up in my mind, and which were not inspired by anything beyond my own nature alone when I applied myself to the consideration of my being. In the first place, then, I considered myself as having a face, hands, arms, and all that system of members composed of bones and flesh as seen in a corpse which I designated by the name of body. In addition to this I considered that I was nourished, that I walked, that I felt, and that I thought, and I referred all these actions to the soul: but I did not stop to consider what the soul was, or if I did stop, I imagined that it was something extremely rare and subtle like a wind, a flame, or an ether, which was spread throughout my grosser parts. As to body I had no manner of doubt about its nature, but thought I had a very clear knowledge of it; and if I had desired to explain it according to the notions that I had then formed of it, I should have described it thus: By the body I understand all that which can be defined by a certain figure: something which can be confined in a certain place, and which can fill a space in such a way that every other body will be excluded from it; which can be perceived either by touch, or by sight, or by hearing, or by taste, or by smell: which can be moved in many ways not, in truth, by itself but by something which is foreign to it, by which it is touched [and from which it receives impressions]: for to have the power of self-movement, as also of feeling or of thinking, I did not consider to appertain to the nature of body: on the contrary, I was rather astonished to find that faculties similar to them existed in some bodies.

But what am I, now that I suppose that there is a certain genius which is extremely powerful, and, if I may say so, malicious, who employs all his powers in deceiving me? Can I affirm that I possess the least of all those things which I have just said pertain to the nature of body? I pause to consider, I revolve all these things in my mind, and I find none of which I can say that it pertains to me. It would be tedious to stop to enumerate them. Let us pass to the attributes of soul and see if there is any one which is in me? What of nutrition or walking [the first mentioned]? But if it is so that I have no body it is also true that I can neither walk nor take nourishment. Another attribute is sensation. But one cannot feel without body, and besides I have thought I perceived many things during sleep that I recognised in my waking moments as not having been experienced at all. What of thinking? I find here that thought is an attribute that belongs to me; it alone cannot be separated from me. I am, I exist, that is certain. But how often? Just when I think; for it might possibly be the case if I ceased entirely to think, that I should likewise cease altogether to exist. I do not now admit anything which is not necessarily true: to speak accurately I am not more than a thing which thinks, that is to say a mind or a soul, or an understanding, or a reason, which are terms whose significance was formerly unknown to me. I am, however, a real thing and really exist; but what thing? I have answered: a thing which thinks.

And what more? I shall exercise my imagination [in order to see if I am not something more]. I am not a collection of members which we call the human body: I am not a subtle air distributed through these members, I am not a wind, a fire, a vapour, a breath, nor anything at all which I can imagine or conceive; because I have assumed that all these were nothing. Without changing that supposition I find that I only leave myself certain of the fact that I am somewhat. But perhaps it is true that these same things which I supposed were non-existent because they are unknown to me, are really not different from the self which I know. I am not sure about this, I shall not dispute about it now; I can only give judgment on things that are known to me. I know that I exist, and I inquire what I am, I whom I know to exist. But it is very certain that the knowledge of my existence taken in its precise significance does not depend on things whose existence is not yet known to me; consequently it does not depend on those which I can feign in imagination. And indeed the very term *feign* in imagination proves to me my error, for I really do this if I image myself a something, since to imagine is nothing else than to contemplate the figure or image of a corporeal thing. But I already know for certain that I am, and that it may be that all these images, and, speaking generally, all things that relate to the nature of body are nothing but dreams [and chimeras]. For this reason I see clearly that I have as little reason to say, 'I shall stimulate my imagination in order to know more distinctly what I am,' than if I were to say, 'I am now awake, and I perceive somewhat that is real and true: but because I do not yet perceive it distinctly enough, I shall go to sleep of express purpose, so that my dreams may represent the perception with greatest truth and evidence.' And, thus, I know for certain that nothing of all that I can understand by means of my imagination belongs to this knowledge which I have of myself, and that it is necessary to recall the mind from this mode of thought with the utmost diligence in order that it may be able to know its own nature with perfect distinctness.

But what then am I? A thing which thinks. What is a thing which thinks? It is a thing which doubts, understands, [conceives], affirms, denies, wills, refuses, which also imagines and feels.

Certainly it is no small matter if all these things pertain to my nature. But why should they not so pertain? Am I not that being who now doubts nearly everything, who nevertheless understands certain things, who affirms that one only is true, who denies all the others, who desires to know more, is averse from being deceived, who imagines many things, sometimes indeed despite his will, and who perceives many likewise, as by the intervention of the bodily organs? Is there nothing in all this which is as true as it is certain that I exist, even though I should always sleep and though he who has given me being employed all his ingenuity in deceiving me? Is there likewise any one of these attributes which can be distinguished from my thought, or which might be said to be separated from myself? For it is so evident of itself that it is I who doubts, who understands, and who desires, that there is no reason here to add anything to explain it. And I have certainly the power of imagining likewise; for although it may happen (as I formerly supposed) that none of the things which I imagine are true, nevertheless this power of imagining does not cease to be really in use, and it forms part of my thought. Finally, I am the same who feels, that is to say, who perceives certain things, as by the organs of sense, since in truth I see light, I hear noise, I feel heat. But it will be said that these phenomena are false and that I am dreaming. Let it be so; still it is at least quite certain that it seems to me that I see light, that I hear noise and that I feel heat. That cannot be false; properly speaking it is what is in me called feeling; and used in this precise sense that is no other thing than thinking. . . .

MEDITATION VI

Of the existence of material things, and of the real distinction between the soul and body of man.

. . . it is right that I should at the same time investigate the nature of sense perception, and that I should see if from the ideas which I apprehend by this mode of thought, which I call feeling, I cannot derive some certain proof of the existence of corporeal objects.

And first of all I shall recall to my memory those matters which I hitherto held to be true, as having perceived them through the senses, and the foundations on which my belief has rested; in the next place I shall examine the reasons which have since obliged me to place them in doubt; in the last place I shall consider which of them I must now believe.

First of all, then, I perceived that I had a head, hands, feet, and all other members of which this body—which I considered as a part, or possibly even as the whole, of myself—is composed. Further I was sensible that this body was placed amidst many others, from which it was capable of being affected in many different ways, beneficial and hurtful, and I remarked that a certain feeling of pleasure accompanied those that were beneficial, and pain those which were harmful. And in addition to this pleasure and pain, I also experienced hunger, thirst, and other similar appetites, as also certain corporeal inclinations towards joy, sadness, anger, and other similar passions. And outside myself, in addition to extension, figure, and motions of bodies, I remarked in them hardness, heat, and all other tactile qualities, and, further, light and colour, and scents and sounds, the variety of which gave me the means of distinguishing the sky, the earth, the sea, and generally all the other bodies, one from the other. And certainly, considering the ideas of all these qualities which presented themselves to my mind, and which alone I perceived properly or immediately, it was not without reason that I believed myself to perceive objects quite different from my thought, to wit, bodies from which those ideas proceeded; for I found by experience that these ideas presented themselves to me without my consent being requisite, so that I could not perceive any object, however desirous I might be, unless it were present to the organs of sense; and it was not in my power not to perceive it, when it was present. And because the ideas which I received through the senses were much more lively, more clear, and even, in their own way, more distinct than any of those which I could of myself frame in meditation, or than those I found impressed on my memory, it appeared as though they could not have proceeded from my mind, so that they must necessarily have been produced in me by some other things. And having no knowledge of those objects excepting the knowledge which the ideas themselves gave me, nothing was more likely to occur to my mind than that the objects were similar to the ideas which were caused. And because I likewise remembered that I had formerly made use of my senses rather than my reason, and recognised that the ideas which I formed of myself were not so distinct as those which I perceived through the senses, and that they were most frequently even composed of portions of these last, I persuaded myself easily that I had no idea in my mind which had not formerly come to me through the senses. Nor was it without some reason that I believed that this body (which by a certain special right I call my own) belonged to me more properly and more strictly than any other; for in fact I could never be separated from it as from other bodies; I experienced in it and on account of it all my appetites and affections, and finally I was touched by the feeling of pain and the titillation of pleasure in its parts, and not in the parts of other bodies which were separated from it. But when I inquired, why, from some, I know not what, painful sensations, there follows sadness of mind, and from the pleasurable sensation there arises joy, or why this mysterious pinching of the stomach which I call hunger causes me to desire to eat, and dryness of throat causes a desire to drink, and so on, I could give no reason excepting that nature taught me so; for there is certainly no affinity (that I at least can understand) between the craving of the stomach and the desire to eat, any more than between the perception of whatever causes pain and the thought of sadness which arises from this perception. And in the same way it appeared to me that I had learned from nature all the other judgments which I formed regarding the objects of my senses, since I remarked that these judgments were formed in me before I had the leisure to weigh and consider any reasons which might oblige me to make them.

But afterwards many experiences little by little destroyed all the faith which I had rested in my senses; for I from time to time observed that those towers which from afar appeared to me to be round, more closely observed seemed square, and that colossal statues raised on the summit of these towers, appeared as quite tiny statues when viewed from the bottom; and so in an infinitude of other cases I found error in judgments founded on the external senses. And not only in those founded on the external senses, but even in those founded on the internal as well; for is there anything more intimate or more internal than pain? And yet I have learned from some persons whose arms or legs have been cut off, that they sometimes seemed to feel pain in the part which had been amputated, which made me think that I could not be quite certain that it was a certain member which pained me, even although I felt pain in it. And to those grounds of doubt I have lately added two others, which are very general; the first is that I never have believed myself to feel anything in waking moments which I cannot also sometimes believe myself to feel when I sleep, and as I do not think that these things which I seem to feel in sleep, proceed from objects outside of me, I do not see any reason why I should have this belief regarding

91

objects which I seem to perceive while awake. The other was that being still ignorant, or rather supposing myself to be ignorant, of the author of my being, I saw nothing to prevent me from having been so constituted by nature that I might be deceived even in matters which seemed to me to be most certain. And as to the grounds on which I was formerly persuaded of the truth of sensible objects, I had not much trouble in replying to them. For since nature seemed to cause me to lean towards many things from which reason repelled me, I did not believe that I should trust much to the teachings of nature. And although the ideas which I receive by the senses do not depend on my will, I did not think that one should for that reason conclude that they proceeded from things different from myself, since possibly some faculty might be discovered in me—though hitherto unknown to me—which produced them.

But now that I begin to know myself better, and to discover more clearly the author of my being, I do not in truth think that I should rashly admit all the matters which the senses seem to teach us, but, on the other hand, I do not think that I should doubt them all universally.

And first of all, because I know that all things which I apprehend clearly and distinctly can be created by God as I apprehend them, it suffices that I am able to apprehend one thing apart from another clearly and distinctly in order to be certain that the one is different from the other, since they may be made to exist in separation at least by the omnipotence of God; and it does not signify by what power this separation is made in order to compel me to judge them to be different: and, therefore, just because I know certainly that I exist, and that meanwhile I do not remark that any other thing necessarily pertains to my nature or essence, excepting that I am a thinking thing, I rightly conclude that my essence consists solely in the fact that I am a thinking thing [or a substance whose whole essence or nature is to think]. And although possibly (or rather certainly, as I shall say in a moment) I possess a body with which I am very intimately conjoined, yet because, on the one side, I have a clear and distinct idea of myself inasmuch as I am only a thinking and unextended thing, and as, on the other, I possess a distinct idea of body, inasmuch as it is only an extended and unthinking thing, it is certain that this I [that is to say, my soul by which I am what I am], is entirely and absolutely distinct from my body, and can exist without it.

I further find in myself faculties employing modes of thinking peculiar to themselves, to wit, the faculties of imagination and feeling, without which I can easily conceive myself clearly and distinctly as a complete being; while, on the other hand, they cannot be so conceived apart from me, that is without an intelligent substance in which they reside, for [in the notion we have of these faculties, or, to use the language of the Schools] in their formal concept, some kind of intellection is comprised, from which I infer that they are distinct from me as its modes are from a thing. I observe also in me some other faculties such as that of change of position, the assumption of different figures and such like, which cannot be conceived, any more than can the preceding, apart from some substance to which they are attached, and consequently cannot exist without it; but it is very clear that these faculties, if it be true that they exist, must be attached to some corporeal or extended substance, and not to an intelligent substance, since in the clear and distinct conception of these there is some sort of extension found to be present, but no intellection at all. There is certainly further in me a certain passive faculty of perception, that is, of receiving and recognising the ideas of sensible things, but this would be useless to me [and I could in no way avail myself of it], if there were not either in me or in some other thing another active faculty capable of forming and producing these ideas. But this active faculty cannot exist in me [inasmuch as I am a thing that thinks] seeing that it does not presuppose thought, and also that those ideas are often produced in me without my contributing in any way to the same, and often even against my will; it is thus necessarily the case that the faculty resides in some substance different from me in which all the reality which is objectively in the ideas that are produced by this faculty is formally or eminently contained, as I remarked before. And this substance is either a body, that is, a corporeal nature in which there is contained formally [and really] all that which is objectively [and by representation] in those ideas, or it is God Himself, or some other creature more noble than body in which that same is contained eminently. But, since God is no deceiver, it is very manifest that He does not communicate to me these ideas immediately and by Himself, nor yet by the intervention of some creature in which their reality is not formally, but only eminently, contained. For since He has given me no faculty to recognise that this is the case, but, on the other hand, a very great inclination to believe [that they are sent to me or] that they are conveyed to me by corporeal objects, I do not see how He could be defended from the accusation of deceit if these ideas were produced by causes other than corporeal objects. Hence we must allow that corporeal things exist. However, they are perhaps not exactly what we perceive by the senses, since this comprehension by the senses is in many instances very obscure and confused; but we must at least admit that all things which

I conceive in them clearly and distinctly, that is to say, all things which, speaking generally, are comprehended in the object of pure mathematics, are truly to be recognised as external objects.

As to other things, however, which are either particular only, as, for example, that the sun is of such and such a figure, etc., or which are less clearly and distinctly conceived such as light, sound, pain and the like, it is certain that although they are very dubious and uncertain, yet on the sole ground that God is not a deceiver, and that consequently He has not permitted any falsity to exist in my opinion which He has not likewise given me the faculty of correcting, I may assuredly hope to conclude that I have within me the means of arriving at the truth even here. And first of all there is no doubt that in all things which nature teaches me there is some truth contained; for by nature, considered in general, I now understand no other thing than either God Himself or else the order and disposition which God has established in created things; and by my nature in particular I understand no other thing than the complexus of all the things which God has given me.

But there is nothing which this nature teaches me more expressly [nor more sensibly] than that I have a body which is adversely affected when I feel pain, which has need of food or drink when I experience the feelings of hunger and thirst, and so on; nor can I doubt there being some truth in all this.

Nature also teaches me by these sensations of pain, hunger, thirst, etc., that I am not only lodged in my body as a pilot in a vessel, but that I am very closely united to it, and so to speak so intermingled with it that I seem to compose with it one whole. For if that were not the case, when my body is hurt, I, who am merely a thinking thing, should not feel pain, for I should perceive this would by the understanding only, just as the sailor perceives by sight when something is damaged in this vessel; and when my body has need of drink or food, I should clearly understand the fact without being warned of it by confused feelings of hunger and thirst. For all these sensations of hunger, thirst, pain, etc. are in truth none other than certain confused modes of thought which are produced by the union and apparent intermingling of mind and body. . . .

. . . in the first place, there is a great difference between mind and body, inasmuch as body is by nature always divisible, and the mind is entirely indivisible. For, as a matter of fact, when I consider the mind, that is to say, myself inasmuch as I am only a thinking thing, I cannot distinguish in myself any parts, but apprehend myself to be clearly one and entire; and although the whole mind seems to be united to the whole body, yet if a foot, or an arm, or some other part, is separated from my body, I am aware that nothing has been taken away from my mind. And the faculties of willing, feeling, conceiving, etc. cannot be properly speaking said to be its parts, for it is one and the same mind which employs itself in willing and in feeling and understanding. But it is quite otherwise with corporeal or extended objects, for there is not one of these imaginable by me which my mind cannot easily divide into parts, and which consequently I do not recognise as being divisible; this would be sufficient to teach me that the mind or soul of man is entirely different from the body, if I had not already learned it from other sources.

12. PERSONS AND THEIR BODIES

Jerome Shaffer

Jerome A. Shaffer (1929–), Professor of Philosophy at the University of Connecticut, has written The Philosophy of Mind *(1968) and several important articles which appeared in philosophical journals. He is also executive secretary of the Council for Philosophical Studies.*

COULD A BODY HAVE MENTAL EVENTS?

Descartes concluded that "no body can think." His argument [1] begins with the sound point that "I have a distinct idea of the body in so far as it is an extended, not a thinking thing"; from this he draws the fatally ambiguous inference that "mind and body are really distinct," from which he concluded that no body can think (ambiguous because "distinct" can mean "intensionally distinct" or "extensionally distinct"; he can prove the former but needs the latter for his conclusion). Spinoza held that one and the same thing could be both bodily and thinking.[2] Locke, in his famous discussion "whether any mere material being thinks or no," argued that we ourselves might be cases of thinking extended matter, but that we could not know one way or the other.[3]

From "Persons and Their Bodies," Philosophical Review, *Vol. 75, No. 1, 1966, pp. 63–67. Reprinted by permission of the author and editor.*

[1] Reply to the Second Set of Objections to the *Meditations*.
[2] Spinoza, *Ethics*, Bk. I, prop. 10.
[3] Locke, *An Essay Concerning Human Understanding*, Bk. IV, ch. iii, sec. 6, ed. by A. S. Pringle-Pattison (Oxford, 1924), pp. 268 ff.

I propose to offer an argument intended to show that the body cannot be the subject of thought or of other mental events.

Persons have bodies; I have a body and so, I dare say, do you. Facts about the person's body are often expressed as facts about the person; for example, in such statements as "He weighs one hundred-eighty pounds" or "He is covered with mud." This might lead one to think a person is identical with his body. But, as Sydney Shoemaker has pointed out, "it no more follows from the truth of such statements that a person *is* his body than it follows from the truth of statements like 'I am out of gas' that a person *is* his automobile." [4] Of course, the relation between a person and his body is different from that between a person and his car; a person's body is not a piece of property owned by him. Yet there is one similarity of great importance. For any car, it is a contingent fact that it is someone's car and, furthermore, a contingent fact that it is one person's car rather than another's; similarly, for any body, it is a contingent fact that it is someone's body and, furthermore, a contingent fact that it is that person's body rather than another person's. Just as that car, which I own, could (logically) have belonged to someone else and can someday belong to someone else or even to no one, so this body, which is mine, could (logically) have been the body of someone else and can someday be the body of someone else or even someday no longer be the body of some person. This last possibility is the most indisputable—namely, that someday, assuming there is no afterlife, my body will exist as a body, but as a dead body or corpse, and at that time will no longer be my body, nor be anyone else's either, for that matter. I think everyone would grant that possibility. But even the possibility of two people switching bodies makes sense, and one can imagine circumstances under which we would be inclined to say that just that had happened. Consider the hypothetical case recently offered by Quinton of the thin, puritanical Scot and the plump, apolaustic Pole.[5] Here suddenly the thin one claims to be the Pole (and, to embellish Quinton's story, passes lie-detector tests), takes on all those features of character and personality formerly possessed by the Pole, speaks familiarly of a past which only the Pole could have known about, speaks a superb and rare Polish, and so forth. Meanwhile, the plump one takes on the mentality of the Scot. Surely we could so work out the hypothetical details that we should be inclined to believe that the miraculous had happened and that somehow the two persons had switched bodies.

If we are willing to admit the possibility that persons could

---

[4] Sydney Shoemaker, *Self Knowledge and Self-Identity* (Ithaca, 1963), p. 18.

[5] Anthony Quinton, "The Soul," *Journal of Philosophy*, LIX, 1962), 401.

switch bodies, then it follows that the fact that any one has the body he has is a *contingent* fact, in that he just happens to have the body he does and might, in the next instant, suddenly find himself with some other body. This is because the identity of the body is logically independent of the identity of the person whose body it is. What makes me the particular person I am is different from what makes my body the particular body it is, and what makes me the same person over time is different from what makes my body the same body over time. Of course, the world being the way it is, the relation between a person and his body is as a matter of fact very stable, so that in general it is reasonable to make the inductive inference from the fact that here we have the same human body to the fact that here we have the same person. Only rarely do we actually make mistakes. Such a case would occur if someone thinks he is talking to a particular person and then discovers that he is not talking to that person, because that person has just died, and only his corpse remains. Here the inference from same body to same person would break down; but such mistakes occur rarely and, when they do occur, are not especially difficult to detect.

The relation between a person and his mental events is quite different, however. Suppose I suddenly feel a pang of anxiety. Would it make any sense to speak of the possibility that exactly that event might occur but to someone else, that someone else might have had just that pang of anxiety rather than I myself? One could easily imagine someone else having an anxiety attack *exactly similar* to mine but not exactly that one.

As P. F. Strawson puts it, "It does not seem to make sense to suggest, for example, that the identical pain which was in fact one's own might have been another's." [6] One must not think that the mental events I have occur but *just happen to occur to me.* It is true that it is a contingent fact that I have the mental events I do but the contingent fact is that such events happen at all, not that they happen *to me.* The identity of a mental event is not logically independent from the identity of the person to whom it occurs. In order to pick out uniquely some mental event it is not sufficient to describe it, or locate it in time (or space, if that makes sense). Two exactly similar mental events could occur simultaneously (and even, in a sense, perhaps, in the same place; for example, that corner). It is a logically essential feature of a mental event that it occurs to a particular person, and to pick it out uniquely we must indicate *whose* mental event it was. It is senseless to say that just that mental event might have occurred, all right, but not to the person to whom it occurred.

If we turn to bodily events, we will notice that a parallel point

---

[6] P. F. Strawson, *Individuals* (London), 1959, p. 97.

can be made about them. If an event occurs to a part of a body—let us say that a part of a body is scratched—it does not make sense to speak of the possibility that exactly that scratch could have occurred to a different part of the body or to a different body altogether. An exactly similar scratch, yes, but not just that scratch. For in picking out uniquely that scratch, we must refer to what the scratch happens to.

When we bring in the concept of a person, however, a crucial difference between a person's mental events and bodily events emerges, a difference which will allow us to prove that we cannot attribute mental events to the body. The difference is that while it does not make sense to say that some particular mental event of mine—for example, a pang of anxiety—might have occurred to someone else, it does make sense to say that some particular bodily event of mine—for example, a scratch —might have occurred to someone else. The latter is possible because someone *else* might have had the body to which the scratch occurred; in that case, he rather than I, would have had precisely that scratch.

Now for the proof that it is wrong to attribute mental events to the body. First, let us put it indirectly. Suppose one could attribute mental events to the body. Since, as we have seen, mental events necessarily occur to a person, those mental events would necessarily be attributed to the person whose body it is. But since, as we have also seen, a body which belongs to a person just *happens* to belong to *that* person, it would follow that the mental events which occur to that person could have occurred but not to *that* person. But that certain mental events could have occurred but not to *that* person is impossible. Hence our supposition that mental events could be attributed to the body is false. Briefly, if mental events happened to bodies, we could imagine them occurring to a different person, but we cannot imagine that. Putting the proof positively, a mental event must happen to some particular person. Events which happen to a body might have happened but not to that particular person. So mental events cannot be events which happen to a body.

Therefore we cannot take a person to be a body which has mental events. . . .[7]

---

[7] This argument also proves effective against the kind of behaviorism that allows for body-switching (see Shoemaker, p. 26) by identifying the person with a set of bodily dispositions and behavior patterns which *could* hold for different bodies at different times. Such a conception runs up against the same objection, namely that of making it seem possible that a particular mental event of some person might have occurred but not to that person, in the event that a different set of dispositions had held for that body. While the latter is possible, the former is not.

13. THE PRIVACY OF THE MENTAL

C. J. Ducasse

Curt J. Ducasse (1881–1969) was for many years Professor of Philosophy at Brown University. He was a president of the American Philosophical Association and the author of numerous books, including Nature, Mind and Death *(1951) and* A Philosophical Scrutiny of Religion *(1953).*

The first point to which attention must be called is that, beyond question, there are things—events, substances, processes, relations, etc.—denominated "material," or "physical," that there are also certain others denominated instead "mental," or "psychical," and that no thing is denominated both "physical" and "psychical," or both "material" and "mental." Rocks, trees, water, air, animal and human bodies, and the processes occurring among them or within them, are examples of the things called "material" or "physical"; emotions, desires, moods, sensations, cravings, images, thoughts, etc., are examples of the things called "mental" or "psychical."

To question whether the first *really* are physical or the second *really* are psychical would be absurd, as it would be absurd to question whether a certain boy whom his parents named "George" really was George. For just as "George" is a name, so "physical" or "material," and "psychical" or "mental," are names; and a name is essentially a *pointer,* which does point at—designates, indicates, denotes, directs attention to—whatever it actually is employed to point at.

It is necessary, however, to ask what characteristic shared by all the things called "physical" or "material" determined their being all designated by one and the same name; and the same question arises with regard to those denominated instead "psychical" or "mental." Evidently, the characteristic concerned had to be an obvious, not a recondite one, since investigation of the recondite characteristics respectively of physical and of psychical things could begin only *after* one knew which things were the physical and which the psychical ones.

In the case of the things called "physical," the patent characteristic common to and peculiar to them, which determined their being all denoted by one and same name, was simply that all of them were,

Reprinted by permission of New York University Press and Curt Ducasse from Dimensions of Mind, *edited by Sidney Hook.* © *1960 by New York University.*

or were capable of being, *perceptually public*—the same tree, the same thunderclap, the same wind, the same dog, the same man, etc., can be perceived by every member of a human public suitably located in space and in time. To be material or physical, then, *basically* means to be, or to be capable of being, perceptually public. And the unperceivable, recondite things physicists discover—electrons, protons, etc., and the processes that occur among them—only have title at all to be also called physical *derivatively*—in virtue, namely, (and *only* in virtue) of their being *constituents* of the things that are perceptually public.

On the other hand, the patent characteristic which functioned as a basis for the application of one identical name to all the things called "psychical" or "mental" was their *inherently private* character, attention *to them*, as distinguished from attention to what they may signify, being accordingly termed "introspection," not "perception."

The events called "psychical," it must be emphasized, are private in a sense radically different from that in which the events occurring inside the body are private. The latter are private only in the sense that visual, tactual, or other exteroceptive perception of them is *difficult*—indeed,.even more difficult for the person whose body is concerned than for other persons—such perception of those events being possible, perhaps, only by means of special instruments, or perhaps only by anatomical "introspection" (!), i.e., by opening up the body surgically and looking at the processes going on inside it. The "privacy" of intra-somatic stimuli, including so-called "covert" behavior, is thus purely adventitious. The privacy of psychical events, on the other hand, is *inherent and ultimate*.

It is sometimes alleged, of course, that their privacy too is only adventitious. But this allegation rests only on failure to distinguish between being *public* and being *published*. Psychical events can be more or less adequately published. That is, perceptually public forms of behavior correlated with occurrence of them can function as *signs* that they are occurring—but *only* as signs, for correlation is not identity. Indeed, correlation presupposes non-identity.

Psychical events *themselves* are never *public* and never can be made so. That, for example, I *now remember* having dreamed of a Siamese cat last night is something which I can *publish* by means of perceptually public words, spoken or written. Other persons are then *informed of it*. But to be informed *that I remember* having so dreamed is one thing, and to *remember* having so dreamed is altogether another thing, and one *inherently private*. The dreaming itself was not, and the remembering itself is not, a *public* event at all and cannot possibly be made so in the way in which my *statement* that I remember that I so dreamed is or can be made public.

How then does it happen that we have names understood by all for events of inherently private kinds? The answer is, of course, that we heard those names—e.g., "anger," "desire," "remembering," etc.,—uttered by other persons when they perceived us behaving in certain more or less stereotyped manners. But the point crucial here is that although each of us acquires his vocabulary for mental events in this way, the words of it, at the times when they are applied by others to *his* behavior, denote *for him* not primarily or perhaps at all his behavior, but the particular kind of inherently private event, i.e., of physical state, which *he* is experiencing at the time. It is only in "behaviorese," i.e., in the language of dogmatic behaviorism, that for example the word "anger," and the words "anger-behavior," both denote the same event, to wit, the event which ordinary language terms "behaving angrily."

There are several varieties of behaviorism, but they agree in that they attempt to account for the behavior of organisms wholly without invoking a psychical cause for any behavior—that is, wholly by reference to physical, perceptually public causes, present and/or past.

Dogmatic behaviorism is the pious belief that the causes of the behavior of organisms, including human organisms, *are never other than physical.* Nothing but this dogma dictates that even when no physical occurrences are actually found that would account for a given behavior, physical occurrences nevertheless *must* be assumed to have taken place.

Empirical or methodological behaviorism, on the other hand, is not thus fideistic. It is simply *a research program,* perfectly legitimate and often fruitful—the program, namely, of *seeking,* for all behavior, causes consisting of physical, i.e., of perceptually public stimulus events, present and past. Evidently, the fact that one undertakes to search for causes of this kind for all behavior leaves entirely open the possibility that, in many of the innumerable cases where no physical causes adequate to account for the given behavior can in fact be observed, the behavior had a psychical not a physical cause.

For, contrary to what is sometimes alleged, causation of a physical by a psychical event, or of a psychical event by stimulation of a physical sense organ, is not in the least paradoxical. The causality relation—whether defined in terms of regularity of succession, or (preferably) in terms of single antecedent difference—does not presuppose at all that its cause-term and its effect-term both belong to the same ontological category, but only that both of them be *events.* . . .

14. MIND AS DISPOSITIONS TO BEHAVE

Gilbert Ryle

Gilbert Ryle (1900–   ) is editor of the well-known philosophical journal Mind, and was for many years Waynflete Professor of Metaphysical Philosophy at Oxford. His major work
is the Concept of Mind (1949), which has provoked as much
discussion as any philosophical work in the twentieth century.
His other books are Dilemmas (1954) and Plato's Progress
(1966). Ryle has contributed numerous significant articles in
philosophical journals as well.

The mental-conduct concepts that I choose to examine first are
those which belong to that family of concepts ordinarily surnamed 'intelligence.' Here are a few of the more determinate adjectives in this
family: 'clever,' 'sensible,' 'careful,' 'methodical,' 'inventive,' 'prudent,'
'acute,' 'logical,' 'witty,' 'observant,' 'critical,' 'experimental,' 'quick-witted,'
'cunning,' 'wise,' 'judicious,' and 'scrupulous.' When a person is deficient
in intelligence he is described as 'stupid' or else by more determinate
epithets such as 'dull,' 'silly,' 'careless,' 'unmethodical,' 'uninventive,'
'rash,' 'dense,' 'illogical,' 'humourless,' 'unobservant,' 'uncritical,' 'unex-
perimental,' 'slow,' 'simple,' 'unwise,' and 'injudicious. . . .'

. . . When a person is described by one or other of the intelli-
gence-epithets such as 'shrewd' or 'silly,' 'prudent' or 'imprudent,' the
description imputes to him not the knowledge, or ignorance, of this or
that truth, but the ability, or inability, to do certain sorts of things.
Theorists have been so preoccupied with the task of investigating the
nature, the source and the credentials of the theories that we adopt that
they have for the most part ignored the question what it is for someone
to know how to perform tasks. In ordinary life, on the contrary, as well
as in the special business of teaching, we are much more concerned with
people's competences than with their cognitive repertoires, with the
operations than with the truths that they learn. . . .

What is involved in our descriptions of people as knowing how to
make and appreciate jokes, to talk grammatically, to play chess, to fish,
or to argue? Part of what is meant is that, when they perform these
operations, they tend to perform them well, i.e. correctly or efficiently
or successfully. Their performances come up to certain standards, or

satisfy certain criteria. But this is not enough. The well-regulated clock keeps good time and the well-drilled circus seal performs its tricks flawlessly, yet we do not call them 'intelligent.' We reserve this title for the persons responsible for their performances. To be intelligent is not merely to satisfy criteria, but to apply them; to regulate one's actions and not merely to be well-regulated. A person's performance is described as careful or skillful, if in his operations he is ready to detect and correct lapses, to repeat and improve upon successes, to profit from the examples of others and so forth. He applies criteria in performing critically, that is, in trying to get things right.

This point is commonly expressed in the vernacular by saying that an action exhibits intelligence, if, and only if, the agent is thinking what he is doing while he is doing it, and thinking what he is doing in such a manner that he would not do the action so well if he were not thinking what he is doing. This popular idiom is sometimes appealed to as evidence in favour of the intellectualist legend. Champions of this legend are apt to try to reassimilate knowing *how* to knowing *that* by arguing that intelligent performance involves the observance of rules, or the application of criteria. It follows that the operation which is characterised as intelligent must be preceded by an intellectual acknowledgment of these rules or criteria; that is, the agent must first go through the internal process of avowing to himself certain propositions about what is to be done ('maxims,' 'imperatives,' or 'regulative propositions' as they are sometimes called); only then can he execute his performance in accordance with those dictates. He must preach to himself before he can practise. The chef must recite his recipes to himself before he can cook according to them; the hero must lend his inner ear to some appropriate moral imperative before swimming out to save the drowning man; the chess-player must run over in his head all the relevant rules and tactical maxims of the game before he can make correct and skillful moves. To do something thinking what one is doing is, according to this legend, always to do two things; namely, to consider certain appropriate propositions, or prescriptions, and to put into practice what these propositions or prescriptions enjoin. It is to do a bit of theory and then do a bit of practice.

Certainly we often do not only reflect before we act but reflect in order to act properly. The chess-player may require some time in which to plan his moves before he makes them. Yet the general assertion that all intelligent performance requires to be prefaced by the consideration of appropriate propositions rings unplausibly, even when it is apologetically conceded that the required consideration is often very swift and may go quite unmarked by the agent. I shall argue that the intellectualist legend is false and that when we describe a performance as intelligent, this does not entail the double operation of considering and executing. . . .

ABSURDITY OF THE CARTESIAN (INNER ACT) THEORY

The crucial objection to the intellectualist legend is this. The consideration of propositions is itself an operation the execution of which can be more or less intelligent, less or more stupid. But if, for any operation to be intelligently executed, a prior theoretical operation had first to be performed and performed intelligently, it would be a logical impossibility for anyone ever to break into the circle.

Let us consider some salient points at which this regress would arise. According to the legend, whenever an agent does anything intelligently, his act is preceded and steered by another internal act of considering a regulative proposition appropriate to his practical problem. But what makes him consider the one maxim which is appropriate rather than any of the thousands which are not? Why does the hero not find himself calling to mind a cooking-recipe, or a rule of Formal Logic? Perhaps he does, but then his intellectual process is silly and not sensible. Intelligently reflecting how to act is, among other things, considering what is pertinent and disregarding what is inappropriate. Must we then say that for the hero's reflections how to act to be intelligent he must first reflect how best to reflect how to act? The endlessness of this implied regress shows that the application of the criterion of appropriateness does not entail the occurrence of a process of considering this criterion. . . .

. . . To put it quite generally, the absurd assumption made by the intellectualist legend is this, that a performance of any sort inherits all its title to intelligence from some anterior internal operation of planning what to do. Now very often we do go through such a process of planning what to do, and, if we are silly, our planning is silly, if shrewd, our planning is shrewd. It is also notoriously possible for us to plan shrewdly and perform stupidly, i.e. to flout our precepts in our practice. By the original argument, therefore, our intellectual planning process must inherit its title to shrewdness from yet another interior process of planning to plan, and this process could in its turn be silly or shrewd. The regress is infinite, and this reduces to absurdity the theory that for an operation to be intelligent it must be steered by a prior intellectual operation. What distinguishes sensible from silly operations is not their parentage but their procedure, and this holds no less for intellectual than for practical performances. 'Intelligent' cannot be defined in terms of 'intellectual' or 'knowing *how*' in terms of 'knowing *that*'; 'thinking what I am doing' does not connote 'both thinking what to do and doing it.'

When I do something intelligently, i.e. thinking what I am doing, I am doing one thing and not two. My performance has a special procedure or manner, not special antecedents. . . .

. . . The cleverness of the clown may be exhibited in his tripping and tumbling. He trips and tumbles just as clumsy people do, except that he trips and tumbles on purpose and after much rehearsal and at the golden moment and where the children can see him and so as not to hurt himself. The spectators applaud his skill at seeming clumsy, but what they applaud is not some extra hidden performance executed 'in his head.' It is his visible performance that they admire, but they admire it not for being an effect of any hidden internal causes but for being an exercise of a skill. Now a skill is not an act. It is therefore neither a witnessable nor unwitnessable act. To recognise that a performance is an exercise of a skill is indeed to appreciate it in the light of a factor which could not be separately recorded by a camera. But the reason why the skill exercised in a performance cannot be separately recorded by a camera is not that it is an occult or ghostly happening, but that it is not a happening at all. It is a disposition, or complex of dispositions, and a disposition is a factor of the wrong logical type to be seen or unseen, recorded or unrecorded. Just as the habit of talking loudly is not itself loud or quiet, since it is not the sort of term of which 'loud' and 'quiet' can be predicated, or just as a susceptibility to headaches is for the same reason not itself unendurable or endurable, so the skills, tastes and bents which are exercised in overt or internal operations are not themselves overt or internal, witnessable or unwitnessable. The traditional theory of the mind has misconstrued the type-distinction between disposition and exercise into its mythical bifurcation of unwitnessable mental causes and their witnessable physical effects.

INTELLIGENCE AS A COMPLEX KIND OF DISPOSITION

The ability to apply rules is the product of practice. It is therefore tempting to argue that competences and skills are just habits. They are certainly second natures or acquired dispositions, but it does not follow from this that they are mere habits. Habits are one sort, but not the only sort, of second nature, and it will be argued later that the common assumption that all second natures are mere habits obliterates distinctions which are of cardinal importance for the inquiries in which we are engaged.

The ability to give by rote the correct solutions of multiplication problems differs in certain important respects from the ability to solve them by calculating. When we describe someone as doing something by pure or blind habit, we mean that he does it automatically and without having to mind what he is doing. He does not exercise care, vigilance, or criticism. After the toddling-age we walk on pavements without minding our steps. But a mountaineer walking over ice-covered rocks in a high wind in the dark does not move his limbs by blind habit; he thinks what he is doing, he is ready for emergencies, he economises in effort, he makes tests and experiments; in short he walks with some degree of skill and judgment. If he makes a mistake, he is inclined not to repeat it, and if he finds a new trick effective he is inclined to continue to use it and to improve on it. He is concomitantly walking and teaching himself how to walk in conditions of this sort. It is of the essence of merely habitual practices that one performance is a replica of its predecessors. It is of the essence of intelligent practices that one performance is modified by its predecessors. The agent is still learning. . . .

. . . There is a further important difference between habits and intelligent capacities, to bring out which it is necessary to say a few words about the logic of dispositional concepts in general.

When we describe glass as brittle, or sugar as soluble, we are using dispositional concepts, the logical force of which is this. The brittleness of glass does not consist in the fact that it is at a given moment actually being shivered. It may be brittle without ever being shivered. To say that it is brittle is to say that if it ever is, or ever had been, struck or strained, it would fly, or have flown, into fragments. To say that sugar is soluble is to say that it would dissolve, or would have dissolved, if immersed in water.

A statement ascribing a dispositional property to a thing has much, though not everything, in common with a statement subsuming the thing under a law. To possess a dispositional property is not to be in a particular state, or to undergo a particular change; it is to be bound or liable to be in a particular state, or to undergo a particular change, when a particular condition is realised. The same is true about specifically human dispositions such as qualities of character. My being an habitual smoker does not entail that I am at this or that moment smoking; it is my permanent proneness to smoke when I am not eating, sleeping, lecturing or attending funerals, and have not quite recently been smoking.

In discussing dispositions it is initially helpful to fasten on the simplest models, such as the brittleness of glass or the smoking habit of a man. For in describing these dispositions it is easy to unpack the hypothetical proposition implicitly conveyed in the ascription of the dispositional properties. To be brittle is just to be bound or likely to fly into fragments in such and such conditions; to be a smoker is just to be bound or likely to fill, light and draw on a pipe in such and such conditions. These are simple, single-track dispositions, the actualisations of which are nearly uniform.

But the practice of considering such simple models of dispositions, though initially helpful, leads at a later stage to erroneous assumptions. There are many dispositions the actualisations of which can take a wide and perhaps unlimited variety of shapes; many disposition-concepts are determinable concepts. When an object is described as hard, we do not mean only that it would resist deformation; we mean also that it would, for example, give out a sharp sound if struck, that it would cause us pain if we came into sharp contact with it, that resilient objects would bounce off it, and so on indefinitely. If we wished to unpack all that is conveyed in describing an animal as gregarious, we should similarly have to produce an infinite series of different hypothetical propositions.

Now the higher-grade dispositions of people with which this inquiry is largely concerned are, in general, not single-track dispositions, but dispositions the exercises of which are indefinitely heterogeneous. When Jane Austen wished to show the specific kind of pride which characterised the heroine of 'Pride and Prejudice,' she had to represent her actions, words, thoughts and feelings in a thousand different situations. There is no one standard type of action or reaction such that Jane Austen could say 'My heroine's kind of pride was just the tendency to do this, whenever a situation of that sort arose. . . .'

. . . In judging that someone's performance is or is not intelligent, we have, as has been said, in a certain manner to look beyond the performance itself. For there is no particular overt or inner performance which could not have been accidentally or 'mechanically' executed by an idiot, a sleepwalker, a man in panic, absence of mind or delirium or even, sometimes, by a parrot. But in looking beyond the performance itself, we are not trying to pry into some hidden counterpart performance enacted on the supposed secret stage of the agent's inner life. We are considering his abilities and propensities of which this performance was an actualisation. Our inquiry is not into causes (and *a fortiori* not into occult causes), but into capacities, skills, habits, liabilities and bents. We observe, for example, a soldier scoring a bull's eye. Was it luck or was it skill? If he has the skill, then he can get on or near the bull's eye again, even if the wind strengthens, the range alters and the target moves. Or if his second shot is an outer, his third, fourth and fifth shots will probably creep nearer and nearer to the bull's eye. He generally checks his breathing before pulling the trigger, as he did on this occasion; he is ready to advise his neighbour what allowances to make for refraction, wind, etc. Marksmanship is a complex of skills, and the question whether he hit the bull's eye by luck or from good marksmanship is the question whether or not he has the skills, and, if he has, whether he used them by making his shot with care, self-control, attention to the conditions and thought of his instructions.

To decide whether his bull's eye was a fluke or a good shot, we need and he himself might need to take into account more than this one success. Namely, we should take into account his subsequent shots, his past record, his explanations or excuses, the advice he gave to his neighbour and a host of other clues of various sorts. There is no one signal of a man's knowing how to shoot, but a modest assemblage of heterogeneous performances generally suffices to establish beyond reasonable doubt whether he knows how to shoot or not. Only then, if at all, can it be decided whether he hit the bull's eye because he was lucky, or whether he hit it because he was marksman enough to succeed when he tried.

A drunkard at the chessboard makes the one move which upsets his opponent's plan of campaign. The spectators are satisfied that this was due not to cleverness but to luck, if they are satisfied that most of his moves made in this state break the rules of chess, or have no tactical connection with the position of the game, that he would not be likely to repeat this move if the tactical situation were to recur, that he would not applaud such a move if made by another player in a similar situation, that he could not explain why he had done it or even describe the threat under which his King had been.

Their problem is not one of the occurrence or non-occurrence of ghostly processes, but one of the truth or falsehood of certain 'could' and 'would' propositions and certain other particular applications of them. For, roughly, the mind is not the topic of sets of untestable categorical propositions, but the topic of sets of testable hypothetical and semi-hypothetical propositions. The difference between a normal person and an idiot is not that the normal person is really two persons while the idiot is only one, but that the normal person can do a lot of things which the idiot cannot do; and 'can' and 'cannot' are not occurrence words but modal words. Of course, in describing the moves actually made by the drunk and the sober players, or the noises actually uttered by the idiotic and the sane men, we have to use not only 'could' and 'would' expressions, but also 'did' and 'did not' expressions. The drunkard's move was made recklessly and the sane man was minding what he was saying. . . .

Knowing *how*, then, is a disposition, but not a single-track disposition like a reflex or a habit. Its exercises are observances of rules or canons or the applications of criteria, but they are not tandem operations of theoretically avowing maxims and then putting them into practice. Further, its exercises can be overt or covert, deeds performed or deeds imagined, words spoken aloud or words heard in one's head, pictures painted on canvas or pictures in the mind's eye. Or they can be amalgamations of the two. . . .

SUMMARY

The central point that is being laboured in this chapter is of considerable importance. It is an attack from one flank upon the category-mistake which underlies the dogma of the ghost in the machine. In unconscious reliance upon this dogma theorists and laymen alike constantly construe the adjectives by which we characterise performances as ingenious, wise, methodical, careful, witty, etc. as signalising the occurrence in someone's hidden stream of consciousness of special processes functioning as ghostly harbingers or more specifically as occult causes of the performances so characterised. They postulate an internal shadow-performance to be the real carrier of the intelligence ordinarily ascribed to the overt act, and think that in this way they explain what makes the overt act a manifestation of intelligence. They have described the overt act as an effect of a mental happening, though they stop short, of course, before raising the next question—what makes the postulated mental happenings manifestations of intelligence and not mental deficiency.

In opposition to this entire dogma, I am arguing that in describing the workings of a person's mind we are not describing a second set of shadowy operations. We are describing certain phases of his one career; namely we are describing the ways in which parts of his conduct are managed. The sense in which we 'explain' his actions is not that we infer to occult causes, but that we subsume under hypothetical and semi-hypothetical propositions. The explanation is not of the type 'the glass broke because a stone hit it,' but more nearly of the different type 'the glass broke when the stone hit it, because it was brittle.' It makes no difference in theory if the performances we are appraising are operations executed silently in the agent's head, such as what he does, when duly schooled to it, in theorising, composing limericks or solving anagrams. Of course it makes a lot of difference in practice, for the examiner cannot award marks to operations which the candidate successfully keeps to himself.

But when a person talks sense aloud, ties knots, feints or sculpts, the actions which we witness are themselves the things which he is intelligently doing, though the concepts in terms of which the physicist or physiologist would describe his actions do not exhaust those which would be used by his pupils or his teachers in appraising their logic, style or technique. He is bodily active and he is mentally active, but he is not being synchronously active in two different 'places,' or with two different 'engines.' There is the one activity, but it is one susceptible of and requiring more than one kind of explanatory description. Somewhat as there is no aerodynamical or physiological difference between the description of one bird as 'flying south' and of another as 'migrating,' though there is a big biological difference between these descriptions, so there need be no physical or physiological differences between the descriptions of one man as gabbling and another talking sense, though the rhetorical and logical differences are enormous.

The statement 'the mind is its own place,' as theorists might construe it, is not true, for the mind is not even a metaphorical 'place.' On the contrary, the chessboard, the platform, the scholar's desk, the judge's bench, the lorry-driver's seat, the studio and the football field are among its places. These are where people work and play stupidly or intelligently. 'Mind' is not the name of another person, working or frolicking behind an impenetrable screen; it is not the name of another place where work is done or games are played; and it is not the name of another tool with which work is done, or another appliance with which games are played.

15. LANGUAGE AND MIND: WITTGENSTEIN'S CRITIQUE OF DUALISM

A. M. Quinton

Ludwig Wittgenstein (1889–1951) was unquestionably one of the most influential philosophers of the twentieth century and many would say that he more than any other philosopher in recent times has shaped the course of contemporary philosophy. His Philosophical Investigations (1953), *although pieced together from notes and containing countless obscure passages, nevertheless presents a new approach to doing philosophy. The major thrust of this method is that philosophical problems arise for us when we are misled or "bewitched" by the language we use in ordinary life. By tracing back a philosophical perplexity to its source or sources in the way we talk about ourselves and*

Reprinted with permission of the Macmillan Company from A Critical History of Western Philosophy, *edited by D. J. O'Connor. Copyright © 1964 by The Free Press of Glencoe, a Division of the Macmillan Company.*

the world, we can in effect "dissolve" these problems. Philosophy, then, comes to be viewed as the application of a very difficult, painstaking and sometimes bewildering kind of therapy intended to cure ourselves and others of the "deep disquietudes" of philosophical perplexity. Anthony M. Quinton (1926–   ) *is a Fellow of New College, Oxford. The following selection is part of a chapter on contemporary British philosophy he contributed to* A Critical History of Western Philosophy, *edited by D. J. O'Connor.*

The particular philosophical problem that takes up most of Wittgenstein's attention in the *Investigations* is that of the nature of mind or, in his terminology, of the language in which we report and describe the mental states of ourselves and others. The metaphysical doctrine against which he is arguing here is that persistent dualism of mind and body, made explicit by Plato and Descartes, but, it would seem, rather deeply lodged in our ordinary way of thinking, which holds that mental states exist in private worlds of their own of which only one person is directly aware. The paradoxes arising from this theory are, first and foremost, the idea that we can never know what is going on in the mind of another person and also perhaps the older difficulty about understanding how things can act upon each other when they are as different from one another as mental and bodily states are according to this theory. The mistaken analogy that lies behind the skeptical absurdities of dualism is that between "I see a tree," or "I touch this stone" on the one hand and "I feel a pain" and "I understand this calculation" on the other. Just as the first two sentences report perception of and action on physical things so, it is supposed, the other two report mental perception and action. The world is then conceived as containing, alongside material objects and acts of manipulating them, mental objects like pains and mental acts or processes like understanding, meaning and thinking.

Wittgenstein maintains that our mental vocabulary does not refer to inner acts and states. It is not so much that he denies the existence of private experiences as that he denies that they could serve as criteria for the employment of mental words. In his view, to say that someone is in a given mental state is to say that he is in any of a large collection of publicly observable situations, that he is doing or disposed to do any of a large collection of publicly observable things. There is no one recurrent kind of thing of which a mental word is the name, nor is it the name of any kind of private thing. He supports this theory with two kinds of argument. In the first place, he examines in detail the working of a representative selection of mental concepts, and, secondly, he has a general argument to prove that a private language, referring to the experiences of which only one person is aware, is an impossibility.

The most important and suggestive particular concept he investigates is that of understanding. The dualist supposes that when someone under instruction says "now I understand," he is reporting a private experience of understanding. But whatever experience he may have, Wittgenstein replies, cannot be the sense, and thus the criterion of truth, of the man's remark. What decides whether or not he really does understand, let us say, long division, is whether or not he can go on to repeat the operation for himself, preferably on new material so as to rule out his having learnt by heart the arrangement of numbers making up the long division sum. To understand something is to be able to apply it. It might be thought that this objection could be countered by a further specification of the purported experience of understanding. Could the experience not take the form of the private awareness of some image or formula which gives the gist of the operation claimed to be understood? Against this suggestion Wittgenstein argues that an image or formula does not dictate its own application. It must itself be understood, and that it has been understood is something that only its correct application can establish. An image or formula as it stands can be interpreted or understood in different ways. Only its publicly observable application can show if the interpretation made of it is the correct one. Essentially the same argument is applied to the concept of meaning something by a word. What a man means by a word is not a private experience, in particular it is not an image which is itself a symbol that can be meant, i.e., used, in very different ways. The meaning a man attaches to a word is only to be discovered by considering the things to which he applies, and from which he withholds, the word and the verbal contexts, the statements and arguments, in which he employs it. It follows from this that thinking is not an interior process that accompanies speech and is the criterion of its being intelligent speech and not babbling. For to think what one is saying is no more than to mean what one is saying. The same general treatment is extended to cover concepts of emotion such as hope and fear. All these concepts derive their significance from the surroundings of the people to whom they are ascribed and not to some private events going on within them. The concepts considered so far all relate to higher forms of mentality and, primarily at any rate, can only be ascribed to creatures that are at least human beings to the extent of being users of language. An important feature of the "surroundings" in these cases is what the people to whom they are ascribed will say. What sense is there, Wittgenstein asks, to the supposition that a dog is afraid of something that may happen next week?

Having argued that the publicly observable surroundings are in fact the criteria for our applications of mental words in these examples, Wittgenstein goes on to prove that this must be so, since there could not be a language whose use was wholly determined by private experiences. It might seem that I could resolve to utter a certain word whenever a sensation like this particular one I am having now took place. This decision would provide a criterion which I should apply whenever the same sensation recurred. But what could be meant, he asks, by the question whether a given sensation was the same as the one chosen as the criterion? We could only compare the present sensation with our memory of its predecessor, and how could we eliminate the possibility that our memory was playing us false? He concludes that language is an essentially social phenomenon. The making of noises does not become linguistic utterance unless it is governed by rules, unless there is an applicable distinction between the correct and mistaken use of words. With a private language, this condition cannot be satisfied, and the uttering of words introduced as names of private sensations would be just an "empty ceremony." It is for this reason that our mental words must be, as they are, connected with features of our situation which anyone can in principle observe. Every inner process must have its outward criteria.

The concept to which this treatment seems least applicable is that of pain, and Wittgenstein considers it at length. Here, as elsewhere, it is important to consider the way in which the use of the words under examination is learnt. Now, we learn how to use the words "it hurts" from other people who tell that we are in pain from our circumstances and behavior. But we do not tell that we are in pain ourselves in this way. In fact, Wittgenstein maintains, we do not discover or find out that we are in pain at all. It is not a thing we can be in doubt about and so not a thing of which it is appropriate to claim knowledge. We use no criteria for our utterances of "it hurts" and it is an incorrigible statement in the sense that we cannot be honestly mistaken about it. If I do hesitate about saying that I am in pain that shows that it is not exactly pain that I am suffering from but something like it, discomfort perhaps. Statements about pain in the first person, Wittgenstein says, are in fact extension of natural pain-behavior, conventionalized alternatives to crying out which we are trained to adopt. They are not so much descriptions of pain but manifestations of it.

The will, in Wittgenstein's opinion, is no more private and internal than thought and feeling. The difference between my raising my arm and my arm's simply going up in the air does not consist in the presence in the former case of an interior act of will. What commonly characterizes voluntary movement is the absence of surprise. Intentions, again, are not private states. I ordinarily know for certain what my intentions are, but this does not rest on any sort of interior observation. There is a parallel here, he asserts, with our knowledge of the movements and positions of our bodies. We do not have to look to see where our arms are but we do not tell by some recognizable feeling either.

The bearing of this theory of mental language on the metaphysical problem about our knowledge of other minds which inspired it is that there is no such general problem. For there could be no mental language with which I could talk about my own mind unless there were a public mental language and I had mastered it. He does not say that any statement about the mind of another person strictly and deductively follows from any set of statements about his behavior. Nevertheless, what others do and say provides all the ground that is required for the justification of our beliefs about them. To believe that other people have feelings in the way we do ourselves does not consist in the acceptance of a definite set of propositions. It is shown, rather, in the way in which we treat other people, in our attitudes of pity and concern for them, for example. . . .

16. THE MENTAL AND THE PHYSICAL AS IDENTICAL

J. J. C. Smart

J. J. C. Smart (1920–   ) is Hughes Professor of Philosophy at the University of Adelaide in Australia. He is the author of An Outline of a System of Utilitarian Ethics *(1961),* Philosophy and Scientific Realism *(1963), and* Between Science and Philosophy *(1960). Perhaps his most influential contribution was a much discussed article entitled "Sensations and Brain Processes," in which he argued that sensations are strictly identical with certain kinds of processes in the brain. He also defends this view in the following selection from* Philosophy and Scientific Realism.

. . . I wish to argue for the view that conscious experiences are simply *brain processes*. This is a view which almost every elementary

From Philosophy and Scientific Realism *(1963), pp. 88–90, 92–97, 99–105. Reprinted by permission of the publishers, Routledge and Kegan Paul, Ltd., London, and The Humanities Press, Inc., New York.*

student of philosophy is taught to refute. I shall try to show that the standard refutations of the view are fallacious.

Many of our ordinary psychological concepts seem to refer to inner processes. Of course this is not so with all of them. Some of them seem to be able to be elucidated in a behaviouristic way: to say that someone is vain is to say that he tends to show off, or look at himself often in the mirror, or something of that sort. To say that he is interested in mathematics is to say that he has a tendency to read mathematical books, to work out problems, to talk in terms of mathematical analogies, and so on. Similarly with the emotions: 'anger,' 'fear,' 'joy,' and the like can plausibly be said to refer to characteristic behaviour patterns. Again various adverbial phrases can be elucidated in a behaviouristic way. As Ryle has pointed out, the phrase 'thinking what he is doing' in 'he is driving the car thinking what he is doing' refers to certain tendencies to behave in various ways: for example, to apply the brakes when one sees a child about to run on to the road. To drive a car thinking what you are doing is not like walking and whistling. You can walk without whistling and you can whistle without walking, but you cannot do the 'thinking what you are doing' part of 'driving the car thinking what you are doing' without the driving of the car. (Similarly, you can walk grace-fully, but you cannot do the being graceful part of the performance without doing the walking part of it.) This helps to elucidate the well-known difficulty of thinking without words. Certain kinds of thinking are pieces of intelligent talking to oneself. Consider the way in which I 'thinkingly' wrote the last sentence. I can no more do the 'thinking' part without the talking (or writing) part than a man can do the being graceful part apart from the walking (or some equivalent activity).

If all our psychological concepts were capable of a behaviouris-tic or quasi-behaviouristic analysis this would be congenial for physi-calism. . . . Unfortunately, however, there are a good many psychologi-cal concepts for which a behaviouristic account seems impossible.

Suppose that I report that I am having an orange-yellow round-ish after-image. Or suppose again that I report that I have a pain. It seems clear that the content of my report cannot be exclusively a set of purely behavioural facts. There seems to be some element of 'pure inner experience' which is being reported, and to which only I have direct access. You can observe my behaviour, but only I can be aware of my own after-image or my own pain. I suspect that the notion of a 'pain' is partly akin to that of an emotion: that is, the notion of pain seems es-sentially to involve the notion of distress, and distress is perhaps capable of an elucidation in terms of a characteristic behaviour pattern. But this is not all that a pain is: there is an immediately felt sensation which we do not have in other cases of distress. (Consider by contrast the distress of a mother because her son goes out gambling. The son gives his mother much pain, but he does not necessarily give her *a* pain.) In the case of the after-image there is not this 'emotional' component of distress, and it seems easier to consider such 'neat' inner experiences. I shall therefore concentrate on the case where I report the experience of having an after-image. . . .

The first argument against the identification of experiences and brain processes can be put as follows: Aristotle, or for that matter an illiterate peasant, can report his images and aches and pains, and yet nevertheless may not know that the brain has anything to do with thinking. (Aristotle thought that the brain was an organ for cooling the blood.) Therefore what Aristotle or the peasant reports cannot *be* a brain process, though it can, of course, be something which is (unknown to Aristotle or the peasant) causally connected with a brain process.

The reply to this argument is simply this: when I say that experiences are brain processes I am asserting this *as a matter of fact*. I am not asserting that 'brain process' is part of what we *mean* by 'experience.' A couple of analogies will show what is wrong with the argument. Suppose that a man is acquainted with Sir Walter Scott and knows him as 'the author of *Waverley*.' He may never have heard of Ivanhoe. Yet the author of *Waverley* can be (and was) the very same person as the author of *Ivanhoe*. Again, consider lightning. According to modern science, lightning is a movement of electric charges from one ionised layer of cloud to another such layer or to the earth. This is what lightning really is. This fact was not known to Aristotle. And yet Aristotle presumably knew the meaning of the Greek word for 'lightning' perfectly well.

I wish to make it clear that I have used these examples mainly to make a *negative* point: I do not wish to claim that the relation between the expression 'I am having an after-image' and 'there is such-and-such a brain process going on in me' is in *all* respects like that between 'there is the author of *Waverley*' and 'there is the author of *Ivanhoe*,' or like that between 'that is lightning' and 'that is a motion of electric charges.' The point I wish to make at present is simply that these analogies show the weakness of the . . . argument against identifying experiences and brain processes. I am, however, suggesting also that it may be the true nature of our inner experiences, as revealed by science, to be brain processes, just as to be a motion of electric charges is the true nature of lightning, what lightning really is. Neither the case of lightning nor the case of inner experiences is like that of explaining a footprint by reference to a burglar. It is not the true nature of a footprint to be a burglar.

In short, there can be contingent statements of the form 'A is identical with B,' and a person may know that something is an A without knowing it is a B. An illiterate peasant might well be able to talk about his sensations without knowing about his brain processes, just as he can talk about lightning, though he knows nothing about lightning. . . .

A related objection which is sometimes put up against the brain process thesis runs as follows. It will be pointed out that the hypothesis that sensations are connected with brain processes shares the tentative character of all scientific hypotheses. It is possible, though in the highest degree unlikely, that our present physiological theories will one day be given up, and it will seem as absurd to connect sensations with the brain as it now does to connect them with the heart. It follows that when we report a sensation we are not reporting a brain process.

This argument falls to the ground once it is realised that assertions of identity can be factual and contingent. The argument certainly does prove that when I say 'I have a yellowish-orange after-image' I cannot *mean* that I have such-and-such a brain process. (Any more than that if a man says 'there goes the author of *Waverley*' he *means* 'there goes the author of *Ivanhoe*.' The two sentences are not inter-translatable.) But the argument does not prove that what we report (e.g. the having of an after-image) is not *in fact* a brain process. It could equally be said that it is conceivable (though in the highest degree unlikely) that the electrical theory of lightning should be given up. This shows indeed that 'that is lightning' does not *mean* the same as 'that is a motion of electric charges.' But for all that, lightning is *in fact* a motion of electric charges. . . . Now it may be said that if we identify an experience and a brain process and if this identification is, as I hold it is, a *contingent* or *factual* one, then the experience must be identified as having some property not logically deducible from the properties whereby we identify the brain process. To return to our analogy of the contingent identification of the author of *Waverley* with the author of *Ivanhoe*. If the property of being the author of *Waverley* is the analogue of the neurophysiological properties of a brain process, what is the analogue of the property of being author of *Ivanhoe*? There is an inclination to say: 'an irreducible, emergent, introspectible property.'

How do I get round this objection? I do so as follows. The man who reports a yellowish-orange after-image does so in effect as follows: '*What is going on in me is like what is going on in me when* my eyes are open, the lighting is normal, etc., etc., and there really is a yellowish-orange patch on the wall.' In this sentence the word 'like' is meant to be used in such a way that something can be like itself: an identical twin is not only like his brother but is like himself too. With this sense of 'like' the above formula will do for a report that one is having a veridical sense datum too. Notice that the italicised words *what is going on in me is like what is going on in me when . . .* are topic-neutral. A dualist will think that what is going on in him when he reports an experience is in fact a non-physical process (though his report does not say that it is), an ancient Greek may think that it is a process in his heart, and I think that it is a process in my brain. The report itself is neutral to all these possibilities. This extreme 'openness' and 'topic neutrality' of reports of experiences perhaps explains why the 'raw feels' or immediate qualia of internal experiences have seemed so elusive. 'What is going on in me is like what is going on in me when . . .' is a colourless phrase, just as the word 'somebody' is colourless. If I say 'somebody is coming through the garden' I may do so because I see my wife coming through the garden. Because of the colourless feel of the word 'somebody' a very naïve hearer (like the king in *Alice in Wonderland,* who got thoroughly confused over the logical grammar of 'nobody') might suspect that 'somebody is coming through the garden' is about some very elusive and ghostly entity, instead of, in fact, that very colourful and flesh and blood person, my wife.

For this account to be successful, it is necessary that we should be able to report two processes as like one another without being able to say in what respect they are alike. An experience of having an after-image may be classified as like the experience I have when I see an orange, and this likeness, on my view, must consist in a similarity of neuro-physiological pattern. But of course we are not immediately aware of the pattern; at most we are able to report the similarity. Now it is tempting, when we think in a metaphysical and *a priori* way, to suppose that reports of similarities can be made only on a basis of the conscious apprehension of the features in respect of which these similarities subsist. But when we think objectively about the human being as a functioning mechanism this metaphysical supposition may come to seem unwarranted. It is surely more easy to construct a mechanism which will record (on a punched tape, for example) bare similarities in a class of stimuli than it is to construct a machine which will provide a report of the features in which these similarities consist. It therefore seems to me quite possible that we should be able to make reports to the effect that 'what is going on in me is like what goes on in me when . . .' without having any idea whatever of what in particular is going on in me (*e.g.* whether a brain process, a heart process, or a spiritual process).

I must make it clear that I am not producing the phrase 'What is going on in me is like what goes on in me when . . .' as a *translation* of a sensation report. It is rather meant to give in an informal way what a sensation report purports to be about. For example, it has been objected that it is no good translating 'I have a pain' as 'what is going on in me is like what goes on when a pin is stuck into me,' since, to put it crudely, pains have nothing in particular to do with pins, and certainly someone might learn the word 'pain' without ever having learned the word 'pin.' When, however, I say that 'I have a pain' is to the effect of 'what is going on in me is like what goes on in me when a pin is stuck into me,' my intention is simply to indicate the way in which learning to make sensation reports is learning to report likenesses and unlikenesses of various internal processes. There is indeed no need to learn the word 'pain' by having a pin stuck into one. A child may, for example, be introduced to the word 'pain' when he accidentally grazes his knee. But sensation talk must be learned with reference to some environmental stimulus or another. Certainly it need not be any *particular* one, such as the sticking in of pins.

The above considerations also show how we can reply to another objection which is commonly brought against the brain-process theory. The experience, it will be said, is not in physical space, whereas the brain process is. Hence the experience is not a brain process. This objection seems to beg the question. If my view is correct the experience *is* in physical space: in my brain. The truth behind the objection is that the experience is not reported as something spatial. It is reported only (in effect) in terms of 'what is going on in me is like what goes on in me when. . . .' This report is so 'open' and general that it is indeed neutral between my view that what goes on in me goes on in physical space and the psychophysical dualist's view that what goes on in me goes on in a non-spatial entity. This is without prejudice to the statement that what goes on in me is something which in fact *is* in physical space. On my view sensations do in fact have all sorts of neurophysiological properties. For they are neurophysiological processes. . . .

We must now pass on to consider another objection. This is that our experiences are private, immediately known only to ourselves, whereas brain processes are public, observable (in principle) by any number of external observers. If someone sincerely says that he is having a certain experience, then no one can contradict him. But if the physiologist reports something in the brain, then it is always *in principle* possible to say: 'Perhaps you are mistaken; you may be having an illusion or hallucination or something of the sort.' It will be remembered that I suggested that in reporting sensations we are in fact reporting likenesses and unlikenesses of brain processes. Now it may be objected (as has been done by K. E. M. Baier): 'Suppose that you had some electro-encephalograph fixed to your brain, and you observed that, according to the electro-encephalograph, you did *not* have the sort of brain process that normally goes on when you have a yellow sense datum. Nevertheless, if you had a yellow sense datum you would not give up the proposition that you had such a sense datum, no matter *what* the encephalograph said.' This part of the objection can be easily answered. I simply reply that the brain-process theory was put forward as a factual identification, not as a logically necessary one. I can therefore agree that it is logically possible that the electro-encephalograph experiment should turn out as envisaged in the objection, but I can still believe *that this will never in fact happen*. If it did happen I should doubtless give up the brain-process theory. . . .

However, it is incumbent on anyone who wishes to dispute the brain-process theory to produce experiences which are known to possess irreducibly 'psychic' properties, not merely 'topic neutral' ones. So far I do not think that anyone has done so.

17. A CRITIQUE OF THE IDENTITY THEORY
Norman Malcolm

Norman Malcolm. *(See essay number 4 for biographical note.)*

I

My main topic will be, roughly speaking, the claim that mental events or conscious experiences or inner experiences are brain processes.[1] I hasten to say, however, that I am not going to talk about 'mental events' or 'conscious experiences' or 'inner experiences.' These expressions are almost exclusively philosophers' terms, and I am not sure that I have got the hang of any of them. Philosophers are not in agreement in their use of these terms. One philosopher will say, for example, that a pain in the foot is a mental event, whereas another will say that a pain *in the foot* certainly is not a *mental* event.

From "*Scientific Materialism and the Identity Theory,*" Dialogue: Canadian Philosophical Review, *Vol. III, 1964. Reprinted by permission of the author and editor.*

[1] This paper was read at the Sixtieth Annual Meeting of the American Philosophical Association, Eastern Division. It is a reply to Professor J. J. C. Smart's essay, "Materialism," published in *The Journal of Philosophy,* LX, No. 22 (October, 1963).

I will avoid these expressions, and concentrate on the particular example of *sudden thoughts*. Suddenly remembering an engagement would be an example of suddenly thinking of something. Suddenly realising, in a chess game, that moving this pawn would endanger one's queen, would be another example of a sudden thought. Professor Smart says that he wishes to 'elucidate thought as an inner process,[2] and he adds that he wants to identify 'such inner processes with brain processes.' He surely holds, therefore, that thinking and thoughts, including sudden thoughts, are brain processes. He holds also that conscious experiences, illusions and aches and pains are brain processes, and that love is a brain state. I will restrict my discussion, however, to sudden thoughts.

My first inclination, when I began to think on this topic, was to believe that Smart's view is false—that a sudden thought certainly is not a brain process. But now I think that I do not know what it *means* to say that a sudden thought is a brain process. In saying this I imply, of course, that the proponents of this view also do not know what it means. This implication is risky for it might turn out, to my surprise and gratification, that Smart will explain his view with great clarity.

In trying to show that there is real difficulty in seeing what his view means, I will turn to Smart's article 'Sensations and brain processes.'[3] He says there that in holding that a sensation is a brain process he is 'using "is" in the sense of strict identity.' 'I wish to make it clear,' he says, 'that the brain process doctrine asserts identity in the *strict sense*.' I assume that he wishes to say the same about the claimed identity of a thought with a brain process. Unfortunately he does not attempt to define this 'strict sense of identity,' and so we have to study his examples.

One of his examples of a 'strict identity' is this: 7 is identical with the smallest prime number greater than 5. We must remember, however, that one feature of 'the identity theory,' as I shall call it, is that the alleged identity between thoughts, sensations, etc., and brain processes, is held to be *contingent*. Since the identity of 7 with the smallest prime greater than 5 is *a priori* and relates to timeless objects, it does not provide me with any clue as to how I am to apply the notion of 'strict identity' to temporal events that are *contingently* related. The example is unsatisfactory, therefore, for the purpose of helping me to deal with the question of whether thoughts are or are not 'strictly identical' with certain brain processes.

Let us move to another example. Smart tells us that the sense in

---

[2] Smart, *op. cit.*, p. 657.
[3] J. J. C. Smart, "Sensations and Brain Processes," *The Philosophical Review*, April, 1959.

which the small boy who stole apples is the same person as the victorious general is *not* the 'strict' sense of 'identity.' He thinks there is a mere spatio-temporal continuity between the apple-stealing boy and the general who won the war. From this *non*-example of 'strict identity' I think I obtain a clue as to what he means by it. Consider the following two sentences: 'General de Gaulle is the tallest Frenchman'; 'The victorious general is the small boy who stole apples.' Each of these sentences might be said to express an identity: yet we can see a difference between the two cases. Even though the victorious general *is* the small boy who stole apples, it is possible for the victorious general to be in this room at a time when there is *no* small boy here. In contrast, if General de Gaulle is the tallest Frenchman, then General de Gaulle is not in this room unless the tallest Frenchman is here. It would be quite natural to say that this latter identity (if it holds) is a *strict* identity, and that the other one is not. I believe that Smart would say this. This suggests to me the following rule for his 'strict identity': If something, x, is in a certain place at a certain time, then something, y, is strictly identical with x only if y is in that same place at that same time.

If we assume that Smart's use of the expression 'strict identity' is governed by the necessary condition I have stated, we can possibly understand why he is somewhat hesitant about whether to say that the Morning Star is strictly identical with the Evening Star. Smart says to an imaginary opponent: 'You may object that the Morning Star is in a sense not the very same thing as the Evening Star, but only something spatio-temporally continuous with it. That is, you may say that the Morning Star is not the Evening Star in the strict sense of "identity" that I distinguished earlier.' Instead of rebutting this objection, Smart moves on to what he calls 'a more plausible example of strict identity.' This suggests to me that Smart is not entirely happy with the case of the stars as an example of strict identity. Why not? Perhaps he has some inclination to feel that the planet that is both the Morning and the Evening Star is not the Morning Star *at the same time* it is the Evening Star. If this were so, the suggested necessary condition for 'strict identity' would not be satisfied. Smart's hesitation is thus a further indication that he wants his use of the expression 'strict identity' to be governed by the rule I have stated.

Let us turn to what Smart calls his 'more plausible' example of strict identity. It is this: Lightning is an electric discharge. Smart avows that this is truly a strict identity. This example provides additional evidence that he wants to follow the stated rule. If an electrical discharge occurred in one region of the sky and a flash of lightning occurred simultaneously in a different region of the sky, Smart would have no inclination to assert (I think) that the lightning was strictly identical with the electrical discharge. Or if electrical discharges and corresponding lightning flashes occurred in the same region of the sky, but not at the same time, there normally being a perceptible interval of time between a discharge and a flash, then Smart (I believe) would not wish to hold that there was anything more strict than a systematic correlation (perhaps causal) between electric discharges and lightning.[4]

The difficulty I have in understanding Smart's identity theory is the following. Smart wants to use a concept of 'strict identity.' Since there are a multitude of uses of the word 'is,' from the mere fact that he tells us that he means 'is' in the sense of 'strict identity' it does not follow that he has explained which use of 'is' he intends. From his examples and non-examples, I surmise that his so-called 'strict identity' is governed by the necessary condition that if x occurs in a certain place at a certain time, then y is strictly identical with x only if y occurs in the same place at the same time. But if x is a brain process and y is a sudden thought, then this condition for strict identity is not (and cannot be) satisfied. Indeed, it does not even make sense to set up a test for it. Suppose we had determined, by means of some instrument, that a certain process occurred inside my skull at the exact moment I had the sudden thought about the milk bottles. How do we make the further test of whether my *thought* occurred inside my skull? For it would have to be a *further* test: it would have to be logically independent of the test for the presence of the brain process, because Smart's thesis is that the identity is *contingent*. But no one has any notion of what it would mean to test for the occurrence of the thought inside my skull *independently* of testing for a brain process. The idea of such a test is not intelligible. Smart's thesis, as I understand it, requires this unintelligible idea. For he is not satisfied with holding that there is a systematic correlation between sudden thoughts and certain brain processes. He wants to take the additional step of holding that there is a 'strict identity.' Now his concept of strict identity either embodies the necessary condition I stated previously, or it does not. If it does not, then I do not know what he means by 'strict identity,' over and above systematic correlation. If his concept of strict identity does embody that necessary condition, then his concept of strict identity cannot be meaningfully applied to the relationship between sudden thoughts and brain processes. My

---

[4] Mr. U. T. Place, in his article "Is Consciousness a Brain Process?" also defends the identity theory. An example that he uses to illustrate the sense of identity in which, according to him, "consciousness" could turn out to be a brain process is this: "A cloud is a mass of water droplets or other particles in suspension." I believe that Place would not be ready to hold that this is a genuine identity, *as contrasted with* a systematic and/or causal correlation, if he did not assume that in the very same region of space occupied by a cloud there is, at the very same time, a mass of particles in suspension.

conclusion is what I said in the beginning: the identity theory has no clear meaning.

I proceed now to take up Smart's claim that a sudden thought is strictly identical with some brain process. It is clear that a brain process has spatial location. A brain process would be a mechanical, chemical or electrical process in the brain substance, or an electric discharge from the brain mass, or something of the sort. As Smart puts it, brain processes take place 'inside our skulls.' [5]

Let us consider an example of a sudden thought. Suppose that when I am in my house I hear the sound of a truck coming up the driveway and it suddenly occurs to me that I have not put out the milk bottles. Now is this sudden thought (which is also a sudden memory) literally inside my skull? I think that in our ordinary use of the terms 'thought' and 'thinking,' we attach no meaning to the notion of determining the bodily location of a thought. We do not seriously debate whether someone's sudden thought occurred in his heart, or his throat, or his brain. Indeed, we should not know what the question meant. We should have no idea what to look for to settle this 'question.' We do say such a thing as 'He can't get the thought out of his head'; but this is not taken as giving the location of a thought, any more than the remark 'He still has that girl on the brain' is taken as giving the location of a girl.

It might be replied that *as things are* the bodily location of thoughts is not a meaningful notion; but if massive correlations were discovered between thoughts and brain processes then we might *begin* to locate thoughts in the head. To this I must answer that our philosophical problem *is* about how things are. It is a question about our *present* concepts of thinking and thought, not about some conjectured future concepts.[6]

---

[5] "Materialism," *loc. cit.*, p. 654.

[6] Mr. Jerome Shaffer proposes an ingenious solution to our problem in "Could Mental States Be Brain Processes?" *The Journal of Philosophy*, LVIII, No. 26 (December 21, 1961). He allows that at present we do not attach any meaning to a bodily location of thoughts. As he puts it, we have no "rules" for asserting or denying that a particular thought occurred in a certain part of the body. But why could we not *adopt* a rule, he asks? Supposing that there was discovered to be a one-to-one correspondence between thoughts and brain processes, we could *stipulate* that a thought is located where the corresponding thoughts are located. Nothing would then stand in the way of saying that thoughts are *identical* with those brain processes! Although filled with admiration for this philosophical technique, I disagree with Shaffer when he says (*ibid.*, p. 818) that the adopted convention for the location of thoughts would not have to be merely an elliptical way of speaking of the location of the corresponding brain processes. Considering the origin of the convention, how could it amount to anything else?

II

I turn now to a different consideration. A thought requires circumstances or, in Wittgenstein's word, surroundings' (*Umgebung*). Putting a crown on a man's head is a coronation only in certain circumstances.[7] The behaviour of exclaiming 'Oh, I have not put out the milk bottles,' or the behaviour of suddenly jumping up, rushing to the kitchen, collecting the bottles and carrying them outside—such behaviour expresses the thought that one has not put out the milk bottles *only in certain circumstances.*

The circumstances necessary for this simple thought are complex. They include the existence of an organised community, of a practice of collecting and distributing milk, of a rule that empty bottles will not be collected unless placed outside the door, and so on. These practices, arrangements and rules could exist only if there was a common language; and this in turn would presuppose shared activities and agreement in the use of language. The thought about the milk bottles requires a background of mutual purpose, activity and understanding.

I assume that if a certain brain process were strictly identical with a certain thought, then the occurrence of that brain process would be an absolutely sufficient condition for the occurrence of that thought. If this assumption is incorrect, then my understanding of what Smart means by 'strict identity' is even *less* than I have believed. In support of this assumption I will point out that Smart has never stated his identity theory in the following way. *In certain circumstances* a particular brain process is identical with a particular thought. His thesis has not carried such a qualification. I believe his thesis is the following: A particular brain process is, *without qualification*, strictly identical with a particular thought. If this thesis were true it would appear to follow that the occurrence of that brain process would be an absolutely sufficient conditions for the occurrence of that thought.

I have remarked that a necessary condition for the occurrence of my sudden thought about the milk bottles is the previous existence of various practices, rules and agreements. If the identity theory were true, then the surroundings that are necessary for the existence of my sudden thought would also be necessary for the existence of the brain process with which it is identical.[8] That brain process would not have

---

[7] *Investigations*, Sec. 584.

[8] It is easy to commit a fallacy here. The circumstances that I have mentioned are *conceptually* necessary for the occurrence of my thoughts. If the identity theory were true it would not follow that they were *conceptually* necessary for the occurrence of the brain process that is identical with that

occurred unless, for example, there was or had been a practice of delivering milk.

This consequence creates a difficulty for those philosophers who, like Smart, hold both to the identity theory and also to the viewpoint that I shall call 'scientific materialism.' According to the latter viewpoint, the furniture of the world 'in the last resort' consists of 'the ultimate entities of physics.' [9] Smart holds that everything in the world is 'explicable in terms of physics.' [10] It does not seem to me that this can be true. My sudden thought about the milk bottles was an occurrence in the world. That thought required a background of common practices, purposes and agreements. But a reference to a practice of e.g. delivering milk could not appear in a proposition of physics. The word 'electron' is a term of physics, but the phrase 'a practice of delivering milk' is not. There could not be an explanation of the occurrence of my thought (an explanation taking account of all the necessary circumstances) which was stated solely in terms of the entities and laws of physics.

My sudden thought about the milk bottles is not unique in requiring surroundings. The same holds for any other thought. No thought would be explicable wholly in the terms of physics (and/or biology) because the circumstances that form the 'stage-setting' for a thought cannot be described in the terms of physics.

Now if I am right on this point, and if the identity theory were true, it would follow that none of those *brain processes* that are identical with thoughts could be given a purely physical explanation. A philosopher who holds both to the identity theory and to scientific materialism is forced, I think, into the self-defeating position of conceding that many brain processes are not explicable solely in terms of physics.[11] The position is self-defeating because such a philosopher regards a brain process as a *paradigm* of something wholly explicable in terms of physics.

---

thought. But it would follow that those circumstances were necessary for the occurrence of the brain process *in the sense* that the brain process *would not* have occurred in the absence of those circumstances.

[9] "Materialism," *loc. cit.*, p. 651.

[10] "Sensations and Brain Processes," p. 34.

[11] I believe this argument is pretty similar to a point made by J. T. Stevenson, in his "Sensations and Brain Processes: A Reply to J. J. C. Smart," *The Philosophical Review* (October, 1960), p. 507. Smart's view, roughly speaking, is that unless sensations are identical with brain processes they are "Nomological danglers." Stevenson's retort is that by insisting that sensations are identical with brain processes we have not got rid of any nomological danglers. He says: "Indeed, on Smart's thesis it turns out that brain processes are danglers, for now brain processes have all those properties that made sensations danglers."

A defender of these two positions might try to avoid this outcome by claiming that the cicumstances required for the occurrence of a thought do themselves consist of configurations of ultimate particles (or of their statistical properties, or something of the sort). I doubt, however, that anyone knows what it would mean to say, for example, that the *rule* that milk bottles will not be collected unless placed outside the door is a configuration of ultimate particles. At the very least, this defence would have to assume a heavy burden of explanation.

III

There is a further point connected with the one just stated. At the foundation of Smart's monism there is, I believe, the desire for a homogeneous system of explanation. Everything in the world, he feels, should be capable of the same *kind* of explanation, namely, one in terms of the entities and laws of physics. He thinks we advance towards this goal when we see that sensations, thoughts, etc., are identical with brain processes.

Smart has rendered a service to the profession by warning us against a special type of fallacy. An illustration of this fallacy would be to argue that a sensation is not a brain process because a person can be talking about a sensation and yet not be talking about a brain process. The verb 'to talk about' might be called an 'intentional' verb, and this fallacy committed with it might be called 'the intentional fallacy.' Other intentional verbs would be 'to mean,' 'to intend,' 'to know,' 'to predict,' to 'describe,' 'to notice,' and so on.

It is easy to commit the intentional fallacy, and I suspect that Smart himself has done so. The verb 'to explain' is also an intentional verb and one must beware of using it to produce a fallacy. Suppose that the Prime Minister of Ireland is the ugliest Irishman. A man might argue that this cannot be so, because someone might be explaining the presence of the Irish Prime Minister in New York and yet not be explaining the presence in New York of the ugliest Irishman. It would be equally fallacious to argue that since the Irish Prime Minister and the ugliest Irishman *are* one and the same person, therefore, to explain the presence of the Prime Minister *is* to explain the presence of the ugliest Irishman.

I wonder if Smart has not reasoned fallaciously, somewhat as follows: If a sudden thought *is* a certain brain process, then to *explain* the occurrence of the brain process *is* to explain the occurrence of the thought. Thus there will be just one kind of explanation for both thoughts and brain processes.

The intentional fallacy here is transparent. If a thought is identical with a brain process, it does not follow that to explain the occurrence of the brain process is to explain the occurrence of the thought. And in fact, an explanation of the one differs in *kind* from an explanation of the other. The explanation of why someone *thought* such and such involves different assumptions and principles and is guided by different interests than is an explanation of why this or that process occurred in his brain. These explanations belong to different *systems* of explanation.

I conclude that even if Smart were right in holding that thoughts are strictly identical with brain processes (a claim that I do not yet find intelligible) he would not have established that there is one and the same explanation for the occurrence of the thoughts and for the occurrence of the brain processes. If he were to appreciate this fact then, I suspect, he would no longer have any *motive* for espousing the identity theory. For this theory, even if true, would not advance us one whit towards the single, homogeneous system of explanation that is the goal of Smart's materialism. . . .

The Problem of Free Action

IV

Am I Ever Justly Held Responsible for Any of My Actions?

18. THE RANGE OF HUMAN FREEDOM

John Hospers

John Hospers *(1918–   ) is Professor of Philosophy at California State College in Los Angeles and editor of* The Personalist. *He has also taught at Columbia, Minnesota, Brooklyn College, and U.C.L.A. He is the author of* Introduction to Philosophical Analysis *(1953) and* Human Conduct *(1961).*

The issue may be put this way: How can anyone be responsible for his actions, since they grow out of his character, which is shaped and molded and made what it is by influences—some hereditary, but most of them stemming from early parental environment—that were not of his own making or choosing? This question, I believe, still troubles many people who would agree to all the distinctions we have just made but still have the feeling that "this isn't all." They have the uneasy suspicion that there is a more ultimate sense, a "deeper" sense, in which we are *not* responsible for our actions, since we are not responsible for the character out of which those actions spring. . . .

Let us take as an example a criminal who, let us say, strangled several persons and is himself now condemned to die in the electric chair. Jury and public alike hold him fully responsible (at least they utter the words "he is responsible"), for the murders were planned down to the minutest detail, and the defendant tells the jury exactly how he planned them. But now we find out how it all came about; we learn of parents who rejected him from babyhood, of the childhood spent in one foster home after another, where it was always plain to him that he was not wanted; of the constantly frustrated early desire for affection, the hard shell of nonchalance and bitterness that he assumed to cover the painful and humiliating fact of being unwanted, and his subsequent attempts to heal these wounds to his shattered ego through defensive aggression.

The criminal is the most passive person in this world, helpless as a baby in his motorically inexpressible fury. Not only does he try to wreak re-

Reprinted by permission of New York University Press and John Hospers from Determinism and Freedom in the Age of Modern Science, *edited by Sidney Hook. © 1958 by New York University.*

venge on the mother of the earliest period of his babyhood; his criminality is based on the inner feeling of being incapable of making the mother even feel that the child seeks revenge on her. The situation is that of a dwarf trying to annoy a giant who superciliously refuses to see these attempts. . . . Because of his inner feeling of being a dwarf, the criminotic uses, so to speak, dynamite. Of that the giant must take cognizance. True, the "revenge" harms the avenger. He may be legally executed. However, the primary inner aim of forcing the giant to acknowledge the dwarf's fury is fulfilled.[1]

The poor victim is not conscious of the inner forces that exact from him this ghastly toll; he battles, he schemes, he revels in pseudo-aggression, he is miserable, but he does not know what works within him to produce these catastrophic acts of crime. His aggressive actions are the wriggling of a worm on a fisherman's hook. And if this is so, it seems difficult to say any longer, "He is responsible." Rather, we shall put him behind bars for the protection of society, but we shall no longer flatter our feeling of moral superiority by calling him personally responsible for what he did.

Let us suppose it were established that a man commits murder only if, sometime during the previous week, he has eaten a certain combination of foods—say, tuna fish salad at a meal also including peas, mushroom soup, and blueberry pie. What if we were to track down the factors common to all murders committed in this country during the last twenty years and found this factor present in all of them, and only in them? The example is of course empirically absurd; but may it not be that there is *some* combination of factors that regularly leads to homicide, factors such as are described in general terms in the above quotation? (Indeed the situation in the quotation is less fortunate than in our hypothetical example, for it is easy to avoid certain foods once we have been warned about them, but the situation of the infant is thrust on him; something has already happened to him once and for all, before he knows it has happened.) When such specific factors are discovered, won't they make it clear that it is foolish and pointless, as well as immoral, to hold human beings responsible for crimes? Or, if one prefers biological to psychological factors, suppose a neurologist is called in to testify at a murder trial and produces X-ray pictures of the brain of the criminal; anyone can see, he argues, that the *cella turcica* was already calcified at the age of nineteen; it should be a flexible bone, growing, enabling the gland to grow.[2] All the defendant's disorders might have resulted from this early calcification. Now, this par-

---

[1] Edmund Bergler, *The Basic Neurosis* (New York: Grune and Stratton, 1949), p. 305.
[2] Meyer Levin, *Compulsion* (New York: Simon and Schuster, 1956), p. 403.

ticular explanation may be empirically false; but who can say that no such factors, far more complex, to be sure, exist?

When we know such things as these, we no longer feel so much tempted to say that the criminal is responsible for his crime; and we tend also (do we not?) to excuse him—not legally (we still confine him to prison) but morally; we no longer call him a monster or hold him personally responsible for what he did. Moreover, we do this in general, not merely in the case of crime: "You must excuse Grandmother for being irritable; she's really quite ill and is suffering some pain all the time." Or: "The dog always bites children after she's had a litter of pups; you can't blame her for it: she's not feeling well, and besides she naturally wants to defend them." Or: "She's nervous and jumpy, but do excuse her: she has a severe glandular disturbance."

Let us note that the more *thoroughly* and *in detail* we know the causal factors leading a person to behave as he does, the more we tend to exempt him from responsibility. When we know nothing of the man except what we see him do, we say he is an ungrateful cad who expects much of other people and does nothing in return, and we are usually indignant. When we learn that his parents were the same way and, having no guilt feelings about this mode of behavior themselves, brought him up to be greedy and avaricious, we see that we could hardly expect him to have developed moral feelings in this direction. When we learn, in addition, that he is not aware of being ungrateful or selfish, but unconsciously represses the memory of events unfavorable to himself, we feel that the situation is unfortunate but "not really his fault." When we know that this behavior of his, which makes others angry, occurs more constantly when he feels tense or insecure, and that he now feels tense and insecure, and that relief from pressure will diminish it, then we tend to "feel sorry for the poor guy" and say he's more to be pitied than censured. We no longer want to say that he is personally responsible; we might rather blame nature or his parents for having given him an unfortunate constitution or temperament.

In recent years a new form of punishment has been imposed on middle-aged and elderly parents. Their children, now in their twenties, thirties or even forties, present them with a modern grievance: "My analysis proves that *you* are responsible for my neurosis." Overawed by these authoritative statements, the poor tired parents fall easy victims to the newest variations on the scapegoat theory.

In my opinion, this senseless cruelty—which disinters educational sins which had been buried for decades, and uses them as the basis for accusations which the victims cannot answer—is unjustified. Yes "the truth loves to be centrally located" (Melville), and few parents—since they are human—have been perfect. But granting their mistakes, they acted as *their* neurotic difficulties forced them to act. To turn the tables and declare the children not guilty because of the *impersonal* nature of their own neuroses, while at the same time the parents are *personally* blamed, is worse than illogical; it is profoundly unjust.[3]

And so, it would now appear, neither of the parties is responsible: "they acted as their neurotic difficulties forced them to act." The patients are not responsible for their neurotic manifestations, but then neither are the parents responsible for theirs; and so, of course, for their parents in turn, and theirs before them. It is the twentieth-century version of the family curse, the curse on the House of Atreus.

"But," a critic complains, "it's immoral to exonerate people indiscriminately in this way. I might have thought it fit to excuse somebody because he was born on the other side of the tracks, if I didn't know so many bank presidents who were also born on the other side of the tracks." Now, I submit that the most immoral thing in this situation is the critic's caricature of the conditions of the excuse. Nobody is excused merely because he was born on the other side of the tracks. But if he was born on the other side of the tracks *and* was a highly narcissistic infant to begin with *and* was repudiated or neglected by his parents *and* . . . (here we list a finite number of conditions), and if this complex of factors is *regularly* followed by certain behavior traits in adulthood, and moreover *unavoidably* so—that is, they occur no matter what he or anyone else tries to do—then we excuse him morally and say he is not responsible for his deed. If he is not responsible for A, a series of events occurring in his babyhood, then neither is he responsible for B, a series of things he does in adulthood, provided that B inevitably—that is, unavoidably—follows upon the occurrence of A. And according to psychiatrists and psychoanalysts, this often happens.

But one may still object that so far we have talked only about neurotic behavior. Isn't nonneurotic or normal or not unconsciously motivated (or whatever you want to call it) behavior still within the area of responsibility? There are reasons for answering "No" even here, for the normal person no more than the neurotic one has caused his own character, which makes him what he is. Granted that neurotics are not responsible for their behavior (that part of it which we call neurotic) because it stems from undigested infantile conflicts that they had no part in bringing about, and that are external to them just as surely as if their behavior had been forced on them by a malevolent deity (which is indeed one theory on the subject); but the so-called normal person is equally the product of causes in which his volition took no part.

---

[3] Edmund Bergler, *The Superego* (New York: Grune and Stratton, 1952), p. 320.

And if, unlike the neurotic's, his behavior is changeable by rational considerations, and if he has the will power to overcome the effects of an unfortunate early environment, this again is no credit to him; he is just lucky. If energy is available to him in a form in which it can be mobilized for constructive purposes, this is no credit to him, for this too is part of his psychic legacy. Those of us who can discipline ourselves and develop habits of concentration of purpose tend to blame those who cannot, and call them lazy and weak-willed; but what we fail to see is that they literally *cannot* do what we expect; if their psyches were structured like ours, they could, but as they are burdened with a tyrannical super-ego (to use psychoanalytic jargon for the moment), and a weak defenseless ego whose energies are constantly consumed in fighting endless charges of the superego, they simply cannot do it, and it is irrational to expect it of them. We cannot with justification blame them for their inability, any more than we can congratulate ourselves for our ability. This lesson is hard to learn, for we constantly and naïvely assume that other people are constructed as we ourselves are. . . .

19. AVOIDABILITY AND RESPONSIBILITY

Roderick Chisholm

Roderick M. Chisholm *(1916–   ) is Professor of Philosophy at Brown University. In addition to numerous articles, he has written* Perceiving: A Philosophical Study *(1957),* Realism and the Background of Phenomenology *(1960), and* The Theory of Knowledge *(1966).*

Edwards and Hospers[1] hold that there is an important sense in which we may be said *not* to be morally responsible for any of our acts or choices. I propose the following as an explicit formulation of their reasoning:

Reprinted by permission of New York University and Roderick Chisholm from Determinism and Freedom in the Age of Modern Science, *edited by Sidney Hook.* © *1958 by New York University.*

[1] *Ed. Note:* Paul Edwards and John Hospers contributed essays to the volume in which this essay appeared.

1. If a choice is one we could not have avoided making, then it is one for which we are not morally responsible.
2. If we make a choice under conditions such that, given those conditions, it is (causally but not logically) impossible for the choice not to be made, then the choice is one we could not have avoided making.
3. Every event occurs under conditions such that, given those conditions, it is (causally but not logically) impossible for that event not to occur.
4. The making of a choice is the occurrence of an event.
5. We are not morally responsible for any of our choices.

If we wish to reject the conclusion (5)—and for most of us (5) is difficult to accept—we must reject at least one of the premises.

Premise (1), I think, may be interpreted as a logical truth. If a man is responsible for what he did, then we may say, "He *could* have done otherwise." And if we may say, "He couldn't help it," then he is not responsible for what he did.

Many philosophers would deny (2), substituting a weaker account of *avoidability*. A choice is avoidable, they might say, provided only it is such that, *if* the agent had reflected further, or had reflected on certain things on which in fact he did not reflect, he would *not* have made the choice. To say of a choice that it "could *not* have been avoided," in accordance with this account, would be to say that, even if the agent *had* reflected further, on anything you like, he would all the same have made the choice. But such conditional accounts of *avoidability* ("An act or choice is avoidable provided only it is such that *if* the agent were to do so-and-so, the act or choice would not occur") usually have this serious defect: the antecedent clause ("if the agent were to do so-and-so") refers to some act or choice, or to the failure to perform some act or to make some choice; hence we may ask, concerning the occurrence or nonoccurrence of this act or choice, whether or not *it* is avoidable. Thus one who accepted (5) could say that, if the agent's failure to reflect further was itself unavoidable, his choice was also unavoidable. And no such conditional account of *avoidability* seems adequate to the use of "avoidable" and "unavoidable" in questions and statements such as these.

If we accept a conditional account of avoidability, we may be tempted to say, of course, that it would be a *misuse* of "avoidable" to ask whether the nonoccurrence of the antecedent event ("the agent does so-and-so") is avoidable. But the philosopher who accepts (5) may well insist that, since the antecedent clause refers to an act or a choice, the use of "avoidable" in question is *not* a misuse.

What, then, if we were to deny (3)? Suppose that some of our choices do not satisfy (3)—that when they are made they are *not* made under any conditions such that it is (causally) impossible (though logically possible) for them not to be made. If there are choices of this sort, then they are merely fortuitous or capricious. And if they are merely fortuitous or capricious, if they "just happen," then, I think, we may say with Blanshard that we are *not* morally responsible for them. Hence denying (3) is not the way to avoid (5).

We seem confronted, then, with a dilemma: either our choices have sufficient causal conditions or they do not; if they do have sufficient causal conditions they are not avoidable; if they do not, they are fortuitous or capricious; and therefore, since our choices are either unavoidable or fortuitous, we are not morally responsible for them.

There are philosophers who believe that by denying the rather strange-sounding premise (4) we can escape the dilemma. Insisting on something like "the primacy of practical reason," they would say that since we are certain that (5) is false we must construct a metaphysical theory about the self, a theory denying (4) and enabling us to reconcile (3) and the denial of (5). I say "metaphysical" because it seems to be necessary for the theory to replace (4) by sentences using such terms as "active power," "the autonomy of the will," "prime mover," or "higher levels of causality"—terms designating something to which we apparently need not refer when expressing the conclusions of physics and the natural sciences. But I believe we cannot know whether such theories enable us to escape our dilemma. For it seems impossible to conceive what the relation is that, according to these theories, holds between the "will," "self," "mover," or "active power," on the one hand, and the bodily events this power is supposed to control, on the other— the relation between the "activities" of the self and the events described by physics.

I am dissatisfied, then, with what philosophers have proposed as alternatives to premises (1) through (4) above, but since I feel certain that (5) is false I also feel certain that at least one of the premises is false.

20. ALL CHOICES ARE PREDETERMINED

P. H. D. d'Holbach

Paul H. D. d'Holbach (1723–1789) was one of the best known figures of the French Enlightenment who advocated atheism and materialism. His frequent and penetrating attacks upon religion earned him the scorn of most of his contemporaries. His major work, The System of Nature *(1770), from which the following selection is taken, was published anonymously.*

. . . The will, as we have elsewhere said, is a modification of the brain, by which it is disposed to action, or prepared to give play to the organs. This will is necessarily determined by the qualities, good or bad, agreeable or painful, of the object or the motive that acts upon his senses, or of which the idea remains with him, and is resuscitated by his memory. In consequence, he acts necessarily, his action is the result of the impulse he receives either from the motive, from the object, or from the idea which has modified his brain, or disposed his will. When he does not act according to this impulse, it is because there comes some new cause, some new motive, some new idea, which modifies his brain in a different manner, gives him a new impulse, determines his will in another way, by which the action of the former impulse is suspended: thus, the sight of an agreeable object, or its idea, determines his will to set him in action to procure it; but if a new object or a new idea more powerfully attracts him, it gives a new direction to his will, annihilates the effect of the former, and prevents the action by which it was to be procured. This is the mode in which reflection, experience, reason, necessarily arrests or suspends the action of man's will: without this he would of necessity have followed the anterior impulse which carried him towards a then desirable object. In all this he always acts according to necessary laws, from which he has no means of emancipating himself.

If when tormented with violent thirst, he figures to himself in idea, or really perceives a fountain, whose limpid streams might cool his feverish want, is he sufficient master of himself to desire or not to desire the object competent to satisfy so lively a want? It will no doubt be conceded, that it is impossible he should not be desirous to satisfy it; but it will be said—if at this moment it is announced to him that the water he so ardently desires is poisoned, he will, notwithstanding his vehement thirst, abstain from drinking it: and it has, therefore, been falsely concluded that he is a free agent. The fact, however, is, that the

138

motive in either case is exactly the same: his own conservation. The same necessity that determined him to drink before he knew the water was deleterious, upon this new discovery equally determines him not to drink; the desire of conserving himself either annihilates or suspends the former impulse; the second motive becomes stronger than the preceding, that is, the fear of death, or the desire of preserving himself, necessarily prevails over the painful sensation caused by his eagerness to drink: but, it will be said, if the thirst is very parching, an inconsiderate man without regarding the danger will risk swallowing the water. Nothing is gained by this remark, in this case the anterior impulse only regains the ascendency; he is persuaded that life may possibly be longer preserved, or that he shall derive a greater good by drinking the poisoned water than by enduring the torment, which, to his mind, threatens instant dissolution: thus the first becomes the strongest and necessarily urges him on to action. Nevertheless, in either case, whether he partakes of the water, or whether he does not, the two actions will be equally necessary; they will be the effect of that motive which finds itself most puissant; which consequently acts in the most coercive manner upon his will.

This example will serve to explain the whole phenomena of the human will. This will, or rather the brain, finds itself in the same situation as a bowl, which, although it has received an impulse that drives it forward in a straight line, is deranged in its course whenever a force superior to the first obliges it to change its direction. The man who drinks the poisoned water appears a madman; but the actions of fools are as necessary as those of the most prudent individuals. The motives that determine the voluptuary and the debauchee to risk their health, are as powerful, and their actions are as necessary, as those which decide the wise man to manage his. But, it will be insisted, the debauchee may be prevailed on to change his conduct: this does not imply that he is a free agent; but that motives may be found sufficiently powerful to annihilate the effect of those that previously acted upon him; then these new motives determine his will to the new mode of conduct he may adopt as necessarily as the former did to the old mode.

Man is said to *deliberate*, when the action of the will is suspended; this happens when two opposite motives act alternately upon him. *To deliberate*, is to hate and to love in succession; it is to be alternately attracted and repelled; it is to be moved, sometimes by one motive, sometimes by another. Man only deliberates when he does not distinctly understand the quality of the objects from which he receives impulse, or when experience has not sufficiently apprised him of the effects, more or less remote, which his actions will produce. He would take the air, but the weather is uncertain; he deliberates in consequence;

he weighs the various motives that urge his will to go out or to stay at home; he is at length determined by that motive which is most probable; this removes his indecision, which necessarily settles his will, either to remain within or to go abroad: his motive is always either the immediate or ultimate advantage he finds, or thinks he finds, in the action to which he is persuaded.

Man's will frequently fluctuates between two objects, of which either the presence or the ideas move him alternately: he waits until he has contemplated the objects, or the ideas they have left in his brain which solicit him to different actions; he then compares these objects or ideas; but even in the time of deliberation, during the comparison, pending these alternatives of love and hatred which succeed each other, sometimes with the utmost rapidity, he is not a free agent for a single instant; the good or the evil which he believes he finds successively in the objects are the necessary motives of these momentary wills; of the rapid motion of desire, or fear, that he experiences as long as his uncertainty continues. From this it will be obvious that deliberation is necessary; that uncertainty is necessary; that whatever part he takes, in consequence of this deliberation, it will always necessarily be that which he has judged, whether well or ill, is most probable to turn to his advantage.

When the soul is assailed by two motives that act alternately upon it, or modify it successively, it deliberates; the brain is in a sort of equilibrium, accompanied with perpetual oscillations, sometimes towards one object, sometimes towards the other, until the most forcible carries the point, and thereby extricates it from this state of suspense, in which consists the indecision of his will. But when the brain is simultaneously assailed by causes equally strong that move it in opposite directions, agreeable to the general law of all bodies when they are struck equally by contrary powers, it stops, it is in *nisu;* it is neither capable to will nor to act; it waits until one of the two causes has obtained sufficient force to overpower the other; to determine its will; to attract it in such a manner that it may prevail over the efforts of the other cause.

This mechanism, so simple, so natural, suffices to demonstrate why uncertainty is painful, and why suspense is always a violent state for man. The brain, an organ so delicate and so mobile, experiences such rapid modifications that it is fatigued; or when it is urged in contrary directions, by causes equally powerful, it suffers a kind of compression, that prevents the activity which is suitable to the preservation of the whole, and which is necessary to procure what is advantageous to its existence. This mechanism will also explain the irregularity, the indecision, the inconstancy of man, and account for that conduct which frequently appears an inexplicable mystery, and which is, indeed, the effect of the received systems. In consulting experience, it will be found that the soul is submitted to precisely the same physical laws as the material body. If the will of each individual, during a given time, was only moved by a single cause or passion, nothing would be more easy than to foresee his actions; but his heart is frequently assailed by contrary powers, by adverse motives, which either act on him simultaneously or in succession; then his brain, attracted in opposite directions, is either fatigued, or else tormented by a state of compression, which deprives it of activity. Sometimes it is in a state of incommodious inaction; sometimes it is the sport of the alternate shocks it undergoes. Such, no doubt, is the state in which man finds himself when a lively passion solicits him to the commission of crime, whilst fear points out to him the danger by which it is attended: such, also, is the condition of him whom remorse, by the continued labour of his distracted soul, prevents from enjoying the objects he has criminally obtained. . . .

. . . Choice by no means proves the free agency of man: he only deliberates when he does not yet know which to choose of the many objects that move him, he is then in an embarrassment, which does not terminate until his will is decided by the greater advantage he believes he shall find in the object he chooses, or the action he undertakes. From whence it may be seen, that choice is necessary, because he would not determine for an object, or for an action, if he did not believe that he should find in it some direct advantage. That man should have free agency it were needful that he should be able to will or choose without motive, or that he could prevent motives coercing his will. Action always being the effect of his will once determined, and as his will cannot be determined but by a motive which is not in his own power, it follows that he is never the master of the determination of his own peculiar will; that consequently he never acts as a free agent. It has been believed that man was a free agent because he had a will with the power of choosing; but attention has not been paid to the fact that even his will is moved by causes independent of himself; is owing to that which is inherent in his own organization, or which belongs to the nature of the beings acting on him.[1] Is he the master of willing not to withdraw his hand from the fire when he fears it will be burnt? Or has he the power to take away from fire the property which makes him

---

[1] Man passes a great portion of his life without even willing. His will depends on the motive by which he is determined. If he were to render an exact account of every thing he does in the course of each day—from rising in the morning to lying down at night—he would find that not one of his actions have been in the least voluntary; that they have been mechanical, habitual, determined by causes he was not able to foresee; to which he was either obliged to yield, or with which he was allured to acquiesce; he would discover, that all the motives of his labours, of his amusements, of his discourses, of his thoughts, have been necessary; that they have evidently either seduced him or drawn him along.

fear it? Is he the master of not choosing a dish of meat, which he knows to be agreeable or analogous to his palate; of not preferring it to that which he knows to be disagreeable or dangerous? Is it always according to his sensations, to his own peculiar experience, or to his suppositions, that he judges of things, either well or ill; but whatever may be his judgment, it depends necessarily on his mode of feeling, whether habitual or accidental, and the qualities he finds in the causes that move him, which exist in despite of himself. . . .

. . . Man's mode of thinking is necessarily determined by his manner of being; it must therefore depend on his natural organization, and the modification his system receives independently of his will. From this, we are obliged to conclude, that his thoughts, his reflections, his manner of viewing things, of feeling, of judging, of combining ideas, is neither voluntary nor free. In a word, that his soul is neither mistress of the motion excited in it, nor of representing to itself, when wanted, those images or ideas that are capable of counterbalancing the impulse it receives. This is the reason, why man, when in a passion, ceases to reason; at that moment reason is as impossible to be heard, as it is during an ecstacy, or in a fit of drunkenness. The wicked are never more than men who are either drunk or mad; if they reason, it is not until tranquillity is re-established in their machine; then, and not till then, the tardy ideas that present themselves to their mind enable them to see the consequence of their actions, and give birth to ideas that bring on them that trouble, which is designated *shame, regret, remorse.*

The errours of philosophers on the free agency of man, have arisen from their regarding his will as the *primum mobile,* the original motive of his actions; for want of recurring back, they have not perceived the multiplied, the complicated causes which, independently of him, give motion to the will itself: or which dispose and modify his brain, whilst he himself is purely passive in the motion he receives. Is he the master of desiring or not desiring an object that appears desirable to him? Without doubt it will be answered, no: but he is the master of resisting his desire, if he reflects on the consequences. But, I ask, is he capable of reflecting on these consequences, when his soul is hurried along by a very lively passion, which entirely depends upon his natural organization, and the causes by which he is modified? Is it in his power to add to these consequences all the weight necessary to counterbalance his desire? Is he the master of preventing the qualities which render an object desirable from residing in it? I shall be told: he ought to have learned to resist his passions; to contract a habit of putting a curb on his desires. I agree to it without any difficulty. But in reply, I again ask, is his nature susceptible of this modification? Does his boiling blood, his unruly imagination, the igneous fluid that circulates in his veins, permit him to make, enable him to apply true experience in the moment when it is wanted? And even when his temperament has capacitated him, has his education, the examples set before him, the ideas with which he has been inspired in early life, been suitable to make him contract this habit of repressing his desires? Have not all these things rather contributed to induce him to seek with avidity, to make him actually desire those objects which you say he ought to resist. . . .

. . . In despite of these proofs of the want of free agency in man, so clear to unprejudiced minds, it will, perhaps, be insisted upon with no small feeling of triumph, that if it be proposed to any one, to move or not to move his hand, an action in the number of those called *indifferent,* he evidently appears to be the master of choosing; from which it is concluded that evidence has been offered of his free agency. The reply is, this example is perfectly simple; man in performing some action which he is resolved on doing, does not by any means prove his free agency: the very desire of displaying this quality, excited by the dispute, becomes a necessary motive, which decides his will either for the one or the other of these actions: what deludes him in this instance, or that which persuades him he is a free agent at this moment, is, that he does not discern the true motive which sets him in action, namely, the desire of convincing his opponent: if in the heat of the dispute he insists and asks, "Am I not the master of throwing myself out of the window?" I shall answer him, no; that whilst he preserves his reason there is no probability that the desire of proving his free agency, will become a motive sufficiently powerful to make him sacrifice his life to the attempt: if, notwithstanding this, to prove he is a free agent, he should actually precipitate himself from the window, it would not be a sufficient warranty to conclude he acted freely, but rather that it was the violence of his temperament which spurred him on to this folly. Madness is a state, that depends upon the heat of the blood, not upon the will. A fanatic or a hero, braves death as necessarily as a more phlegmatic man or a coward flies from it.[2]

---

[2] There is, in point of fact, no difference between the man that is cast out of the window by another and the man who throws himself out of it, except that the impulse in the first instance comes immediately from without, whilst that which determines the fall in the second case, springs from his own peculiar machine, having its more remote cause also exterior. When Mutius Scaevola held his hand in the fire, he was as much acting under the influence of necessity (caused by interior motives) that urged him to this strange action, as if his arm had been held by strong men: pride, despair, the desire of braving his enemy, a wish to astonish him, an anxiety to intimidate him, &c., were the invisible chains that held his hand bound to the fire. The love of glory, enthusiasm for their country, in like manner caused Codrus and Decius to devote themselves for their fellow-citizens. The Indian Colanus and the Philosopher Peregrinus were equally obliged to burn themselves, by desire of exciting the astonishment of the Grecian assembly.

It is said that free agency is the absence of those obstacles competent to oppose themselves to the actions of man, or to the exercise of his faculties: it is pretended that he is a free agent whenever, making use of these faculties, he produces the effect he has proposed to himself. In reply to this reasoning, it is sufficient to consider that it in nowise depends upon himself to place or remove the obstacles that either determine or resist him; the motive that causes his action is no more in his own power than the obstacle that impedes him, whether this obstacle or motive be within his own machine or exterior of his person: he is not master of the thought presented to his mind, which determines his will; this thought is excited by some cause independent of himself.

To be undeceived on the system of his free agency, man has simply to recur to the motive by which his will is determined; he will always find this motive is out of his own control. It is said: that in consequence of an idea to which the mind gives birth, man acts freely if he encounters no obstacle. But the question is, what gives birth to this idea in his brain? Was he the master either to prevent it from presenting itself, or from renewing itself in his brain? Does not this idea depend either upon objects that strike him exteriorly and in despite of himself, or upon causes, that without his knowledge, act within himself and modify his brain? Can he prevent his eyes, cast without design upon any object whatever, from giving him an idea of this object, and from moving his brain? He is not more master of the obstacles; they are the necessary effects of either interior or exterior causes, which always act according to their given properties. A man insults a coward, this necessarily irritates him against his insulter, but his will cannot vanquish the obstacle that cowardice places to the object of his desire, because his natural conformation, which does not depend upon himself, prevents his having courage. In this case, the coward is insulted in despite of himself; and against his will is obliged patiently to brook the insult he has received.

The partisans of the system of free agency appear ever to have confounded constraints with necessity. Man believes he acts as a free agent, every time he does not see any thing that places obstacles to his actions; he does not perceive that the motive which causes him to will, is always necessary and independent of himself. A prisoner loaded with chains is compelled to remain in prison; but he is not a free agent in the desire to emancipate himself; his chains prevent him from acting, but they do not prevent him from willing; he would save himself if they would loose his fetters; but he would not save himself as a free agent; fear or the idea of punishment would be sufficient motives for his action.

Man may, therefore, cease to be restrained, without, for that

144

reason, becoming a free agent: in whatever manner he acts, he will act necessarily, according to motives by which he shall be determined. He may be compared to a heavy body that finds itself arrested in its descent by any obstacle whatever: take away this obstacle, it will gravitate or continue to fall; but who shall say this dense body is free to fall or not? Is not its descent the necessary effect of its own specific gravity? The virtuous Socrates submitted to the laws of his country, although they were unjust; and though the doors of his jail were left open to him, he would not save himself; but in this he did not act as a free agent: the invisible chains of opinion, the secret love of decorum, the inward respect for the laws, even when they are iniquitous, the fear of tarnishing his glory, kept him in his prison; they were motives sufficiently powerful with this enthusiast for virtue, to induce him to wait death with tranquillity; it was not in his power to save himself, because he could find no potential motive to bring him to depart, even for an instant, from those principles to which his mind was accustomed.

Man, it is said, frequently acts against his inclination, from whence it is falsely concluded he is a free agent; but when he appears to act contrary to his inclination, he is always determined to it by some motive sufficiently efficacious to vanquish this inclination. A sick man, with a view to his cure, arrives at conquering his repugnance to the most disgusting remedies: the fear of pain, or the dread of death, then becomes necessary motives; consequently this sick man cannot be said to act freely.

When it is said, that man is not a free agent, it is not pretended to compare him to a body moved by a simple impulsive cause: he contains within himself causes inherent to his existence; he is moved by an interior organ, which has its own peculiar laws, and is itself necessarily determined in consequence of ideas formed from perceptions resulting from sensations which it receives from exterior objects. As the mechanism of these sensations, of these perceptions, and the manner they engrave ideas on the brain of man, are not known to him; because he is unable to unravel all these motions; because he cannot perceive the chain of operations in his soul, or the motive principle that acts within him, he supposes himself a free agent; which, literally translated, signifies, that he moves himself by himself; that he determines himself without cause: when he rather ought to say, that he is ignorant how or for why he acts in the manner he does. It is true the soul enjoys an activity peculiar to itself; but it is equally certain that this activity would never be displayed, if some motive or some cause did not put it in a condition to exercise itself: at least it will not be pretended that the soul is able either to love or to hate without being moved, without knowing the objects, without having some idea of their qualities. Gunpowder has

145

unquestionably a particular activity, but this activity will never display itself, unless fire be applied to it; this, however, immediately sets it in motion.

It is the great complication of motion in man, it is the variety of his action, it is the multiplicity of causes that move him, whether simultaneously or in continual succession, that persuades him he is a free agent: if all his motions were simple, if the causes that move him did not confound themselves with each other, if they were distinct, if his machine were less complicated, he would perceive that all his actions were necessary, because he would be enabled to recur instantly to the cause that made him act. A man who should be always obliged to go towards the west, would always go on that side; but he would feel that, in so going, he was not a free agent: if he had another sense, as his actions or his motion, augmented by a sixth, would be still more varied and much more complicated, he would believe himself still more a free agent than he does with his five senses.

It is, then, for want of recurring to the causes that move him; for want of being able to analyze, from not being competent to decompose the complicated motion of his machine, that man believes himself a free agent; it is only upon his own ignorance that he founds the profound yet deceitful notion he has of his free agency; that he builds those opinions which he brings forward as a striking proof of his pretended freedom of action. If, for a short time, each man was willing to examine his own peculiar actions, search out their true motives to discover their concatenation, he would remain convinced that the sentiment he has of his natural free agency, is a chimera that must speedily be destroyed by experience.

Nevertheless it must be acknowledged that the multiplicity and diversity of the causes which continually act upon man, frequently without even his knowledge, render it impossible, or at least extremely difficult for him to recur to the true principles of his own peculiar actions, much less the actions of others: they frequently depend upon causes so fugitive, so remote from their effects, and which, superficially examined, appear to have so little analogy, so slender a relation with them, that it requires singular sagacity to bring them into light. This is what renders the study of the moral man a task of such difficulty; this is the reason why his heart is an abyss, of which it is frequently impossible for him to fathom the depth. He is then obliged to content himself with a knowledge of the general and necessary laws by which the human heart is regulated: for the individuals of his own species these laws are pretty nearly the same; they vary only in consequence of the organization that is peculiar to each, and of the modification it undergoes: this, however, cannot be rigorously the same in any two. It suffices to know, that by his essence, man tends to conserve himself, and to render his existence happy: this granted, whatever may be his actions, if he recur back to this first principle, to this general, this necessary tendency of his will, he never can be deceived with regard to his motives.

21. SOME CHOICES ARE NOT PREDETERMINED
C. A. Campbell

C. A. Campbell *(1897–   ) is Professor Emeritus at the University of Glasgow and a Fellow of the British Academy. His major works are* Scepticism and Construction *(1931) and* On Selfhood and Godhood *(1956).*

. . . 3. Let me, then, briefly sum up the answer at which we have arrived to our question about the kind of freedom required to justify moral responsibility. It is that a man can be said to exercise free will in a morally significant sense only in so far as his chosen act is one of which he is the sole cause or author, and only if—in the straightforward, categorical sense of the phrase—he 'could have chosen otherwise.'

I confess that this answer is in some ways a disconcerting one, disconcerting, because most of us, however objective we are in the actual conduct of our thinking, would *like* to be able to believe that moral responsibility is real: whereas the freedom required for moral responsibility, on the analysis we have given, is certainly far more difficult to establish than the freedom required on the anayses we found ourselves obliged to reject. If, e.g. moral freedom entails only that I could have acted otherwise *if* I had chosen otherwise, there is no real 'problem' about it at all. I am 'free' in the normal case where there is no external obstacle to prevent my translating the alternative choice into action, and not free in other cases. Still less is there a problem if all that moral freedom entails is that I could have acted otherwise *if* I had been a differently constituted person, or been in different circumstances. Clearly I am *always* free in *this* sense of freedom. But, as I have argued, these so-called 'freedoms' fail to give us the pre-conditions of moral responsibility, and hence leave the freedom of the traditional

From On Selfhood and Godhood, *Lecture IX, pp. 164–165; 167–178. Reprinted by permission of the publisher, George Allen & Unwin Ltd.*

free-will problem, the freedom that people are really concerned about, precisely where it was. . . .

. . . 5. That brings me to the second, and more constructive, part of this lecture. From now on I shall be considering whether it is reasonable to believe that man does in fact possess a free will of the kind specified in the first part of the lecture. If so, just how and where within the complex fabric of the volitional life are we to locate it?— for although free will must presumably belong (if anywhere) to the volitional side of human experience, it is pretty clear from the way in which we have been forced to define it that it does not pertain simply to volition as such; not even to all volitions that are commonly dignified with the name of 'choices.' It has been, I think, one of the more serious impediments to profitable discussion of the Free Will problem that Libertarians and Determinists alike have so often failed to appreciate the comparatively narrow area within which the free will that is necessary to 'save' morality is required to operate. It goes without saying that this failure has been gravely prejudicial to the case for Libertarianism. I attach a good deal of importance, therefore, to the problem of locating free will correctly within the volitional orbit. Its solution forestalls and annuls, I believe, some of the more tiresome clichés of Determinist criticism.

We saw earlier that Common Sense's practice of 'making allowances' in its moral judgments for the influence of heredity and environment indicates Common Sense's conviction, both that a just moral judgment must discount determinants of choice over which the agent has no control, and also (since it still accepts moral judgments as legitimate) that *something* of moral relevance survives which can be regarded as genuinely self-originated. We are now to try to discover what this 'something' is. And I think we may still usefully take Common Sense as our guide. Suppose one asks the ordinary intelligent citizen *why* he deems it proper to make allowances for X, whose heredity and/or environment are unfortunate. He will tend to reply, I think, in some such terms as these: that X has more and stronger temptations to deviate from what is right than Y or Z, who are normally circumstanced, so that he must put forth *a stronger moral effort* if he is to achieve the same level of external conduct. The intended implication seems to be that X is just as morally praiseworthy as Y or Z *if* he exerts an equivalent moral effort, even though he may not thereby achieve an equal success in conforming his will to the 'concrete' demands of duty. And this implies, again, Common Sense's belief that *in moral effort* we have something for which a man is responsible *without qualification*, something that is *not* affected by heredity and environment but depends *solely* upon the self itself.

Now in my opinion Common Sense has here, in principle, hit upon the one and only defensible answer. Here, and here alone, so far as I can see, in the act of deciding whether to put forth or withhold the moral effort required to resist temptation and rise to duty, is to be found an act which is free in the sense required for moral responsibility; an act of which the self is sole author, and of which it is true to say that 'it could be' (or, after the event, 'could have been') 'otherwise.' Such is the thesis which we shall now try to establish.

6. The species of argument appropriate to the establishment of a thesis of this sort should fall, I think, into two phases. First, there should be a consideration of the evidence of the moral agent's own inner experience. What *is* the act of moral decision, and what does it imply, from the standpoint of the actual participant? Since there is no way of knowing the act of moral decision—or for that matter any other form of activity—except by actual participation in it, the evidence of the subject, or agent, is on an issue of this kind of palmary importance. It can hardly, however, be taken as in itself conclusive. For even if that evidence should be overwhelmingly to the effect that moral decision does have the characteristics required by moral freedom, the question is bound to be raised—and in view of considerations from other quarters pointing in a contrary direction is *rightly* raised—Can we *trust* the evidence of inner experience? That brings us to what will be the second phase of the argument. We shall have to go on to show, if we are to make good our case, that the extraneous considerations so often supposed to be fatal to the belief in moral freedom are in fact innocuous to it.

In the light of what was said in the last lecture about the self's experience of moral decision as a *creative* activity, we may perhaps be absolved from developing the first phase of the argument at any great length. The appeal is throughout to one's own experience in the actual taking of the moral decision in the situation of moral temptation. 'Is it possible,' we must ask, 'for anyone so circumstanced to *dis*-believe that we could be deciding otherwise?' The answer is surely not in doubt. When we decide to exert moral effort to resist a temptation, we feel quite certain that we *could* withhold the effort; just as, if we decide to withhold the effort and yield to our desires, we feel quite certain that we *could* exert it—otherwise we should not blame ourselves afterwards for having succumbed. It may be indeed, that this conviction is mere self-delusion. But that is not at the moment our concern. It is enough at present to establish that the act of deciding to exert or to withhold moral effort, as we know it from the inside in actual moral living, belongs to the category of acts which 'could have been otherwise.'

149

Mutatis mutandis, the same reply is forthcoming if we ask, 'Is it possible for the moral agent in the taking of his decision to *dis*believe that he is the *sole* author of that decision?' Clearly he cannot disbelieve that it is *he* who takes the decision. That, however, is not in itself sufficient to enable him, on reflection, to regard himself as *solely* responsible for the act. For his 'character' as so far formed might conceivably be a factor in determining it, and no one can suppose that the constitution of his 'character' is uninfluenced by circumstances of heredity and environment with which *he* has nothing to do. But as we pointed out in the last lecture, the very essence of the moral decision as it is experienced is that it is a decision whether or not to *combat* our strongest desire, and our strongest desire *is* the expression in the situation of our character as so far formed. Now clearly our character cannot be a factor in determining the decision whether or not to *oppose* our character. I think we are entitled to say, therefore, that the act of moral decision is one in which the self is for itself not merely 'author' but 'sole author.'

7. We may pass on, then, to the second phase of our constructive argument; and this will demand more elaborate treatment. Even if a moral agent *qua* making a moral decision in the situation of 'temptation' cannot help believing that he has free will in the sense at issue—a moral freedom between real alternatives, between genuinely open possibilities—are there, nevertheless, objections to a freedom of this kind so cogent that we are bound to distrust the evidence of 'inner experience'?

I begin by drawing attention to a simple point whose significance tends, I think, to be under-estimated. If the phenomenological analysis we have offered is substantially correct, no one while functioning as a moral agent can help believing that he enjoys free will. Theoretically he may be completely convinced by Determinist arguments, but when actually confronted with a personal situation of conflict between duty and desire he is quite certain that it lies with him here and now whether or not he will rise to duty. It follows that if Determinists could produce convincing theoretical aruguments against a free will of this kind, the awkward predicament would ensue that man has to deny as a theoretical being what he has to assert as a practical being. Now I think the Determinist ought to be a good deal more worried about this than he usually is. He seems to imagine that a strong case on general theoretical grounds is enough to prove that the 'practical' belief in free will, even if inescapable for us as practical beings, is mere illusion. But in fact it proves nothing of the sort. There is no reason whatever why a belief that we find ourselves obliged to hold *qua* theoretical beings; or, for that matter, *vice versa*. All that the theoretical arguments of Determinism can prove, unless they are reinforced by a refutation of the phenomenological analysis that supports Libertarianism, is that there is a radical conflict between the theoretical and the practical sides of man's nature, an antimony at the very heart of the self. And this is a state of affairs with which no one can easily rest satisfied. I think therefore that the Determinist ought to concern himself a great deal more than he does with phenomenological analysis, in order to show, if he can, that the assurance of free will is not really an inexpugnable element in man's practical consciousness. There is just as much obligation upon him, convinced though he may be of the soundness of his theoretical arguments, to expose the errors of the Libertarian's phenomenological analysis, as there is upon us, convinced though we may be of the soundness of the Libertarian's phenomenological analysis, to expose the errors of the Determinist's theoretical arguments.

8. However, we must at once begin the discharge of our own obligation. The rest of this lecture will be devoted to trying to show that the arguments which seem to carry most weight with Determinists are, to say the least of it, very far from compulsive.

Fortunately a good many of the arguments which at an earlier time in the history of philosophy would have been strongly urged against us make almost no appeal to the bulk of philosophers today, and we may here pass them by. That applies to any criticism of 'open possibilities' based on a metaphysical theory about the nature of the universe as a whole. Nobody today *has* a metaphysical theory about the nature of the universe as a whole! It applies also, with almost equal force, to criticisms based upon the universality of causal law as a supposed postulate of science. There have always been, in my opinion, sound philosophic reasons for doubting the validity, as distinct from the convenience, of the causal postulate in its universal form, but at the present time, when scientists themselves are deeply divided about the need for postulating causality even within their own special field, we shall do better to concentrate our attention upon criticisms which are more confidently advanced. I propose to ignore also, on different grounds, the type of criticism of free will that is sometimes advanced from the side of religion, based upon religious postulates of Divine Omnipotence and Omniscience. So far as I can see, a postulate of human freedom is every bit as necessary to meet certain religious demands (e.g. to make sense of the 'conviction of sin'), as postulates of Divine Omniscience and Omnipotence are to meet certain other religious demands. If so, then it can hardly be argued that religious experience as such tells more strongly against than for the position we are defending; and we may be satisfied, in the present context, to leave the matter there. It will be more profitable to discuss certain arguments which contemporary philosophers do think important, and which recur with a somewhat monotonous regularity in the literature of anti-Libertarianism.

These arguments can, I think, be reduced in principle to no more than two: first, the argument from 'predictability'; second, the argument from the alleged meaninglessness of an act supposed to be the self's act and yet not an expression of the self's character. Contemporary criticism of free will seems to me to consist almost exclusively of variations of these two themes. I shall deal with each in turn.

9. On the first we touched in passing at an earlier stage. Surely it is beyond question (the critical urges) that when we know a person intimately we can foretell with a high degree of accuracy how he will respond to at least a large number of practical situations. One feels safe in predicting that one's dog-loving friend will not use his boot to repel the little mongrel that comes yapping at his heels; or again that one's wife will not pass with incurious eyes (or indeed pass at all) the new hat-shop in the city. So to behave would not be (as we say) 'in character.' But, so the criticism runs, you with your doctrine of 'genuinely open possibilities,' of a free will by which the self can diverge from its own character, remove all rational basis from such prediction. You require us to make the absurd supposition that the success of countless predictions of the sort in the past has been mere matter of chance. If you *really* believed in your theory, you would not be surprised if tomorrow your friend with the notorious horror of strong drink should suddenly exhibit a passion for whisky and soda, or if your friend whose taste for reading has hitherto been satisfied with the sporting columns of the newspapers should be discovered on a fine Saturday afternoon poring over the works of Hegel. But of course you *would* be surprised. Social life would be sheer chaos if there were not well-grounded social expectations; and social life is not sheer chaos. Your theory is hopelessly wrecked upon obvious facts.

Now whether or not this criticism holds good against some versions of Libertarian theory I need not here discuss. It is sufficient if I can make it clear that against the version advanced in this lecture, according to which free will is localised in a relatively narrow field of operation, the criticism has no relevance whatsoever.

Let us remind ourselves briefly of the setting within which, on our view, free will functions. There is X, the course which we believe we ought to follow, and Y, the course towards which we feel our desire is strongest. The freedom which we ascribe to the agent is the freedom to put forth or refrain from putting forth the moral effort required to resist the pressure of desire and do what he thinks he ought to do.

But then there is surely an immense range of practical situations

—covering by far the greater part of life—in which there is no question of a conflict within the self between what he most desires to do and what he thinks he ought to do? Indeed such conflict is a comparatively rare phenomenon for the majority of men. Yet over that whole vast range there is nothing whatever in our version of Libertarianism to prevent our agreeing that character determines conduct. In the absence, real or supposed, of any 'moral' issue, what a man chooses will be simply that course which, after such reflection as seems called for, he deems most likely to bring him what he most strongly desires; and that is the same as to say the course to which his present character inclines him.

Over by far the greater area of human choices, then, our theory offers no more barrier to successful prediction on the basis of character than any other theory. For where there is no clash of strongest desire with duty, the free will we are defending has no business. There is just nothing for it to do.

But what about the situations—rare enough though they may be—in which there *is* this clash and in which free will does therefore operate? Does our theory entail that there at any rate, as the critic seems to suppose, 'anything may happen'?

Not by any manner of means. In the first place, and by the very nature of the case, the range of the agent's possible choices is bounded by what he thinks he ought to do on the one hand, and what he most strongly desires on the other. The freedom claimed for him is a freedom of decision to make or withhold the effort required to do what he thinks he ought to do. There is no question of a freedom to act in some 'wild' fashion, out of all relation to his characteristic beliefs and desires. This so-called 'freedom of caprice,' so often charged against the Libertarian, is, to put it bluntly, a sheer figment of the critics' imagination, with no *habitat* in serious Libertarian theory. Even in situations where free will does come into play it is perfectly possible, on a view like ours, given the appropriate knowledge of a man's character, to predict within certain limits how he will respond.

But 'probable' prediction in such situations can, I think, go further than this. It is obvious that where desire and duty are at odds, the felt 'gap' (as it were) between the two may vary enormously in breadth in different cases. The moderate drinker and the chronic tippler may each want another glass, and each deem it his duty to abstain, but the felt gap between desire and duty in the case of the former is trivial beside the great gulf which is felt to separate them in the case of the latter. Hence it will take a far harder moral effort for the tippler than for the moderate drinker to achieve the same external result of abstention. So much is matter of common agreement. And we are entitled, I think, to take it into account in prediction, on the simple principle that the harder the moral effort required to resist desire the less likely it is to occur. Thus in the example taken, most people would predict that the tippler will very probably succumb to his desires, whereas there is a reasonable likelihood that the moderate drinker will make the comparatively slight effort needed to resist them. So long as the prediction does not pretend to more than a measure of probability, there is nothing in our theory which would disallow it.

I claim, therefore, that the view of free will I have been putting forward is consistent with predictability of conduct on the basis of character over a very wide field indeed. And I make the further claim that that field will cover all the situations in life concerning which there is any empirical evidence that successful prediction is possible.

10. Let us pass on to consider the second main line of criticism. This is, I think, much the more illuminating of the two, if only because it compels the Libertarian to make explicit certain concepts which are indispensable to him, but which, being desperately hard to state clearly, are apt not to be stated at all. The critic's fundamental point might be stated somewhat as follows:

'Free will as you describe it is completely unintelligible. On your own showing no *reason* can be given, because there just *is* no reason, why a man decides to exert rather than to withhold moral effort, or *vice versa*. But such an act—or more properly, such an "occurrence"—it is nonsense to speak of as an act of a *self*. If there is nothing in the self's character to which it is, even in principle, in any way traceable, the self has nothing to do with it. Your so-called "freedom," therefore, so far from supporting the self's moral responsibility, destroys it as surely as the crudest Determinism could do.'

If we are to discuss this criticism usefully, it is important, I think, to begin by getting clear about two different senses of the word 'intelligible.'

If, in the first place, we mean by an 'intelligible' act one whose occurrence is in principle capable of being inferred, since it follows necessarily from something (though we may not know in fact from what), then it is certainly true that the Libertarian's free will is unintelligible. But that is only saying, is it not, that the Libertarian's 'free' act is not an act which follows necessarily from something! This can hardly rank as *a criticism* of Libertarianism. It is just a description of it. That there can be nothing unintelligible in *this* sense is precisely what the Determinist has got to *prove*.

Yet is is surprising how often the critic of Libertarianism involves himself in this circular mode of argument. Repeatedly it is urged against the Libertarian, with a great air of triumph, that on his view he can't say *why* I now decide to rise to duty, or now decide to follow my strongest desire in defiance of duty. Of course he can't. If he could he wouldn't be a Libertarian. To 'account for' a 'free' act is a contradiction in terms. A free will is *ex hypothesi* the sort of thing of which the request for an *explanation* is absurd. The assumption that an explanation must be in principle possible for the act of moral decision deserves to rank as a classic example of the ancient fallacy of 'begging the question.'

But the critic usually has in mind another sense of the word 'unintelligible.' He is apt to take it for granted that an act which is unintelligible in the *above* sense (as the morally free act of the Libertarian undoubtedly is) is unintelligible in the *further* sense that we can attach no meaning to it. And this is an altogether more serious matter. If it could really be shown that the Libertarian's 'free will' were unintelligible in this sense of being meaningless, that, for myself at any rate, would be the end of the affair. Libertarianism would have been conclusively refuted.

But it seems to me manifest that this can *not* be shown. The critic has allowed himself, I submit, to become the victim of a widely accepted but fundamentally vicious assumption. He has assumed that whatever is meaningful must exhibit its meaningfulness to those who view it from the standpoint of external observation. Now if one chooses thus to limit one's self to the role of external observer, it is, I think, perfectly true that one can attach no meaning to an act which is the act of something we call a 'self' and yet follows from nothing in that self's character. But then *why should we* so limit ourselves, when what is under consideration is a subjective activity? For the apprehension of subjective acts there is *another* standpoint available, that of *inner experience*, of the practical consciousness in its actual functioning. If our free will should turn out to be something to which we can attach a meaning from *this* standpoint, no more is required. And no more ought to be expected. For I must repeat that only from the inner standpoint of living experience *could* anything of the nature of 'activity' be directly grasped. Observation from without is in the nature of the case impotent to apprehend the active *qua* active. We can from without observe sequences of states. If into these we read activity (as we sometimes do), this can only be on the basis of what we discern in ourselves from the inner standpoint. It follows that if anyone insists upon taking his criterion of the meaningful simply from the standpoint of external observation, he is really deciding in advance of the evidence that the notion of activity, and *a fortiori* the notion of a free will, is 'meaningless.' He looks for the free act through a medium which is in the nature of the case incapable of revealing it, and then, because inevitably he doesn't find it, he declares that it doesn't exist!

But if, as we surely ought in this context, we adopt the inner standpoint, then (I am suggesting) things appear in a totally different light. From the inner standpoint, it seems to me plain, there is no difficulty whatever in attaching meaning to an act which is the self's act and which nevertheless does not follow from the self's character. So much I claim has been established by the phenomenological analysis, in this and the previous lecture, of the act of moral decision in face of moral temptation. It is thrown into particularly clear relief where the moral decision is to make the moral effort required to rise to duty. For the very function of moral effort, as it appears to the agent engaged in the act, is to enable the self to act against the line of least resistance, against the line to which his character as so far formed most strongly inclines him. But if the self is thus conscious here of *combating* his formed character, he surely cannot possibly suppose that the act, although his own act, *issues from* his formed character? I submit, therefore, that the self knows very well indeed—from the inner standpoint—what is meant by an act which is the *self's* act and which nevertheless does not follow from the self's *character*.

What this implies—and it seems to me to be an implication of cardinal importance for any theory of the self that aims at being more than superficial—is that the nature of the self is for itself something more than just its character as so far formed. The 'nature' of the self and what we commonly called the 'character' of the self are by no means the same thing, and it is utterly vital that they should not be confused. The 'nature' of the self comprehends, but is not without remainder reducible to, its 'character'; it must, if we are to be true to the testimony of our experience of it, be taken as including *also* the authentic creative power of fashioning and re-fashioning 'character.'

The misguided, and as a rule quite uncritical, belittlement, of the evidence offered by inner experience has, I am convinced, been responsible for more bad argument by the opponents of Free Will than has any other single factor. How often, for example, do we find the Determinist critic saying, in effect, '*Either* the act follows necessarily upon precedent states, *or* it is a mere matter of chance and accordingly of no moral significance.' The disjunction is invalid, for it does not exhaust the possible alternatives. It seems to the critic to do so only because he *will* limit himself to the standpoint which is proper, and indeed alone possible, in dealing with the physical world, the standpoint of the external observer. If only he would allow himself to assume the standpoint which is not merely proper for, but necessary to, the apprehension of subjective activity, the inner standpoint of the practical consciousness in its actual functioning, he would find himself obliged to recognise the falsity of his disjunction. Reflection upon the act of moral decision as apprehended from the inner standpoint would force him to recognise a *third* possibility, as remote from chance as from necessity, that, namely, of *creative activity,* in which (as I have ventured to express it) nothing determines the act save the agent's doing of it. . . .

22. A PRAGMATIC ARGUMENT AGAINST DETERMINISM

William James

William James (1842–1910) along with C. S. Pierce and John Dewey developed the philosophical approach known as pragmatism, perhaps the only "home grown" philosophical movement to develop in America. Prior to becoming Professor of Philosophy at Harvard in 1880, James taught physiology and psychology. His Principles *of* Psychology *(1890) became a classic in the field and more recently has evoked the interest of phenomenology, a contemporary philosophical movement spearheaded by Husserl, Sartre, and Merleau-Ponty. James' most important works are* The Will to Believe and Other Essays *(1897),* The Varieties of Religious Experience *(1902), and* Pragmatism *(1907).*

. . . We have seen what determinism means: we have seen that indeterminism is rightly described as meaning chance; and we have seen that chance, the very name of which we are urged to shrink from as from a metaphysical pestilence, means only the negative fact that no part of the world, however big, can claim to control absolutely the destinies of the whole. But although, in discussing the word 'chance,' I may at moments have seemed to be arguing for its real existence, I have not meant to do so yet. We have not yet ascertained whether this be a world of chance or no; at most, we have agreed that it seems so. And I now repeat what I said at the outset, that, from any strict theoretical point of view, the question is insoluble. To deepen our theoretic sense of the *difference* between a world with chances in it and a deterministic world is the most I can hope to do; and this I may now at last begin upon, after all our tedious clearing of the way.

I wish first of all to show you just what the notion that this is a deterministic world implies. The implications I call your attention

157

to are all bound up with the fact that it is a world in which we constantly have to make what I shall, with your permission, call judgments of regret. Hardly an hour passes in which we do not wish that something might be otherwise; and happy indeed are those of us whose hearts have never echoed the wish of Omar Khayam—

> That we might clasp, ere closed, the book of fate,
>   And make the writer on a fairer leaf
> Inscribe our names, or quite obliterate.
> Ah! Love, could you and I with fate conspire
> To mend this sorry scheme of things entire,
>   Would we not shatter it to bits, and then
> Remould it nearer to the heart's desire?

Now, it is undeniable that most of these regrets are foolish, and quite on a par in point of philosophic value with the criticisms on the universe of that friend of our infancy, the hero of the fable The Atheist and the Acorn,—

> Fool! had that bough a pumpkin bore,
> Thy whimsies would have worked no more, etc.

Even from the point of view of our own ends, we should probably make a botch of remodelling the universe. How much more then from the point of view of ends we cannot see! Wise men therefore regret as little as they can. But still some regrets are pretty obstinate and hard to stifle,—regrets for acts of wanton cruelty or treachery, for example, whether performed by others or by ourselves. Hardly any one can remain *entirely* optimistic ofter reading the confession of the murderer at Brockton the other day: how, to get rid of the wife whose continued existence bored him, he inveigled her into a desert spot, shot her four times, and then, as she lay on the ground and said to him, "You didn't do it on purpose, did you, dear?" replied, "No, I didn't do it on purpose," as he raised a rock and smashed her skull. Such an occurrence, with the mild sentence and self-satisfaction of the prisoner, is a field for a crop of regrets, which one need not take up in detail. We feel that, although a perfect mechanical fit to the rest of the universe, it is a bad moral fit, and that something else would really have been better in its place.

But for the deterministic philosophy the murder, the sentence, and the prisoner's optimism were all necessary from eternity; and nothing else for a moment had a ghost of a chance of being put into their place. To admit such a chance, the determinists tell us, would be to make a suicide of reason; so we must steel our hearts against the thought. And here our plot thickens, for we see the first of those difficult implications of determinism and monism which it is my purpose to make you feel.

If this Brockton murder was called for by the rest of the universe, if it had to come at its preappointed hour, and if nothing else would have been consistent with the sense of the whole, what are we to think of the universe? Are we stubbornly to stick to our judgment of regret, and say, though it *couldn't* be, yet it *would* have been a better universe with something different from this Brockton murder in it? That, of course, seems the natural and spontaneous thing for us to do; and yet it is nothing short of deliberately espousing a kind of pessimism. The judgment of regret calls the murder bad. Calling a thing bad means, if it mean anything at all, that the thing ought not to be, that something else ought to be in its stead. Determinism, in denying that anything else can be in its stead, virtually defines the universe as a place in which what ought to be is impossible,—in other words, as an organism whose constitution is afflicted with an incurable taint, an irremediable flaw. The pessimism of a Schopenhauer says no more than this,—that the murder is a symptom; and that it is a vicious symptom because it belongs to a vicious whole, which can express its nature no otherwise than by bringing forth just such a symptom as that at this particular spot. Regret for the murder must transform itself, if we are determinists and wise, into a larger regret. It is absurd to regret the murder alone. Other things being what they are, *it* could not be different. What we should regret is that whole frame of things of which the murder is one member. I see no escape whatever from this pessimistic conclusion, if being determinists, or judgment of regret is to be allowed to stand at all.

The only deterministic escape from pessimism is everywhere to abandon the judgment of regret. That this can be done, history shows to be not impossible. The devil, *quoad existentiam*, may be good. That is, although he be a *principle* of evil, yet the universe, with such a principle in it, may practically be a better universe than it could have been without. On every hand, in a small way, we find that a certain amount of evil is a condition by which a higher form of good is brought. There is nothing to prevent anybody from generalizing this view, and trusting that if we could but see things in the largest of all ways, even such matters as this Brockton murder would appear to be paid for by the uses that follow in their train. An optimism *quand même*, a systematic and infatuated optimism like that ridiculed by Voltaire in his Candide, is one of the possible ideal ways in which a man may train himself to look on life. Bereft of dogmatic hardness and lit up with the expression of a tender and pathetic hope, such an optimism has been the grace of some of the most religious characters that ever lived.

> Throb thine with Nature's throbbing breast,
> And all is clear from east to west.

Even cruelty and treachery may be among the absolutely blessed fruits of time, and to quarrel with any of their details may be blasphemy. The only real blasphemy, in short, may be that pessimistic temper of the soul which lets it give way to such things as regrets, remorse, and grief.

Thus, our deterministic pessimism may become a deterministic optimism at the price of extinguishing our judgments of regret.

But does not this immediately bring us into a curious logical predicament? Our determinism leads us to call our judgments of regret wrong, because they are pessimistic in implying that what is impossible yet ought to be. But how then about the judgments of regret themselves? If they are wrong, other judgments, judgments of approval presumably, ought to be in their place. But as they are necessitated, nothing else *can* be in their place; and the universe is just what it was before,—namely, a place in which what ought to be appears impossible. We have got one foot out of the pessimistic bog, but the other one sinks all the deeper. We have rescued our actions from the bonds of evil, but our judgments are now held fast. When murders and treacheries cease to be sins, regrets are theoretic absurdities and errors. The theoretic and the active life thus play a kind of see-saw with each other on the ground of evil. The rise of either sends the other down. Murder and treachery cannot be good without regret being bad: regret cannot be good without treachery and murder being bad. Both, however, are supposed to have been foredoomed; so something must be fatally unreasonable, absurd, and wrong in the world. It must be a place of which either sin or error forms a necessary part. From this dilemma there seems at first sight no escape. . . .

The only consistent way of representing a pluralism and a world whose parts may affect one another through their conduct being either good or bad is the indeterministic way. What interest, zest, or excitement can there be in achieving the right way, unless we are enabled to feel that the wrong way is also a possible and a natural way,—nay, more, a menacing and an imminent way? And what sense can there be in condemning ourselves for taking the wrong way, unless we need have done nothing of the sort, unless the right way was open to us as well? I cannot understand the willingness to act, no matter how we feel, without the belief that acts are really good and bad. I cannot understand the belief that an act is bad, without regret at its happening. I cannot understand regret without the admission of real, genuine possibilities in the world. Only *then* is it other than a mockery to feel, after we have failed to do our best, that an irreparable opportunity is gone from the universe, the loss of which it must forever after mourn.

If you insist that this is all superstition, that possibility is in the eye of science and reason impossibility, and that if I act badly 'tis that the universe was foredoomed to suffer this defect, you fall right back into the dilemma, the labyrinth, of pessimism, from out of whose toils we have just wound our way.

Now, we are of course free to fall back, if we please. For my own part, though, whatever difficulties may beset the philosophy of objective right and wrong, and the indeterminism it seems to imply, determinism, with its alternative of pessimism or romanticism, contains difficulties that are greater still. But you will remember that I expressly repudiated awhile ago the pretension to offer any arguments which could be coercive in a so-called scientific fashion in this matter. And I consequently find myself, at the end of this long talk, obliged to state my conclusions in an altogether personal way. This personal method of appeal seems to be among the very conditions of the problem; and the most any one can do is to confess as candidly as he can the grounds for the faith that is in him, and leave his example to work on others as it may.

Let me, then, without circumlocution say just this. The world is enigmatical enough in all conscience, whatever theory we may take up toward it. The indeterminism I defend, the free-will theory of popular sense based on the judgment of regret, represents that world as vulnerable, and liable to be injured by certain of its parts if they act wrong. And it represents their acting wrong as a matter of possibility or accident, neither inevitable nor yet to be infallibly warded off. In all this, it is a theory devoid either of transparency or of stability. It gives us a pluralistic, restless universe, in which no single point of view can ever take in the whole scene; and to a mind possessed of the love of unity at any cost, it will, no doubt, remain forever inacceptable. A friend with such a mind once told me that the thought of my universe made him sick, like the sight of the horrible motion of a mass of maggots in their carrion bed.

But while I freely admit that the pluralism and the restlessness are repugnant and irrational in a certain way, I find that every alternative to them is irrational in a deeper way. The indeterminism with its maggots, if you please to speak so about it, offends only the native absolutism of my intellect,—an absolutism which, after all, perhaps, deserves to be snubbed and kept in check. But the determinism with its necessary carrion, to continue the figure of speech, and with no possible maggots to eat the latter up, violates my sense of moral reality through and through. When, for example, I imagine such carrion as the Brockton murder, I cannot conceive it as an act by which the universe, as a whole, logically and necessarily expresses its nature without shrinking from complicity with such a whole. And I deliberately refuse to keep

161

on terms of loyalty with the universe by saying blankly that the murder, since it does flow from the nature of the whole, is not carrion. There are *some* instinctive reactions which I, for one, will not tamper with. . . .

23. THE UNPREDICTABILITY OF CHOICES

D. M. MacKay

Donald M. MacKay (1922–   ) is Research Professor of Communication at the University of Keele, England. The following selection is based on the first of two BBC talks which were later published in The Listener, *May 9, 1957.*

Everyone admits that some human actions may sometimes be determined by the physical state of the brain. No one doubts that the convulsions of epilepsy or the tremors of Parkinson's disease have, as we say, a physical cause; and most of us would admit that many of our less spectacular actions could probably also be traced back continuously to the physical action of our central nervous system. At least it would not worry us if it were so.

It worries nobody, as long as the actions concerned are not of a kind to which we attach moral significance. But as soon as we come to acts of choice in which questions of responsibility might arise, we find ourselves in the middle of a well-trodden battlefield. On the one hand, there are those who believe that if my choice is to be morally valid, the physical activity of my brain must at some point "change its course" in a way which is not determined by purely physical factors. They do not mean only that the change would be too complicated to work out in practice—though in fact it probably would be. They believe that even with unlimited powers of calculation, and complete physical information about every part of the brain, it would be impossible to know the change in advance, because, they would say, the change does not depend only on physical factors. If it did, then the choice would not be a morally valid one.

From "Brain and Will," first of two talks presented on the BBC and later published in The Listener, *May 9, 1957. Reprinted by permission of the author and the British Broadcasting Corporation. (Both talks may be found in* Body and Mind, *1964, edited by G. N. A. Vesey, and published by Allen & Unwin.)*

162

According to this view, then, the brain is to be thought of as an instrument often likened to a pianoforte, with at least a few controlling keys open to influences of a non-physical kind. I shall refer to it, for short, as the "open-system" view.

Over against this view we have a strong body of opinion, particularly among scientists, which maintains that even when I make a moral choice, the physical changes in my brain depend entirely on the physical events that lead up to them. On this view there would be no discontinuity in the chain of physical cause and effect. A complete knowledge of the immediately preceding state, it is believed, would always be sufficient in principle to indicate beforehand which choice would be made. No openings are admitted for any non-physical influences to disrupt the expected pattern. We may refer to this as the "closed-system" view of the brain.

On both sides there are plenty of varieties of opinion. Some who hold the "open-system" view would maintain that each morally valid choice—each choice for which I may properly be held responsible—requires a miraculous physical change to take place in the brain. Others, such as Dr. E. L. Mascall in his recent Bampton Lectures, hold that the well-known indeterminacy of small-scale physical events, first explicated by Heisenberg, could allow the brain to respond to non-physical influences without disobeying physical laws.[1]

In the "closed-system" camp there are even more varieties of opinion about the "mental" aspect. Some robustly deny that there are any morally valid choices. They agree with the "open-system" people that a choice could not be valid unless it falsified or went beyond what was indicated beforehand by the state of the brain—but they do not believe that human choices do so. Others, again, would argue that questions of moral validity are "meaningless"; and so we could go on.

A PRIOR QUESTION

But I am not concerned here to come down on one side or the other of this traditional fence. I simply do not know—nobody knows—to what extent the processes going on in the brain are physically determined. We are gradually accumulating evidence which suggests that brain tissue does behave according to the same physical principles as the rest of the body; and we now know also that no behaviour-pattern [2] which we can observe and specify is beyond the capabilities of a physi-

---

[1] *Christian Theology and Natural Science* (1956), p. 241.

[2] I.e., no information-processing operation. We are not here concerned with feats of physical strength, but with the kind of behaviour usually taken as evidence of intelligence.

cal mechanism. On the other hand, it is undeniable that some processes in the brain might occasionally be affected by physically indeterminate events of the sort which Heisenberg's Principle allows.

No, what I want to do is to undercut all discussion of this kind
by raising a group of prior questions which might profitably have been
asked before sides were picked on the traditional ground. The central
question is: Could I be *excused* from responsibility if a choice of mine
did *not* involve any physically indeterminate changes in my brain?

At first sight the answer may seem obvious. "Surely," we may
say, "a choice which is uniquely indicated beforehand by the state of
the brain cannot be called a 'free' choice? If you could in principle predict how I shall choose before I make my choice, surely my choosing
has no moral validity?" In one sense this *is* obvious. We should all
agree that if we could be given a description of our action beforehand,
and had no power to help or hinder its fulfilment, then we should have
to admit that this action was not "free" but involuntary. A sneeze, for
example, at a sufficiently advanced stage, might be judged involuntary
by this criterion. So would a simple reflex action like a knee-jerk or an
eye-blink.

But—and this is the point—even supposing that the necessary
brain-processes were determined only by physical factors, are we sure
that what we normally call a "free choice" could be described to us in
advance? I think not. In fact I believe that whether the brain-mecha-
nism is physically determinate or not, the activity which we call "making
a free choice" is of a special kind which could never be described to
us with certainty beforehand. Suppose we are asked to choose between
porridge and prunes for breakfast. We think: "Let's see: I've had
prunes all last week; I'm sick of prunes; I'll have porridge." We would
normally claim now to have made a "free choice." But suppose that
some super-physiologist has been observing our brain-workings all this
time, and suppose he declares that our brain went through nothing but
physically determinate actions. Does this mean that he could have told
us in advance that we would certainly choose porridge? Of course not.
However carefully calculated the super-physiologist's proffered description of our choice, we know—and he would know—that we still
had power to alter it.

LOGICAL INDETERMINACY

No matter how much he tried to allow in advance for the effects
of his telling us, we could still defy him to give us a valid description [3]

---

[3] Here and later, I use "description" as shorthand for "complete determination in detail."

of what our choice would be. This is our plain everyday experience of what most people mean by our free choice: a choice which nobody could (even in principle) describe to us in advance. My point is that this vital criterion of freedom of choice, which we shall see later can be extended and strengthened, would apply equally well whether the brain were physically determinate in its workings or not. In either case, the state of our brain after receiving his description would not (and could not) be the state on which he based his calculations. If he were to try to allow beforehand for the effects of his description upon us, he would be doomed to an endless regression—logically chasing his own tail in an effort to allow for the effects of allowing for the effects of allowing . . . indefinitely. This sort of logical situation was analysed some years ago in another connection by Professor Karl Popper,[4] and the conclusion I think is watertight. Any proffered description of our choice as already certain would automatically be self-invalidating for us.

It is necessary, however, to carry the argument a stage further. One might get the impression from what I have said that our choice could not be proved free in this sense unless we succeeded in actually falsifying a would-be description of it. But this is not so. If we are supposing that our super-physiologist has access to all our brain-workings, then our freedom to nullify predictions of our choices can in principle be established simply by examining the structure—the blue-print, so to speak—of those brain-workings. It is not necessary actually to make the experiment of presenting us with an alleged "prediction," in order to verify that the basis of the prediction would be invalidated. The point is simply that the brain is always altered by receiving information; so that the brain which has received a hitherto valid description of itself cannot possibly be in the state described. Provided that the parts of our brain concerned with receiving and understanding the information are lined up with the mechanisms concerned with our taking the decision (and nobody doubts this even on the "closed-system" view), then it is logically impossible to give us—or even to make ourselves imagine—a valid complete description of a decision we are still deliberating, whether on the basis of advance observation or anything else. It is not that we are unable to ascertain the true description. It is that for us *there is no true description to ascertain.* For us the decision is something not be be ascertained but to be *made.* In fact, any description would be for us *logically indeterminate* (neither true nor false) because it would be self-referring in a contradictory way, rather like the statement: "This sentence I am now uttering is false."

It is this *logical* indeterminacy, of statements predicting our

---

[4] "Indeterminism in Quantum Physics and in Classical Physics," *British Journal for the Philosophy of Science* (1950–51), pp. 117–133, 173–195.

decisions, which has tended in the past to be confused with *physical* indeterminacy, as something which was thought to be necessary if a choice were to be morally valid. We all feel intuitively that there is something queerly "undetermined" about the decisions we take—that there is something absurd and self-contradictory in trying to believe or even consider as "true now" any advance description of them. I hope I have shown that this intuitive feeling is entirely justified—but on grounds which have nothing to do with physical indeterminacy in the matter of our brains. We appear to be so constructed that any would-be prediction of our voluntary actions becomes for us merely an invitation to choose how to act. This is not only theory, but also empirical fact. If anyone tries to predict to us that we are about to choose porridge rather than prunes, then no matter how scientific the basis of his statement, we can easily verify that he is simply giving us a fresh opportunity to make up our minds. Whether we decide in the end to fall in with this would-be prediction or to contradict it, we know—and he knows—that it has lost any scientific validity by being offered to us.

"I KNEW YOU'D CHOOSE THAT"

But, we may well ask, what if our super-physiologist does *not* tell me of his prediction? What if he just keeps his mouth shut and watches how I choose, and then says, "Aha, I knew you'd choose that"? We must admit straight away that we should feel rather upset if anybody could do that to us every time we made a choice; and I must agree that I do not believe it could ever be done consistently in practice. Consistent success would be possible only if our brains *were* physically determinate, and if the super-physiologist could know the whole of our brain-workings, together with all the influences which would act on them from the outside world. The first supposition is doubtful and the second is certainly impossible on practical grounds of sheer complexity; and between them I think these considerations are enough to account for—and justify—our feeling of incredulity.

But suppose for the sake of argument that it *were* so: that although we can defy anyone to tell us how we are going to choose, yet a successful prediction of our choice could in principle be made by someone who keeps quiet about it. What then? Could we excuse ourselves from responsibility for our choice on these grounds? I do not think so. If we had no power to falsify his prediction, we might indeed excuse ourselves. But in this case there is no doubt that we have the power. Our silent observer is only denying us the opportunity to demonstrate it. He knows, as well as we, that in fact his prediction is only conditionally "certain": certain just so long as we do not know it; and it is rather an odd sort of "certainty" that you have to hide from someone in case it turns false! Clearly even when he kept quiet the sense in which his prediction was "certain" would be a rather limited one.

As a matter of fact, the great majority of our choices day by day could be predicted with great success without even opening our heads, by anyone who knows us sufficiently well; but it never occurs to us to question our responsibility for them on these grounds. At least if it does I do not think it ought to, for all it means is that we make most of our choices "in character"; not that we could not have chosen otherwise (if confronted with the allegedly "certain" prediction), but simply that we were not inclined to—and might not have felt so inclined even if the prediction had been offered to us.

In short, the super-physiologist's knowledge, if our brain-workings accurately reflected what we were thinking, would do no more than enable him to make predictions as if he knew what was going on in our minds. In that case it would be surprising if he were not successful, so long as he kept quiet; but we could never appeal to his evidence in order to excuse ourselves from responsibility for such choices, for at most it could only offer *confirmation*—and not contradiction—of the mental processes in terms of which our moral responsibility would be judged.

To sum up, I believe that brain-processes may well include some events which are physically indeterminate as well as many which are not. But I am suggesting that our responsibility for moral choices rests not on any physical indeterminateness of our brains, but on the logical indeterminateness to us of any advance description of our decisions. It is the unique organisation of our brains which gives this peculiar status to our decisions—not anything physically queer about their workings.

24. AN ATTEMPT TO RECONCILE DETERMINISM AND MORAL RESPONSIBILITY

P. H. Nowell-Smith

P. H. Nowell-Smith (1914–   ) is Professor of Philosophy at
the University of Kent, England. He has written a number of
significant papers in various areas of philosophy, but his chief
work is Ethics, published in 1954.

The traditional problem of free will has been so adequately
covered in recent philosophical literature that some excuse must be
offered for reopening it; and I do so because, although I believe that
the traditional problem has been solved, I believe also that the solution
leaves open certain further problems that are both interesting and important. It is to these problems that I propose to devote most of this
paper; but, even at the risk of flogging dead horses, I feel bound to say
something about the traditional problem itself.

I

The problem arises out of a *prima facie* incompatibility between
the freedom of human action and the universality of causal law. It was
raised in an acute form when universal determinism was believed to be
a necessary presupposition of science; but it was not then new, because
the incompatibility, if it exists at all, exists equally between human
freedom and the fore-knowledge of God. As it appears to the "plain
man" the problem may be formulated as follows: "Very often I seem to
myself to be acting freely, and this freedom, if it exists, implies that I
could have acted otherwise than I did. If this freedom is illusory, I
shall need a very convincing argument to prove that it is so, since it
appears to be something of which I am immediately aware. Moreover,
if there is no freedom, there is no moral responsibility; for it would not
be right to praise or blame a man for something that he could not help
doing. But, if a man could have acted otherwise than he did, his action
must have been uncaused, and universal determinism is therefore untrue."

Broadly, there are two methods of resolving this, as any other,

From "Free Will and Moral Responsibility" (Parts 1 & 2), Mind,
Vol. 57, No. 225, 1948. Reprinted by permission of the author and
the editor.

antinomy. We can either assume that the incompatibility is a genuine one at a certain level of thought and try to resolve it at a higher plane in which either or both the terms "freedom" and "necessity" lose their ordinary meaning or we can try to show by an analysis of these terms that no such incompatibility exists. If the latter method is successful, it will show that what is essential in our concept of freedom does not conflict with what is essential in our concept of causal necessity and that the incompatibility arises only because, at some stage in our development of one or both of these concepts, we have been tempted into making a false step. This method seems to me the better (provided always that it is successful), on the ground that it does not resort to any metaphysical conception imported *ad hoc* to solve this problem, which might be objectionable on other grounds. In the first two sections of this paper I shall give a brief outline of the analysis of the problem that I believe to be correct; and for this analysis I claim no originality. The method of presentation will, however, throw into relief the partial nature of the solution and help to indicate the further problems to be discussed in the last three sections.

Freedom, so far from being incompatible with causality, implies it. When I am conscious of being free, I am not directly conscious that my actions are uncaused, because absence of causation is not something of which one could be directly aware. That the plain man and the Libertarian philosopher are right in claiming to know directly the difference between voluntary and involuntary actions, at least in some cases, I have no doubt; but we can never have this direct knowledge that something is uncaused, since this is a general proposition and, like other general propositions, could only be established by reflection on empirical evidence. Fortunately it is not necessary here either to attempt an analysis of causality or to answer the question whether or not it is a necessary presupposition of science. It is now widely recognised that the considerations which lead scientists to suppose that strict determinism is not true are irrelevant to the problem of free will, since these considerations lend no support to the view that the phenomena with which we are concerned are not predictable; and it is to predictability, not to any special theory of the grounds of predictability, that the Libertarian objects. He claims that if our actions are predictable we are "pawns in the hands of fate" and cannot choose what we shall do. If, it is argued, someone can know what I shall do, then I have no choice but to do it.

The fallacy of this argument has often been exposed and the clearest proof that is is mistaken or at least muddled lies in showing that I could not be free to choose what I do *unless* determinism is correct. There are, indeed, grounds for supposing that strict determinism

169

in psychology is not correct; but this, if true, constitutes not an increase but a limitation of our freedom of action. For the simplest actions could not be performed in an indeterministic universe. If I decide, say, to eat a piece of fish, I cannot do so if the fish is liable to turn into a stone or to disintegrate in mid-air or to behave in any other utterly unpredictable manner. It is precisely because physical objects have determinate causal characteristics that we are able to do what we decide to do. To this it is no answer to say that perhaps the behaviour of physical objects is determined while that of volitions is not. For we sometimes cause people to make decisions as well as to act on them. If someone shouts: "Look out! There is a bull," I shall probably run away. My action is caused by my decision to run; but my decision is itself caused by my fear, and that too is caused by what I have heard. Or, again, someone may try to influence my vote by offering me a bribe. If I accept the bribe and vote accordingly, the action is caused by the bribe, my avarice and my sense of obligation to the donor; yet this would certainly be held to be a blameworthy action, and therefore a voluntary one. A genuinely uncaused action could hardly be said to be an action *of* the agent at all; for in referring the action to an agent we are referring it to a cause.

In calling a man "honest" or "brave" we imply that he can be relied on to act honestly or bravely, and this means that we predict such actions from him. This does not mean that we can predict human actions with the same degree of assurance as that with which we predict eclipses. Psychology and the social sciences have not yet succeeded in establishing laws as reliable as those that we have established in some of the natural sciences, and maybe they never will. But any element of unreliability in our predictions of human actions decreases rather than increases the reliability of our moral judgments about them and of our consequent attributions of praise and blame. An expert chess player has less difficulty in defeating a moderate player than in defeating a novice, because the moves of the moderate player are more predictable; but they could hardly be said to be less voluntary. In calling an action "voluntary" we do not, therefore, mean that it is unpredictable; we mean that no one compelled the agent to act as he did. To say that, on the determinist view, we are "mere pawns in the hands of fate" is to confuse causality with compulsion, to confuse natural laws (descriptions) with social laws (prescriptions) and to think of fate as a malignant deity that continually thwarts our aims. What the protagonist of freedom requires, in short, is not uncaused actions, but actions that are the effects of a peculiar kind of causes. I shall be as brief as possible in saying what these causes are, since this has often been said before. But it is one thing to state the criteria by which we decide whether or not an action is voluntary and another to say why this distinction is important for ethics. The problem which the analysts have not, in my view, sufficiently considered is that of analysing the peculiar relation of "merit" or "fittingness" that is held to exist between voluntary actions and moral responsibility.

II

If someone overpowers me and compels me to fire a gun which causes a death, I should not be held guilty of murder. It would be said that my action was not voluntary; for I could not, had I so wished, have acted otherwise. On the other hand, if I kill someone because I hope to benefit under his will, my action is still caused, namely by my greed; but my action would be held to be voluntary and I should be blamed for it. The citerion here is that, while in the first case the cause is external to me, in the second it is my decision. A similar criterion would be used to distinguish a kleptomaniac from a thief. A kleptomaniac is held to be one who steals without having decided to do so, perhaps even in spite of a decision not to do so. He is not held morally responsible for his action because his action is not held to be voluntary. But in this case it is not true, as it was in the last, that his action is called involuntary because it is caused by some outside force. The cause of kleptomania is obscure; but it is not external compulsion. And, if the cause is not external, how can we say that the kleptomaniac is "compelled"? As used by psychologists, the term "compulsion" is evidently a metaphor, similar to that by which we speak of a man's doing something when "he is not himself." Evidently our moral judgements imply not merely a distinction between voluntary and compelled actions, but a further distinction among actions that are not compelled.

A third example will make it clear that some such distinction must be made. Suppose that a schoolmaster has two pupils A and B, who fail to do a simple sum correctly. A has often done sums of similar difficulty before and done them correctly, while B has always failed. The schoolmaster will, perhaps, threaten A with punishment, but he will give B extra private tuition. On the traditional view his action might be explained as follows: "A has done these sums correctly before; therefore he could have done them correctly on this occasion. His failure is due to carelessness or laziness. On the other hand, B is stupid. He has never done these sums correctly; so I suppose that he *cannot* do them. A's failure is due to a moral delinquency, B's to an intellectual defect. A therefore deserves punishment, but B does not." This is, I think, a fair summary of what the "plain man" thinks about a typical case, and the points to which I wish to draw attention are these:

(*a*) Neither failure is said to be "uncaused."

(*b*) The causes assigned are divided into two classes, moral and intellectual. (Cases of physical deficiency, *e.g.* not being strong or tall enough would go along with the intellectual class, the point being that such deficiencies are nonmoral.)

(*c*) Praise and blame are thought appropriate to moral but not to nonmoral defects.

(*d*) The criterion for deciding whether a defect is moral is "Could the agent have acted otherwise?"

I do not wish to suggest that the reasoning attributed to the plain man in this case is in any way incorrect, only that, particularly in regard to point (*c*) and (*d*) it needs explaining.

It is evident that one of the necessary conditions of moral action is that the agent "could have acted otherwise" and it is to this fact that the Libertarian is drawing attention. His case may be stated as follows: "It is a well-known maxim that 'I ought' implies 'I can.' If I cannot do a certain action, then that action cannot be my duty. On the other hand, 'I ought' as clearly implies 'I need not'; for if I cannot possibly refrain from a certain action, there can be no merit or demerit in doing it. Therefore, in every case of moral choice it is possible for the agent to do the action and also possible for him not to do it; were it not so, there would be no *choice;* for choice is between possibilities. But this implies that the action is uncaused, because a caused action cannot but occur." The fallacy in this argument lies in supposing that, when we say "A could have acted otherwise," we mean that A, being what he was and being placed in the circumstances in which he was placed, could have done something other than what he did. But in fact we never do mean this; and if we believe that voluntary action is uncaused action, that is only because we believe erroneously that uncaused action is a necessary condition of moral responsibility. The Libertarian believes that an action cannot be a moral one if the agent could not have acted otherwise, and he takes no account of possible differences in the causes that might have prevented him from acting otherwise. The Determinist, on the other hand, holds that the objective possibility of alternative actions is an illusion and that, if A in fact did X, then he could not have done any action incompatible with X. But he holds also that differences in the various causes that might have led to X may be of great importance and that it is in fact from the consideration of such differences that we discover the criterion by which we judge an action to be voluntary, and so moral.

We all blame Nero for murdering Agrippina, and the Libertarian holds that this implies that Nero could have abstained from his action. But this last phrase is ambiguous. Even if we admit that it would have been impossible for anyone to predict Nero's action with the degree of assurance with which we predict eclipses, yet an acute observer at Nero's court might have laid longish odds that Nero, being what he was and being placed in the circumstances in which he was placed, would sooner or later murder his mother. To say that Nero might have acted otherwise is to say that he could have decided to act otherwise and that he would have so decided if he had been of a different character. If Nero had been Seneca, for example, he would have preferred suicide to matricide. But what could "If Nero had been Seneca . . ." possibly mean? Unfulfilled conditionals in which both terms are names of individuals constitute, admittedly, a thorny philosophical problem; but it is clear, I think, that if "If Nero had seen Seneca . . ." means anything at all, it is a quasi-general proposition which can be analysed either as "If Nero had had the character of Seneca" or "If Seneca had been emperor" or in some similar fashion. None of these analyses are incompatible with the Determinist's contention that, as things stood, Nero could not have abstained. But, adds the Determinist, the cause of his inability to abstain was not external compulsion nor some inexplicable and uncharacteristic quirk. His action was predictable because it was characteristic, and it is for the same reason that he is held to blame.

But the Libertarian's case is not yet fully answered. He might reply: "But, on this analysis, I still cannot blame Nero which in fact I do, and feel that I do justly. If the murder was caused by his character, *he* may not have been to blame. For his character may have been caused by hereditary and environmental factors over which he had no control. Can we justly blame a man if his vicious actions are due to hereditary epilepsy or to the influence of a corrupt and vicious court?" To this the answer is that we can and do. So long as we persist in supposing that, to be moral, an action must be uncaused, we can only push the moral responsibility back in time; and this, so far from solving the problem, merely shows the impossibility of any solution on these lines.

This is made abundantly clear by Aristotle's discussion of the subject, which I shall paraphrase somewhat freely in order to show that it must raise a difficulty which Aristotle does not squarely face. Aristotle says that, if a man plead that he could not help doing X because he was "the sort of man to do X," then he should be blamed for being this sort of man. His character was caused by his earlier actions, Y and Z, that made him the sort of person who would, in the given situation, inevitably do X. But suppose the criminal pleads that at the time of doing Y and Z he did not know that these were vicious actions and did not know that doing vicious actions causes a vicious character? Then, says Aristotle, all we can say in such a case is that not to know that actions create character is the mark of a singularly senseless person. But this is clearly inadequate. For the criminal might proceed: "Very well then, I was a singularly senseless person; I neither knew that Y and Z were vicious actions nor that, if I did them, I would become the sort of person to do X. And, anyhow, at the time of doing Y and Z, I was the sort of person to do Y and Z. These actions were just as much caused as was X. You say that blaming me for doing X is really blaming me for having done Y and Z. Now apply the same argument to Y and Z and see where it leads you. Furthermore my ignorance at the time of doing Y and Z which, according to you, is the real source of the trouble, was not my fault either. My father did not have me properly educated. Blame him, if you must blame somebody; but he will offer the same reply as I have done, and so *ad infinitum*." This argument carries no conviction; but it admits of no reply, and it is here that the temptation to invoke a metaphysical *deus ex machina* becomes inviting. If we proceed on the assumption that, to be moral, an action must be uncaused, either we shall find a genuinely uncaused action at the beginning of the chain or we shall not. If we do not, then, according to the Libertarian, there can be no moral praise and blame at all (and it was to account for these that Libertarianism was invented); and, if we do, then we must suppose that, while almost all our actions are caused, and therefore amoral, there was in the distant past some one action that was not caused and for which we can justly be praised or blamed. This bizarre theory has in fact been held; but the objections to it are clear. We praise and blame people for what they do now, not for what they might have done as babies, and any theory of moral responsibility must account for this. Secondly the same man is subjected to judgements both of praise and of blame: therefore the subject of these judgements cannot be one solitary act; and, thirdly, even if we were able to discover this one hypothetical infantile act, would it in fact to be a fit subject for either praise or blame. If it were genuinely uncaused, it could hardly be either, since it would not be an action *of* the agent. . . .

25. REASONS FOR ACTIONS DISTINGUISHED FROM CAUSES OF ACTIONS

S. I. Benn / R. S. Peters

S. I. Benn *(1920–   ) is Senior Fellow in Philosophy at the Australian National University. He was formerly Lecturer in Political Theory at the University of Southampton, England. He has contributed numerous articles to learned journals and is co-author with R. S. Peters of* The Principles of Political Thought *(1959).* R. S. Peters *(1919–   ) is Professor of the Philosophy of Education at the University of London. He is the author of a book on the philosophy of Hobbes and has edited two volumes of Hobbes' works. But Peters' main contributions have been in the areas of philosophical psychology and philosophy of education. His works include* The Concept of Motivation *(1958),* Authority, Responsibility and Education *(1959),* Ethics and Education *(1966), and* The Principles of Political Thought *(1959), of which he is the co-author with S. I. Benn.*

Determinism to a scientist conveys the general proposition that every event has a cause. Whether this general proposition is true is a very difficult question to decide, but it is certainly assumed to be true by most scientists. To say that an event has a cause is to say that there are universal laws together with statements about initial conditions prevailing at particular times, and that from these two together we can predict an event which we call an 'effect.' For example, given that under the conditions x,y,z, iron expands when it is heated, and given that the conditions x,y,z, prevail and that this is a case of iron being heated, we can make the prediction that iron will expand. Here we have a typical causal relation. The so-called 'cause' is then the event referred to in the statement of initial conditions. And these conditions are regarded as being *sufficient* to explain the effect, if it is a full-blooded causal *explanation.*

Have we such relations in human affairs? The initial difficulty about saying that we have is that it is difficult to maintain that there are any psychological or sociological laws which would enable us to make such definite predictions. There are also difficulties connected with our knowledge of particular situations which constitute the initial conditions; for when we are dealing with stones and bodies falling, their past history is scarcely part of the present situation. But when we are dealing with human beings, their past history is very much part of the present situation, and it is very difficult to know whether a given case is really of the type to which the particular law we have in mind applies. Nevertheless, there are some generalizations in psychology and the social sciences which are reasonably well established. They do not enable us to make detailed predictions; they merely enable us to state the sort of thing that will *tend* to happen under certain typical conditions. In this respect psychology is in no worse plight than other sciences like meteorology. The difficulties arise from the complexity of the subject-matter, and, it might be argued, can be remedied in time.

If, however, we look more closely at these so-called laws in psychology we find, in the main, that they do not give sufficient explanations of human *actions*, of what human beings do deliberately, knowing what they are doing and for which they can give reasons. Freud's brilliant discoveries, for instance, were not of the causes of *actions* like signing contracts or shooting pheasants; rather they were of things that *happen* to a man like dreams, hysteria, and slips of the tongue. These might be called 'passions' more appropriately than 'actions,' and in this respect they are similar to what we call 'fits of passion' or 'gusts of emotion.' Men do not dream or forget a name 'on purpose' any more than they are deliberately subject to impulses or gusts of emotion. One class of laws in psychology, then, gives causal explanations which seem sufficient to account for what *happens* to a man, but not for what he does.

There is another class of laws, however, which concern not what happens to me, but what they do—their actions, performances and achievements. But such laws state necessary rather than sufficient conditions. We have in mind here the contributions made by physiological psychologists and those who have studied cognitive skills like learning, remembering and perceiving. Part of what we mean by such terms is that human beings attain a norm or standard. Remembering is not just a psychological process; for to remember is to be *correct* about what happened in the past. Knowing is not just a mental state; it is to be sure that we are *correct* and to have *good grounds* for our conviction. To perceive something is to be *right* in our claims about what is before our eyes; to learn something is to *improve* at something or to get something *right*. All such concepts have norms written into them. In a similar way, as we have previously argued, a human action is typically something done in order to bring about a result or in accordance with a standard. Such actions can be said to be done more or less intelligently and more or less correctly only because of the norms defining what are

176

ends and what are efficient and correct means to them. It follows that a psychologist who claims that such performances depend on antecedent physiological conditions or mental processes, can at the most be stating necessary conditions. For processes, of themselves, are not appropriately described as correct or incorrect, intelligent or stupid. They only become so in the context of standards laid down by men. As Protagoras taught, nature knows no norms. It may well be true that a man cannot remember without part of his brain being stimulated, or that learning is a function, in part, of antecedent 'tension.' But the very meaning of 'remembering' and 'learning' precludes a sufficient explanation in these sorts of naturalistic terms.

Furthermore the problem of the freedom of the will arose mainly in connection with a type of action that is palpably different from a mere movement or process—an action that is preceded by deliberation and choice. For, roughly speaking, a 'willed action' was usually taken to mean one in which we think before we act, when we make up our minds in terms of considerations which are relevant to the matter in hand before we act. There are difficulties about developing causal laws for actions of this type which are additional to those already stated about actions in general. Such difficulties are similar to those which the social scientist, as well as the psychologist, has in predicting what human beings will do. This is connected with the fact that into the human being's deliberations about what he is going to do will be introduced considerations about what he is likely to do, which the social scientist may have published. A scientist may discover a causal law connecting the properties of clover with a certain effect upon the digestive organs of sheep. But, when he publishes his findings, the sheep cannot take account of them and modify their behaviour accordingly. But with men it is different. Many causal connections discovered by psychologists may only hold good provided that the people whose actions are predicted in accordance with the law remain ignorant of what it asserts. And it is practically impossible to ensure that this is the case. So, if people know the causes on which a prediction of a certain type of behaviour is based, and if they deliberate before acting they may do something different from what is predicted, just because they recognize these causes. A prediction may thus be valid only on the assumption that the people concerned remain unconscious of the causes on which it is based. Otherwise it may be no more than a warning.

But why cannot causal explanations *also* be given of such informed deliberations which precede actions? We are here confronted with the difficulty of accounting for *logical* thought in casual terms, of giving a causal explanation for rational actions done after deliberation which involves logically relevant considerations. This is an extreme case

177

of the difficulty already cited of giving sufficient explanations in causal terms for actions and performances which involve norms and standards. Yet, as has already been pointed out, such premeditated actions are particularly important in the free-will controversy, as the exercise of 'will' has usually been associated with rational deliberation before acting. When a man is solving a geometrical problem and his thoughts are proceeding in accordance with certain logical canons, it is logically absurd to suggest that any causal explanation in terms of movements in his brain, his temperament, his bodily state, and so on, is sufficient *by itself* to explain the movement of his thought. For logical canons are normative and cannot be sufficiently explained in terms of states and processes which are not. Of course there are any number of necessary conditions which must be taken account of. A man cannot think *without* a brain, for instance. But any *sufficient* explanation would have to take account of the *reasons* for his actions. We would have to know the rules of chess, for instance, which gave some *point* to a chess-player's move. Indeed we would only ask for the cause of a chess-player's behaviour if he did something which could not be explained in terms of the rules of chess and the objective at which he was aiming. If, for instance, he refrained from taking his opponent's queen, when this was the obvious and the best move, we might ask 'What made him do that?' and we would be asking for a causal explanation, like 'he was tired'. But this would now be an explanation of what *happened* to him, not of what he did deliberately. We would not ask for such an explanation if there was an obvious reason for his move.[1]

This example can be generalized and the point made that behaviour is usually explicable not because we know its causes, but because people act in accordance with certain known rules and conventions and adopt appropriate means to objectives which are accepted as legitimate goals. We know why a parson is mounting the pulpit not because we know much about the causes of his behaviour but because we know the conventions governing church services. We would only ask what were the causes of his behaviour if he fainted when he peered out over the congregation or if something similar *happened* to him. Most of our explanations of human behaviour are couched in terms of a purposive, rule-following model, not in casual terms. Moral behavior, above all other sorts, falls into this purposive, rule-following category. For, as

---

[1] Of course the category of 'action' is much wider than that of premeditated action, though it may be co-extensive with that of 'rationality.' For this covers the sort of things for which a man could have a reason—i.e. which fall under what we call the purposive rule-following model. Premeditated action is a particular case of action where action is *preceded* by rehearsals and deliberation; but often reasons can be given by people for what they do even though they do not deliberate *before* they act.

Aristotle put it in his Ethics,[2] it is not a man's passions which are the object of moral appraisal nor his capacity to be subject to such passions; rather we praise or blame a man for what he does about his passions, for the extent to which he controls or fails to control them in various situations. Deliberation and choice may not precede every action, but habits are set up as a result of such deliberation and choice. It is for the exercise of such habits that men are praised and blamed—for the ends which they seek and for the means which they adopt to bring about their ends. Punishment, too, as we have pointed out, presupposes that men can foresee the consequences of their actions and that they can learn to avoid those to which penalties are attached. Praise and blame, reward and punishment, act as rudders to steer human actions precisely because men deliberate and choose and can be influenced by considerations of consequences. There is a radical difference between actions of this sort and cases where things happen to a man—where he acts 'on impulse,' has a dream, a vision, or lapse of memory, or where he is afflicted by a feeling of nausea or hysterical paralysis. Questions of the 'freedom of the will' do not arise where things happen to a man; only where a man acts and can be praised or blamed, punished or rewarded for what he does. Yet it is precisely in these cases of human actions, as distinct from passions, that causal explanations seem inappropriate as sufficient explanations.

Two sorts of objection might be mounted against this attempt to limit the role of causal explanations of human behaviour. In the first place it might be said that by substituting concepts like rule-following and the pursuit of objectives we were in fact introducing other sorts of causes. Now the word 'cause' can be used in this very wide sense. But the terminological question is largely irrelevant; for two sorts of explanations which are logically quite different would then be included under the enlarged concept of 'cause.' To follow rules, to take steps which are seen to be necessary to reach some sort of objective, to see the point of something, these may be 'causes'; but they are causes in quite a different sense of 'cause' from things like stomach contractions, brain lesions, acute pains, and so on. The types of explanation must be distinguished whether we use the term 'cause' to cover both or not. And certainly seeing the point of something is quite different—even if it is called a 'cause'—from the causes prevalent in the physical world. In the early days of the determinist controversy philosophers like Spinoza and Kant used the term 'self-determined' to distinguish rational actions from those which could be explained in terms of mechanical causes like movements of the brain and body. Indeed Kant's suggestion that man lives in two worlds, and is subject to two different sorts of causation, is

---

[2] Aristotle, *Nichomachean Ethics*.

a metaphysical way of bringing out the logical distinction between these two sorts of explanation.

The second objection is the suggestion that all reasons might be rationalizations—a smoke screen for what we are going to do anyway. We are, as it were, pushed by causes in the mechanical, physical sense, whatever we do; but sometimes we throw up an elaborate smokescreen of excuses which make no difference to what we in fact do. If, however, we say that *all* reasons are rationalizations, we make no difference between the behaviour of an obsessive or a compulsive and that of a rational man. If a compulsive believes that his hands are covered in blood and spends his time continually washing them, no relevant considerations will make any difference to his behaviour. All the known tests fail to show blood; yet he still goes on washing his hands. But a civil servant making a complex decision about policy does not proceed like this. He will change his mind and alter policy in the light of relevant considerations. Indeed it is only because people *sometimes* alter their behaviour because of relevant considerations that it makes any *sense* to talk of rationalizations as well as of reasons. A term like 'rationalization,' which casts aspersions on the reasons given for action, is a verbal parasite. It flourishes because there *are* cases of genuine reasons with which rationalizations can be contrasted. Thus even if all behaviour has causes, in the sense of *necessary* conditions, there are objections to saying that all behaviour—especially rational behaviour—can be *sufficiently* explained by causes of the sort suggested by physical scientists, and by mechanistic philosophers like Hobbes.

THE PROBLEM
OF MORALITY
V

Can I Know What Is Morally Right?

26. ETHICAL RELATIVISM

Paul Taylor

Paul W. Taylor (1923–   ) is Professor of Philosophy at
Brooklyn College. He is the author of Normative Discourse
(1961) and has co-edited Knowledge and Value (1959).

I

A number of recent studies in ethics have investigated the possibility of giving *good reasons* for or against moral statements. These
studies have thrown new light on the argument between ethical relativism and ethical absolutism. A reconstruction of that argument is in
order, and this paper is an attempt to carry out such a reconstruction.
The argument will be presented in four stages. The first stage deals
with ethical relativism in its usual sense; each subsequent stage, involving
the problem of giving good reasons in matters of ethics, presents a new
type of ethical relativism for consideration.

Are moral values relative to a given society or historical period,
or are they validly applicable to all men everywhere at all times? This
is the central issue of the first stage of the argument. The ethical relativist maintains that nothing is "really" or "simply" good or bad but is
only good or bad in relation to the moral code of a given culture or historical era. The widespread acceptance of this view among educated
people in our century has perhaps been primarily the result of their
increasing awareness of certain findings in sociology, anthropology, and
psychology. These findings may be summed up in three broad statements of fact:

(1) The moral consciousness of man is environmentally conditioned. Each individual learns from his social environment to feel
guilty about certain things, to approve of this way of acting and to
disapprove of that, to hold himself and others responsible in certain
circumstances and not in others, to judge that these aims are right and
those are wrong, etc.

(2) The moral feelings and beliefs of individuals from different

From Philosophical Review, Vol. LXIII, No. 4, 1954, pp. 500–516.
Reprinted by permission of the author and the editor.

cultures, different eras in the history of a culture, and different groups within a culture may be extremely diverse and even contradictory.

(3) Most human beings have claimed that the moral beliefs of their own culture, era, or group are the only true ones. That is, most human beings are ethnocentric.[1]

From these factual statements the ethical relativist draws the following conclusions: (a) It is narrow-minded dogmatism on the part of any individual to presume that the moral beliefs of his society are more "advanced," "enlightened," or "true" than those of another society. (b) There *is* no set of moral values which is more "advanced," "enlightened," or "true" than another set. (c) Therefore it is unjustifiable to apply one set of moral values to all men everywhere at all times. Ethical relativism thus appears to be "proved by science."

It should be noted that this type of relativism does not imply that value statements cannot in *any* sense be called true or false, nor does it imply that they are unverifiable, that there is no way of finding out whether they are (in *some* sense) true or false. The truth or falsity of a value statement is, from this point of view, relative to the value beliefs of a given society. If all the members of a society believe that slavery is right then the statement "Slavery is right" is valid or correct for that society. Slavery "really is" right *relatively to the society.* But the assertion that slavery is right makes no claim upon the assent of anyone outside the society. In this respect the terms "true" and "false" as applied to moral statements do not have the same meaning as applied to factual or mathematical statements. (One may, if one wishes, conclude that therefore moral statements for the relativist are neither true nor false, but it is disputable whether having a claim upon universal assent is a defining characteristic of truth. At least at this point no further theoretical difficulty is present, and the issue becomes verbal.)

In order to refute ethical relativism in this first sense it is sufficient to discover some acceptable procedure for rationally justifying moral statements, that is, a method whereby such statements will be found to be true or false independently of the moral beliefs of those who utter the statements. It must be a method which makes no appeal to what as a matter of fact people do judge to be right or wrong, good or bad. (It need not, however, be a method which appeals to some kind of "objective" realm of values or to some kind of "nonnatural" properties of things.) As an example of such a procedure we need only cite that of the hedonistic utilitarian. An act is right, according to this view, if it is instrumental in bringing about a greater amount of

---

[1] Ethnocentrism has been defined as "the point of view that one's own way of life is to be preferred to all others" (Melville J. Herskovits, *Man and His Works* [New York, 1948], p. 68).

pleasure in human life than could have been brought about by any alternative act in the situation. Suppose x is such a maximally pleasure-yielding act. Then the statement "x is right" is true. The assertion that "x is right" is true is not contradicted by any discovery to the effect that people in a certain society believe x to be wrong. When the utilitarian says that the statement "x is right" is true he does not imply that everyone believes it or even that anyone (except perhaps himself) believes it. But he does intend to claim that the person who does not believe it, whatever might be the social and historical sources of his disbelief, is making a mistake.

It may be the case, of course, that the ethical relativist will not accept the utilitarian's or anyone else's procedure for justifying moral statements. But as soon as the argument centers upon whether there is such a procedure, and if there is one, whether it is acceptable or valid, the dispute has entered a new phase. It has been placed on a new level of discourse, the meta-language of the first-order language of morals. Instead of the question, Is slavery wrong only for us or is it wrong absolutely? we have the question, Is "Slavery is wrong" verifiable, and if so, how? The general problem of ethical relativism *vs.* ethical absolutism then becomes: Are moral statements verifiable,[2] and if they are, what method of verification is to be used and on what grounds is this method to be chosen? It is in terms of this problem that the three remaining types of relativism are formulated.

II

The second type of relativism is a corollary of what has come to be known as the "emotive" or "imperative" theory of ethics.[3] According to this theory moral statements are not really statements at all. They do not express propositions which are true or false; they express emotions or commands which are neither true nor false. Consequently they are unverifiable in the sense that good reasons cannot be given for or against them. Many sentences *appear* to express moral propositions which actually express factual propositions. The sentence "Stealing is wrong" might be used in certain common circumstances to mean that stealing is one of the things forbidden by the Bible or by the authorities of a specified religion, and this is a factual matter. The sentence is

---

[2] "Verifiable," of course, in a sense other that that which the relativist himself grants.

[3] See C. L. Stevenson, *Ethics and Language* (New Haven, 1944), *passim;* A. J. Ayer, *Language, Truth and Logic,* 2nd ed. (London, 1946), pp. 20–22, 102–114; S. Toulmin, *An Examination of the Place of Reason in Ethics* (Cambridge, 1950), pp. 46–60; W. Sellars and J. Hospers, *Readings in Ethical Theory* (New York, 1952), pp. 391–440.

verifiable, and the way to verify it is to consult the Bible or the proper religious authorities. Or when the utilitarian says, "Stealing is wrong," he might mean that stealing is not the best means to personal happiness, and this also is a question of fact, not of value. Genuine questions of value are not matters of fact but matters of attitude and emotion. When a person utters the sentence "Stealing is wrong" and he does not mean (implicitly or explicitly) to describe anything by it, he is then merely evincing his disapproval of stealing or is commanding his hearers not to steal or is trying by persuasion to make their attitudes about stealing agree with his. He is making a genuine moral utterance, and it is in the nature of such an utterance that good reasons cannot be given for or against it. As soon as the utilitarian, for example, offers as a good reason for the wrongness of stealing that stealing is not the best means to personal happiness, the emotivist would reply that the sentence "Stealing is wrong" is being used descriptively, not normatively, or else that it is being used only normatively in part, namely, in that part which involves the "emotive" or "quasi-imperative" meaning of the term "wrong." It is perfectly possible for a sentence to have both a normative and a descriptive function at the same time. But the normative function is an emotive or imperative one, and purely normative utterances cannot be deduced from factual statements and cannot be confirmed by inductive procedures. They can be *caused* (aroused, stimulated) by the reading or hearing of factual sentences, but they cannot be *justified* by them.

A normative sentence, then, is relative to the emotive situation from which it arises and in reference to which it is uttered. It may be uttered to give expression to inner feelings or it may be uttered to bring about changes in the feelings of others. As such it can be critically examined as to its appropriateness or its usefulness but it cannot be rationally justified. No *valid* argument can be formulated which would obligate a reasonable person to give intellectual assent to the utterance.

The relativistic aspect of the emotive theory becomes even clearer if we consider how moral conflicts are analyzed by those who hold it. Moral conflicts are conceived as essentially "disagreements in attitude," although "disagreements in belief" may comprise part of the total conflict situation.[4] Disagreement in belief can be settled in a rational manner, that is to say, by appeal to empirical knowledge and by use of the rules of logic. Disagreement in attitude, on the other hand, can only be settled by those means which are as a matter of fact instrumental in so altering attitudes that the conflict is brought to an end. The latter process, however, cannot be said to provide a rational justification of one moral position or a rational refutation of another.[5] Validity is not prop-

---

[4] Stevenson, *op. cit.*, ch. i.
[5] *Ibid.*, chs. v., vii.

erly attributable to it, even when such procedures as the following are used in settling the conflict: citing facts, clarifying the meanings of the statements uttered in the dispute, setting up a competent judge to decide the issue or to decide relevant subordinate issues, appealing to the imagination of each party in the dispute to think how it would feel to be in the position of the opposite party or in the position of a third party affected by the situation in question, referring to principles or norms acceptable to both disputants, etc. These procedures have the same function in moral conflicts as the following: use of force, emotive use of language in propaganda, advertizing and exhortation, intimidation and threats, application of legal sanctions and prohibitions, etc. Both kinds of procedure are merely more or less effective instruments in terminating the conflict. Even if procedures of the first kind alone are used in the process, nothing in the process constitutes *good reasons* for one side or against the other. Such procedures are merely one sort of causal determinant tending to settle the dispute; they do not provide a rational ground for claiming that the moral values finally agreed upon are "true," "valid," or "justified." Moral values, then, are *relative to the causal determinants which produce them* (including the procedures used in arriving at them). If one set of procedures causally determines the disputants to agree that slavery is wrong, for example, all we can conclude is that the wrongness of slavery has been established by means of these procedures; we cannot conclude that therefore slavery is "really" wrong or even that it is "probably" wrong. If another set of procedures causally determine the disputants to agree that slavery is right, the same results apply to the rightness of slavery.

The difficulty with this kind of ethical relativism can now be stated: Are we willing to grant that this is all there is to be said about such an issue as whether slavery is right or wrong? Let us consider the matter in this way. Suppose a group of men were able to gain enough power to conquer the world and were able, by means of thought control, intimidation, torture, etc., to convert the entire population of the world to a way of life based on cruelty, suspicion, and cowardice. Certain means of settling moral conflicts having been used to maximum efficiency, a universal set of values has now been established. Wouldn't we say that, nevertheless, the values so established are in some very real sense *unjustifiable* or *mistaken?* Wouldn't we wish to assert that good reasons can be given for repudiating such values and that good reasons can be given to justify a different set of values, meaning by this not merely that a different procedure (giving good reasons) would psychologically yield a different set of value utterances, but that this procedure would provide a rational *argument* against the given values and a rational *argument* for other values?

The believer in the emotive theory might reply that perhaps *we* would wish to assert this, but "we" are presumably reasonable people, people who want to have *enlightened* moral values. That is, we want to approve or disapprove of an object only after we know something about it, about the probable consequences of realizing it, about the means necessary to realize it, about a "wise" person's judgment of it, etc. And this simply means that we are people who will accept a moral utterance only as a result of rational procedures. A person who did not want to be reasonable, who did not want to use such procedures, would not feel this "difficulty."

Can any argument be given in answer to this? We could say that even if no one felt the difficulty, the difficulty would still be there. But it must be admitted that the difficulty itself (rather than the feeling of it) is a real difficulty only if one assumes that it is *justifiable* to attempt to find good reasons for or against moral statements. On what grounds can this assumption be made? Can one give good reasons for being reasonable, that is, is the attempt to justify rationally a set of moral values itself rationally justifiable? This question may be taken to signify the emergence of a new type of relativism.

III

The third type of ethical relativist asserts that a person who attempts to justify his moral statements by giving reasons for them can claim them to be true only by presupposing the value of reasonableness. But *this* value cannot be justified, since to try to justify it is to be reasonable and thus to assume the thing you are trying to prove. It would not be incumbent upon anyone who did not want to be reasonable to accept moral statements which, to a reasonable person, were rationally justified, for he could say: "You have shown your beliefs to be true only by using rational methods. Since I do not wish to use such methods but rather to impose my moral beliefs upon you by force, you can make no claim that your beliefs are superior to mine. You may claim reasonableness, but this is not to make a legitimate claim upon me. By forcing you to agree with me I can change your beliefs and still maintain my own. You cannot say I am 'really' wrong unless you use your reason, and since I do not respect reason I am not obligated to give assent to your appeal to reason. An *argument* for a moral belief has a claim only upon those who want to be reasonable, it has no claim upon those who deny the value of reasonableness."

Is there any rational objection to this argument? Can the question, Why be reasonable? be answered without assuming the value of being reasonable and thereby begging the question? The issue is of great importance because it goes to the very heart of the attacks now so violently set in motion throughout the world upon the attempt to lead a rational life.

The question, Why be reasonable? may mean in this context any of three things.[6]

(1) It may be a demand for a *moral* justification of being reasonable. It is another way of asking, "Am I morally obligated to be reasonable in these circumstances?" This is a meaningful question and can be answered, without redundancy or circularity, by giving reasons for being reasonable. The phrase "giving reasons for being reasonable" involves *two* meanings of "reasonableness," which may be designated "second-order" and "first-order" reasonableness, respectively. First-order reasonableness occurs when a person goes through a reasoning process before arriving at a decision or before committing himself in action or when a person tries to persuade others by giving reasons for doing one thing rather than another. That is, first-order reasonableness is the use of rational procedures in making moral decisions and in resolving moral conflicts. Now in certain circumstances we may question the moral rightness of being reasonable in this first-order sense, and we may demand *reasons* for being reasonable in that sense. The satisfying of such a demand by giving reasons is being reasonable in the *second-order* sense. Thus if we give reasons to show that a person ought to be reasonable (in the first-order sense) when he is deciding how many more drinks he should take before driving his friends home from a party, we are being reasonable (in the second-order sense). And if we give reasons to show that a person ought *not* to be reasonable (in the first-order sense) with an escaped madman who is about to do harm to his family, we are also being reasonable (in the second-order sense). To try to give good reasons against the use of reason in certain situations is not to contradict oneself, since one is being reasonable in the second-order sense in opposing being reasonable in the first-order sense. Any attempt to morally justify being reasonable or not being reasonable does imply some method of giving good reasons in support of moral judgments. But there is no circularity here because good reasons can be given which justify either (first-order) reasonableness or (first-order) unreasonableness. Indeed, the very same person may be trying to reason whether or not to be reasonable in the first-order sense. And if in a certain situation his reasoning leads him to decide not to be reasonable (that is, not to use rational procedures) because to do so would be morally wrong, he does not contradict himself, even though he uses rational procedures in opposing the use of rational procedures.

---

[6] The three meanings of the question were first suggested to me by my colleague, Martin Lean.

(2) The second possible interpretation of the question, Why be reasonable? is that it is a demand for a *pragmatic* justification of being reasonable. It is another way of asking, "Is it useful or prudent in these circumstances to be reasonable?" or, "If I am seeking such-and-such ends, is being reasonable a means to them?" This also is a meaningful question. It may be answered in the affirmative or in the negative. It is prudent for a person to be reasonable about what is good for his health but we should hardly say a soldier should try to be reasonable with his enemy on the battlefield.[7] Here again it is perfectly consistent to use reason to justify not using reason, that is, to be reasonable in the second-order sense in deciding not to be reasonable in the first-order sense.

(3) The third interpretation of the question is that it is a demand for a *theoretical* justification of being reasonable. It means: Give me reasons for using reason *at all*. It asks: Is it reasonable *ever* to be reasonable? Now this is a very peculiar question. In fact it is a question which would never be asked by anyone who thought about what he was saying, since the question, to speak loosely, answers itself. It is admitted that no amount of arguing in the world can make a person who does not want to be reasonable want to be. For to argue would be to give reasons, and to give reasons already assumes that the person to whom you give them is *seeking* reasons. That it, it assumes he is reasonable. A person who did not want to be reasonable in *any* sense would never ask the question, Why be reasonable? For in asking the question, Why? he is seeking reasons, that is, he is being reasonable in asking the question. The question calls for the use of reason to justify *any* use of reason, including the use of reason to answer the question. No distinction is made between a first-order and a second-order use of reason. It is qute true that as soon as one attempted to use reason to answer the question one would be committed to the assumption that such use of reason was justified. But no logical error would be involved beyond that which is made in asking the question in the first place. The question, Why be reasonable? under this third interpretation is the same as the question, What are good reasons for being reasonable? or, What are good reasons for seeking good reasons? The questioner is thus seeking good reasons for seeking good reasons. The peculiarity of this situation actually derives from the fact that in a strict sense the ques-

---

[7] It is true that ordinarily we would be likely to say, not that it was reasonable for the soldier to be unreasonable with his enemy, but that it was unreasonable for him to try to be reasonable with the enemy. But what would be intended by either statement is perfectly clear and not self-contradictory: that good reasons can be given to show that it is "unreasonable" (or that it is useless, imprudent, or unwise) to try to reason with the enemy.

tion is meaningless, since every answer which could possibly be accepted as a satisfactory answer would be a tautology to the effect that it is reasonable to be reasonable. A negative answer to the question, Is it reasonable to be reasonable? would express a self-contradiction.

Now it is this third interpretation which is intended by the ethical relativist who claims that we can never ultimately justify our moral beliefs because (1) to try to justify them is to commit ourselves to the position that reasonableness is superior to unreasonableness, (2) hence any result of such attempt at justification is not an absolute value but only a value relative to the presupposed value of being reasonable, and (3) this latter value cannot itself be justified without begging the question. This argument, however, has no weight because, although one cannot give reasons for being reasonable at all, such a demand cannot meaningfully be made. A person who does not care to be reasonable will not accept any proposed justification of being reasonable. (And if he is consistent he will not try to justify his *un*reasonableness.) He can claim that the reasonable person's values are relative to the appeal to reason but no logical difficulty results from this allegation. The reasonable person is neither inconsistent nor "ultimately" unreasonable in seeking good reasons for his moral beliefs. If someone challenges him with the questions, "Why seek good reasons to support your moral judgments? Why use rational ways of settling moral conflicts?" he can only reply, "Because I want to be reasonable." The person cannot then ask, "Why be reasonable?" without himself being reasonable in asking the question and thus rendering the question meaningless.

IV

The three types of relativism that have been distinguished may be labeled: (1) social or cultural relativism (moral values are relative to a given society), (2) psychological or contextural relativism (moral utterances are relative to the situations in which they arise and the purposes for which they are used; they can be justified pragmatically and perhaps aesthetically by reference to those situations and purposes, but they cannot be justified in any other sense), (3) theoretical or logical relativism (moral statements can be rationally justified but only by presupposing the value of reasonableness, which cannot itself be justified). The fourth and most important type of relativism may be called *methodological relativism*. This view arises from recognizing the fact that every theory of ethics other than the emotive theory declares moral statements to be verifiable or rationally justifiable, but each theory differs with the others as to the *proper method* of such verification. The methodological relativist then demands: "By what method is one to choose the correct method among all those proposed for verifying moral statements? If we attempt to justify our moral beliefs by using a certain method, how can we justify use of this method itself?" The relativist says that we cannot. He will admit that moral beliefs can be said to be true or false, that they are true or false no matter who agrees or disagrees with them, and that the true moral beliefs apply to all men everywhere at all times. But he goes on to say that these beliefs are true only *in relation to the method of justifying them.* Values are relative not to culture or to psychological and practical conditions or to reasonableness in general, but to method.

The same principle applies with equal force to the use of rational procedures for settling moral conflicts. The resolution of a moral conflict between two reasonable people will depend upon what specific rational procedure is used to justify or invalidate the moral beliefs in question. But if one person chooses one procedure and the other person chooses another they might arrive at opposite conclusions regarding the truth or falsity of the beliefs. Hence the conflict could not be settled rationally unless one particular procedure was first agreed upon by both disputants. But on what grounds is such agreement to be reached? Won't some other procedure be needed for choosing between the two procedures which led to contradictory results? And won't still another procedure be needed to choose a procedure for choosing between the two procedures? And so on *ad infinitum.* . . .

. . . The principle of ethical relativism of the fourth type is this: Granted that there are various methods for justifying moral statements, the truth or falsity of any given statement will depend on which method is used. Moral values are relative either to the particular deductive language system from which they are derived or to whatever qualified persons are appealed to for valid intuitions.

I think the challenge of the methodological relativist can be met successfully only in the following manner. The proper answer to the question, Why ought this method rather than that be used to verify moral statements? is simply that this, and not that, is what we *ordinarily mean* by saying that a moral statement is true (what we ordinarily mean, that is, when we have articulated no special theory of ethics). Instead of constructing logical systems or appealing to intuitive feelings to justify moral beliefs, suppose we examine the procedures and reasoning actually used in everyday life by ordinary people (that is, people who are not professional moralists or philosophers) in resolving moral conflicts, in justifying moral statements, and in arriving at moral decisions, and then explicate (make explicit) the principles or reasons implicit in this use. Three ways of carrying out this process of "explication" have been proposed in contemporary writing in ethics and I shall conclude with a brief summary of each of these proposals.[8] Further work in this area must, I think, develop out of these or similar investigations. It is sufficient for the purposes of this paper to point out how these modes of "explication" provide the *kind* of argument necessary to refute methodological relativism.

The first mode of explication is to *describe* how people in various circumstances actually use the sentences expressing their moral beliefs, how they go about giving reasons in justification of their beliefs, and what their purposes are when they utter normative statements. Then with reference to this description an analysis is made of *what are ordinarily taken to be* "good reasons" for moral beliefs. A set of criteria is thus arrived at which will distinguish good reasoning from bad reasoning in moral disputes. For if we examine what we ordinarily mean by giving good reasons for or against moral beliefs we find certain characteristics which reasons must possess in order to be called "good reasons." We then simply make explicit just what those characteristics are so that it can always be decided in any given case whether a reason offered in justification of a moral belief is a good one or a poor one.[9] This method of explication is not, therefore, merely inductive or descriptive. It yields standards of validity which can be applied to arguments for the purpose of judging the intellectual obligation we have to accept or reject them. It is an explication not only of the *facts* but of the *logic* of moral reasoning.

A second way of explicating the ordinary methods and reasons used in practical life for settling moral disputes, justifying moral beliefs, and arriving at moral decisions is (1) to define a certain class of men whom we would ordinarily accept as competent judges, (2) to define a certain class of judgments made by these men which would ordinarily be accepted as reasonable judgments, and (3) to stipulate a set of principles or standards which, if they were applied to moral disputes and decisions by a competent person, would render the judgments of that person the same as the reasonable judgments of competent judges.[10] A

---

[8] Among classical philosophers I should mention Hume and Kant as having made a beginning in the adoption of this approach to ethics.

[9] This is essentially the method used by Stephen Toulmin (*op. cit.*) and by Arthur E. Murphy in his unpublished Matchette Foundation Lectures, "How Can Moral Judgments Be Universally Valid?" and "How Can Moral Conflicts Be Rationally Resolved?" The method is also used in J. B. Pratt's *Reason in the Art of Living* (New York, 1949), ch. xiv, R. M. Hare's *The Language of Morals* (Oxford, 1952), and P. H. Nowell-Smith's *Ethics* (London, 1954).

[10] This method has been presented very cogently by John Rawls in "Outline of a Decision Procedure for Ethics," *Philosophical Review*, LX (April, 1951). I owe my use of the term "explication" to Rawls, although he might not accept as broad a usage for the term as mine.

somewhat similar method of explication is suggested by Roderick Firth in his article, "Ethical Absolutism and the Ideal Observer." [11] Here the method consists in making explicit the characteristics an observer would have if he were an ideal observer in settling a moral conflict in a rational way or in giving reasons for a moral belief or in arriving at a reasonable decision. The characteristics of an ideal observer are found, says Firth, "by examining the procedures which we actually regard, implicitly or explicitly, as the rational ones for deciding ethical questions." [12]

The third method of explication is that used by Everett W. Hall in his *What Is Value?* (New York, 1952). Hall is more concerned with syntactical and semantical than with logical or epistemological questions. He explicates what is involved in the use of normative sentences by a linguistic analysis which is constantly referred to what we ordinarily intend by uttering normative sentences in everyday life. This linguistic analysis attempts to make clear the syntax and semantics of moral discourse as it occurs in practical (nonphilosophical) situations. In particular, it attempts to make clear that which, in the case of normative sentences, is analogous to the truth-value of descriptive statements and to the facts or states of affairs which make descriptive statements true. Hall is in search of a "clarified language" which will reveal what is implicit but hidden in ordinary normative discourse. His careful account of the syntax and semantics of this "clarified language" provides one sort of explication of moral reasoning.

In conclusion, if the methodological relativist still persists in asking, "Why choose this method rather than that?" and demands an answer to the question, Why choose *explication* as a method? the reply is simply that explication does what we start out trying to do. We begin by seeing whether there is a *rational* procedure for settling moral conflicts, or whether *good reasons* can be given for justifying moral beliefs, or whether there is a *reasonable* way of arriving at a moral decision. What does this mean? It means what we *ordinarily* mean by using the terms "rational," "good reasons," and "reasonable." Why should it mean anything else? Explication is simply the process by which this ordinary meaning is brought to light and made precise. If it is then asked, "But why seek a rational way of settling a dispute, or good reasons for justifying moral beliefs, or a reasonable way of arriving at a moral decision?" the answer is that we start out to do this because it is a real problem in practical life. People just do try to find out how to be reasonable in questions of ethics. And explanation clarifies for them what is ordinarily meant, that is, what *they* mean, by being reasonable in such matters.

---

[11] *Philosophy and Phenomenological Research,* XII (March, 1952).
[12] *Ibid.,* p. 332.

27. EGOISM IN ETHICS

Kai Nielsen

Kai Nielsen *is Professor of Philosophy at the University of Calgary, Canada. For many years he taught at New York University. He has written* Reason and Practice: A Modern Introduction to Philosophy *(1971) and numerous articles in philosophical journals.*

I

Egoism in ethics may be divided into psychological egoism and ethical egoism. The former, which must be clearly distinguished from ethical egoism, is a theory of human motivation. Stated most simply, the psychological egoist argues that man always in fact seeks his own good. And ethical egoism, in any form, argues that man *ought* always to seek his own good. Ethical egoism may take two logically independent forms: it may be developed as an ethical egoism of *ends* or an ethical egoism of *means*.

The initial plausibility of egoism stems from taking it as a psychological doctrine of human motivation. If psychological egoism is false, this certainly does not entail that ethical egoism is also false, but it undermines the rather superficial persuasiveness of the doctrine. In fact, the truth of ethical egoism implies the falsity of psychological egoism.[1] This can be seen to be the case by examining the very use of terms like 'ethical egoism' and 'psychological egoism.' The ethical egoist wishes to say that man *ought* always to seek his own good. But 'ought'—at least when used in moral discourse—is taken to imply 'can.' This means that for any act about which it is appropriate to say that it ought to be done, it follows that one can choose either to do it or not to do it. This is usually taken to mean that man *in fact* is physically and psychologically able to choose between alternative courses of action.[2]

From Philosophy and Phenomenological Research, *Vol. XIX, No. 4, 1959, pp. 502–510. Reprinted by permission of author and the editor.*

---

[1] At this point, as well as several other places in this paper, I am indebted to Professor Charles A. Baylis although I would not like to hold him responsible for any shortcomings that my argument may exhibit.

[2] I do not wish this to be confused with any decision for or against the doctrine of "free will." A deterministic view could well be developed that would not conflict with anything said above. For one such formulation see Charles A. Baylis, "Rational Preference, Determinism and Moral Obligation," *The Journal of Philosophy,* Vol. XLVII, No. 3, February 2, 1950, pp. 57–63.

The psychological egoist is asserting that as a matter of *fact* man always does seek his own good. But if this is the case, then the truth of psychological egoism is incompatible with the truth of ethical egoism. This is true for the following reasons: ethical egoism asserts that man *ought* always to seek his own good. 'Ought' is taken to imply 'can' in the quite unexceptional sense in which the ethical egoist wishes to use it, but if psychological egoism, in asserting that man always *in fact* does seek his own good, denies 'can' in the sense of 'factually can,' then it trivially follows as merely a matter of logic that psychological and ethical egoism cannot both be true.

II

However, in saying that the initial plausibility of all forms of **ethic**al egoism stems from psychological egoism a much simpler point was intended. The point is simply this: the initial "convincing" character of egoism stems from the rather obvious psychological observation that an extraordinary amount of our behavior, even that which is "officially" nonegoistic, is often revealed, in even a relatively superficial introspection, as egoistic.

The truth or falsity of a doctrine of psychological egoism is, of course, a complicated psychological question, but it is apparent that man, in the vast majority of his dealings, acts, as Spinoza put it, so as to inhere in his own being. To meet the many obvious examples of at least apparently altruistic behavior, psychological egoism is driven, in attempting to make its theory plausible at all, to the doctrine that man is not always *consciously* egoistic. There is no question, as psychoanalytic studies have made increasingly apparent, that the "self-sacrifice" of many a mother for her children is at bottom an effort of a rather crushed personality to gain or regain lost or wavering self-esteem; or, the "self-sacrifice" may be a maneuver on the part of a woman, disappointed in her relationships with her husband, to bind her children to her through acts of "self-sacrifice." [3]

This contention of the psychological egoist is ostensibly, at least, an empirical claim. It is important to realize that it is not just a claim that people *sometimes* act this way, but rather the much stronger claim that *all* people *always* act this way. But how could the psychological egoist prove this? It is not, on his own admission, analytically true. How would we ever know whether all men always act in that way? If we mean by 'all men' all men who are now living, the statement is verifiable in principle, that is, it is logically possible to verify it. It may

---

[3] The mother in D. H. Lawrence's *Sons and Lovers* is a fictional example of this unfortunately not infrequent character trait.

even be physically or technically possible to verify that all men always consciously seek their own good even in the above context.[4] But to say in any of the three mentioned senses that the egoist's claim is verifiable is only to say that it is a meaningful empirical statement, not that it is a *true* or even a verified empirical statement. It only means that it *might* be true. It does not entail that it *is* true or that there is any evidence for it at all. We have only to ask the psychological egoist what the evidence for his claim is, or what he would take as a falsification of his claim, to bring out the "metaphysical" nature of his contention. True enough, people often do seek their own good and neglect what is called "the common good." These two things do not prove, however, that all people *always* do so or even that they *ever* do what commonsensically would be regarded as paradigm cases of altruistic behavior for essentially selfish reasons. The egoist must supply some evidence that some people do in fact go to their death willingly because the prior anticipatory good is so great that it outweighs the resultant evil of death and violent destruction. But such a proof even *if* it were forthcoming is not enough. The psychological egoist must prove that it is at least probable that all men always act on such egoistic motives in such contexts. I do not see that there is the slightest evidence for this contention of the egoist. Without this proof the psychological egoist's contention is mere dogma.

There is a Freudian tack the psychological egoist might take. It might be possible for a psychological egoist to argue that unconsciously each man is seeking his own death. There are in all human beings, according to one theory, "two fundamentally different kinds of instincts, the sexual instincts, in the widest sense of the word (Eros) and the aggressive instincts, whose aim is destruction."[5] The so-called death instinct (Thanatos) as it is fused (as on Freud's theory it always is) with Eros is exhibited in sadism and masochism. Man's altruistic behavior is really, on this theory, a form of masochism (pleasure in self-torture) erotically bound.

While the phenomenon of masochism is too well established in psychological theory to be reasonably denied, it is well to distinguish this frequent clinical phenomenon from a *metapsychological* theory which would argue that there is this form of self-aggression in all human beings which, together with sadistic impulses, constitute an all-pervasive impulse toward death. If this theory is used to bolster psychological egoism, it is not conclusively refutable, but it is also without

---

[4] For the distinction between physical, technical and logically possible verification see Hans Reichenbach, "The Verifiability Theory of Meaning," in *Readings in the Philosophy of Science* (Feigl and Brodbeck, eds.), p. 97, and Hans Reichenbach, *Elements of Symbolic Logic*, Chapter VIII.

[5] Sigmund Freud, *Three Contributions to the Theory of Sex*, p. 77.

a crucial test that would establish its truth. Overtly, egoistic behavior can be explained by the pleasure principle, and all exceptions as cases of either sadism or masochism. But if this "theory" is to be more than a dogma, we must be able to say what it would be like for it to be wrong.

The skeptic might say at this point that although my reasoning seems plausible I must have missed the point of psychological egoism. Psychological egoism has occurred and reoccurred throughout the history of ethics from Democritus to Gardner Williams. And in addition to the philosophers, it is a "theory" that frequently recommends itself to reflective common sense. If it is so patently absurd, why has it been such a hardy perennial and why has it seemed so plausible to so many "tough-minded" people? While neither longevity nor common consent is a good test for truth, it is the better part of wisdom to pay close attention to such a recurrent theory as psychological egoism. Now, if my above argument is correct, the plausibility of psychological egoism is very slight indeed: but, I still need to show why people have come to think it so plausible, and to lay bare the philosophical *malaise* that motivates psychological egoism.

It is an analytic truth that we would not do any of the acts we commonly regard as voluntary acts unless we were *motivated* to do them. In ordinary language, we might restate this so: *We only do what we prefer doing or (in some contexts) dislike least.* Let us call this (1). But we easily confuse (1) with (2), i.e., we only do that which satisfies our own personal (selfish) desires, or with (3), i.e., we only do that which promotes our own good. The psychological egoist mistakenly takes (1), (2), and (3) to be equivalent; but they are not equivalent in any of the usual senses of that word.

I will now try to make good my claim that (1) and (2) are not equivalent. After the explication of the differences between (1) and (2), the reader will be able to see readily that a similar explication would apply to (1) and (3).

It is, of course, a truism that all my preferences must be my own personal preferences, for only I can have them; but this does not mean (in any ordinary sense) that my preferences must be selfish preferences. If we concentrate our attention on the subject of the preferences rather than on the objects of preference we are apt to think (1) and (2) have the same meaning. But we must recall that our preferences also are *for something*, that is, they have some object. Sometimes we prefer our own pleasure, happiness, or our own maximum satisfaction of desire (another vague phrase); but food, sex, companionship, recognition, the welfare of family and friends and sometimes even mankind as a whole are also the objects of our preferences.

Williams in defending egoism (reflecting in all probability Butler's classic critique of psychological egoism) is willing to acknowledge this. He remarks: "Love is absolutely unselfish in the ordinary sense that it aims wholly at the welfare of others. But it is absolutely selfish in a Pickwickian sense; since it is a part of a self, its expression is that self's *self*-expression, and its satisfaction is that self's satisfaction." [6] In an ordinary sense we may say that at least some preferences are unselfish or not egoistic, though in a Pickwickian sense of 'selfish' all our preferences are "selfish preferences," i.e., they spring from a person or are located in a given organism. All preferences are located in some organism (human or infrahuman), but this is not to say in any ordinary sense that all preferences are "selfish preferences." Yet it is the ordinary sense of 'selfish preference' that causes worry when we say that all human acts are rooted in preferences. If the psychological egoist says that egoistic aims (i.e., selfish antisocial aims) are the only *ultimate* aims people have he must give some evidence for this. And it will not help him in the slightest to say that no one would ever do anything if he didn't want to do it, for this only shows that a voluntary act, to be a 'voluntary act,' must be a preferred act or an act toward which the actor has a pro-attitude. It says nothing at all about the goals or objects of our preferences.

Alternatively, the psychological egoist may take a different tack. If he says that egoistic aims are the only aims a rational and tough-minded man ought to have he has left psychological egoism for ethical egoism; and, as we have seen in Part I, psychological egoism and ethical egoism are logically incompatible.

Thus (1) is radically different from (2). It is obviously also radically different from (3). The truth of (1) does not entail the truth of (2) and/or (3). (1) does not even serve as good evidence for (2) or (3). But if we do *not* pay careful heed to the uses or functions of our language it is very easy to confuse truisms like (1) with statements like (2) and (3). We *misunderstand* the logic of our language. Perplexed by this, we then recall how often it is that people rationalize and how often it is that intentions which parade as altruistic and high-minded are actually egoistic and selfish in the extreme. We remember our Ibsen and Cellini as well as our Mill and Epicurus, though we forget our Tolstoy and Dickins. We combine our odd linguistic beliefs, which result from a faulty understanding of the functions of our lan-

---

[6] Gardner Williams, "The Inevitability of Egoism in Ethics," *Papers of the Michigan Academy of Science and Letters,* Vol. XXXVII (1951), p. 494. E. W. Hall's review of Williams' *Humanistic Ethics* is worth noting with respect to this issue and with respect to the issue noted in Footnote 9. See E. W. Hall, *Ethics,* Vol. LXIII, October, 1952, pp. 69–70.

guage, with confirmed empirical beliefs, and conclude, plausibly (though falsely), that psychological egoism is true. From both the vantage point of language and from factual observation our vision is blurred by a one-sided diet.

III

A purely ethical egoism divorced from a psychological egoism is also difficult to render plausible. Taken as a doctrine of *ends* the ethical egoist might argue that all value or good terminates in immediate prizings and disprizings. The final test of the valuable is what I like in the way of experience. This experience in its most primitive state is irreducibly personal, and only later in a state of partly settled inquiry does it become "shared." Thus, when A says "X is valuable," he is really only saying in a confusing and elliptical way, "I value X." To be meaningful all valuings must be identified with a valuer. Good, then, is always "good for me." That there are "shared goods" and that occasionally self-sacrifice is deemed fitting, only reflects that some men have gone beyond "human bondage" and have an "adequate idea" of their own needs and the means by which they are realized. In short, they have become "enlightened" egoists and realize that their personal good can be insured in the long run only if at least occasionally they do perform "altruistic" and "nonegoistic" acts and urge others to do likewise.[7]

An ethical egoism would not have to explain away instances of what would ordinarily be called altruistic behavior as disguised instances of egoistic behavior, but could simply assert altruistic ideals are mistaken moral ideals and that we *ought* to seek only our own good.

It is plausible to contend that an ethical egoism of ends could justify a goodly number of our obviously nonegoistic acts as instrumental to an enlightened self-interest, but again the difficulty returns of explaining *all* nonegoistic ethical action on this basis. It is most paradoxical on such a theory to say that a man who volunteers for a rearguard action that will most probably result in his death considers this as a good instrumental to his welfare. This might be plausible if the egoist in question were also a supernaturalist and felt that this action would be instrumental to his reward in heaven. But it is at least thinkable that the egoist might be an atheist and how, if he were an atheist, this act could then be viewed as personally instrumentally good is far from clear.

---

[7] This type of view has been briefly but baldly stated by Gardner Williams in "Ethics for Scientific Humanists" and "The Relativity of Right" in *Humanist World Digest*, November, 1956, and February, 1957, respectively.

When Professor X (an ethical egoist) claims that the end of all moral action ought to be the self-interest of the individual involved, what is he claiming? He may be taken to mean that all men ought to seek their own self-interest as an end, but how then will the fact—if it is a fact—that all valuings terminate in the immediately prized help him? The latter is a factual statement, but Professor X's statement is a *normative* statement stating a moral criterion. The fact that all valuings are "for me" in the sense that all value is derivative from direct prizings does not entail, in any usual sense of 'entail,' that "all men ought to seek their own interest as an end." From the factual premise *about* valuings we could with as much (or as little) justification derive the normative premise, "the only worthy moral end is the cultivation of a Good Will," or any other normative premise that might be desired.

Alternatively, Professor X might be taken, though with less plausibility, to be asserting not the universal statement that all men ought to seek their own good, but only that he, Professor X, ought to seek solely his own good. But then this statement would only tell us what Professor X ought to do and not what all men, a group of men, or even any other men ought to do. A moral criterion is public. Thus his statement could not possibly serve as a moral criterion for any morality no matter how iconoclastic. The very uses of both 'moral' and 'criterion' make the above egotistic use of 'moral criterion' completely unintelligible. The egoist's use of 'moral criterion' does not even bear a family resemblance to the ordinary uses of 'moral criterion.' We have only similar tokens (sign vehicles) with completely different uses.

The final alternative for egoism in ethics is ethical egoism as a doctrine of *means*. As a doctrine of means, ethical egoism could be completely compatible with an altruistic doctrine of ends or with an objective ethical theory. This last variety of ethical egoist (Professor Y may serve as its protagonist) need merely assert that good-on-the-whole or what is commonly called "the common good" can best be achieved by each man consciously seeking his own good. Yet in the face of the above-mentioned exceptions to what would normally be considered egoistic behavior, an ethical egoism of means is also difficult to hold. It is usually felt that certain acts involving self-sacrifice ought, under certain conditions, to be performed to insure the common good. An ethical egoist of this type might argue that a common good that is nobody's individual good would not be a suitable ideal and would not be in fact what is usually meant by 'good' at all. This seems to be obviously (and tritely) true. Certainly, it is important to take proper account, in constructing criteria for good-on-the-whole, of the goods of particular individuals. Yet if psychological egoism is given up and an ethical egoism of ends is given up, an ethical egoism as a doctrine of means seems at a loss to explain the obvious "fact" of everyday moral experience that self-sacrifice—and sometimes even extreme self-sacrifice—is upon occasion necessary for the common good. Ethical egoism must contend that it is *never* right for a soldier to volunteer for a rear-guard action that will almost certainly mean his own death. This must be so, no matter how just the war or how great the needs of his comrades and country. An ethical egoism of this type makes the *factual* claim that the exclusive seeking one's own good always best contributes to good-on-the-whole. We are not dealing here with purely moral principles but with whether certain moral principles will be more casually effective in achieving certain goals, e.g., good-on-the-whole. Yet clearly sometimes in cases like that of a man or group of men fighting a rear-guard action more total good is realized in the universe than if the rear-guard fighters had followed through on egotistic principles.

The ethical egoist can save himself here only by offering some bizarre persuasive definition of 'good-on-the-whole.' Yet, at least within Western Culture, there is, generally speaking, a fairly stable conception of the common good. If this last extra-ordinary kind of egoist denied this conception and redefined 'good-on-the-whole' in some other fashion to make it consonant with his *theory*, his critic might finally have to smile tolerantly and grant him that this, in some "Alice-In-Wonderland world," is a "consistently thinkable" view. If 'good' is so defined, then he cannot be refuted conclusively; but it can be held against his view that it does not fit the usual use of moral words and that if he will use moral language as it is usually used his view cannot be sustained.

The ethical egoist might reply that his opponent is here making only a rather interesting sociological and philological observation, but that the objection does not even tend to disprove his theory. To follow this rebuttal through would be to launch into a discussion of the role of conceptual analysis or linguistic analysis in ethics. This, of course, would require a paper of some considerable length. Here I can only make a few brief comments.

Whether we start out talking about common moral experience or about the actual language of moral discourse, our *subject matter* in ethics remains the moral assessments and moral arguments we actually make.[8] Egoists, by and large, have recognized this in practice. Hobbes

---

[8] This has been well put by A. I. Melden, "Two Comments on Utilitarianism," *Philosophical Review*, October, 1951, Vol. LX, pp. 512–513. In the above broad sense both Edwards and Mandelbaum agree about the subject matter of ethics, though the former explicates actual moral discourse via a Wittgenstein linguistic method and the latter turns to actual moral experience with a modified phenomenological method. See Paul Edwards, *The Logic of Moral Discourse*, pp. 19–21 and 77–81, and Maurice Mandelbaum, *The Phenomenology of Moral Experience*, Chapter 1.

had a different rationale for accepting many of our common-sense moral appraisals but he accepted them nonetheless. Gardner Williams (a latter-day egoist) does much the same thing.[9] They do not make actual moral recommendations of an iconoclastic or nihilistic kind. Finally we may, as Nietszche, wish to go beyond moral good and evil altogether. Perhaps (if we do not put too much weight on the 'ethical' in 'ethical egoism') that is what the "ethical egoist" wishes to account for. He may want to point out that finally we can give no further reason for being moral than that being moral is a good *for us*. If another person does not find that being moral is a good for him, there is, in the last analysis, nothing of an intellectual sort that we can say to him. A good, finally, is not a good unless it is a good for the individual. We will only take a moral point of view if taking a moral point of view meets our long-range satisfaction. In that case, though the *egoist's* remarks may be of great interest and though they may be relevant to ethics, his remarks are not 'moral remarks' or remarks about or explicative of moral remarks, that is to say, they are not made from within the mode of moral reasoning nor are they metaethical explications of moral reasoning.[10] His value judgments may be maxims of prudence or of self love, but they are not, literally speaking, moral judgments.

I have in my critique proceeded on the assumption that the ethical egoist was sticking to the subject matter and was not asking the question, or "alleged question," "Why be moral?" I have assumed in criticizing ethical egoism that when the ethical egoist refers to his position as an 'ethical position' or speaks of 'moral standards' he uses these phrases in the same way they are used in ordinary language. Within these limitations, I have tried to show that a psychological egoism and an ethical egoism of ends or means are either false or unintelligible. If the "ethical egoist" replies that he is *not* using language as it is ordinarily used, I will reply that he has then changed the subject. If he replies that he is not trying to justify egoism in ethics but is asking, as a candid amoral egoist, "Why should I be moral?" I will again say he has changed the subject. I do not deny his right to do either and

---

[9] Note how Hobbes restates the traditional virtues of the natural law and commonsense tradition while giving them a completely different basis. Thomas Hobbes, *Leviathan* Chapters XIV, XV. See also Gardner Williams, "Comments and Criticism: Universalistic Hedonism vs. Hedonic Individual Relativism," *The Journal of Philosophy*, Vol. LII, February 3, 1955, pp. 72–77, and most particularly Gardner Williams, "The Inevitability of Egoism in Ethics," *Papers of the Michigan Academy of Science, Arts and Letters*, Vol. XXXVII, 1951, pp. 494–495.

[10] For the conception of the mode of ethical reasoning relevant here see Stephen Toulmin, *An Examination of the Place of Reason in Ethics*, pp. 102–104 and Chapters 9, 10, and 11.

I do not regard the question "Why should I be moral?" as self-contradictory or patently absurd;[11] but I would insist that none of these moves by the "ethical egoist" will at all weaken my argument that there is no good reason to accept the view of egoism *in* ethics.[12]

28. RIGHT ACTS AS THOSE WHICH PRODUCE THE MOST HAPPINESS

John Stuart Mill

John Stuart Mill (1806–1873) was the most influential British philosopher in the nineteenth century, his major contributions being made in the areas of logic and ethics. His education as a child was received from his father, James Mill, who was a utilitarian philosopher and economist. John Stuart Mill's major published works were completed while he was employed by the East Endia Company. Those works are: The System of Logic *(1843),* The Principles of Political Economy *(1848),* On Liberty *(1859), and* Utilitarianism *(1861). The following selection is taken from the latter work, one of the most important and influential books to appear in the area of moral philosophy.*

The creed which accepts as the foundation of morals "utility" or the "greatest happiness principle" holds that actions are right in proportion as they tend to promote happiness; wrong as they tend to produce the reverse of happiness. By happiness is intended pleasure and the absence of pain; by unhappiness, pain and the privation of pleasure. To give a clear view of the moral standard set up by the theory, much more requires to be said; in particular, what things it includes in the ideas of pain and pleasure, and to what extent this is

---

[11] I have argued for this as against Toulmin and Melden elsewhere. See my "Is 'Why Should I be Moral?' an Absurdity?" *Australasian Journal of Philosophy*, Vol. 36, No. 1 (1958), pp. 25–31.

[12] For my remarks about the relation of philosophy to language I am, of course, deeply indebted to Ludwig Wittgenstein's *Philosophical Investigations*. For an elaborate and brilliant defense of a "linguistic method in ethics" see Everett W. Hall, *What is Value?*, Chapter 7.

left an open question. But these supplementary explanations do not affect the theory of life on which this theory of morality is grounded —namely, that pleasure and freedom from pain are the only things desirable as ends; and that all desirable things (which are as numerous in the utilitarian as in any other scheme) are desirable either for pleasure inherent in themselves or as means to the promotion of pleasure and the prevention of pain.

Now such a theory of life excites in many minds, and among them in some of the most estimable in feeling and purpose, inveterate dislike. To suppose that life has (as they express it) no higher end than pleasure—no better and nobler object of desire and pursuit—they designate as utterly mean and groveling, as a doctrine worthy only of swine, to whom the followers of Epicurus were, at a very early period, contemptuously likened; and modern holders of the doctrine are occasionally made the subject of equally polite comparisons by its German, French, and English assailants.

When thus attacked, the Epicureans have always answered that it is not they, but their accusers, who represent human nature in a degrading light, since the accusation supposes human beings to be capable of no pleasures except those of which swine are capable. If this supposition were true, the charge could not be gainsaid, but would then be no longer an imputation; for if the sources of pleasure were precisely the same to human beings and to swine, the rule of life which is good enough for the one would be good enough for the other. The comparison of the Epicurean life to that of beasts is felt as degrading, precisely because a beast's pleasures do not satisfy a human being's conceptions of happiness. Human beings have faculties more elevated than the animal appetites and, when once made conscious of them, do not regard anything as happiness which does not include their gratification. I do not, indeed, consider the Epicureans to have been by any means faultless in drawing out their scheme of consequences from the utilitarian principle. To do this in any sufficient manner, many Stoic, as well as Christian, elements require to be included. But there is no known Epicurean theory of life which does not assign to the pleasures of the intellect, of the feelings and imagination, and of the moral sentiments a much higher value as pleasures than to those of mere sensation. It must be admitted, however, that utilitarian writers in general have placed the superiority of mental over bodily pleasures chiefly in the greater permanency, safety, uncostliness, etc., of the former—that is, in their circumstantial advantages rather than in their intrinsic nature. And on all these points utilitarians have fully proved their case; but they might have taken the other and, as it may be called, higher ground with entire consistency. It is quite compatible with the principle of utility to recognize the fact that some kinds of pleasure are more desirable and more valuable than others. It would be absurd that, while in estimating all other things quality is considered as well as quantity, the estimation of pleasure should be supposed to depend on quantity alone.

If I am asked what I mean by difference of quality in pleasures, or what makes one pleasure more valuable than another, merely as a pleasure, except its being greater in amount, there is but one possible answer. Of two pleasures, if there be one to which all or almost all who have experience of both give a decided preference, irrespective of any feeling of moral obligation to prefer it, that is the more desirable pleasure. If one of the two is, by those who are competently acquainted with both, placed so far above the other that they prefer it, even though knowing it to be attended with a greater amount of discontent, and would not resign it for any quantity of the other pleasure which their nature is capable of, we are justified in ascribing to the preferred enjoyment a superiority in quality so far outweighing quantity as to render it, in comparison, of small account.

Now it is an unquestionable fact that those who are equally acquainted with and equally capable of appreciating and enjoying both do give a most marked preference to the manner of existence which employs their higher faculties. Few human creatures would consent to be changed into any of the lower animals for a promise of the fullest allowance of a beast's pleasures; no intelligent human being would consent to be a fool, no instructed person would be an ignoramus, no person of feeling and conscience would be selfish and base, even though they should be persuaded that the fool, the dunce, or the rascal is better satisfied with his lot than they are with theirs. They would not resign what they possess more than he for the most complete satisfaction of all the desires which they have in common with him. If they ever fancy they would, it is only in cases of unhappiness so extreme that to escape from it they would exchange their lot for almost any other, however undesirable in their own eyes. A being of higher faculties requires more to make him happy, is capable probably of more acute suffering, and certainly accessible to it at more points, than one of an inferior type; but in spite of these liabilities, he can never really wish to sink into what he feels to be a lower grade of existence. We may give what explanation we please of this unwillingness; we may attribute it to pride, a name which is given indiscriminately to some of the most and to some of the least estimable feelings of which mankind are capable; we may refer it to the love of liberty and personal independence, an appeal to which was with the Stoics one of the most effective means for the inculcation of it; to the love of power or to the love of excitement, both of which do really enter into and contribute to it; but its most appropriate appellation is a sense of dignity, which all human beings possess in one form or other, and in some, though by no means in exact, proportion to their higher faculties, and which is so essential a part of the happiness of those in whom it is strong that nothing which conflicts with it could be otherwise than momentarily an object of desire to them. Whoever supposes that this preference takes place at a sacrifice of happiness—that the superior being, in anything like equal circumstances, is not happier than the inferior—confounds the two very different ideas of happiness and content. It is indisputable that the being whose capacities of enjoyment are low has the greatest chance of having them fully satisfied; and a highly endowed being will always feel that any happiness which he can look for, as the world is constituted, is imperfect. But he can learn to bear its imperfections, if they are at all bearable; and they will not make him envy the being who is indeed unconscious of the imperfections, but only because he feels not at all the good which those imperfections qualify. It is better to be a human being dissatisfied than a pig satisfied; better to be Socrates dissatisfied than a fool satisfied. And if the fool, or the pig, are of a different opinion, it is because they only know their own side of the question. The other party to the comparison knows both sides.

It may be objected that many who are capable of the higher pleasures occasionally, under the influence of temptation, postpone them to the lower. But this is quite compatible with a full appreciation of the intrinsic superiority of the higher. Men often, from infirmity of character, make their election for the nearer good, though they know it to be the less valuable; and this no less when the choice is between two bodily pleasures than when it is between bodily and mental. They pursue sensual indulgences to the injury of health, though perfectly aware that health is the greater good. It may be further objected that many who begin with youthful enthusiasm for everything noble, as they advance in years, sink into indolence and selfishness. But I do not believe that those who undergo this very common change voluntarily choose the lower description of pleasures in preference to the higher. I believe that, before they devote themselves exclusively to the one, they have already become incapable of the other. Capacity for the nobler feelings is in most natures a very tender plant, easily killed, not only by hostile influences, but by mere want of sustenance; and in the majority of young persons it speedily dies away if the occupations to which their position in life has devoted them, and the society into which it has thrown them, are not favorable to keeping that higher capacity in exercise. Men lose their high aspirations as they lose their intellectual tastes, because they have not time or opportunity for indulging them; and they addict themselves to inferior pleasures, not because they deliberately prefer them, but because they are either the only ones to which they have access or the only ones which they are any longer capable of enjoying. It may be questioned whether anyone who has remained equally susceptible to both classes of pleasures ever knowingly and calmly preferred the lower, though many, in all ages, have broken down in an ineffectual attempt to combine both.

From this verdict of the only competent judges, I apprehend there can be no appeal. On a question which is the best worth having of two pleasures, or which of two modes of existence is the most grateful to the feelings, apart from its moral attributes and from its consequences, the judgment of those who are qualified by knowledge of both, or, if they differ, that of the majority among them, must be admitted as final. And there needs be the less hesitation to accept this judgment respecting the quality of pleasures, since there is no other tribunal to be referred to even on the question of quantity. What means are there of determining which is the acutest of two pains, or the intensest of two pleasurable sensations, except the general suffrage of those who are familiar with both? Neither pains nor pleasures are homogeneous, and pain is always heterogeneous with pleasure. What is there to decide whether a particular pleasure is worth purchasing at the cost of a particular pain, except the feelings and judgment of the experienced? When, therefore, those feelings and judgment declare the pleasures derived from the higher faculties to be preferable *in kind,* apart from the question of intensity, to those of which the animal nature, disjoined from the higher faculties, is susceptible, they are entitled on this subject to the same regard.

I have dwelt on this point as being a necessary part of a perfectly just conception of utility or happiness considered as the directive rule of human conduct. But it is by no means an indispensable condition to the acceptance of the utilitarian standard; for that standard is not the agent's own greatest happiness, but the greatest amount of happiness altogether; and if it may possibly be doubted whether a noble character is always the happier for its nobleness, there can be no doubt that it makes other people happier, and that the world in general is immensely a gainer by it. Utilitarianism, therefore, could only attain its end by the general cultivation of nobleness of character, even if each individual were only benefited by the nobleness of others, and his own, so far as happiness is concerned, were a sheer deduction from the benefit. But the bare enunciation of such an absurdity as this last renders refutation superfluous.

According to the greatest happiness principle, as above explained, the ultimate end, with reference to and for the sake of which all other things are desirable—whether we are considering our own good or that of other people—is an existence exempt as far as possible from pain, and as rich as possible in enjoyments, both in point of quantity and quality; the test of quality and the rule for measuring it against quantity being the preference felt by those who, in their opportunities of experience, to which must be added their habits of self-consciousness and self-observation, are best furnished with the means of comparison. This, being according to the utilitarian opinion the end of human action, is necessarily also the standard of morality, which may accordingly be defined "the rules and precepts for human conduct," by the observance of which an existence such as has been described might be, to the greatest extent possible, secured to all mankind; and not to them only, but, so far as the nature of things admits, to the whole sentient creation. . . .

The objectors to utilitarianism cannot always be charged with representing it in a discreditable light. On the contrary, those among them who entertain anything like a just idea of its disinterested character sometimes find fault with its standard as being too high for humanity. They say it is exacting too much to require that people shall always act from the inducement of promoting the general interests of society. But this is to mistake the very meaning of a standard of morals and confound the rule of action with the motive of it. It is the business of ethics to tell us what are our duties, or by what test we may know them; but no system of ethics requires that the sole motive of all we do shall be a feeling of duty; on the contrary, ninety-nine hundredths of all our actions are done from other motives, and rightly so done if the rule of duty does not condemn them. It is the more unjust to utilitarianism that this particular misapprehension should be made a ground of objection to it, inasmuch as utilitarian moralists have gone beyond almost all others in affirming that the motive has nothing to do with the morality of the action, though much with the worth of the agent. He who saves a fellow creature from drowning does what is morally right, whether his motive be duty or the hope of being paid for his trouble; he who betrays the friend that trusts him is guilty of a crime, even if his object be to serve another friend to whom he is under greater obligations.[1] But to speak only of actions done from the motive of duty,

---

[1] An opponent, whose intellectual and moral fairness it is a pleasure to acknowledge (the Rev. J. Llewellyn Davies), has objected to this passage, saying, "Surely the rightness or wrongness of saving a man from drowning does depend very much upon the motive with which it is done. Suppose that a tyrant, when his enemy jumped into the sea to escape from him, saved him from drowning simply in order that he might inflict upon him more exquisite tortures, would it tend to clearness to speak of that rescue as 'a morally right action'? Or suppose again, according to one of the stock illustrations of ethical

and in direct obedience to principle: it is a misapprehension of the utilitarian mode of thought to conceive it as implying that people should fix their minds upon so wide a generality as the world, or society at large. The great majority of good actions are intended not for the benefit of the world, but for that of individuals, of which the good of the world is made up; and the thoughts of the most virtuous man need not on these occasions travel beyond the particular persons concerned, except so far as is necessary to assure himself that in benefiting them he is not violating the rights, that is, the legitimate and authorized expectations, of anyone else. The multiplication of happiness is, according to the utilitarian ethics, the object of virtue: the occasions on which any person (except one in a thousand) has it in his power to do this on an extended scale—in other words, to be a public benefactor—are but exceptional; and on these occasions alone is he called on to consider public utility; in every other case, private utility, the interest or happiness of some few persons, is all he has to attend to. Those alone the influence of whose actions extends to society in general need concern themselves habitually about so large an object. In the case of abstinences indeed— of things which people forbear to do from moral considerations, though the consequences in the particular case might be beneficial—it would be unworthy of an intelligent agent not to be consciously aware that the action is of a class which, if practiced generally, would be generally injurious, and that this is the ground of the obligation to abstain from it. The amount of regard for the public interest implied in this recogni-

---

inquiries, that a man betrayed a trust received from a friend, because the discharge of it would fatally injure that friend himself or someone belonging to him, would utilitarianism compel one to call the betrayal 'a crime' as much as if it had been done from the meanest motive?"

I submit that he who saves another from drowning in order to kill him by torture afterwards does not differ only in motive from him who does the same thing from duty or benevolence; the act itself is different. The rescue of the man is, in the case supposed, only the necessary first step of an act far more atrocious than leaving him to drown would have been. Had Mr. Davies said, "The rightness or wrongness of saving a man from drowning does depend very much" not upon the motive, but "upon the *intention*," no utilitarian would have differed from him. Mr. Davies, by an oversight too common not to be quite venial, has in this case confounded the very different ideas of Motive and Intention. There is no point which utilitarian thinkers (and Bentham preeminently) have taken more pains to illustrate than this. The morality of the action depends entirely upon the intention—that is, upon what the agent *wills to do*. But the motive, that is, the feeling which makes him will so to do, if it makes no difference in the act, makes none in the morality: though it makes a great difference in our moral estimation of the agent, especially if it indicates a good or a bad habitual *disposition*—a bent of character from which useful, or from which hurtful actions are likely to arise.

tion is no greater than is demanded by every system of morals, for they all enjoin to abstain from whatever is manifestly pernicious to society. . . .

   . . . Again, utility is often summarily stigmatized as an immoral doctrine by giving it the name of "expediency," and taking advantage of the popular use of that term to contrast it with principle. But the expedient, in the sense in which it is opposed to the right, generally means that which is expedient for the particular interest of the agent himself; as when a minister sacrifices the interests of this country to keep himself in place. When it means anything better than this, it means that which is expedient for some immediate object, some temporary purpose, but which violates a rule whose observance is expedient in a much higher degree. The expedient in this sense, instead of being the same thing with the useful, is a branch of the hurtful. Thus it would often be expedient, for the purpose of getting over some momentary embarrassment, or attaining some object immediately useful to ourselves or others, to tell a lie. But inasmuch as the cultivation in ourselves of a sensitive feeling on the subject of veracity is one of the most useful, and the enfeeblement of that feeling one of the most hurtful, things to which our conduct can be instrumental; and inasmuch as any, even unintentional, deviation from truth does that much toward weakening the trustworthiness of human assertion, which is not only the principal support of all present social wellbeing, but the insufficiency of which does more than any one thing that can be named to keep back civilization, virtue, everything on which human happiness on the largest scale depends—we feel that the violation, for a present advantage, of a rule of such transcendent expediency is not expedient, and that he who, for the sake of convenience to himself or to some other individual, does what depends on him to deprive mankind of the good, and inflict upon them the evil, involved in the greater or less reliance which they can place in each other's word, acts the part of one of their worst enemies. Yet that even this rule, sacred as it is, admits of possible exceptions is acknowledged by all moralists; the chief of which is when the withholding of some fact (as of information from a malefactor, or of bad news from a person dangerously ill) would save an individual (especially an individual other than oneself) from great and unmerited evil, and when the withholding can only be effected by denial. But in order that the exception may not extend itself beyond the need, and may have the least possible effect in weakening reliance on veracity, it ought to be recognized and, if possible, its limits defined; and, if the principle of utility is good for anything, it must be good for weighing these conflicting utilities against one another and marking out the region within which one or the other preponderates. . . .

OF WHAT SORT OF PROOF THE PRINCIPLE
OF UTILITY IS SUSCEPTIBLE

. . . Questions of ultimate ends do not admit of proof, in the ordinary acceptation of the term. To be incapable of proof by reasoning is common to all first principles, to the first premises of our knowledge, as well as to those of our conduct. But the former, being matters of fact, may be the subject of a direct appeal to the faculties which judge of fact—namely, our senses and our internal consciousness. Can an appeal be made to the same faculties on questions of practical ends? Or by what other faculty is cognizance taken of them?

Questions about ends are, in other words, questions about what things are desirable. The utilitarian doctrine is that happiness is desirable, and the only thing desirable, as an end; all other things being only desirable as means to that end. What ought to be required of this doctrine, what conditions is it requisite that the doctrine should fulfill —to make good its claim to be believed?

The only proof capable of being given that an object is visible is that people actually see it. The only proof that a sound is audible is that people hear it; and so of the other sources of our experience. In like manner, I apprehend, the sole evidence it is possible to produce that anything is desirable is that people do actually desire it. If the end which the utilitarian doctrine proposes to itself were not, in theory and in practice, acknowledged to be an end, nothing could ever convince any person that it was so. No reason can be given why the general happiness is desirable, except that each person, so far as he believes it to be attainable, desires his own happiness. This, however, being a fact, we have not only all the proof which the case admits of, but all which it is possible to require, that happiness is a good, that each person's happiness is a good to that person, and the general happiness, therefore, a good to the aggregate of all persons. Happiness has made out its title as *one* of the ends of conduct and, consequently, one of the criteria of morality.

But it has not, by this alone, proved itself to be the sole criterion. To do that, it would seem, by the same rule, necessary to show, not only that people desire happiness, but that they never desire anything else. Now it is palpable that they do desire things which, in common language, are decidedly distinguished from happiness. They desire, for example, virtue and the absence of vice no less really than pleasure and the absence of pain. The desire of virtue is not as universal, but it is as authentic a fact as the desire of happiness. And hence, the opponents of the utilitarian standard deem that they have a right to infer that there are other ends of human action besides happiness, and that happiness is not the standard of approbation and disapprobation.

But does the utilitarian doctrine deny that people desire virtue, or maintain that virtue is not a thing to be desired? The very reverse. It maintains not only that virtue is to be desired, but that it is to be desired disinterestedly, for itself. Whatever may be the opinion of utilitarian moralists as to the original conditions by which virtue is made virtue, however they may believe (as they do) that actions and dispositions are only virtuous because they promote another end than virtue, yet this being granted, and it having been decided, from considerations of this description, what *is* virtuous, they not only place virtue at the very head of the things which are good as means to the ultimate end, but they also recognize as a psychological fact the possibility of its being, to the individual, a good in itself, without looking to any end beyond it; and hold that the mind is not in a right state, not in a state conformable to utility, not in the state most conducive to the general happiness, unless it does love virtue in this manner—as a thing desirable in itself, even although, in the individual instance, it should not produce those other desirable consequences which it tends to produce, and on account of which it is held to be virtue. This opinion is not, in the smallest degree, a departure from the happiness principle. The ingredients of happiness are very various, and each of them is desirable in itself, and not merely when considered as swelling an aggregate. The principle of utility does not mean that any given pleasure, as music, for instance, or any given exemption from pain, as for example health, is to be looked upon as means to a collective something termed happiness, and to be desired on that account. They are desired and desirable in and for themselves; besides being means, they are a part of the end. Virtue, according to the utilitarian doctrine, is not naturally and originally part of the end, but it is capable of becoming so; and in those who live it disinterestedly it has become so, and is desired and cherished, not as a means to happiness but as a part of their happiness. . . .

29. RIGHT ACTS AS THOSE WHICH CONFORM TO OPTIMIFIC RULES

John Rawls

John Rawls (1921–   ) is Professor of Philosophy at Harvard
and has taught at Cornell University and the Massachusetts
Institute of Technology. His writings, which have appeared in
leading philosophical journals, have made important contributions to moral theory.

In this paper I want to show the importance of the distinction
between justifying a practice [1] and justifying a particular action falling
under it, and I want to explain the logical basis of this distinction and
how it is possible to miss its significance. While the distinction has
frequently been made,[2] and is now becoming commonplace, there remains the task of explaining the tendency either to overlook it altogether,
or to fail to appreciate its importance.

From Philosophical Review, *Vol. 64, No. 1, 1955, pp. 3–4; 13–18;
22–24; 28; 32. Reprinted by permission of the author and the editor.*

---

[1] I use the word "practice" throughout as a sort of technical term
meaning any form of activity specified by a system of rules which defines
offices, roles, moves, penalties, defenses, and so on, and which gives the
activity its structure. As examples one may think of games and rituals, trials
and parliaments.

[2] The distinction is central to Hume's discussion of justice in *A Treatise
of Human Nature*, bk. III, pt. II, esp. secs. 2–4. It is clearly stated by John
Austin in the second lecture of *Lectures on Jurisprudence* (4th ed.; London,
1873), I, 116ff. (1st ed., 1832). Also it may be argued that J. S. Mill took
it for granted in *Utilitarianism;* on this point cf. J. O. Urmson, "The Interpretation of the Moral Philosophy of J. S. Mill," *Philosophical Quarterly,* vol. III
(1953). In addition to the arguments given by Urmson there are several clear
statements of the distinction in *A System of Logic* (8th ed.; London, 1872),
bk. VI, ch. xii pars. 2, 3, 7. The distinction is fundamental to J. D. Mabbott's
important paper, "Punishment," *Mind,* n.s., vol. XLVIII (April, 1939). More
recently the distinction has been stated with particular emphasis by S. E.
Toulmin in *The Place of Reason in Ethics* (Cambridge, 1950), see esp. ch. xi,
where it plays a major part in his account of moral reasoning. Toulmin doesn't
explain the basis of the distinction, nor how one might overlook its importance,
as I try to in this paper, and in my review of his book (*Philosophical Review,*
vol. LX [October, 1951]), as some of my criticisms show, I failed to understand the force of it. See also H. D. Aiken, "The Levels of Moral Discourse,"
Ethics, vol. LXII (1952), A. M. Quinton, "Punishment," *Analysis,* vol. XIV
(June, 1954), and P. H. Nowell-Smith, *Ethics* (London, 1954), pp. 236–239,
271–273.

To show the importance of the distinction I am going to defend utilitarianism against those objections which have traditionally been made against it in connection with punishment and the obligation to keep promises. I hope to show that if one uses the distinction in question then one can state utilitarianism in a way which makes it a much better explication of our considered moral judgments than these traditional objections would seem to admit.[3] Thus the importance of the distinction is shown by the way it strengthens the utilitarian view regardless of whether that view is completely defensible or not.

To explain how the significance of the distinction may be overlooked, I am going to discuss two conceptions of rules. One of these conceptions conceals the importance of distinguishing between the justification of a rule or pactice and the justification of a particular action falling under it. The other conception makes it clear why this distinction must be made and what is its logical basis. . . .

II

I shall now consider the question of promises. The objection to utilitarianism in connection with promises seems to be this: it is believed that on the utilitarian view when a person makes a promise the only ground upon which he should keep it, if he should keep it, is that by keeping it he will realize the most good on the whole. So that if one asks the question "Why should I keep *my* promise?" the utilitarian answer is understood to be that doing so in *this* case will have the best consequences. And this answer is said, quite rightly, to conflict with the way in which the obligation to keep promises is regarded.

Now of course critics of utilitarianism are not unaware that one defense sometimes attributed to utilitarians is the consideration involving the practice of promise-keeping.[4] In this connection they are supposed to argue something like this: it must be admitted that we feel strictly about keeping promises, more strictly than it might seem our view can account for. But when we consider the matter carefully it is always necessary to take into account the effect which our action will have on the practice of making promises. The promisor must weigh, not

---

[3] On the concept of explication see the author's paper *Philosophical Review,* vol. LX (April, 1951).

[4] Ross, *The Right and the Good,* pp. 37–39, and *Foundations of Ethics* (Oxford, 1939), pp. 92–94. I know of no utilitarian who has used this argument except W. A. Pickard-Cambridge in "Two Problems about Duty," *Mind,* n.s., XLI (April, 1932), 153–157, although the argument goes with G. E. Moore's version of utilitarianism in *Principia Ethica* (Cambridge, 1903). To my knowledge it does not appear in the classical utilitarians; and if one interprets their view correctly this is no accident.

only the effects of breaking his promise on the particular case, but also the effect which his breaking his promise will have on the practice itself. Since the practice is of great utilitarian value, and since breaking one's promise always seriously damages it, one will seldom be justified in breaking one's promise. If we view our individual promises in the wider context of the practice of promising itself we can account for the strictness of the obligation to keep promises. There is always one very strong utilitarian consideration in favor of keeping them, and this will insure that when the question arises as to whether or not to keep a promise it will usually turn out that one should, even where the facts of the particular case taken by itself would seem to justify one's breaking it. In this way the strictness with which we view the obligation to keep promises is accounted for.

Ross has criticized this defense as follows: [5] however great the value of the practice of promising, on utilitarian grounds, there must be some value which is greater, and one can imagine it to be obtainable by breaking a promise. Therefore there might be a case where the promisor could argue that breaking his promise was justified as leading to a better state of affairs on the whole. And the promisor could argue in this way no matter how slight the advantage won by breaking the promise. If one were to challenge the promisor his defense would be that what he did was best on the whole in view of all the utilitarian considerations, which in this case *include* the importance of the practice. Ross feels that such a defense would be unacceptable. I think he is right insofar as he is protesting against the appeal to consequences in general and without further explanation. Yet it is extremely difficult to weigh the force of Ross's argument. The kind of case imagined seems unrealistic and one feels that it needs to be described. One is inclined to think that it would either turn out that such a case came under an exception defined by the practice itself, in which case there would not be an appeal to consequences in general on the particular case, or it would happen that the circumstances were so peculiar that the conditions which the practice presupposes no longer obtained. But certainly Ross is right in thinking that it strikes us as wrong for a person to defend breaking a promise by a general appeal to consequences. For a general utilitarian defense is not open to the promisor: it is not one of the defenses allowed by the practice of making promises.

Ross gives two further counterarguments: [6] First, he holds that

---

[5] Ross, *The Right and the Good*, pp. 38–39.

[6] Ross, *ibid.*, p. 39. The case of the nonpublic promise is discussed again in *Foundations of Ethics*, pp. 95–96, 104–105. It occurs also in Mabbott, "Punishment," *op. cit.*, pp. 155–157, and in A. I. Melden, "Two Comments on Utilitarianism," *Philosophical Review*, LX (October, 1951), 519–523, which discusses Carritt's example in *Ethical and Political Thinking*, p. 64.

it overestimates the damage done to the practice of promising by a failure to keep a promise. One who breaks a promise harms his own name certainly, but it isn't clear that a broken promise always damages the practice itself sufficiently to account for the strictness of the obligation. Second, and more important, I think, he raises the question of what one is to say of a promise which isn't known to have been made except to the promisor and the promisee, as in the case of a promise a son makes to his dying father concerning the handling of the estate.[7] In this sort of case the consideration relating to the practice doesn't weigh on the promisor at all, and yet one feels that this sort of promise is as binding as other promises. The question of the effect which breaking it has on the practice seems irrelevant. The only consequence seems to be that one can break the promise without running any risk of being censured; but the obligation itself seems not the least weakened. Hence it is doubtful whether the effect on the practice ever weighs in the particular case; certainly it cannot account for the strictness of the obligation where it fails to obtain. It seems to follow that a utilitarian account of the obligation to keep promises cannot be successfully carried out.

. . . [these arguments and counterarguments] . . . fail to make the distinction between the justification of a practice and the justification of a particular action falling under it, and therefore they fall into the mistake of taking it for granted that the promisor, like Carritt's official, is entitled without restriction to bring utilitarian considerations to bear in deciding whether to keep *his* promise. But if one considers what the practice of promising is one will see, I think, that it is such as not to allow this sort of general discretion to the promisor. Indeed, the point of the practice is to abdicate one's title to act in accordance with utilitarian and prudential considerations in order that the future may be tied down and plans coordinated in advance. There are obvious utilitarian advantages in having a practice which denies to the promisor, as a defense, any general appeal to the utilitarian principle in accordance with which the practice itself may be justified. There is nothing contradictory, or surprising, in this: utilitarian (or aesthetic) reasons might properly be given in arguing that the game of chess, or baseball, is satisfactory just as it is, or in arguing that it should be changed in various respects, but a player in a game cannot properly appeal to such considerations as reasons for his making one move rather than another.

---

[7] Ross's example is described simply as that of two men dying alone where one makes a promise to the other. Carritt's example (cf, n. 17 supra) is that of two men at the North Pole. The example in the text is more realistic and is similar to Mabbott's. Another example is that of being told something in confidence by one who subsequently dies. Such cases need not be "desert-island arguments" as Newell-Smith seems to believe (cf. his *Ethics*, pp. 239–244).

It is a mistake to think that if the practice is justified on utilitarian grounds then the promisor must have complete liberty to use utilitarian arguments to decide whether or not to keep his promise. The practice forbids this general defense; and it is a purpose of the practice to do this. Therefore what the above arguments presuppose—the idea that if the utilitarian view is accepted then the promisor is bound if, and only if, the application of the utilitarian principle to his own case shows that keeping it is best on the whole—is false. The promisor is bound because he promised: weighing the case on its merits is not open to him.[8]

Is this to say that in particular cases one cannot deliberate whether or not to keep one's promise? Of course not. But to do so is to deliberate whether the various excuses, exceptions and defenses, which are understood by, and which constitute an important part of, the practice, apply to one's own case.[9] Various defenses for not keeping one's promise are allowed, but among them there isn't the one that, on general utilitarian grounds, the promisor (truly) thought his action best on the whole, even though there may be the defense that the consequences of keeping one's promise would have been *extremely* severe. While there are too many complexities here to consider all the necessary details, one can see that the general defense isn't allowed if one asks the following question: what would one say of someone who, when asked why he broke his promise, replied simply that breaking it was best on the whole? Assuming that his reply is sincere, and that his belief was reasonable (i.e., one need not consider the possibility that he was mistaken), I think that one would question whether or not he knows what it means to say "I promise" (in the appropriate circumstances). It would be said of someone who used this excuse without further explanation that he didn't understand what defenses the practice, which defines a promise, allows to him. If a child were to use this excuse one would correct him; for it is part of the way one is taught the concept of a promise to be corrected if one uses this excuse. The point of having the practice would be lost if the practice did allow this excuse.

It is no doubt part of the utilitarian view that every practice should admit the defense that the consequences of abiding by it would have been extremely severe; and utilitarians would be inclined to hold that some reliance on people's good sense and some concession to hard cases is necessary. They would hold that a practice is justified by serving the interests of those who take part in it; and as with any set of rules

---

[8] What I have said in this paragraph seems to me to coincide with Hume's important discussion in the *Treatise of Human Nature*, bk. III, pt. ii, sec. 5; and also sec. 6, par. 8.

[9] For a discussion of these, see H. Sidgwick, *The Methods of Ethics* (6th ed.; London, 1901), bk. III, ch. vi.

there is understood a background of circumstances under which it is expected to be applied and which need not—indeed which cannot—be fully stated. Should these circumstances change, then even if there is no rule which provides for the case, it may still be in accordance with the practice that one be released from one's obligation. But this sort of defense allowed by a practice must not be confused with the general option to weigh each particular case on utilitarian grounds which critics of utilitarianism have thought it necessarily to involve. . . .

III

So far I have tried to show the importance of the distinction between the justification of a practice and the justification of a particular action falling under it by indicating how this distinction might be used to defend utilitarianism against two longstanding objections. One might be tempted to close the discussion at this point by saying that utilitarian considerations should be understood as applying to practices in the first instance and not to particular actions falling under them except insofar as the practices admit of it. One might say that in this modified form it is a better account of our considered moral opinions and let it go at that. But to stop here would be to neglect the interesting question as to how one can fail to appreciate the significance of this rather obvious distinction and can take it for granted that utilitarianism has the consequence that particular cases may always be decided on general utilitarian grounds.[10] I want to argue that this mistake may be connected with misconceiving the logical status of the rules of practices; and to show this I am going to examine two conceptions of rules, two ways of placing them within the utilitarian theory.

-----

[10] So far as I can see it is not until Moore that the doctrine is expressly stated in this way. See, for example, *Principia Ethica,* p. 147, where it is said that the statement "I am morally bound to perform this action" is identical with the statement *"This* action will produce the greatest possible amount of good in the Universe" (my italics). It is important to remember that those whom I have called the classical utilitarians were largely interested in social institutions. They were among the leading economists and political theorists of their day, and they were not infrequently reformers interested in practical affairs. Utilitarianism historically goes together with a coherent view of society, and is not simply an ethical theory, much less an attempt at philosophical analysis in the modern sense. The utilitarian principle was quite naturally thought of, and used, as a criterion for judging social institutions (practices) and as a basis for urging reforms. It is not clear, therefore, how far it is necessary to amend utilitarianism in its classical form. For a discussion of utilitarianism as an integral part of a theory of society, see L. Robbins, *The Theory of Economic Policy in English Classical Political Economy* (London, 1952).

The conception which conceals from us the significance of the distinction I am going to call the summary view. It regards rules in the following way: one supposes that each person decides what he shall do in particular cases by applying the utilitarian principle; one supposes further that different people will decide the same particular case in the same way and that there will be recurrences of cases similar to those previously decided. Thus it will happen that in cases of certain kinds the same decision will be made either by the same person at different times or by different persons at the same time. If a case occurs frequently enough one supposes that a rule is formulated to cover that sort of case. I have called this conception the summary view because rules are pictured as summaries of past decisions arrived at by the *direct* application of the utilitarian principle to particular cases. Rules are regarded as reports that cases of a certain sort have been found on *other* grounds to be properly decided in a certain way (although, of course, they do not *say* this). . . .

1. The point of having rules derives from the fact that similar cases tend to recur and that one can decide cases more quickly if one records past decisions in the form of rules. If similar cases didn't recur, one would be required to apply the utilitarian principle directly, case by case, and rules reporting past decisions would be of no use.

2. The decisions made on particular cases are logically prior to rules. Since rules gain their point from the need to apply the utilitarian principle to many similar cases, it follows that a particular case (or several cases similar to it) may exist whether or not there is a rule covering that case. We are pictured as recognizing particular cases prior to there being a rule which covers them, for it is only if we meet with a number of cases of a certain sort that we formulate a rule. Thus we are able to describe a particular case as a particular case of the requisite sort whether there is a rule regarding *that* sort of case or not. Put another way: what the A's and the B's refer to in rules of the form 'Whenever A do B' may be described as A's and B's whether or not there is the rule 'Whenever A do B', or whether or not there is any body of rules which make up a practice of which that rule is a part.

To illustrate this consider a rule, or maxim, which could arise in this way: suppose that a person is trying to decide whether to tell someone who is fatally ill what his illness is when he has been asked to do so. Suppose the person to reflect and then decide, on utilitarian grounds, that he should not answer truthfully; and suppose that on the basis of this and other like occasions he formulates a rule to the effect that when asked by someone fatally ill what his illness is, one should not tell him. The point to notice is that someone's being fatally ill and asking what his illness is, and someone's telling him, are things that can be described as such whether or not there is this rule. The performance of the action to which the rule refers doesn't require the stage-setting of a practice of which this rule is a part. This is what is meant by saying that on the summary view particular cases are logically prior to rules.

3. Each person is in principle always entitled to reconsider the correctness of a rule and to question whether or not it is proper to follow it in a particular case. As rules are guides and aids, one may ask whether in past decisions there might not have been a mistake in applying the utilitarian principle to get the rule in question, and wonder whether or not it is best in this case. The reason for rules is that people are not able to apply the utilitarian principle effortlessly and flawlessly; there is need to save time and to post a guide. On this view a society of rational utilitarians would be a society without rules in which each person applied the utilitarian principle directly and smoothly, and without error, case by case. On the other hand, ours is a society in which rules are formulated to serve as aids in reaching these ideally rational decisions on particular cases, guides which have been built up and tested by the experience of generations. If one applies this view to rules, one is interpreting them as maxims, as "rules of thumb"; and it is doubtful that anything to which the summary conception did apply would be called a *rule*. Arguing as if one regarded rules in this way is a mistake one makes while doing philosophy.

4. The concept of a *general* rule takes the following form. One is pictured as estimating on what percentage of the cases likely to arise a given rule may be relied upon to express the correct decision, that is, the decision that would be arrived at if one were to correctly apply the utilitarian principle case by case. If one estimates that by and large the rule will give the correct decision, or if one estimates that the likelihood of making a mistake by applying the utilitarian principle directly on one's own is greater than the likelihood of making a mistake by following the rule, and if these considerations held of persons generally, then one would be justified in urging its adoption as a general rule. In this way *general* rules might be accounted for on the summary view. It will still make sense, however, to speak of applying the utilitarian principle case by case, for it was by trying to foresee the results of doing this that one got the initial estimates upon which acceptance of the rule depends. That one is taking a rule in accordance with the summary conception will show itself in the naturalness with which one speaks of the rule as a guide, or as a maxim, or as a generalization from experience, and as something to be laid aside in extraordinary cases where there is no assurance that the generalization will hold and the case must therefore be treated on its merits. Thus there goes with this conception the

notion of a particular exception which renders a rule suspect on a particular occasion.

The other conception of rules I will call the practice conception. On this view rules are pictured as defining a practice. Practices are set up for various reasons, but one of them is that in many areas of conduct each person's deciding what to do on utilitarian grounds case by case leads to confusion, and that the attempt to coordinate behavior by trying to foresee how others will act is bound to fail. As an alternative one realizes that what is required is the establishment of a practice, the specification of a new form of activity; and from this one sees that a practice necessarily involves the abdication of full liberty to act on utilitarian and prudential grounds. It is the mark of a practice that being taught how to engage in it involves being instructed in the rules which define it, and that appeal is made to those rules to correct the behavior of those engaged in it. Those engaged in a practice recognize the rules as defining it. The rules cannot be taken as simply describing how those engaged in the practice in fact behave: it is not simply that they act as if they were obeying the rules. Thus it is essential to the notion of a practice that the rules are publicly known and understood as definitive; and it is essential also that the rules of a practice can be taught and can be acted upon to yield a coherent practice. On this conception, then, rules are not generalizations from the decisions of individuals applying the utilitarian principle directly and independently to recurrent particular cases. On the contrary, rules define a practice and are themselves the subject of the utilitarian principle. . . .

If one compares the two conceptions of rules I have discussed, one can see how the summary conception misses the significance of the distinction between justifying a practice and justifying actions falling under it. On this view rules are regarded as guides whose purpose it is to indicate the ideally rational decision on the given particular case which the flawless application of the utilitarian principle would yield. One has, in principle, full option to use the guides or to discard them as the situation warants without one's moral office being altered in any way: whether one discards the rules or not, one always holds the office of a rational person seeking case by case to realize the best on the whole. But on the practice conception, if one holds an office defined by a practice then questions regarding one's actions in this office are settled by reference to the rules which define the practice. If one seeks to question these rules, then one's office undergoes a fundamental change: one then assumes the office of one empowered to change and criticize the rules, or the office of a reformer, and so on. The summary conception does away with the distinction of offices and the various forms of argument appropriate to each. On that conception there is one office and so no offices at all. It therefore obscures the fact that the utilitarian principle must, in the case of actions and offices defined by a practice, apply to the practice, so that general utilitarian arguments are not available to those who act in offices so defined. . . .

I have tried to show that when we fit the utilitarian view together with the practice conception of rules, where this conception is appropriate,[11] we can formulate it in a way which saves it from several traditional objections. I have further tried to show how the logical force of the distinction between justifying a practice and justifying an action falling under it is connected with the practice conception of rules and cannot be understood as long as one regards the rules of practices in accordance with the summary view. Why, when doing philosophy, one may be inclined to so regard them, I have not discussed. The reasons for this are evidently very deep and would require another paper.

30. RIGHT ACTS AS THOSE WHICH ARE UNIVERSALIZABLE

Immanuel Kant

Immanuel Kant (1726–1806) is considered by many to be the most profound and influential philosopher in the western world, surpassing even those great Greeks, Plato and Aristotle. His most famous work, Critique of Pure Reason *(1781), is generally regarded by philosophers as the most profound, original and important philosophical treatise ever written. In it, Kant attempted to prove that what we take to be features of the real world outside our minds are actually ways in which the human mind organizes and structures the perceptions it receives. In ethics, Kant maintained that valid moral principles are supplied by reason alone independently of experience and feeling. His*

From The Fundamental Principles of the Metaphysic of Morals, *translated by H. J. Paton, 1948. Published by the Hutchinson Publishing Group, Ltd., London, and by Harper Torchbooks, New York. Reprinted by permission of the Hutchinson Publishing Group, Ltd.*

---

[11] As I have already stated, it is not always easy to say where the conception is appropriate. Nor do I care to discuss at this point the general sorts of cases to which it does apply except to say that one should not take it for granted that it applies to many so-called "moral rules." It is my feeling that relatively few actions of the moral life are defined by practices and that the practice conception is more relevant to understanding legal and legal-like arguments than it is to the more complex sort of moral arguments. Utilitarianism must be fitted to different conceptions of rules depending on the case, and no doubt the failure to do this has been one source of difficulty in interpreting it correctly.

Critique of Practical Reason (1788) and The Foundations of the Metaphysics of Morals (1785) are his major works in moral philosophy. The following selection is taken from the latter.

Everything in nature works in accordance with laws. Only a rational being has the power to act *in accordance with his ideas* of laws —that is, in accordance with principles—and only so has he a *will*. Since *reason* is required in order to derive actions from laws, the will is nothing but practical reason. If reason infallibly determines the will, then in a being of this kind the actions which are recognized to be objectively necessary are also subjectively necessary—that is to say, the will is then a power to choose *only that* which reason independently of inclination recognizes to be practically necessary, that is, to be good. But if reason solely by itself is not sufficient to determine the will; if the will is exposed also to subjective conditions (certain impulsions) which do not always harmonize with the objective ones; if, in a word, the will is not *in itself* completely in accord with reason (as actually happens in the case of men); then actions which are recognized to be objectively necessary are subjectively contingent, and the determining of such a will in accordance with objective laws is *necessitation*. That is to say, the relation of objective laws to a will not good through and through is conceived as one in which the will of a rational being, although it is determined by principles of reason, does not necessarily follow these principles in virtue of its own nature.

The conception of an objective principle so far as this principle is necessitating for a will is called a command (of reason), and the formula of this command is called an *Imperative*.

All imperatives are expressed by an *'ought'* (*Sollen*). By this they mark the relation of an objective law of reason to a will which is not necessarily determined by this law in virtue of its subjective constitution (the relation of necessitation). They say that something would be good to do or to leave undone, only they say it to a will which does not always do a thing because it has been informed that this is a good thing to do. . . .

A perfectly good will would thus stand quite as much under objective laws (laws of the good), but it could not on this account be conceived as *necessitated* to act in conformity with law, since of itself, in accordance with its subjective constitution, it can be determined only by the concept of the good. Hence for the *divine* will, and in general for a *holy* will, there are no imperatives: 'I ought' is here out of place, because 'I will' is already of itself necessarily in harmony with the law. Imperatives are in consequence only formulae for expressing the relation of objective laws of willing to the subjective imperfection of the will of this or that rational being—for example, of the human will.

CLASSIFICATION OF IMPERATIVES

All *imperatives* command either *hypothetically* or *categorically*. Hypothetical imperatives declare a possible action to be practically necessary as a means to the attainment of something else that one wills (or that one may will). A categorical imperative would be one which represented an action as objectively necessary in itself apart from its relation to a further end. . . . [Hence] if the action would be good solely as a means to *something else*, the imperative is *hypothetical*; if the action is represented as good *in itself* and therefore as necessary, in virtue of its principle, for a will which of itself accords with reason, then the imperative is *categorical*.

An imperative therefore tells me which of my possible actions would be good; and it formulates a practical rule for a will that does not perform an action straight away because the action is good—whether because the subject does not always know that it is good or because, even if he did know this, he might still act on maxims contrary to the objective principles of practical reason.

A hypothetical imperative thus says only that an action is good for some purpose or other, either *possible* or *actual*. In the fist case it is a *poblematic* practical principle; in the second case an *assertoric* practical principle. A categorical imperative, which declares an action to be objectively necessary in itself without reference to some purpose—that is, even without any further end—ranks as an *apodeictic* practical principle. . . .

All sciences have a practical part consisting of problems which suppose that some end is possible for us and of imperatives which tell us how it is to be attained. Hence the latter can in general be called imperatives of *skill*. Here there is absolutely no question about the rationality or goodness of the end, but only about what must be done to attain it. A prescription required by a doctor in order to cure his man completely and one required by a poisoner in order to make sure of killing him are of equal value so far as each serves to effect its purpose perfectly. Since in early youth we do not know what ends may present themselves to us in the course of life, parents seek above all to make their children learn things *of many kinds;* they provide carefully for *skill* in the use of means to all sorts of *arbitrary* ends, of none of which can they be certain that it could not in the future become an actual purpose of their ward, while it is always *possible* that he might adopt it. Their care in this matter is so great that they commonly neglect on this account to form and correct the judgement of their children about the worth of the things which they might possibly adopt as ends.

There is, however, *one* end that can be presupposed as actual in all rational beings (so far as they are dependent beings to whom imperatives apply); and thus there is one purpose which they not only *can* have, but which we can assume with certainty that they all *do* have by a natural necessity—the purpose, namely, of *happiness*. A hypothetical imperative which affirms the practical necessity of an action as a means to the furtherance of happiness is *assertoric*. We may represent it, not simply as necessary to an uncertain, merely possible purpose, but as necessary to a purpose which we can presuppose *a priori* and with certainty to be present in every man because it belongs to his very being. Now skill in the choice of means to one's own greatest well-being can be called *prudence* in the narrowest sense. Thus an imperative concerned with the choice of means to one's own happiness—that is, a precept of prudence—still remains *hypothetical:* an action is commanded, not absolutely, but only as a means to a further purpose.

Finally, there is an imperative which, without being based on, and conditioned by, any further purpose to be attained by a certain line of conduct, enjoins this conduct immediately. This imperative is *categorical*. It is concerned, not with the matter of the action and its presumed results, but with its form and with the principle from which it follows; and what is essentially good in the action consists in the mental disposition, let the consequences be what they may. This imperative may be called the imperative of *morality*. . . .

HOW ARE IMPERATIVES POSSIBLE?

The question now arises 'How are all these imperatives possible?' This question does not ask how we can conceive the execution of an action commanded by the imperative, but merely how we can conceive the necessitation of the will expressed by the imperative in setting us a task. How an imperative of skill is possible requires no special discussion. Who wills the end, wills (so far as reason has decisive influence on his actions) also the means which are indispensably necessary and in his power. So far as willing is concerned, this proposition is analytic: for in my willing of an object as an effect there is already conceived the causality of myself as an acting cause—that is, the use of means; and from the concept of willing an end the imperative merely extracts the concept of actions necessary to this end. (Synthetic propositions are required in order to determine the means to a proposed end, but these are concerned, not with the reason for performing the act of will, but with the cause which produces the object.) That in order to divide a line into two equal parts on a sure principle I must from its ends describe two intersecting arcs—this is admittedly taught by mathematics only in synthetic propositions; but when I know that the aforesaid effect can be produced only by such an action, the proposition 'If I fully will the effect, I also will the action required for it' is analytic; for it is one and the same thing to conceive something as an effect possible in a certain way through me and to conceive myself as acting in the same way with respect to it. . . .

[With the] categorical imperative or law of morality the reason for our difficulty (in comprehending its possibility) is a very serious one. We have here a synthetic *a priori* practical proposition,[1] and since in theoretical knowledge there is so much difficulty in comprehending the possibility of propositions of this kind, it may readily be gathered that in practical knowledge the difficulty will be no less.

THE FORMULA OF UNIVERSAL LAW

In this task we wish first to enquire whether perhaps the mere concept of a categorical imperative may not also provide us with the formula containing the only proposition that can be a categorical imperative; for even when we know the purport of such an absolute command, the question of its possibility will still require a special and troublesome effort, which we postpone to the final chapter.

When I conceive a *hypothetical* imperative in general, I do not know beforehand what it will contain—until its condition is given. But if I conceive a *categorical* imperative, I know at once what it contains. For since besides the law this imperative contains only the necessity that our maxim [2] should conform to this law, while the law, as we have seen, contains no condition to limit it, there remains nothing over to which the maxim has to conform except the universality of a law as

---

[1] Without presupposing a condition taken from some inclination I connect an action with the will *a priori* and therefore necessarily (although only objectively so—that is, only subject to the Idea of a reason having full power over all subjective impulses to action). Here we have a practical proposition in which the willing of an action is not derived analytically from some other willing already presupposed (for we do not possess any such perfect will), but is on the contrary connected immediately with the concept of the will of a rational being as something which is not contained in this concept.

[2] A *maxim* is a subjective principle of action and must be distinguished from an *objective principle*—namely, a practical law. The former contains a practical rule determined by reason in accordance with the conditions of the subject (often his ignorance or again his inclinations): it is thus a principle on which the subject *acts*. A law, on the other hand, is an objective principle valid for every rational being; and it is a principle on which he *ought to act*—that is, an imperative.

such; and it is this conformity alone that the imperative properly asserts to be necessary.

There is therefore only a single categorical imperative and it is this: '*Act only on that maxim through which you can at the same time will that it should become a universal law.*'

Now if all imperatives of duty can be derived from this one imperative as their principle, then even although we leave it unsettled whether what we call duty may be an empty concept, we shall still be able to show at least what we understand by it and what the concept means.

THE FORMULA OF THE LAW OF NATURE

Since the universality of the law governing the production of effects constitutes what is properly called *nature* in its most general sense (nature as regards its form)—that is, the existence of things so far as determined by universal laws—the universal imperative of duty may also run as follows: '*Act as if the maxim of your action were to become through your will a universal law of nature.*'

ILLUSTRATIONS

We will now enumerate a few duties, following their customary division into duties towards self and duties towards others and into perfect and imperfect duties.

1. A man feels sick of life as the result of a series of misfortunes that has mounted to the point of despair, but he is still so far in possession of his reason as to ask himself whether taking his own life may not be contrary to his duty to himself. He now applies the test 'Can the maxim of my action really become a universal law of nature?' His maxim is 'From self-love I make it my principle to shorten my life if its continuance threatens more evil than it promises pleasure.' The only further question to ask is whether this principle of self-love can become a universal law of nature. It is then seen at once that a system of nature by whose law the very same feeling whose function (*Bestimmung*) is to stimulate the furtherance of life should actually destroy life would contradict itself and consequently could not subsist as a system of nature. Hence this maxim cannot possibly hold as a universal law of nature and is therefore entirely opposed to the supreme principle of all duty.

2. Another finds himself driven to borrowing money because of need. He well knows that he will not be able to pay it back; but he sees too that he will get no loans unless he gives a firm promise to pay it

back within a fixed time. He is inclined to make such a promise; but he has still enough conscience to ask 'Is it now unlawful and contrary to duty to get out of difficulties in this way?' Supposing, however, he did resolve to do so, the maxim of his action would run thus: 'Whenever I believe myself short of money, I will borrow money and promise to pay it back, though I know that this will never be done.' Now this principle of self-love or personal advantage is perhaps quite compatible with my own entire future welfare; only there remains the question 'Is it right?' I therefore transform the demand of self-love into a universal law and frame my question thus: 'How would things stand if my maxim became a universal law?' I then see straight away that this maxim can never rank as a universal law of nature and be self-consistent, but must necessarily contradict itself. For the universality of a law that every one believing himself to be in need can make any promise he pleases with the intention not to keep it would make promising, and the very purpose of promising, itself impossible, since no one would believe he was being promised anything but would laugh at utterances of this kind as empty shams.

3. A third finds in himself a talent whose cultivation would make him a useful man for all sorts of purposes. But he sees himself in comfortable circumstances, and he prefers to give himself up to pleasure rather than to bother about increasing and improving his fortunate natural aptitudes. Yet he asks himself further 'Does my maxim of neglecting my natural gifts, besides agreeing in itself with my tendency to indulgence, agree also with what is called duty?' He then sees that a system of nature could indeed always subsist under such a universal law, although (like the South Sea Islanders) every man should let his talents rust and should be bent on devoting his life solely to idleness, indulgence, procreation, and, in a word, to enjoyment. Only he cannot possibly *will* that this should become a universal law of nature or should be implanted in us as such a law by a natural instinct. For as a rational being he necessarily wills that all his powers should be developed, since they serve him, and are given him, for all sorts of possible ends.

4. Yet a *fourth* is himself flourishing, but he sees others who have to struggle with great hardships (and whom he could easily help); and he thinks 'What does it matter to me? Let every one be as happy as Heaven wills or as he can make himself; I won't deprive him of anything; I won't even envy him; only I have no wish to contribute anything to his well-being or to his support in distress!' Now admittedly if such an attitude were a universal law of nature, mankind could get on perfectly well—better no doubt than if everybody prates about sympathy and goodwill, and even takes pains, on occasion, to

practise them, but on the other hand cheats where he can, traffics in human rights, or violates them in other ways. But although it is possible that a universal law of nature could subsist in harmony with this maxim, yet it is impossible to *will* that such a principle should hold everywhere as a law of nature. For a will which decides in this way would be in conflict with itself, since many a situation might arise in which the man needed love and sympathy from others, and in which, by such a law of nature sprung from his own will, he would rob himself of all hope of the help he wants for himself.

THE CANON OF MORAL JUDGEMENT

These are some of the many actual duties—or at least of what we take to be such—whose derivation from the single principle cited above leaps to the eye. We must *be able to will* that a maxim of our action should become a universal law—this is the general canon for all moral judgement of action. Some actions are so constituted that their maxim cannot even be *conceived* as a universal law of nature without contradiction, let alone be *willed* as what *ought* to become one. In the case of others we do not find this inner impossibility, but it is still impossible to *will* that their maxim should be raised to the universality of a law of nature, because such a will would contradict itself. It is easily seen that the first kind of action is opposed to strict or narrow (rigorous) duty, the second only to wider (meritorious) duty; and thus that by these examples all duties—so far as the type of obligation is concerned (not the object of dutiful action)—are fully set out in their dependence on our single principle.

If we now attend to ourselves whenever we transgress a duty, we find that we in fact do not will that our maxim should become a universal law—since this is impossible for us—but rather that its opposite should remain a law universally: we only take the liberty of making an *exception* to it for ourselves (or even just for this once) to the advantage of our inclination. . . .

We have thus at least shown this much—that if duty is a concept which is to have meaning and real legislative authority for our actions, this can be expressed only in categorical imperatives and by no means in hypothetical ones. At the same time—and this is already a great deal—we have set forth distinctly, and determinately for every type of application, the content of the categorical imperative, which must contain the principle of all duty (if there is to be such a thing at all). But we are still not so far advanced as to prove *a priori* that there actually is an imperative of this kind—that there is a practical law which by itself commands absolutely and without any further motives, and that the following of this law is duty. . . .

Our question therefore is this: 'Is it a necessary law *for all rational beings* always to judge their actions by reference to those maxims of which they can themselves will that they should serve as universal laws?' If there is such a law, it must already be connected (entirely *a priori*) with the concept of the will of a rational being as such. But in order to discover this connexion we must, however much we may bristle, take a step beyond it—that is, into metaphysics, although into a region of it different from that of speculative philosophy, namely, the metaphysic of morals. . . . Here . . . we are discussing objective practical laws, and consequently the relation of a will to itself as determined solely by reason. Everything related to the empirical then falls away of itself; for if *reason entirely by itself* determines conduct (and it is the possibility of this which we now wish to investigate), it must necessarily do so *a priori*.

THE FORMULA OF THE END IN ITSELF

The will is conceived as a power of determining oneself to action in *accordance with the idea of certain laws*. And such a power can be found only in rational beings. Now what serves the will as a subjective ground of its self-determination is an *end;* and this, if it is given by reason alone, must be equally valid for all rational beings. What, on the other hand, contains merely the ground of the possibility of an action whose effect is an end is called a *means*. The subjective ground of a desire is an *impulsion* (*Triebfeder*); the objective ground of a volition is a *motive* (*Bewegungsgrund*). Hence the difference between subjective ends, which are based on impulsions, and objective ends, which depend on motives valid for every rational being. Practical principles are *formal* if they abstract from all subjective ends; they are *material*, on the other hand, if they are based on such ends and consequently on certain impulsions. Ends that a rational being adopts arbitrarily as *effects* of his action (material ends) are in every case only relative; for it is solely their relation to special characteristics in the subject's power of appetition which gives them their value. Hence this value can provide no universal principles, no principles valid and necessary for all rational beings and also for every volition—that is, no practical laws. Consequently all these relative ends can be the ground only of hypothetical imperatives.

Suppose, however, there were something *whose existence* has *in itself* an absolute value, something which as *an end in itself* could be a ground of determinate laws; then in it, and in it alone, would there be the ground of a possible categorical imperative—that is, of a practical law.

Now I say that man, and in general every rational being, *exists* as an end in himself, *not merely as a means* for arbitrary use by this or that will: he must in all his actions, whether they are directed to himself or to other rational beings, always be viewed *at the same time as an end*. All the objects of inclination have only a conditioned value; for if there were not these inclinations and the needs grounded on them, their object would be valueless. Inclinations themselves, as sources of needs, are so far from having an absolute value to make them desirable for their own sake that it must rather be the universal wish of every rational being to be wholly free from them. Thus the value of all objects that can *be produced* by our action is always conditioned. Beings whose existence depends, not on our will, but on nature, have none the less, if they are non-rational beings, only a relative value as means and are consequently called *things*. Rational beings, on the other hand, are called *persons* because their nature already marks them out as ends in themselves—that is, as something which ought not to be used merely as a means—and consequently imposes to that extent a limit on all arbitrary treatment of them (and is an object of reverence). Persons therefore, are not merely subjective ends whose existence as an object of our actions has a value *for us*: they are *objective ends*—that is, things whose existence is in itself an end, and indeed an end such that in its place we can put no other end to which they should serve *simply* as means; for unless this is so, nothing at all of *absolute* value would be found anywhere. But if all value were conditioned—that is, contingent—then no supreme principle could be found for reason at all.

If then there is to be a supreme practical principle and—so far as the human will is concerned—a categorical imperative, it must be such that from the idea of something which is necessarily an end for every one because it is an *end in itself* it forms an *objective* principle of the will and consequently can serve as a practical law. The ground of this principle is: *Rational nature exists as an end in itself.* This is the way in which a man necessarily conceives his own existence: it is therefore so far a *subjective* principle of human actions. But it is also the way in which every other rational being conceives his existence on the same rational ground which is valid also for me; hence it is at the same time an *objective* principle, from which, as a supreme practical ground, it must be possible to derive all laws for the will. The practical imperative will therefore be as follows: *Act in such a way that you always treat humanity, whether in your own person or in the person of any other, never simply as a means, but always at the same time as an end.* We will now consider whether this can be carried out in practice.

ILLUSTRATIONS

Let us keep to our previous examples.

First, as regards the concept of necessary duty to oneself, the man who contemplates suicide will ask 'Can my action be compatible with the Idea of humanity *as and end in itself?*' If he does away with himself in order to escape from a painful situation, he is making use of a person merely as *a means* to maintain a tolerable state of affairs till the end of his life. But man is not a thing—not something to be used *merely* as a means: he must always in all his actions be regarded as an end in himself. Hence I cannot dispose of man in my person by maiming, spoiling, or killing. (A more precise determination of this principle in order to avoid all misunderstanding—for example, about having limbs amputated to save myself or about exposing my life to danger in order to preserve it, and so on—I must here forego: this question belongs to morals proper.)

Secondly, so far as necessary or strict duty to others is concerned, the man who has a mind to make a false promise to others will see at once that he is intending to make use of another man *merely as a means* to an end he does not share. For the man whom I seek to use for my own purposes by such a promise cannot possibly agree with my way of behaving to him, and so cannot himself share the end of the action. This incompatibility with the principle of duty to others leaps to the eye more obviously when we bring in examples of attempts on the freedom and property of others. For then it is manifest that a violator of the rights of man intends to use the person of others merely as a means without taking into consideration that, as rational beings, they ought always at the same time to be rated as ends—that is, only as beings who must themselves be able to share in the end of the very same action.

Thirdly, in regard to contingent (meritorious) duty to oneself, it is not enough that an action should refrain fom conflicting with humanity in our own person as an end in itself: it must also *harmonize with this end.* Now there are in humanity capacities for greater perfection which form part of nature's purpose for humanity in our person. To neglect these can admittedly be compatible with the *maintenance* of humanity as an end in itself, but not with the *promotion* of this end.

Fourthly, as regards meritorious duties to others, the natural end which all men seek is their own happiness. Now humanity could no doubt subsist if everybody contributed nothing to the happiness of others but at the same time refrained from deliberately impairing their happiness. This is, however, merely to agree negatively and not positively with *humanity as an end in itself* unless every one endeavours also, so far as in him lies, to further the ends of others. For the ends of a subject who is an end in himself must, if this conception is to have its *full* effect in me, be also, as far as possible, *my* ends.

31. WHAT IF EVERYONE DID THAT?

Colin Strang

Colin Strang *(1922–   ) teaches philosophy at the University of Newcastle in England.*

. . . We are evidently concerned with communities of people and with things that must be done, or not done, if the community is to be saved from damage or destruction; and we want to know whose duty it is to do, or not to do, these things. The complexity of the problem is no longer in doubt. (1) There are some things that need doing once, some that need doing at regular intervals, and some that need doing all the time. (2) Some things need doing by one person, some by a number of people which can be roughly estimated, and some by as many as possible. (3) In practice, who shall do what (though not who *ought* to do what) is determined by economic factors, or by statutory direction (e.g. service with the armed forces in war, paying income tax), or merely by people's inclinations generally, i.e. when enough people are inclined to do the thing anyway.

Somewhere in this territory our quarry has its lair. The following dialogue betwen defaulter and moralist on the evasion of income tax and military service begins the hunt. Our first steps are taken on already familiar ground:

Defaulter: £ 100 is a drop in the ocean to the exchequer. No one will suffer from their loss of £ 100, but it means a good deal to me.

Moralist: But what if everyone did that and offered the same excuse?

Defaulter: But the vast majority won't, so no one will suffer.

From The Durham University Journal, *Vol. 53, No. 1, 1960, pp. 5–10. Reprinted by permission of the author and the editor.*

Moralist: Still, would you say it was *in order* for anyone whatever to evade tax and excuse himself on the same grounds as you do?

Defaulter: Certainly.

Moralist: So it would be quite in order for *everyone* to do the same and offer the same excuse?

Defaulter: Yes.

Moralist: Even though disaster would ensue for the exchequer and for everyone?

Defaulter: Yes. The exchequer would no more miss my £ 100 if *everyone* evaded than they would if only I evaded. They wouldn't miss anyone's individual evasion. What they would miss would be the aggregate £ 1,000,000,000 or so, and that isn't my default or yours or anyone's. So even if everyone evades it is still all right for me to evade; and if it's all right for me to evade it's all right for everyone to evade.

Moralist: You seem now to be in the paradoxical position of saying that if everyone evaded it would be disastrous, and yet no one would be to blame.

Defaulter: Paradoxical, perhaps, but instructive. I am not alarmed. Let me recur to one of your previous questions: you asked whether it would be in order for all to evade and give the same excuse. I now want to reply: No, it would not be in order, but only in the sense that it would be disastrous; but it *would* be in order in the sense that each person's grounds for evasion would still be as valid as they would have been if he had been the *only* evader and no disaster had ensued. In other words, none of the defaulters would be to blame for the disaster —and certainly not one of them would blame himself: on the contrary, each one would argue that had he paid he would have been the only one to pay and thus lost his £ 100 without doing himself or anyone else any good. He would have been a mug to pay.

Moralist: But surely there can't be a disaster of this kind for which no one is to blame.

Defaulter: If anyone is to blame it is the person whose job it is to circumvent evasion. If too few people vote, then it should be made illegal not to vote. If too few people volunteer, then you must introduce conscription. If too many people evade taxes, then you must tighten up your system of enforcement. My answer to your 'If everyone did that' is 'Then someone had jolly well better see to it that they don't; it doesn't impress me as a reason why *I* should, however many people do or don't.'

Moralist: But surely you are being inconsistent here. Take the case of evading military service.

Defaulter: You mean not volunteering in time of crisis, there being no conscription? I do that too.

Moralist: Good. As I was saying, aren't you being inconsistent? You think *both* that it is all right not to volunteer even if too few other people volunteer (because one soldier more or less could make no difference), *and* think that you ought to be conscripted.

Defaulter: But that is not at all inconsistent. Look: the enemy threatens, a mere handful volunteer, and the writing is on the wall; my volunteering will not affect the outcome, but conscript me with the rest to stay the deluge and I will come without a murmur. In short, no good will come of my volunteering, but a great good will come of a general conscription which gathers me in with the rest. There is no inconsistency. I should add that my volunteering would in fact do positive harm; all who resist and survive are to be executed forthwith. There will be one or two heroes, but I did not think you were requiring me to be heroic.

Moralist: I confirm that I was not, and I concede that your position is not inconsistent, however unedifying. As I see it, the nub of your position is this: Given the premiss 'if everyone did that the result would be disastrous' you cannot conclude 'therefore *you* oughtn't' but only 'therefore someone ought to see to it that they don't.' If you are right, the 'if everyone did' argument, as usually taken, is invalid. But then we are left with the question: Whence does it derive its apparent force?

Defaulter: Whence, indeed?

(*interval*)

Moralist: Suppose when you give your justification for evading ('no one will miss *my* contribution') I reply: But don't you think it *unfair* that other people should bear the burden which you shirk and from the bearing of which by others you derive benefit for yourself?

Defaulter: Well, yes, it is rather unfair. Indeed you make me feel a little ashamed; but I wasn't prepared, and I'm still not, to let your pet argument by without a fight. Just where does fairness come into it?

Moralist: I think I can see. Let me begin by pushing two or three counters from different points on the periphery of the problem with the hope that they will meet at the centre. First, then: if someone is morally obliged (or permitted or forbidden) to do some particular thing, then there is a reason why he is so obliged. Further, if someone is obliged to do something for a particular reason, then anyone else whatever is equally obliged provided the reason applies to him also. The reason why a particular person is obliged to do something will be expressible in general terms, and could be expressed by describing some class to which he belongs. My principle then reads as follows: If someone is obliged to do something *just because* he is a member of a certain class, then any other member of that class will be equally obliged to do that thing. You yourself argued, remember, that any member of the class of people whose contribution would not be missed (here I allude to your reason for evasion) was no less entitled to evade than you.

Defaulter: Agreed.

Moralist: My second counter now comes into play. 'Fairness,' you will agree, is a moral term like 'rightness.' An act is unfair if it results in someone getting a greater or lesser share of something (whether pleasant or unpleasant) than he ought to get—more or less than his fair share, as we say.

Now there are a number of things, burdensome or otherwise, which need to be done if the community is not to suffer. But who precisely is to do them? Why me? Why not me? You will also agree, I hope, to the wide principle that where the thing to be done is burdensome the burden should be fairly distributed?

Defaulter: Certainly. I seldom dispute a truism. But in what does a fair distribution consist?

Moralist: In other words: given two people and a burden, how much of it ought each to bear? I say: *unless there is some reason why one should bear more or less of it than the other, they should both bear the same amount.* This is my Fairness Principle. It concerns both the fair allocation of the burden to some class of community members and the fair distribution of it within that class (and this may mean dividing the class into sub-classes of 'isophoric' members): there must always be a *reason* for treating people differently. For instance, people who are unfit or above or below a certain age are exempted or excluded from military service, and for good reasons; women are exempted or excluded from certain kinds of military service, for what Plato regarded as bad reasons; those with more income pay more tax, while those with more children pay less, and for good reasons—and so on. You will have noticed that the typical complaint about unfair dealing begins with a 'why': 'Why did they charge me more than him?' (unfair distribution), or 'Why should married couples be liable for so much surtax?' (unfair allocation). The maxim governing differential treatment, i.e. which is behind the reasons given for it, seems to be: From each according to his resources, to each according to his need. You might argue that my principle about equal burdens is no more than a special case of this maxim. But that principle is all I need for my argument and all I insist on; I shall not stick my neck out further than necessary.

Defaulter: It is not, thus far, too dangerously exposed, I think.

Moralist: Good. We are now ready to move a little nearer to the core of the problem. But first compare the two principles I have advanced. The first was: if a thing is obligatory etc. for one person, then

237

it is obligatory etc. for anyone in the same class (i.e. the class relevant to the reason given). This is a license to argue from one member of a class to all its members; we will call it the Universalization Principle (U-Principle). The second, which is my Fairness Principle, is: A burden laid on a particular class is to be shared equally by all its members, unless there is reason to the contrary. This, in contrast to the first, is a license to argue from the class itself to each of its members. I take it, by the way, that these two principles are independent, that neither follows from the other.

Defaulter: Granted, granted. I am impatient to know what light all this throws on your 'if everyone did' argument.

Moralist: I am coming to that. You will remember that you used the U-Principle yourself to argue that if it's all right for you to evade it's all right for everyone else. But it was no use to me in pressing my case, and we can now see why: it argues from one to all, and there was no *one* to argue from. Nor, of course, could I argue from the consequences of your act. 'Why me?' you asked, and I had then no reply. But I did at least have a retort: 'Why not you?'. Now it seems to me that it is just my Fairness principle that lies behind the effectiveness of this retort, for by it you can be shown to have a duty in cases like this unless you can show that you have not. You would have to show, in the military service example, that you were not a member of the class on which the duty of military service is normally (and we will assume, fairly) regarded as lying. But you cannot show this: you cannot claim to be under age or over age or blind or lame. All you claim is that you have a certain property, the property of being one whose contribution won't be missed, which is shared by every other member of the military class; and this claim, so far from being a good reason for not volunteering, now stands revealed as no reason at all.

Defaulter: Still, you didn't dispute my point that the blame for a disaster following upon wholesale evasion lay upon those duty it was, or in whose power it lay, to prevent such evasion.

Moralist: You certainly had a point, but I can see now that you made too much of it. I concede that the authorities failed in their duty, but then the military class as a whole failed in theirs too. The duty of both was ultimately the same, to ensure the safety of the state, just as the duty of wicket-keeper and long-stop is the same, to save byes. To confine the blame to the authorities is like saying that it's all right to burn the house down so long as its insured or that the mere existence of a police force constitutes a general license to rob banks. As for the individual defaulter, you wanted to absolve him from all blame—a claim which seemed at once plausible and paradoxical: plausible because he was not, as you rightly pointed out, to blame for the disaster (it was not his duty to prevent that, since it was not in his power to do so); paradoxical because he was surely to blame for *something*, and we now know what for: failure to bear his share of the burden allotted to his class.

Defaulter: Maybe, but it still seems to me that if I volunteer and others don't I shall be taking on an unfair share of it, and *that* can't be fair. Then again if I don't volunteer I shall be doing less than my share and *that* can't be fair either. Whichever I do, there's something wrong. And that can't be right.

Moralist: There are two mistakes here. Whichever you do there's something wrong, but nothing unfair; the only wrong is people failing in their duty. Fairness is an attribute of distributions, and whether you volunteer or not neither you nor anyone else are distributing anything. Nor, for that matter, are fate or circumstances, for they are not persons. That is your first mistake. Your second is this: you talk as if the lone volunteer will necessarily do more than his fair share. He may, but he needn't. If he does, that is his own look out: *volenti non fit iniuria.*

Defaulter: It's more dangerous to fight alone than as one among many. How can he ration the danger?

Moralist: He can surrender or run away. Look, he isn't expected to be heroic or to do, or even attempt, the impossible. If two are needed to launch and man the lifeboat, the lone volunteer can only stand and wait: *he also* serves. The least a man can do is offer and hold himself ready, though sometimes it is also the most he can do.

Defaulter: Let it be so. But I am still in trouble about one thing: suppose I grant all you say about fairness and the defaulter, I'm still not clear why you choose to make your point against him in just the mysterious way you do, i.e. by fixing him with your glittering eye and beginning 'If everyone did that.'

Moralist: It is a little puzzling, isn't it? But not all that puzzling. After all, the premiss states and implies a good deal; (1) It states that wholesale evasion will have such and such results; (2) it states or implies that the results will be bad; (3) it implies strongly that a duty to prevent them must lie *somewhere;* (4) it implies that the duty does not lie solely on the person addressed (otherwise a quite different kind of argument would apply); (5) it implies, rather weakly, that nevertheless the person addressed has no better excuse for doing nothing about it than anyone else has. The conclusion is then stated that he ought to do something about it. A gap remains, to be sure; but it can't be a very big one, or people wouldn't, as they sometimes do, feel the force of the argument, however obscurely. The 'Why me?' retort brings out implication (4), while the 'Why not you?' counter-retort brings out implication (5); and we didn't really have very far to go from there.

The argument is clearly elliptical and needs filling out with some explicit reference to the Fairness principle. I would formalize it as follows:

> Unless such and such is done, undesirable consequences X will ensue;
>
> the burden of preventing X lies upon class Y as a whole;
>
> each member of class Y has a *prima facie* duty to bear an equal share of the burden by doing Z;
>
> you are a member of class Y;
>
> therefore you have a *prima facie* duty to do Z.

I have introduced the notion of a *prima facie* duty at this late stage to cover those cases where only a few members of class Y are required to do Z and it would be silly to put them all to work. In the latrine case only one person needs to dig, and in America only a small proportion of fit persons are required for short-term military service. In such cases it is considered fair to select the requisite number by lot. Until the lot is cast I must hold myself ready; if I am selected my *prima facie* duty becomes an actual duty; if I am spared, it lapses. Why selection by lot should be a fair method I leave you to work out for yourself.

Notice that the argument only holds if the thing to be done is burdensome. Voting isn't really very burdensome; indeed a lot of people seem to enjoy it, and this accounts for the weakness of the argument in this application. If the thing to be done were positively enjoyable one might even have to invoke the Fairness principle against over-indulgence.

Notice, finally, that the argument doesn't apply unless there is a fairly readily isolable class to which a burden can be allotted. This rules out the farming and such like cases. You can't lay it down that the burden of providing food for the nation (if it *is* a burden) lies on the farmers (i.e. the class that provides food for the nation), for that is a tautology, or perhaps it implies the curious proposition that everyone *ought* to be doing the job he *is* doing. Might one say instead that *everyone* has a *prima facie* duty to farm, but that the duty lapses when inclination, ability and economic reward conspire to select a sufficient farming force? Far-fetched, I think. The matter might be pursued, but only at the risk of tedium. Well, are you satisfied?

Defaulter: Up to a point. Your hypothesis obviously calls for a lot more testing yet. But I have carried the burden a good deal further than my fair share of the distance; let others take it from here.

32. MORAL OBLIGATIONS AS SELF-EVIDENT

W. D. Ross

W. D. Ross (1877–   ) is a distinguished translator and inter-
preter of Aristotle's philosophy in addition to being an influential moral philosopher. He was a fellow and tutor of Oriel
College, Oxford, and later became provost of Oriel. He has
been President of the British Academy and chairman of the
Council of the Royal Institute of Philosophy. Ross edited the
Oxford Translations of Aristotle (1908–31) and translated Aristotle's Metaphysics (1908) and the Ethics (1925). In the area of
ethics, Ross has written The Right and the Good (1930) and
Foundations of Ethics (1939).

When a plain man fulfils a promise because he thinks he ought
to do so, it seems clear that he does so with no thought of its total
consequences, still less with any opinion that these are likely to be the
best possible. He thinks in fact much more of the past than of the
future. What makes him think it right to act in a certain way is the
fact that he has promised to do so—that and, usually, nothing more.
That his act will produce the best possible consequences is not his
reason for calling it right. What lends colour to the theory we are
examining, then, is not the actions (which form probably a great majority of our actions) in which some such reflection as 'I have promised'
is the only reason we give ourselves for thinking a certain action right,
but the exceptional cases in which the consequences of fulfilling a
promise (for instance) would be so disastrous to others that we judge
it right not to do so. It must of course be admitted that such cases
exist. If I have promised to meet a friend at a particular time for some
trivial purpose, I should certainly think myself justified in breaking
my engagement if by doing so I could prevent a serious accident or
bring relief to the victims of one. And the supporters of the view we are
examining hold that my thinking so is due to my thinking that I shall
bring more good into existence by the one action than by the other.
A different account may, however, be given of the matter, an account
which will, I believe, show itself to be the true one. It may be said
that besides the duty of fulfilling promises I have and recognize a duty
of relieving distress, and that when I think it right to do the latter at the
cost of not doing the former, it is not not because I think I shall produce

From The Right and the Good, 1930, Clarendon Press. Reprinted by
permission of the publisher, Clarendon Press, Oxford.

more good thereby but because I think it the duty which is in the circumstances more of a duty. This account surely corresponds much more closely with what we really think in such a situation. If, so far as I can see, I could bring equal amounts of good into being by fulfilling my promise and by helping some one to whom I had made no promise, I should not hesitate to regard the former as my duty. Yet on the view that what is right is right because it is productive of the most good I should not so regard it.

There are two theories, each in its way simple, that offer a solution of such cases of conscience. One is the view of Kant, that there are certain duties of perfect obligation, such as those of fulfilling promises, of paying debts, of telling the truth, which admit of no exception whatever in favour of duties of imperfect obligation, such as that of relieving distress. The other is the view of, for instance, Professor Moore and Dr. Rashdall, that there is only the duty of producing good, and that all 'conflicts of duties' should be resolved by asking 'by which action will most good be produced?' But it is more important that our theory fit the facts than that it be simple, and the account we have given above corresponds (it seems to me) better than either of the simpler theories with what we really think, viz. that normally promise-keeping, for example, should come before benevolence, but that when and only when the good to be produced by the benevolent act is very great and the promise comparatively trivial, the act of benevolence becomes our duty.

In fact the theory of 'ideal utilitarianism, if I may for brevity refer so to the theory of Professor Moore, seems to simplify unduly our relations to our fellows. It says, in effect, that the only morally significant relation in which my neighbours stand to me is that of being possible beneficiaries by my action.[1] They do stand in this relation to me, and this relation is morally significant. But they may also stand to me in the relation of promisee to promiser, of creditor to debtor, of wife to husband, of child to parent, of friend to friend, of fellow countryman to fellow countryman, and the like; and each of these relations is the foundation of a *prima facie* duty, which is more or less incumbent on me according to the circumstances of the case. When I am in a situation, as perhaps I always am, in which more than one of these *prima facie* duties is incumbent on me, what I have to do is to study the situation as fully as I can until I form the considered opinion (it is never more) that in the circumstances one of them is more incumbent than

---

[1] Some will think it, apart from other considerations, a sufficient refutation of this view to point out that I also stand in that relation to myself, so that for this view the distinction of oneself from others is morally insignificant.

242

any other; then I am bound to think that to do this *prima facie* duty is my duty *sans phrase* in the situation.

I suggest '*prima facie* duty' or 'conditional duty' as a brief way of referring to the characteristic (quite distinct from that of being a duty proper) which an act has, in virtue of being of a certain kind (e.g. the keeping of a promise), of being an act which would be a duty proper if it were not at the same time of another kind which is morally significant. Whether an act is a duty proper or actual duty depends on *all* the morally significant kinds it is an instance of. . . .

There is nothing arbitrary about these *prima facie* duties. Each rests on a definite circumstance which cannot seriously be held to be without moral significance. Of *prima facie* duties I suggest, without claiming completeness or finality for it, the following division.[2]

(1) Some duties rest on previous acts of my own. These duties seem to include two kinds, (*a*) those resting on a promise or what may fairly be called an implicit promise, such as the implicit undertaking not to tell lies which seems to be implied in the act of entering into conversation (at any rate by civilized men), or of writing books that purport to be history and not fiction. These may be called the duties of fidelity. (*b*) Those resting on a previous wrongful act. These may be called the duties of reparation. (2) Some rest on previous acts of other men, i.e. services done by them to me. These may be loosely described as the duties of gratitude. (3) Some rest on the fact or possibility of a distribution of pleasure or happiness (or of the means thereto) which is not in accordance with the merit of the persons concerned; in such cases there arises a duty to upset or prevent such a distribution. These are the duties of justice. (4) Some rest on the mere fact that there are other beings in the world whose condition we can make better in respect of virtue, or of intelligence, or of pleasure. These are the duties of beneficence. (5) Some rest on the fact that we can improve our own condition in respect of virtue or of intelligence. These

---

[2] I should make it plain at this stage that I am *assuming* the correctness of some of our main convictions as to *prima facie* duties, or, more strictly, am claiming that we *know* them to be true. To me it seems as self-evident as anything could be, that to make a promise, for instance, is to create a moral claim on us in someone else. Many readers will perhaps say that they do *not* know this to be true. If so, I certainly cannot prove it to them; I can only ask them to reflect again, in the hope that they will ultimately agree that they also know it to be true. The main moral convictions of the plain man seem to me to be, not opinions which it is for philosophy to prove or disprove, but knowledge from the start; and in my own case I seem to find little difficulty in distinguishing these essential convictions from other moral convictions which I also have, which are merely fallible opinions based on an imperfect study of the working for good or evil of certain institutions or types of action.

are the duties of self-improvement. (6) I think that we should distinguish from (4) the duties that may be summed up under the title of 'not injuring others.' No doubt to injure others is incidentally to fail to do them good; but it seems to me clear that non-maleficence is apprehended as a duty distinct from that of beneficence, and as a duty of a more stringent character. It will be noticed that this alone among the types of duty has been stated in a negative way. An attempt might no doubt be made to state this duty, like the others, in a positive way. It might be said that it is really the duty to prevent ourselves from acting either from an inclination to harm others or from an inclination to seek our own pleasure, in doing which we should incidentally harm them. But on reflection it seems clear that the primary duty here is the duty not to harm others, this being a duty whether or not we have an inclination that if followed would lead to our harming them; and that when we have such an inclination the primary duty not to harm others gives rise to a consequential duty to resist the inclination. The recognition of this duty of non-maleficence is the first step on the way to the recognition of the duty of beneficence; and that accounts for the prominence of the commands 'thou shalt not kill,' 'thou shalt not commit adultery,' 'thou shalt not steal,' 'thou shalt not bear false witness,' in so early a code as the Decalogue. But even when we have come to recognize the duty of beneficence, it appears to me that the duty of non-maleficence is recognized as a distinct one, and as *prima facie* more binding. We should not in general consider it justifiable to kill one person in order to keep another alive, or to steal from one in order to give alms to another.

The essential defect of the 'ideal utilitarian' theory is that it ignores, or at least does not do full justice to, the highly personal character of duty. If the only duty is to produce the maximum of good, the question who is to have the good—whether it is myself, or my benefactor, or a person to whom I have made a promise to confer that good on him, or a mere fellow man to whom I stand in no such special relation—should make no difference to my having a duty to produce that good. But we are all in fact sure that it makes a vast difference. . . .

If the objection be made, that this catalogue of the main types of duty is an unsystematic one resting on no logical principle, it may be replied, first, that it makes no claim to being ultimate. It is a *prima facie* classification of the duties which reflection on our moral convictions seems actually to reveal. And if these convictions are, as I would claim that they are, of the nature of knowledge, and if I have not misstated them, the list will be a list of authentic conditional duties, correct as far as it goes though not necessarily complete. The list of *goods* put forward by the rival theory is reached by exactly the same method—

the only sound one in the circumstances—viz. that of direct reflection on what we really think. Loyalty to the facts is worth more than a symmetrical architectonic or a hastily reached simplicity. If further reflection discovers a perfect logical basis for this or for a better classification, so much the better.

It may, again, be objected that our theory that there are these various and often conflicting types of *prima facie* duty leaves us with no principle upon which to discern what is our actual duty in particular circumstances. But this objection is not one which the rival theory is in a position to bring forward. For when we have to choose between the production of two heterogeneous goods, say knowledge and pleasure, the 'ideal utilitarian' theory can only fall back on an opinion, for which no logical basis can be offered, that one of the goods is the greater; and this is no better than a similar opinion that one of two duties is the more urgent. And again, when we consider the infinite variety of the effects of our actions in the way of pleasure, it must surely be admitted that the claim which *hedonism* sometimes makes, that it offers a readily applicable criterion of right conduct, is quite illusory.

I am unwilling, however, to content myself with an *argumentum ad hominem*, and I would contend that in principle there is no reason to anticipate that every act that is our duty is so for one and the same reason. Why should two sets of circumstances, or one set of circumstances, *not* possess different characteristics, any one of which makes a certain act our *prima facie* duty? When I ask what it is that makes me in certain cases sure that I have a *prima facie* duty to do so and so, I find that it lies in the fact that I have made a promise; when I ask the same question in another case, I find the answer lies in the fact that I have done a wrong. And if on reflection I find (as I think I do) that neither of these reasons is reducible to the other, I must not on any *a priori* ground assume that such a reduction is possible. . . .

It is necessary to say something by way of clearing up the relation between *prima facie* duties and the actual or absolute duty to do one particular act in particular circumstances. If, as almost all moralists except Kant are agreed, and as most plain men think, it is sometimes right to tell a lie or to break a promise, it must be maintained that there is a difference between *prima facie* duty and actual or absolute duty. When we think ourselves justified in breaking, and indeed morally obliged to break, a promise in order to relieve some one's distress, we do not for a moment cease to recognize a *prima facie* duty to keep our promise, and this leads us to feel, not indeed shame or repentance, but certainly compunction, for behaving as we do; we recognize further, that it is our duty to make up somehow to the promisee for the breaking of the promise. We have to distinguish from the characteristic of being our duty that of tending to be our duty. Any act that we do contains various elements in virtue of which it falls under various categories. In virtue of being the breaking of a promise, for instance, it tends to be wrong; in virtue of being an instance of relieving distress it tends to be right. Tendency to be one's duty may be called a parti-resultant attribute, i.e. one which belongs to an act in virtue of some one component in its nature. *Being* one's duty is a toti-resultant attribute, one which belongs to an act in virtue of its whole nature and of nothing less than this. . . .

Another instance of the same distinction may be found in the operation of natural laws. *Qua* subject to the force of gravitation towards some other body, each body tends to move in a particular direction with a particular velocity; but its actual movement depends on *all* the forces to which it is subject. It is only by recognizing this distinction that we can preserve the absoluteness of laws of nature, and only by recognizing a corresponding distinction that we can preserve the absoluteness of the general principles of morality. But an important difference between the two cases must be pointed out. When we say that in virtue of gravitation a body tends to move in a certain way, we are referring to a causal influence actually exercised on it by another body or other bodies. When we say that in virtue of being deliberately untrue a certain remark tends to be wrong, we are referring to no causal relation, to no relation that involves succession in time, but to such a relation as connects the various attributes of a mathematical figure. And if the word 'tendency' is thought to suggest too much a causal relation, it is better to talk of certain types of act as being *prima facie* right or wrong (or of different persons as having different and possibly conflicting claims upon us), than of their tending to be right or wrong.

Something should be said of the relation between our apprehension of the *prima facie* rightness of certain types of act and our mental attitude towards particular acts. It is proper to use the word 'apprehension' in the former case and not in the latter. That an act, *qua* fulfilling a promise, or *qua* effecting a just distribution of good, or *qua* returning services rendered, or *qua* promoting the good of others, or *qua* promoting the virtue or insight of the agent, is *prima facie* right, is self-evident; not in the sense that it is evident from the beginning of our lives, or as soon as we attend to the proposition for the first time, but in the sense that when we have reached sufficient mental maturity and have given sufficient attention to the proposition it is evident without any need of proof, or of evidence beyond itself. It is self-evident just as a mathematical axiom, or the validity of a form of inference, is evident. The moral order expressed in these propositions is just as much part of the fundamental nature of the universe (and, we may add, of any possible universe in which there were moral agents at all) as is the spatial or numerical structure expressed in the axioms of geometry or arithmetic. In our confidence that these propositions are true there is involved the same trust in our reason that is involved in our confidence in mathematics; and we should have no justification for trusting it in the latter sphere and distrusting it in the former. In both cases we are dealing with propositions that cannot be proved, but that just as certainly need no proof. . . .

Our judgements about our actual duty in concrete situations have none of the certainty that attaches to our recognition of the general principles of duty. A statement is certain, i.e. is an expression of knowledge, only in one or other of two cases: when it is either self-evident, or a valid conclusion from self-evident premises. And our judgements about our particular duties have neither of these characters. (1) They are not self-evident. Where a possible act is seen to have two characteristics, in virtue of one of which it is *prima facie* right, and in virtue of the other *prima facie* wrong, we are (I think) well aware that we are not certain whether we ought or ought not to do it; that whether we do it or not, we are taking a moral risk. We come in the long run, after consideration, to think one duty more pressing than the other, but we do not feel certain that it is so. And though we do not always recognize that a possible act has two such characteristics, and though there *may* be cases in which it has not, we are never certain that any particular possible act has not, and therefore never certain that it is right, nor certain that it is wrong. For, to go no further in the analysis, it is enough to point out that any particular act will in all probability in the course of time contribute to the bringing about of good or of evil for many human beings and thus have a *prima facie* rightness or wrongness of which we know nothing. (2) Again, our judgements about our particular duties are not logical conclusions from self-evident premises. The only possible premises would be the general principles stating their *prima facie* rightness or wrongness *qua* having the different characteristics they do have; and even if we could (as we cannot) apprehend the extent to which an act will tend on the one hand, for example, to bring about advantages for our benefactors, and on the other hand to bring about disadvantages for fellow men who are not our benefactors, there is no principle by which we can draw the conclusion that it is on the whole right or on the whole wrong. In this respect the judgement as to the rightness of a particular act is just like the judgement as to the beauty of a particular natural object or work of art. A poem is, for instance, in respect of certain qualities beautiful and in respect of certain others not beautiful; and our judgement as to the degree of beauty it possesses on the whole is never reached by logical reasoning from the apprehension of its particular beauties or particular defects. Both in this and in the moral case we have more or less probable opinions which are not logically justified conclusions from the general principles that are recognized as self-evident.

There is therefore much truth in the description of the right act as a fortunate act. If we cannot be certain that it is right, it is our good fortune if the act we do is the right act. This consideration does not, however, make the doing of our duty a mere matter of chance. There is a parallel here between the doing of duty and the doing of what will be to our personal advantage. We never *know* what act will in the long run be to our advantage. Yet it is certain that we are more likely in general to secure our advantage if we estimate to the best of our ability the probable tendencies of our actions in this respect, than if we act on caprice. And similarly we are more likely to do our duty if we reflect to the best of our ability on the *prima facie* rightness or wrongness of various possible acts in virtue of the characteristics we perceive them to have, than if we act without reflection. With this greater likelihood we must be content.

Many people would be inclined to say that the right act for me is not that whose general nature I have been describing, viz. that which if I were omniscient I should see to be my duty, but that which on all the evidence available to me I should think to be my duty. But suppose that from the state of partial knowledge in which I think act A to be my duty, I could pass to a state of perfect knowledge in which I saw act B to be my duty, should I not say 'act B was the right act for me to do'? I should no doubt add 'though I am not to be blamed for doing act A.' But in adding this, am I not passing from the question 'what is right' to the question 'what is morally good'? At the same time I am not making the *full* passage from the one notion to the other; for in order that the act should be morally good, or an act I am not to be blamed for doing, it must not merely be the act which it is reasonable for me to think my duty; it must also be done for that reason, or from some other morally good motive. Thus the conception of the right act as the act which it is reasonable for me to think my duty is an unsatisfactory compromise between the true notion of the right act and the notion of the morally good action.

The general principles of duty are obviously not self-evident from the beginning of our lives. How do they come to be so? The answer is, that they come to be self-evident to us just as mathematical axioms do. We find by experience that this couple of matches and that couple make four matches, that this couple of balls on a wire and that couple make four balls; and by reflection on these and similar discoveries we come to see that it is of the nature of two and two to make four. In a precisely similar way, we see the *prima facie* rightness of an act which would be the fulfilment of a particular promise, and of another which would be the fulfilment of another promise, and when we have reached sufficient maturity to think in general terms, we apprehend *prima facie* rightness to belong to the nature of any fulfilment of promise. What comes first in time is the apprehension of the self-evident *prima facie* rightness of an individual act of a particular type. From this we come by reflection to apprehend the self-evident general principle of *prima facie* duty. From this, too, perhaps along with the apprehension of the self-evident *prima facie* rightness of the same act in virtue of its having another characteristic as well, and perhaps in spite of the apprehension of its *prima facie* wrongness in virtue of its having some third characteristic, we come to believe something not self-evident at all, but an object of probable opinion, viz. that this particular act is (not *prima facie* but) actually right. . . .

Supposing it to be agreed, as I think on reflection it must, that no one *means* by 'right' just 'productive of the best possible consequences,' or 'optimific,' the attributes 'right' and 'optimific' might stand in either of two kinds of relation to each other. (1) They might be so related that we could apprehend *a priori*, either immediately or deductively, that any act that is optimific is right and any act that is right is optimific, as we can apprehend that any triangle that is equilateral is equiangular and *vice versa*. Professor Moore's view is, I think, that the coextensiveness of 'right' and 'optimific' is apprehended immediately. He rejects the possibility of any proof of it. Or (2) the two attributes might be such that the question whether they are invariably connected had to be answered by means of an inductive inquiry. Now at first sight it might seem as if the constant connexion of the two attributes could be immediately apprehended. It might seem absurd to suggest that it could be right for any one to do an act which would produce consequences less good than those which would be produced by some other act in his power. Yet a little thought will convince us that this is not absurd. The type of case in which it is easiest to see that this is so is, perhaps, that in which one has made a promise. In such a case we all think that *prima facie* it is our duty to fulfill the promise irrespective of the precise goodness of the total consequences. And though we do not think it is necessarily our actual or absolute duty to do so, we are far from thinking that any, even the slightest, gain in the value of the total consequences will necessarily justify us in doing something else instead. Suppose, to simplify the case by abstraction, that the fulfilment of a promise to A would produce 1,000 units of good [3] for him, but that by doing some other act I could produce 1,001 units of good

---

[3] I am assuming that good is objectively quantitative, but not that we can accurately assign an exact quantitative measure to it. Since it is of a definite amount, we can make the *supposition* that its amount is so-and-so, though we cannot with any confidence *assert* that it is.

for *B,* to whom I have made no promise, the other consequences of the two acts being of equal value; should we really think it self-evident that it was our duty to do the second act and not the first? I think not. We should, I fancy, hold that only a much greater disparity of value between the total consequences would justify us in failing to discharge our *prima facie* duty to A. After all, a promise is a promise, and is not to be treated so lightly as the theory we are examining would imply. What, exactly, a promise is, is not so easy to determine, but we are surely agreed that it constitutes a serious moral limitation to our freedom of action. To produce the 1,001 units of good for *B* rather than fulfil our promise to A would be to take, not perhaps our duty as philanthropists too seriously, but certainly our duty as makers of promises too lightly. . . .

Such instances—and they might easily be added to—make it clear that there is no self-evident connexion between the attributes 'right' and 'optimific.' The theory we are examining has a certain attractiveness when applied to our decision that a particular act is our duty (though I have tried to show that it does not agree with our actual moral judgements even here). But it is not even plausible when applied to our recognition of *prima facie* duty. For if it were self-evident that the right coincides with the optimific, it should be self-evident that what is *prima facie* right is *prima facie* optimific. But whereas we are certain that keeping a promise is *prima facie* right, we are not certain that it is *prima facie* optimific (though we are perhaps certain that it is *prima facie* bonific). Our certainty that it is *prima facie* right depends not on its consequences but on its being the fulfilment of a promise. The theory we are examining involves too much difference between the evident ground of our conviction about *prima facie* duty and the alleged ground of our conviction about actual duty. . . .

I conclude that the attributes 'right' and 'optimific' are not identical, and that we do not know either by intuition, by deduction, or by induction that they coincide in their application, still less that the latter is the foundation of the former. It must be added, however, that if we are ever under no special obligation such as that of fidelity to a promisee or of gratitude to a benefactor, we ought to do what will produce most good; and that even when we are under a special obligation the tendency of acts to promote general good is one of the main factors in determining whether they are right.

In what has preceded, a good deal of use has been made of 'what we really think' about moral questions; a certain theory has been rejected because it does not agree with what we really think. It might

250

be said that this is in principle wrong; that we should not be content to expound what our present moral consciousness tells us but should aim at a criticism of our existing moral consciousness in the light of theory. Now I do not doubt that the moral consciousness of men has in detail undergone a good deal of modification as regards the things we think right, at the hands of moral theory. But if we are told, for instance, that we should give up our view that there is a special obligatoriness attaching to the keeping of promises because it is self-evident that the only duty is to produce as much good as possible, we have to ask ourselves whether we really, when we reflect, *are* convinced that this is self-evident, and whether we really *can* get rid of our view that promise-keeping has a bindingness independent of productiveness of maximum good. In my own experience I find that I cannot, in spite of a very genuine attempt to do so; and I venture to think that most people will find the same, and that just because they cannot lose the sense of special obligation, they cannot accept as self-evident, or even as true, the theory which would require them to do so. In fact it seems, on reflection, self-evident that a promise, simply as such, is something that *prima facie* ought to be kept, and it does *not,* on reflection, seem self-evident that production of maximum good is the only thing that makes an act obligatory. And to ask us to give up at the bidding of a theory our actual apprehension of what is right and what is wrong seems like asking people to repudiate their actual experience of beauty, at the bidding of a theory which says 'only that which satisfies such and such conditions can be beautiful.' If what I have called our actual apprehension is (as I would maintain that it is) truly an apprehension, i.e. an instance of knowledge, the request is nothing less than absurd.

I would maintain, in fact, that what we are apt to describe as 'what we think' about moral questions contains a considerable amount that we do not think but know, and that this forms the standard by reference to which the truth of any moral theory has to be tested, instead of having itself to be tested by reference to any theory. I hope that I have in what precedes indicated what in my view these elements of knowledge are that are involved in our ordinary moral consciousness.

It would be a mistake to found a natural science on 'what we really think,' i.e. on what reasonably thoughtful and well-educated people think about the subjects of the science before they have studied them scientifically. For such opinions are interpretations, and often misinterpretations, of sense-experience; and the man of science must appeal from these to sense-experience itself, which furnishes his real data. In ethics no such appeal is possible. We have no more direct way of access to the facts about rightness and goodness and about what things are right or good, than by thinking about them; the moral convictions of thoughtful and well-educated people are the data of ethics just as sense-perceptions are the data of a natural science. Just as some of the latter have to be rejected as illusory, so have some of the former; but as the latter are rejected only when they are in conflict with other more accurate sense-perceptions, the former are rejected only when they are in conflict with other convictions which stand better the test of reflection. The existing body of moral convictions of the best people is the cumulative product of the moral reflection of many generations, which has developed an extremely delicate power of appreciation of moral distinctions; and this the theorist cannot afford to treat with anything other than the greatest respect. The verdicts of the moral consciousness of the best people are the foundation on which he must build; though he must first compare them with one another and eliminate any contradictions they may contain.

33. A CRITIQUE OF ETHICAL INTUITIONISM

P. F. Strawson

P. F. Strawson (1919–   ) is a fellow of University College, Oxford, and one of the most influential philosophers working within the "ordinary language" analytic tradition. His best known work is Individuals, *which Strawson considers to be "descriptive metaphysics." In addition, he has written* The Bounds of Sense *(1966) and* An Introduction to Logical Theory *(1952).*

North.—What is the trouble about moral facts? When someone denies that there is an objective moral order, or asserts that ethical propositions are pseudo-propositions, cannot I refute him (rather as Moore refuted those who denied the existence of the external world) by saying: "You know very well that Brown did wrong in beating his wife. You know very well that you ought to keep promises. You know very well that human affection is good and cruelty bad, that many actions are wrong and some are right"?

From Philosophy, *Vol. 24, No. 88, 1949, pp. 23–28. Reprinted by permission of the author and the editor.*

West.—Isn't the trouble about formal facts another case of trouble about knowing, about learning? We find out facts about the external world by looking and listening; about ourselves, by feeling; about other people, by looking and listening *and* feeling. When this is noticed, there arises a wish to say that the facts *are* what is seen, what is heard, what is felt; and, consequently, that moral facts fall into one of these classes. So those who have denied that there are "objective moral characteristics" have not wanted to deny that Brown's action was wrong or that keeping promises is right. They have wanted to point out that rightness and wrongness are a matter of what is felt in the heart, not of what is seen with the eyes or heard with the ears. They have wanted to emphasise the way in which "Promise-keeping is right" resembles "Going abroad is exciting," "Stories about mothers-in-law are comic," "Bombs are terrifying"; and differs from "Roses are red" and "Sea-water is salt." This does not prevent you from talking about the moral order, or the moral world, if you want to; but it warns you not to forget that the only access to the moral world is through remorse and approval and so on; just as the only access to the world of comedy is through laughter; and the only access to the coward's world is through fear.

North.—I agree, of course, that we cannot see the goodness of something as we see its colour, or identify rightness by the sense of touch; though I think you should add that the senses are indispensable as a means of our becoming aware of those characteristics upon which moral characteristics depend. You may be partly right, too, in saying that access to the moral world is obtained through experience of the moral emotions; for it may be that only when our moral feelings have been strongly stirred do we first become clearly aware of the characteristics which evoke these feelings. But these feelings are not identical with that awareness. "Goodness" does not stand to "feeling approval," "guilt" to "feeling guilty," "obligation" to "feeling bound," as "exciting-ness" stands to "being excited" and "humorousness" to "feeling amused." To use the jargon for a moment: moral characteristics and relations are non-empirical, and awareness of them is neither sensory nor intro-spectual. It is a different kind of awareness, which the specialists call "intuition": and it is only empiricist prejudice which prevents your acknowledging its existence. Once acknowledged, it solves our problems: and we see that while "Promise-keeping is right" differs from "The sea is salt," this is not because it resembles "Detective-stories are exciting"; it differs from *both* in being the report neither of a sensible nor an introspectible experience, but of an intuition. We may, perhaps, know some moral characteristics mediately, through others. ("Obligation" is, perhaps, definable in terms of "goodness.") But at least one such characteristic—rightness or goodness—is unanalysable, and known by intuition alone. The fundamental cognitive situation in morals is that in which we intuit the rightness of a particular action or the goodness of a particular state of affairs. We see this moral characteristic as present in virtue of some other characteristics, themselves capable of being described in empirical terms, which the action or state of affairs possesses. (This is why I said that sense-perception is a necessary, though not a sufficient, condition of obtaining information about the moral order). Our intuition, then, is not a bare intuition of the moral characteristic, but also the intuition of its dependence on some others: so that this fundamental situation yields us, by intuitive induction, knowledge of moral rules, generalisations regarding the right and the good, which we can apply in other cases, even when an actual intuition is lacking. So much do these rules become taken for granted, a part of our habitual moral life, that most of our everyday moral judgments involve merely an implicit reference to them: [1] a reference which becomes explicit only if the judgment is challenged or queried. Moral emotions, too, assume the character of habitual reactions. But emotions and judgments alike are grounded upon intuitions. Emotion may be the gatekeeper to the moral world; but intuition is the gate.

West.—Not so fast. I understand you to say that at least one fundamental moral characteristic—rightness or goodness—is unanalysable. Perhaps both are. The experts are divided. In any case, the fundamental characteristic (or characteristics) can be known only by intuitive awareness of its presence in some particular contemplated action or state of affairs. There is, then, a kind of analogy between the word "right" (or "good") and the name of some simple sensible characteristic such as "red." [2] Just as everybody who understands the word "red" has seen some red things, so everybody who understands the word "right" or the word "good" has intuited the character, rightness, in some actions, or the character, goodness, in some states of affairs; and nobody who has not intuited these characters understands the words "right" or "good." But this is not quite enough, is it? In order for me to know *now* the meaning of an indefinable word, it is not enough that a certain perceptual or intuitional event should have occurred at some particular point in my history; for I might not only have forgotten the details of that event; I might have forgotten what *kind* of an event it was; I might not know *now* what it would be like for such an event to occur. If the word "red" expresses an indefinable visual concept, then it is self-contradictory to say: "I know what the word 'red' means, but I can't remember ever *seeing* red and I don't know what it would be *like* to see

---

[1] Cf. D. Daiches Raphael, *The Moral Sense*, Chapters V and VI.
[2] Cf. G. E. Moore, *Principia Ethica*, p. 7 *et seq.*

red." Similarly, if the word "right," or the word "good," expresses an indefinable intuitive concept, then it is self-contradictory to say: "I know what the word 'right' or the word 'good' means, but I can't remember ever *intuiting* rightness or goodness, and I don't know what it would be *like* to intuit rightness or goodness." If your theory is true, then this statement is a contradiction.

But it is not at all obvious to me that it is a contradiction. I should be quite prepared to assert that I understood the words "right" and "good," but that I couldn't remember ever intuiting rightness or goodness and that I couldn't imagine what it would be like to do so. And I think it is quite certain that I am not alone in this, but that there are a large number of people who are to be presumed capable of accurate reporting of their own cognitive experience, and who would find nothing self-contradictory in saying what I say. And if this is so, you are presented with a choice of two possibilities. The first is that the words "right" and "good" have quite a different meaning for one set of people from the meaning which they have for another set. But neither of us believes this. The second is that the intuitionist theory is a mistake; that the phrase "intuitional event having a moral characteristic as its object (or a part of its object)" is a phrase which describes nothing at all; or describes misleadingly the kind of emotional experience we both admit. There is no third possibility. It is no good saying: "All people who succeed in learning the meaning of moral words do as a matter of fact have moral intuitions, but unfortunately many people are inclined to forget them, to be quite unable to remember what they are like." True, there would be nothing self-contradictory in saying this: but it would simply be a variant of the first possibility; for I cannot be said to know *now* the meaning of a word expressing an intuitive concept unless I know now what it would be like to intuit the characteristic of which it is a concept. The trouble with your intuitionist theory is that, if true, it should be a truism. There should be no doubt about the occurrence of the distinctive experience of intuiting rightness (or goodness), and about its being the only way to learn the meaning of the primary moral words; just as there is no doubt about the occurrence of seeing red (or blue), and about this being the only way to learn the meaning of the primary colour words. But there *is* doubt; and over against this doubt there rises a certainty: the certainty that we all know what it is to *feel* guilty, to *feel* bound, to *feel* approving.

North.—What I have said *is* a truism; and that is its strength. It is not I who am inventing a mythical faculty, but you, irritated, perhaps, by the language of intuitionism, who are denying the obvious. When you said that you couldn't *imagine* what it would be like to have moral intuitions, isn't it clear that you wanted "intuiting a moral characteristic" to be like seeing a colour or hearing a sound? Naturally you couldn't *imagine* anything of the sort. But I have already pointed out that moral characteristics are dependent on others of which the presence *is* ascertainable by looking and listening. You do not intuit rightness or goodness independently of the other features of the situation. You intuit *that* an action is (or would be) right, a state of affairs good, *because* it has (or would have) certain other empirically ascertainable qualities. The total content of your intuition includes the "because" clause. Of course, our ordinary moral judgments register unreflective reactions. Nevertheless "This act is right (or this state of affairs is good) because it has P, Q, R"—where "P, Q, R" stands for such empirically ascertainable qualities—expresses the type of fundamental cognitive situation in ethics, of which our normal judgments are copies, mediated by habit, but ready, if challenged, to become explicit as their original. Consider what happens when someone dissents from your opinion. You produce reasons. And this is not a matter of accounting for an emotional condition; but of bringing evidence in support of a verdict.

West.—When the jury brings in a verdict of guilty on a charge of murder, they do so because the facts adduced in evidence are of the kind covered by the definition of "murder." When the chemical analyst concludes that the material submitted for analysis is a salt, he does so because it exhibits the defining properties of a salt. The evidence is the sort of thing that is *meant* by "murder," by "salt." But the fundamental moral word, or words, you say, cannot be defined; their concepts are unanalysable. So it cannot be in this way that the "because" clause of your ethical sentence functions as evidence. "X is a right action because it is a case of promise-keeping" does not work like "X is a salt because it is a compound of basic and acid radicals"; for, if "right" is indefinable, "X is right" does not *mean* "X is an act of promise-keeping or of relieving distress or of telling the truth or . . ."

When I say "It will be fine in the morning; for the evening sky is red," the evidence is of a different sort. For I might observe the fine morning without having noticed the state of the evening sky. But you have rightly stressed the point that there is no *independent* awareness of *moral* qualities: that they are always "seen" as dependent on those other features mentioned in the "because" clause. So it is not in this way, either, that the "because" clause of your ethical sentence functions as evidence. And there is no other way. Generally, we may say that whenever q is evidence for p, *either* q is the sort of thing we mean by "p" ("p" is definable in terms of "q") or we can have knowledge of the state of affairs described by "p" independently of knowledge of the state of affairs described by "*q*." But neither of these conditions is satisfied by the *q*, the "because" clause, of your ethical sentence.

The "because" clause, then, does not, as you said it did, constitute evidence for the ethical judgment. And this, it seems to me, should be a serious matter for you. For where is such evidence to be found? It is no good saying that, after all, the ethical judgments of other people (or your own at other times) may corroborate your own present judgment. They may agree with it; but their agreement strengthens the probability of your judgment only on the assumption that their moral intuitions tend on the whole to be correct. But the only possible evidence for the existence of a *tendency* to have correct intuitions is the correctness of *actual* intuitions. And it is precisely the correctness of actual intuitions for which we are seeking evidence, and failing to find it.

And evidence you must have, if your account of the matter is correct. You will scarcely say that ethical intuitions are infallible; for ethical disagreements may survive the resolution of factual disagreements. (You might, of course, say that *genuine* intuitions were infallible: then the problem becomes one of finding a criterion for distinguishing between the genuine ones and those false claimants that carry the same inner conviction.) So your use of the language of "unanalysable predicates ascribed in moral judgment to particular actions and states of affairs" leads to contradiction. For to call such a judgment "non-infallible" would be meaningless unless there were some way of checking it; of confirming or confuting it, by producing evidence for or against it. But I have just shown that your account of these judgments is incompatible with the possibility of producing evidence for or against them. So, if your account is true, these judgments are both corrigible and incorrigible; and this is absurd.

But the absurdity points to the solution. Of course these judgments are corrigible: but not in the way in which the diagnosis of a doctor is corrigible; rather in the way in which the musical taste of a child is corrigible. Correcting them is not a matter of *producing evidence* for them or their contraries, though it is (partly) a matter of *giving reasons* for them or their contraries. We say, warningly, that ethical judgments are corrigible, because ethical disagreement sometimes survives the resolution of factual disagreement. We say, encouragingly, that ethical judgments are corrigible, because the resolution of factual disagreement sometimes leads to the resolution of ethical disagreement. But the one kind of agreement leads (when it *does* lead) to the other, not in the way in which agreed evidence leads to an agreed conclusion, but in the way in which common experience leads to sympathy. The two kinds of agreement, the two kinds of judgment, are as different as chalk from cheese. Ordinary language can accommodate the difference without strain: it is the pseudo-precise philosophical use of "judgment" which slurs over the difference and raises the difficulty. It is not clear, then, what people have meant when they said that ethical disagreements were like disagreemets in taste, in choice, in practical attitude? [3] Of course, as you said, when we produce our reasons, we are not often simply giving the causes of our emotional condition. But neither are we producing evidence for a verdict, for a moral diagnosis. We are using the facts to back our attitudes, to appeal to the capacity of others to feel as we feel, to respond as we respond. . . .

34. WHY BE MORAL?

Kurt Baier

Kurt Baier (1917–   ) was educated at the University of Vienna, the University of Melbourne, and Oxford. He is currently professor of Philosophy at the University of Pittsburgh. He has written The Moral Point of View (1958) and numerous essays in philosophical periodicals.

THE SUPREMACY OF MORAL REASONS

Are moral reasons really superior to reasons of self-interest as we all believe? Do we really have reason on our side when we follow moral reasons against self-interest? What reasons could there be for being moral? Can we really give an answer to "Why should we be moral?" It is obvious that all these questions come to the same thing. When we ask, "Should we be moral?" or "Why should we be moral?" or "Are moral reasons superior to all others?" we ask to be shown the reason for being moral. What is this reason?

Let us begin with a state of affairs in which reasons of self-interest are supreme. In such a state everyone keeps his impulses and inclinations in check when and only when they would lead him into behavior detrimental to his own interest. Everyone who follows reason

Reprinted from Kurt Baier: The Moral Point of View. © 1958 by Cornell University. Used by permission of Cornell University Press.

[3] Cf. Charles Stevenson, Ethics and Language, Chapter 1. See also his paper "The Emotive Meaning of Ethical Terms."

will discipline himself to rise early, to do his exercises, to refrain from excessive drinking and smoking, to keep good company, to marry the right sort of girl, to work and study hard in order to get on, and so on. However, it will often happen that people's interests conflict. In such a case, they will have to resort to ruses or force to get their own way. As this becomes known, men will become suspicious, for they will regard one another as scheming competitors for the good things in life. The universal supremacy of the rules of self-interest must lead to what Hobbes called the state of nature. At the same time, it will be clear to everyone that universal obedience to certain rules overriding self-interest would produce a state of affairs which serves everyone's interest much better than his unaided pursuit of it in a state where everyone does the same. Moral rules are universal rules designed to override those of self-interest when following the latter is harmful to others. "Thou shalt not kill," "Thou shalt not lie," "Thou shalt not steal" are rules which forbid the inflicting of harm on someone else even when this might be in one's interest.

The very *raison d'être* of a morality is to yield reasons which overrule the reasons of self-interest in those cases when everyone's following self-interest would be harmful to everyone. Hence moral reasons are superior to all others.

"But what does this mean?" it might be objected. "If it merely means that we do so regard them, then you are of course right, but your contention is useless, a mere point of usage. And how could it mean any more? If it means that we not only do so regard them, but *ought* so to regard them, then there must be *reasons* for saying this. But there could not be any reasons for it. If you offer reasons of self-interest, you are arguing in a circle. Moreover, it cannot be true that it is always in my interest to treat moral reasons as superior to reasons of self-interest. If it were, self-interest and morality could never conflict, but they notoriously do. It is equally circular to argue that there are moral reasons for saying that one ought to treat moral reasons as superior to reasons of self-interest. And what other reasons are there?"

The answer is that we are now looking at the world from the point of view of *anyone*. We are not examining particular alternative courses of action before this or that person; we are examining two alternative worlds, one in which moral reasons are always treated by everyone as superior to reasons of self-interest and one in which the reverse is the practice. And we can see that the first world is the better world, because we can see that the second world would be the sort which Hobbes describes as the state of nature.

This shows that I ought to be moral for when I ask the question "What ought I to do?" I am asking, "Which is the course of action supported by the best reasons?" But since it has just been shown that moral reasons are superior to reasons of self-interest, I have been given a reason for being moral, for following moral reasons rather than any other, namely, they are better reasons than any other.

But is this always so? Do we have a reason for being moral whatever the conditions we find ourselves in? Could there not be situations in which it is not true that we have reasons for being moral, that, on the contrary, we have reasons for ignoring the demands of morality? Is not Hobbes right in saying that in a state of nature the laws of nature, that is, the rules of morality, bind only *in foro interno?*

Hobbes argues as follows.

(i) To live in a state of nature is to live outside society. It is to live in conditions in which there are no common ways of life and, therefore, no reliable expectations about other people's behavior other than that they will follow their inclination or their interest.

(ii) In such a state reason will be the enemy of co-operation and mutual trust. For it is too risky to hope that other people will refrain from protecting their own interests by the preventive elimination of probable or even possible dangers to them. Hence reason will counsel everyone to avoid these risks by preventive action. But this leads to war.

(iii) It is obvious that everyone's following self-interest leads to a state of affairs which is desirable from no one's point of view. It is, on the contrary, desirable that everybody should follow rules overriding self-interest whenever that is to the detriment of others. In other words, it is desirable to bring about a state of affairs in which all obey the rules of morality.

(iv) However, Hobbes claims that in the state of nature it helps nobody if a single person or a small group of persons begins to follow the rules of morality, for this could only lead to the extinction of such individuals or groups. In such a state, it is therefore contrary to reason to be moral.

(v) The situation can change, reason can support morality, only when the presumption about other people's behavior is reversed. Hobbes thought that this could be achieved only by the creation of an absolute ruler with absolute power to enforce his laws. We have already seen that this is not true and that it is quite different if people live in a society, that is, if they have common ways of life, which are taught to all members and somehow enforced by the group. Its members have reason to expect their fellows generally to obey its rules, that is, its religion, morality, customs, and law, even when doing so is not, on certain occasions, in their interest. Hence they too have reason to follow these rules.

In this argument sound? One might, of course, object to step (i) on the grounds that this is an empirical proposition for which there is little or no evidence. For how can we know whether it is true that people in a state of nature would follow only their inclinations or, at best, reasons of self-interest, when nobody now lives in that state or has ever lived in it?

However, there is some empirical evidence to support this claim. For in the family of nations, individual states are placed very much like individual persons in a state of nature. The doctrine of the sovereignty of nations and the absence of an effective international law and police force are a guarantee that nations live in a state of nature, without commonly accepted rules that are somehow enforced. Hence it must be granted that living in a state of nature leads to living in a state in which individuals act either on impulse or as they think their interest dictates. For states pay only lip service to morality. They attack their hated neighbors when the opportunity arises. They start preventive wars in order to destroy the enemy before he can deliver his knockout blow. Where interests conflict, the stronger party usually has his way, whether his claims are justified or not. And where the relative strength of the parties is not obvious, they usually resort to arms in order to determine "whose side God is on." Treaties are frequently concluded but, morally speaking, they are not worth the paper they are written on. Nor do the partners regard them as contracts binding in the ordinary way, but rather as public expressions of the belief of the governments concerned that for the time being their alliance is in the interest of the allies. It is well understood that such treaties may be canceled before they reach their predetermined end or simply broken when it suits one partner. In international affairs, there are very few examples of *Nibelungentreue,* although statesmen whose countries have profited from keeping their treaties usually make such high moral claims.

It is, moreover, difficult to justify morality in international affairs. For suppose a highly moral statesman were to demand that his country adhere to a treaty obligation even though this meant its ruin or possibly its extinction. Suppose he were to say that treaty obligations are sacred and must be kept whatever the consequences. How could he defend such a policy? Perhaps one might argue that someone has to make a start in order to create mutual confidence in international affairs. Or one might say that setting a good example is the best way of inducing others to follow suit. But such a defense would hardly be sound: The less skeptical one is about the genuineness of the cases in which nations have adhered to their treaties from a sense of moral obligation, the more skeptical one must be about the effectiveness of such examples of virtue in effecting a change of international practice. Power politics still govern in international affairs.

We must, therefore, grant Hobbes the first step in his argument and admit that in a state of nature people, as a matter of psychological fact, would not follow the dictates of morality. But we might object to the next step that knowing this psychological fact about other people's behavior constitutes a reason for behaving in the same way. Would it not still be immoral for anyone to ignore the demands of morality even though he knows that others are likely or certain to do so, too? Can we offer as a justification for morality the fact that no one is entitled to do wrong just because someone else is doing wrong? This argument begs the question whether it *is* wrong for anyone in this state to disregard the demands of morality. It cannot be wrong to break a treaty or make preventive war if we have no reason to obey the moral rules. For to say that it is wrong to do so is to say that we ought not to do so. But if we have no reason for obeying the moral rule, then we have no reason overruling self-interest, hence no reason for keeping the treaty when keeping it is not in our interest, hence it is not true that we have a reason for keeping it, hence not true that we ought to keep it, hence not true that it is wrong not to keep it.

I conclude that Hobbes's argument is sound. Moralities are systems of principles whose acceptance by everyone as overruling the dictates of self-interest is in the interest of everyone alike, though following the rules of a morality is not of course identical with following self-interest. If it were, there could be no conflict between a morality and self-interest and no point in having moral rules overriding self-interest. Hobbes is also right in saying that the application of this system of rules is in accordance with reason only in social conditions, that is, when there are well-established ways of behavior.

The answer to our question "Why should we be moral?" is therefore as follows. We should be moral because being moral is following rules designed to overrule self-interest whenever it is in the interest of everyone alike that everyone should set aside his interest. It is not self-contradictory to say this, because it may be in one's interest *not* to follow one's interest at times. We have already seen that enlightened self-interest acknowledges this point. But while enlightened self-interest does not require any genuine sacrifice from anyone, morality does. In the interest of the possibility of the good life for everyone, voluntary sacrifices are sometimes required from everybody. Thus, a person might do better for himself by following enlightened self-interest rather than morality. It is not possible, however, that *everyone* should do better for himself by following enlightened self-interest rather than morality. The best possible life *for everyone* is possible only by everyone's following the rules of morality, that is, rules which quite frequently may require individuals to make genuine sacrifices.

It must be added to this, however, that such a system of rules has the support of reason only where people live in societies, that is, in conditions in which there are established common ways of behavior. Outside society, people have no reason for following such rules, that is, for being moral. In other words, outside society, the very distinction between right and wrong vanishes.

35. CAN THE MORAL POINT OF VIEW BE JUSTIFIED?

J. C. Thornton

J. C. Thornton *teaches philosophy at the University of Canterbury in New Zealand.*

Does Baier succeed in showing that there are weightier reasons for doing what is right than for following our own interests? In one sense he does, but unfortunately not in the sense required by his original "fundamental" question. All he succeeds in showing is Hobbes' point, viz. that there are weightier reasons for everyone doing what is right than for everyone following self-interest. Baier asks us to examine "the two alternative worlds, one in which moral reasons are always treated by everyone as superior to reasons of self-interest and one in which the reverse is the practice. And we can see that the first world is the better world, because we can see that the second world would be the sort which Hobbes describes as the state of nature." Baier concludes that the answer to the question 'Why should we be moral?' is as follows: "We should be moral because being moral is following rules designed to overrule self-interest whenever it is in the interest of everyone alike that everyone should set aside his interest. . . . It is not possible that *everyone* should do better for himself by following enlightened self-interest rather than morality. The best possible life *for everyone* is attainable only by

From The Australasian Journal of Philosophy, *Vol. 42, 1964, pp. 26–28. Reprinted by permission of the author and the editor.*

everyone's following the rules of morality, that is, rules which quite frequently may require individuals to make genuine sacrifices."

It is clear, I think, that Baier has not answered his original question. His mistake was to think that what we have to do to answer it is to consider two alternative worlds, the one in which moral rules are universally followed and the one in which the rules of enlightened self-interest are universally followed, and then decide which is the better world to live in, i.e. in our own better interests. But if we are going to answer along these lines his fundamental question of ethics, viz. 'Why should I be moral when doing so is not to my advantage?', then there are not just two alternative worlds which we have to compare but *three*. The third possible world is the one in which moral rules are obeyed by everyone else *except me*, who follow enlightened self-interest. The first world is admittedly, from everyone's point of view, a better alternative to the second, but is not the third world, from *my* point of view, a better alternative to either of the other two? Of course, one can hold that the third world is not a practical possibility, but Baier has made it plain that he does not support this view. He makes it quite clear that following morality entails making "genuine sacrifices" and he is not convinced by those who would argue that following morality is in the long run identical with following enlightened self-interest. Inevitably, then, his attempt to give the moral point of view a rational basis comes to grief because, in spite of what he says to the contrary, he has assumed that the only *really* ultimate reason justifying an action is in fact self-interest, and so he is logically prevented from justifying doing one's moral duty in those situations in which duty and interest really do conflict.

My guess is that he was probably prevented from seeing the glaring self-contradiction in his argument by a simple verbal confusion. It is significant that in the early stages of his book he frequently expresses his "fundamental question of ethics" in the words "Why should *I* be moral?" (my italics). However, at the end of the book, when he is at last ready to try to answer the question, he invariably expresses it in the words "Why should *we* be moral?" This latter question can easily be interpreted as a demand for a rational justification for the institution of morality in general, and, of course, a plausible answer can be given to this question along more or less Hobbist lines. But to answer this general question is not automatically to have answered the particular and very different question, "Why should *I* be moral (in the particular situation x at time t)?", and yet Baier has tended to use these two ways of expressing his question indifferently as if they meant the same thing.

My conclusion at this point is that Baier has not succeeded in answering his "fundamental question of ethics" and therefore not succeeded in showing that it is a genuine question demanding a serious answer. But, of course, it may still be true that the question is in fact a genuine one.

36. RACISM

R. M. Hare

R. M. Hare *(1919–) is a Fellow of Balliol College at Oxford University. His first book,* The Language of Morals *(1952), has been one of the most influential and widely discussed books in ethics since Moore's* Principia Ethica. *More recently, Hare wrote* Freedom and Reason *(1963), which he calls a "progress report" on his thinking concerning the nature of morality since the publication of his first work.*

. . . Let us ask, first, why it is that we think what I have called factual arguments to be relevant to moral questions. Why did I say that certain factual arguments (for example about the predictable results of certain policies) were prefectly admissible; and why, on the other hand, do we have this strange phenomenon of Nazis and others inventing obviously spurious factual arguments in order to justify their actions morally? Why not just get on with the job of exterminating the Jews? What need is supplied by the bogus claim that Germans have some special element in their heredity which distinguishes them from other men? Or why does it make a difference to the moral argument that a certain policy would have a certain result? It looks as if facts (or some sorts of facts) are held to be relevant to moral arguments; so much so that if one has not got any genuine facts one invents some make-believe ones. But why is this? In short, what is the bearing of facts on moral arguments? This is one of the central problems of moral philosophy, and I have tried in this and my earlier book to sketch an answer to it. Without further references back, let us set out the answer as clearly and briefly as possible.

An obvious, and so far as it goes true, but incomplete answer to the question 'Why are facts relevant to moral arguments?' is this:

From Freedom and Reason, *1963, Clarendon Press, Oxford. Reprinted by permission of The Clarendon Press, Oxford.*

moral judgements have to be *about something*; and it is the facts of the case which determine what we are judging. Thus, when we are asking moral questions about a proposed action, it is relevant to know what the person would be doing who did the action; for, if we do not know this, we literally shall not know what we are talking about.

I say that this answer is incomplete for two reasons. The first is that it does not explain why we think some facts, and not others, relevant to moral arguments. The second is that it does not explain why it makes a difference if it is a *moral* argument. If I were deciding just what *to do*, without any thought of what I *ought* to do, it would still be important to me to know *what* I should be doing if I did so and so. We shall see that these two incompletenesses are related to each other.

There are some philosophers, to whom I have referred often enough before, who can see only one possible way in which facts might have relevance in moral arguments. This is by there being some logical link, holding in virtue of the meanings of words, between factual premisses and moral conclusions. Now I do not think that there is any such link. And because these philosophers have eyes only for this sort of relevance, they think that if I deny the possibility of such a link, I am committed to holding that facts are not relevant to moral arguments; and this would be an absurd position. But what I have been maintaining is that facts are relevant to moral arguments, but not in the way that these people think.

Facts are relevant to moral arguments because they make a difference between cases which would otherwise be similar. Let us illustrate this by considering again why the Nazis set so much store by the claim that there is something in the blood of Germans which differentiates them from other races. The explanation is that they were proposing to treat other races in a markedly different way from Germans, and wanted a reason why they *ought* to do this. A Nazi might say, as he contemplated the Jews that he was just driving into the gas-chamber, 'These men look just as I would look if I were starved and naked like them; they have the same feelings and aspirations, and there is, apparently, no other relevant difference between them and myself or my German friends. And I would not think it right to treat a German in this way. But there is something that makes a difference; although Germans and Jews are often indistinguishable to the naked eye, there is this all-important thing about them, that they lack that factor in their heredity which true Germans have, and which entitles Germans to send them to the gas-chamber.' Put thus crudely, the argument sounds grotesque; yet something of the sort undoubtedly lies behind many claims of racial superiority. And this parody of moral thinking, just because it is a parody of moral thinking, illustrates extremely well the

266

role which even bogus facts can play in moral arguments—even bad ones. This argument of the Nazis is pretending to be like a perfectly good moral argument, and thus shows us something about what a good moral argument would be like.

The point is this: it is part of the meanings of the moral words that we are logically prohibited from making different moral judgements about two cases, when we cannot adduce any difference between the cases which is the ground for the difference in moral judgements. This is one way of stating the requirement of universalizability which, as we have seen, is fundamental to all moral reasoning. Since the Nazi cannot justify his different treatment of Germans and Jews without adducing some difference between their cases, he invents a difference.

Other participants in race conflicts are more fortunate: they do not have to invent anything; the difference is there, for all to see, in the colour of their victims' skins. This is why it seems so much easier to justify racial discrimination when there is a colour difference than when there is not. But even less obvious differences than those of colour will serve if they have to. What is important to the would-be discriminator is that there should be *some* qualitative difference (i.e. not merely a numerical difference) between the class of people whom he wishes to oppress, exploit, or persecute and those whom he does not. Some of us remember how, at school, the wearing of shoes of a different pattern was enough to mark out some poor boy for maltreatment.

These caricatures of moral reasoning teach us something about the real thing. It is indeed required that, to justify different treatment of people, qualitative differences have to be produced between them or between their actions or circumstances. We try to justify our singular moral judgements by producing principles involved in them: one may or ought to do such and such a *kind* of thing in such and such a *kind* of situation to people of a certain *kind*.

11.7. Now these examples of spurious moral reasoning are parodies. The question which next arises, therefore, is, How do we distinguish the parody from its original? If we do not think that it is an adequate justification for discriminating against a person that his skin is black, how would we distinguish those features of the man or his situation which do justify different treatment from those which do not? There seems at first sight to be no formal difference between saying 'It is right to kill him because his skin is black' and saying 'It is right to kill him because he has killed another man'. Some people regard both of these as good reasons; some, neither; and some, one but not the other. We have therefore to ask, can moral philosophy point out any means of distinguishing between good and bad reasons of this sort; or, in other words, between relevant differences, such as really do justify discrimination, and those which are not relevant? Have we any reason for saying that black skin is not relevant, but being a murderer is?

There are those who try to answer this question in the following way. They take a look at the kind of differences that people *do* call morally relevant; and they make a list of them, reduce them if they can to some sort of system, and then say that we *mean* by 'morally relevant difference' just these differences and no others, and *mean* by 'morality' just that system of evaluations which takes these, and no other, differences into account. There are many objections to this procedure; I will here mention just two. First, how do we know that we could not get a different list if we did the investigation in South Africa or Soviet Russia or ancient Sparta? Secondly, to make such a list does not explain anything; we want to know what leads to things getting put on the list or left off it. The proponents of this view do not seem to have gone far enough in their search for an explanation.

Now, if the argument of this book is correct, we can in fact go a good deal further, by a step which is really no different in principle from one which we took a moment ago. We saw that it follows from the meanings of the moral terms that if different moral judgements are made, relevant differences must be adduced; and we saw that this was a version of the requirement of universalizability. But we have not yet exhausted the potency of this principle; we still have the use of it left which was explained in 6.8 and 9.4.

In order to illustrate this use again, let us suppose that we are having an argument with a man who maintains that a black skin, by itself, is a sufficient ground for discriminating against its possessor. We tell him, and he, being a credulous person, believes, the following story. The Soviet Institute of Race Relations (which is a much more enterprising and scientific body than its Western counterparts) has just succeeded in breeding a new kind of bacillus, which Soviet agents are at this very moment broadcasting in areas of racial conflict throughout the world. This bacillus is very catching and the symptom of the disease which it induces is that, if the patient's skin was white, it turns permanently black, and vice versa. Now when the person with whom we are arguing has absorbed the implications of this story, we ask him whether he still thinks that skin-colour by itself is a sufficient ground for moral discrimination. It is unlikely that he will go on saying that it is; for then he will have to say that if he catches the disease the former blacks who have also had it will have acquired the right to oppress *him*, and all his formerly white friends.

What do we learn from this simple piece of science fiction? What we have got our opponent to do by this innocent deception is to perform an intellectual operation which, if he had really been wanting to reason morally, he would have performed without the deception. This operation is to consider the hypothetical case in which he himself has lost the quality which he said was a sufficient ground for discrimination, and his present victims have gained it—and to consider this hypothetical case as if it were actual. There are two stages in the process of universalization. The first is passed when we have found a universal principle, not containing proper names or other singular terms, from which the moral judgement which we want to make follows, given the facts of our particular situation. This stage is comparatively easy to pass, even for the proponent of the most scandalous moral views. It is passed, for example, by adducing the principle that it is all right for black people to be oppressed by white people. But the next stage is more difficult. It is necessary, not merely that this principle should be produced, but that the person who produces it should actually hold it. It is necessary not merely to *quote* a maxim, but (in Kantian language) to *will* it to be a universal law. It is here that prescriptivity, the second main logical feature of moral judgements, makes its most decisive appearance. For willing it to be a universal law involves willing it to apply even when the roles played by the parties are reversed. And this test will be failed by all maxims or principles which look attractive to oppressors and persecutors on the first test. It will indeed be found that, if we apply these two tests, both founded on the logical, formal features of moral terms, we shall be able to sort out, in the field of race relations at least, the grounds of discrimination which we are really prepared to count as morally relevant from those which we are not.

11.8. From this satisfactory conclusion, however, there is, as we have seen, a way of escape for the sufficiently determined racialist. It remains to illustrate, in terms of the present example, what price he has to pay for his escape. Let us suppose that there is a racialist the mainspring of whose racialism is a horror of miscegenation; and let us suppose that the source of this horror is not any belief about the consequences, social or biological, of miscegenation. That is to say, he is not moved by alleged facts about the weakening of the human stock by mating between people of different colours, or about the unsatisfactory life lived by people of mixed descent or by anything of that kind. If these were his grounds, we could argue with him in a scientific way, trying to show that the offspring of mixed marriages are just as likely to be vigorous and intelligent as those of other marriages; or that any bad social effects of miscegenation would be removed if *he* and people like him abandoned their attempts to enforce a colour bar. Let us suppose, however, that his grounds are not these, but simply a horror of the very idea of a black man mating with a white woman. This cannot be touched by any scientific or factual argument of the sort described. And it may well be true that, if miscegenation is to be prevented, it is necessary to have a rigid colour bar; and that if this is enforced, and leads to resentment, other repressive measures will be necessary for the maintenance of public order, and thus we shall have the whole apparatus of racial repression. If this is true, then it will be hard for us to argue with this man. He detests miscegenation so much that he is prepared to live in a police state in order to avoid it.

And he must be prepared for more than this. He must, if he is going to universalize his moral judgements, be prepared that he himself should not merely live in a police state, but live in it in the same conditions as he is now prepared to make the blacks live in—conditions which are getting steadily worse. He must be prepared that *he* should be subject to arbitrary arrest and maltreatment just on grounds of skin colour, and to butchery if he tries, in collaboration with his fellows, to protest.

Now it may be that there are people so fanatical as to be prepared for all these things in order to avoid miscegenation. But they are surely very few. The repression happens because these few people have on their side a multitude of other people who are not prepared at all to suffer thus, but who have not really thought through the argument. They think, perhaps, that all will be well without too much repression; or that blacks do not mind being treated like this as much as whites would; or that there is a scientific basis for belief in racial superiority —or some of the many other things that racialists tend to believe. All these beliefs can perhaps be refuted severally by scientists and others without any help from the philosopher; but they are apt, collectively, to form an amalgam in the minds of racialists which makes into allies of the fanatic many people who are not, in themselves, in the least fanatical. The contribution of the philosopher is to take this amalgam apart, deposit such beliefs as are open to scientific refutation in the in-trays of the scientists, and, when the scientists have dealt with them, exhibit the prescriptive remainder of racialism for what it is—something that fanatics may hold but which the bulk of a people—even a people as hard-pressed as the white South Africans—never will.

11.9. We are now in a position to explain why, in spite of the inadequacy of an argument which we mentioned earlier, it *is* morally relevant that blacks are people. Saying that they are people is saying that they are like us in certain respects. It is not clear yet in *what* respects; this will be found to vary from case to case, as we shall see. But the principle of this argument from the fact that blacks are people can now be exposed as follows. If a black man whom I am contemplating maltreating has, as I have every reason to suppose that he has, certain characteristics in common with myself—if, to use an example from an earlier century, it causes him great suffering if he and his wife are separated and sent as slaves to different countries—then I can reason as follows. I am not prepared in general to accept the maxim that it is all right for people to separate husbands from wives for commercial gain; for this would be committing myself to the judgement that it would be all right for somebody to do this to me if he were in a position to do so. But can I say that it is all right to do this to blacks? The answer must be 'No'; for if I envisage myself becoming a black, but retaining my other characteristics, and in particular the characteristic of being attached to my wife, I am not (since I am not a fanatic for the liberty of commerce) prepared to accept a maxim which permits people to do this to me.

On the other hand, if we take the example of the murderer mentioned above, the position is altered. I may very well be prepared to prescribe that, if I commit a murder, I should be hanged. In actual fact I am not; for I am not a supporter of capital punishment—for reasons which are irrelevant to the present argument. But let us, in order to avoid this difficulty, substitute 'put in prison' for 'hanged' or 'killed.' I am prepared to prescribe that if I commit a murder I should be put in prison: and my reasons are utilitarian ones comparable to those given by the judge in 7.2 ff. But reasons of this sort are not available to racialists. Thus we see why it is thought not to be relevant that the man is black, but is thought to be relevant that a man is a murderer. More important, we see why it is thought to be relevant that a slave loves his wife. The duties which we acknowledge towards people are not derived from the 'essence of man' or from any philosophical mystifications of that sort; they are acknowledged because we say 'There, but for my good fortune, go I. That man is like me in important respects; in particular, the same things as cause me to suffer cause him to suffer; therefore, unless I am prepared to accept a maxim which would permit me to be treated like him were I to acquire a black skin (which I am not), I cannot say that it is all right for me to treat him thus.'

This line of reasoning also helps to explain why we recognize certain duties towards both men and animals, but certain others towards men only. For example, nobody would be thought to be oppressing animals because he did not allow way of putting this is to say that these people are not paying attention to the relevant similarities between themselves and their victims. If we like to revert to the metaphor, having understood what it stands for, the bear-baiter is not thinking of the bear as his brother—or even cousin.

It is also possible that, though fully aware of what they are doing to their victims, they are not reasoning morally about it. That is to say, they are not asking themselves whether they can universalize their prescriptions; though they may make play with the moral *words* which they have heard other people use, they are not, in their own thinking, using these words according to the logical rules which are implicit in their meaning. And there are other possibilities, too numerous to mention here, which have been examined in the body of this book.

It may be asked: What is to be done about this? Can the philosopher, in particular, do anything about it? When South African believers in white supremacy read this book, will they at once hasten to repeal the pass laws and make the blacks their political equals? This is highly unlikely; and in any case they will not read the book. To get people to think morally it is not sufficient to tell them how to do it; it is necessary also to induce in them the wish to do it. And this is not the province of the philosopher. It is more likely that enlightened politicians, journalists, radio commentators, preachers, novelists, and all those who have an influence on public opinion will gradually effect a change for the better—given that events do not overtake them. Perhaps people in areas of racial conflict can be, in the end, brought to think of the resemblances between themselves and members of other races as morally relevant, and of the differences as morally irrelevant. Perhaps, even, they may learn to cultivate their imaginations. But this much can be claimed for philosophy, that it is sometimes easier to bring something about if we understand clearly what it is we are trying to do.

37. WAR

Richard Wasserstrom

Richard A. Wasserstrom (1936–   ) *is Professor of Law and Philosophy at the University of California at Los Angeles. He has written* The Judicial Decision *(1961) and edited* War and Morality *(1970). He has also published a number of articles in the area of legal philosophy.*

I propose in this paper to consider three arguments having to do with the morality of war. The first two are concerned with the question of whether it makes sense at all to make moral judgments about wars. The third is concerned to establish the absolute immorality of all

From The Journal of Philosophy, *Vol. 65, No. 19, 1968, pp. 578; 581–590. Reprinted by permission of the author and the editor.*

war and of ever waging war. To an appreciable extent these are only preliminary arguments that require consideration before other more central issues can be taken up. Yet, to analyze even these with any care is a more complicated matter than one might suppose—sufficiently complicated at least to exhaust the space limitations of this symposium. I want to record at the outset, therefore, my awareness of the fact that this paper is at best an introduction to the problem of the morality of war, and neither a final nor an adequate analysis of it. . . .

II

I want now to consider the claim that it is not possible to assess war in moral terms. This is the position that asserts that moral predicates either cannot be applied meaningfully to wars or should not be applied to wars. For want of a better name for this general view, I shall call it *moral nihilism*.

It is apparent that anyone who believes that all moral predicates are meaningless, or that all morality (and not just conventional morality) is a sham and a fraud, will regard the case of the morality of war simply as an instantiation of this general view. This is not the position I am interested in considering.

In contrast, the view that I call *moral nihilism* is, I think, more interesting at least in the sense that it is restricted to the case of war. What I have in mind is this: During the controversy over the rightness of the Vietnam war there have been any number of persons—including a large number in the university—who very frequently claim to hold the view that in matters of war (but not in other matters) morality has no place. The war in Vietnam may, they readily concede, be stupid, unwise, against the best interests of the United States, and absurd; but it is neither immoral nor unjust. Not because it is moral or right, but because these predicates are *in this context* either senseless or inapplicable.

Nor is this view limited to the Vietnam war. Consider, for instance, the following passage from a speech given only a few years ago by Dean Acheson, the former Secretary of State.

. . . [T]hose involved in the Cuban crisis of October, 1962, will remember the irrelevance of the supposed moral considerations brought out in the discussions. Judgment centered about the appraisal of dangers and risks, the weighing of the need for decisive and effective action against considerations of prudence; the need to do enough, against the consequences of doing too much. Moral talk did not bear on the problem. Nor did it bear upon the decision of those called upon to advise the President in 1949 whether and with what degree of urgency to press the attempt to produce a thermonuclear weapon. A respected colleague advised me that it would be better that our nation and people should perish rather than be party to a course so evil as producing that weapon. I told him that on the Day of Judgment his view might be confirmed and that he was free to go forth and preach the necessity for salvation. It was not, however, a view which I could entertain as a public servant.[1]

Admittedly, the passage just reproduced is susceptible of different interpretations. Acheson may be putting forward the view that moral evaluation is relevant to the "ends" pursued by any country (including our own) but not to the policies *adopted* in furtherance of these ends. But at times, at least, he appears to be an exponent of a quite different view, namely that in the realm of foreign affairs moral judgments, as opposed to strategic or prudential ones, are simply misplaced, and any attempts at moral assessment misdirected.

Irrespective of what may be the correct exegesis of the text, I want to treat it as illustrative of the position that morality has no place in the assessment of war.[2]

There are several things it is worth considering in respect to a view such as this one. In the first place, the claim that in matters of war morality has no place is an ambiguous claim. To put it somewhat loosely, the claim may be descriptive, or it may be prescriptive, or it may be analytic. Thus, it might be the factual claim that matters relating to war uniformly turn out to be decided on grounds of national interest or expediency rather than by appeal to what is moral.[3] This claim I will not consider further; it is an empirical claim better answered by students of American (and foreign) diplomatic relations.

It would be a prescriptive claim were it to be taken to assert that matters relating to war ought always be decided by appeal to (say) national interest rather than by appeal to the moral point of view. For reasons that have yet to be elucidated, on this view the moral point of view is capable of being employed, but it is undesirable to employ it. I shall say something more about this view in a moment, and I shall consider it in appreciably more detail in part III of the paper, below.

The analytic point is not that morality ought not be used, but rather that it cannot be. On this view the statement "The United States is behaving immorally in the way it is waging war in Vietnam" (or "in waging war in Vietnam") is not wrong but meaningless.

What are we to make of the analytic view? As I have indicated,

---

[1] Dean Acheson, "Ethics in International Relations Today," quoted in Marcus G. Raskin and Bernard B. Fall, eds., *The Viet-Nam Reader* (New York: Vintage Books, 1965), p. 13.

[2] Admittedly, Acheson's view is somewhat broader than this since it appears to encompass all foreign relations.

[3] Such a view could also hold, although it need not, that it would be desirable that these matters be determined on moral grounds.

it could, of course, be advanced simply as an instantiation of a more sweeping position concerning the general meaninglessness of the moral point of view. What I want to consider, though, is the degree to which this view is held as a special view about war and not as a part of a more general claim that all morality is meaningless.[4]

I think that there are at least four reasons why this special view gets to be held. I consider three of them in this section and the fourth in the next.

First, the accusation that one's own country is involved in an immoral war is one that is very threatening in a number of respects. For one thing, if the accusation is well founded it may be thought to imply that certain types of behavior are forbidden to the citizen and that other kinds are obligatory upon him. Yet, in time of war it is just this obligatory sort of behavior that will be treated most harshly by the actor's own government. Hence the morally responsible citizen is put in the most troublesome of all possible moral dilemmas. If his country is engaged in an immoral war then he may have a duty to oppose and resist; yet opposition and resistance will typically carry extraordinarily severe penalties. The stakes for the person who is concerned to be moral could not be higher.

The pressure is, I suspect, simply too great for many of us. We are unwilling to pay the fantastically high personal price that goes with the moral point of view, and we are equally unwilling to plead guilty to a charge of immorality of this most serious sort. So we solve the problem by denying the possibility that war can be immoral. The relief is immediate; the moral "heat" is off. If war cannot be immoral, then one's country cannot be engaged in an immoral war—only a stupid, or unwise one. And whatever one's obligations may be to keep one's country from behaving stupidly or improvidently, they are vastly less stringent and troublesome than obligations imposed by the specter of complicity in an immoral war. And so, in a kind of desperation, the distinctions between the conduct of the United States in 1941–45 and the conduct of the United States in 1967–68 in Vietnam—to say nothing of the distinctions between the Axis powers and the Allies, are collapsed if not obliterated.[5]

---

[4] Much of what I say in this section applies, I believe, with equal force to what I call the *prescriptive view*, which I discuss more fully in part III. For stylistic reasons I refer just to the analytic view, but I mean to include them both where appropriate.

[5] One of the very important matters that I do not discuss at all adequately in this paper is the relationship between judgments about the morality of war, judgments about the morality of a particular country's role in a war, and judgments about the morality of citizens of a country engaged in war. Although I tend to treat these three kinds of judgments as indistinguishable, I realize there are important and complicated differences and connections.

Second, I think the nihilistic view sometimes seems plausible because of the existence of differences between personal behavior and the behavior of states. In particular, the plausibility of this view can, perhaps, be explained in part by the fact that there are not laws governing the behavior of states in the same way in which there are positive laws governing the behavior of citizens. International law is a notoriously troublesome notion just because it is both like and unlike our concept of positive law.

Now, how does skepticism about the lawlike quality of international law lead to the claim that it is impossible for war to be either moral or immoral? I do not know, but perhaps it is because there is at least one sense of justice that is intimately tied up with the notion of a rule violation, namely, that which relates justice to the following of rules and to the condemnation and punishment of those who break rules. In the absence of laws that govern the behavior of states, it may be inferred (although I think mistakenly) that it is impossible for states to behave either justly or unjustly.[6] But even if justice were analyzable solely in terms of the following of rules, morality certainly is not. Hence, the absence of international laws cannot serve to make the moral appraisal of war impossible.

Third, there is a view that is substantially more plausible than the one just considered. This asserts that, in the absence of positive laws and in the absence of any machinery by which to punish even the grossest kinds of immorality, behavior cannot be regarded as morally obligatory. This is one way to take Hobbes when he asserts that in the state of nature the natural laws bind in conscience but not in action. Even this view, however, would not render the moral assessment of the behavior of states meaningless; it would only excuse immorality in the absence of effective international law. More importantly, though, it, too, misunderstands the nature and demands of the moral point of view in its insistence that morality depends for its *meaning* on the existence of guarantees of moral conformity by others.

In short, although I understand how it is that persons come to embrace this kind of nihilism in repect to war, I see no reason to believe the nihilistic view more plausible here than in respect to human action generally.

III

There is, as I have indicated, another way to take the claim that in matters of war morality has no place. That is the view I have called

---

[6] Mistakenly, because justice is not analyzable solely in terms of rule-following and rule-violating behavior.

prescriptive: the view that national interest ought to determine policies in respect to war, not morality. This is surely one way to take the remarks of Dean Acheson reproduced earlier. It is also, perhaps, involved in the following defense given by President Truman for the dropping of the atomic bomb on Hiroshima. What he said was this:

> Having found the bomb, we have to use it. We have used it against those who attacked us without warning at Pearl Harbor, against those who have starved and beaten and executed American prisoners of war, against those who have abandoned all pretense of obeying international laws of warfare. We have used it in order to shorten the agony of war, in order to save the lives of thousands and thousands of young Americans.[7]

Although this passage has many interesting features, I am concerned only with President Truman's insistence that the dropping of the bomb was justified because to do so saved the lives "of thousands and thousands of young Americans."

Conceivably, this is unobjectionable. Conceivably, it is an elliptical way of saying that on balance fewer lives were lost through the dropping of the bomb and the accelerated cessation of hostilities than through any alternative course of conduct. Suppose, though, that this was not the argument. Suppose instead that the justification was regarded as adequate provided only that it was reasonably clear that fewer *American* lives would be lost than through any alternative course of conduct. Thus, to quantify the example, we can imagine someone maintaining that Hiroshima was justified because 20,000 fewer Americans died in the Pacific theater than would have died if the bomb had not been dropped. And this is justified even though 30,000 more Japanese died than would have been killed had the war been fought to an end with conventional means. Thus, even though 10,000 more people died than would otherwise have been the case, the bombing was justified because of the greater number of American lives saved.

On this interpretation it would appear that the argument depends upon a valuing of the lives of Americans higher than the lives of persons from other countries. As such, is there anything to be said for the argument?

One strong argument, and the only one I shall consider, might go like this: Truman was the President of the United States and as such had an obligation always to choose that course of conduct which appeared to offer the greatest chance of maximizing the interests of the United States. As President, he was obligated to prefer the lives of American soldiers over those from any other country, and he was obli-

---

[7] *Address to the Nation,* August 9, 1945.

gated to prefer them just because they were Americans and he was their President. The case is analogous to that of a lawyer or that of a parent. A lawyer has a duty to be an advocate for the interests of his client. He has an obligation to present his client's case in the fashion most calculated to ensure his client's victory; and he has this obligation irrespective of the objective merits of his client's case. Similarly, we are neither surprised nor dismayed when a parent prefers the interests of *his* child over those of other children elsewhere. A parent qua parent is certainly not behaving immorally when he acts so as to secure satisfactions for his child, again, irrespective of the objective merits of his child's needs or wants. Thus, *as public servants,* Dean Acheson and Harry Truman had no moral choice but to pursue those policies which appeared to them to be in the best interest of the United States. And to a lesser degree, all persons qua citizens of the United States have a similar if slightly more attenuated obligation. It is for this reason that morality has no real place in war.

This, then, or something like it is an argument that could be made in support of the consistent application of a standard of national interest to all decisions involving the waging of war. Up to a point the argument clearly has merit, but only up to a point. It is certainly both correct and important to observe that public officials, like parents and lawyers, do have special moral obligations that are imposed by virtue of the position or role they fill. A lawyer does have a duty to prefer his client's interests in a way that would be improper were the person anyone other than his client. And the same, I think, holds for a parent, a President, and, doubtless, countless others.

The point becomes distorted, however, when it is supposed that such an obligation always, under all circumstances, overrides any and all other obligations that the person might have. The case of the lawyer is instructive. While he has an obligation to attend to his client's interests in very special ways, there are many other things that it is impermissible for the lawyer to do in furtherance of his client's interests—irrespective, this time, of how significantly they might advance that interest.

The case for the President, or for public servants generally, is similar. Although the President may indeed have an obligation to prefer and pursue the national interests, this obligation could only be justifiable—could only be a moral obligation—if it were enmeshed in a comparable range of limiting and competing obligations. If we concede that the President has certain obligations to prefer the national interest that no one else has, we must be equally sensitive to the fact that the President also has some of the same obligations to other persons that all other men have—if for no other reason than that all persons have the right to be treated or not treated in certain ways. So, whatever special obligations the President may have cannot by themselves support the view that in war considerations of morality ought have no place.[8]

IV

I find appreciably more persuasive, although still not convincing, what could in some sense be regarded as the opposite of those just considered; namely, the view that all wars under all circumstances are immoral. This is the view that I call the view of *absolute pacifism*. There is a weak sense in which I think this view is correct and a strong sense in which it is probably not. The weak sense is the claim that every war is to some degree unjust or immoral. The strong sense is the claim that no war can be morally justifiable.

The claim that war is always immoral might derive from an argument such as the following: War has as one of its inevitable consequences the fact that persons who are in some intelligible sense innocent will be wounded and killed. Among the persons who will be killed in any war are children, innocent persons, and this alone is sufficient to make any such war immoral.

In order to see that this is the case, so the argument continues, consider the following: we can imagine a thoroughly unprovoked attack upon another country, an attack committed moreover from the worst of motives and with the most despicable of ends in mind. And let us assume, too, for the moment, that under such circumstances there is nothing immoral about fighting back and even killing those who are attacking. But in fighting back, we will be killing children of the aggressor country. Yet, it would not be the children of the aggressor country who were attacking. Children are simply not capable of making war, or even of deciding whether to make war. In this sense, at least, even the children of the aggressor are innocent. To kill them is immoral.

There are three different objections or qualifications that I want to consider in respect to this view.[9]

First, someone might point out that it is possible for a war to

---

[8] It is, I am convinced, the seductiveness of this particular view—the ease with which we move from giving the national interest its due to giving it unquestioned primacy—that makes plausible, as alternatives, movements that seek to develop a single world government and a notion of *world* rather than *national* citizenship.

[9] One that I do not consider concerns the use of children as one clear case of innocents. There are, of course, others who probably qualify: women, the aged, conscriptees, those who do everything possible to oppose the war their country is waging. I acknowledge a need to work out with greater care what is involved in the notion of innocence, how it would apply to these classes of persons, and its precise relevance to moral assessments of war.

be fought without any noncombatants being killed or seriously wounded. If so, this argument would not apply. Actually, given the development of weapons of mass destruction, I think it extraordinarily unlikely that a war could be fought today in which large numbers of innocent persons would not be killed. But that is an empirical matter that could be disputed. It is sufficient if the argument in question is treated as a hypothetical one; engaging in war is immoral if it is the case that one (or one's country) will engage in acts that will bring about the death of innocent persons, i.e., noncombatants such as children.

Second, it is clear that the fact that children will die in a war—as in many other activities—is not itself sufficient to render their deaths immoral. For that to be the case the deaths must be intentionally, knowingly, recklessly, or negligently brought about. And there are gradations of culpability here just as there are in other spheres of behavior. Thus, if a country engages in acts of war that are done with the intention of bringing about the deaths of children (say, to weaken the will of the enemy), this is one thing. If a country engages in acts of war aimed at killing combatants but which, it is known, will also kill children, this is another. And both of these are different from engaging in conduct in which the foreseeable harm to noncombatants is consciously disregarded or only carelessly taken into account. In all cases, however, the killing of innocent noncombatants under such circumstances would, I believe, make immoral to some degree or other the activities in question.

A different sort of problem arises if someone asks how we are to differentiate the deaths of children in war from, for example, the deaths of children that accompany the use of highways or airplanes in times of peace. Someone might, that is, argue that we permit children to ride in cars on highways and to fly in airplanes even though we *know* that there will be accidents and that as a result of these accidents innocent children will die. And since we know this to be the case, the situation appears to be indistinguishable from that of engaging in acts of war where it is known that the death of children will be a direct, although not intended, consequence.

I think that there are two sorts of response that can be made to a question of this sort. In the first place, it simply does seem to me one thing to act where one knows that certain more or less identifiable persons will be killed (say, bombing a troop camp when one knows that those children who live in the vicinity of the camp will also be killed) and quite another thing to engage in conduct in which all one can say is that it can be predicted with a high degree of confidence that over a given period of time a certain number of persons (including children) will be killed. The difference seems to lie partly in the lack of specificity concerning the identity of the persons and to lie partly in the kind of causal connection involved.

In the second place, there is certainly a difference in the two cases in respect to the possibility of deriving benefits from the conduct. That is to say when a highway is used, one is participating in a system or set of arrangements in which benefits are derived from that use (even though risks, and hence costs, are also involved). It is not easy to see how a similar sort of analysis can *plausibly* be proposed in connection with typical acts of war.

V

It is clear that, under even the most favorable interpretation, the argument of absolute pacifism establishes only that to engage in war today is immoral. It does not by itself demonstrate that to engage in war would necessarily be morally unjustifiable. Such a demonstration, if indeed it can be made, is beyond the scope of this paper. Any inquiry in this direction would require a consideration of a number of issues which, as I have indicated, I have avoided altogether. It is, I think, nonetheless appropriate to conclude by indicating something of what such a demonstration would involve. At a minimum, it would involve a consideration of the relevance and import of at least the following topics:

(1) The circumstances that transpired before the war began; the incidents or conditions that occasioned the war, the presence or absence of aggression, the existence of past grievances and injustices;

(2) To the extent to which it makes sense to think of war as a rule-governed activity, the quality of these rules and the degree of conformity to them;

(3) The aims or goals sought to be achieved through the war;

(4) The presence or absence of a claim of self-defense.

What weight each of these perspectives ought to receive in any moral assessment of war is a large and important matter. Given the awesomeness and awfulness of war, however, this and other such questions certainly deserve more attention than they have so far received from philosophers.

38. CIVIL DISOBEDIENCE

John Rawls

John Rawls. *(See essay number 29 for biographical note.)*

I. INTRODUCTION

I should like to discuss briefly, and in an informal way, the grounds of civil disobedience in a constitutional democracy. Thus, I shall limit my remarks to the conditions under which we may, by civil disobedience, properly oppose legally established democratic authority; I am not concerned with the situation under other kinds of government nor, except incidentally, with other forms of resistance. My thought is that in a reasonably just (though of course not perfectly just) democratic regime, civil disobedience, when it is justified, is normally to be understood as a political action which addresses the sense of justice of the majority in order to urge reconsideration of the measures protested and to warn that in the firm opinion of the dissenters the conditions of social cooperation are not being honored. This characterization of civil disobedience is intended to apply to dissent on fundamental questions of internal policy, a limitation which I shall follow to simplify our question.

II. THE SOCIAL CONTRACT DOCTRINE

It is obvious that the justification of civil disobedience depends upon the theory of political obligation in general, and so we may appropriately begin with a few comments on this question. The two chief virtues of social institutions are justice and efficiency, where by the efficiency of institutions I understand their effectiveness for certain social conditions and ends the fulfillment of which is to everyone's advantage. We should comply with and do our part in just and efficient social arrangements for at least two reasons: first of all, we have a natural duty not to oppose the establishment of just and efficient institutions (when they do not yet exist) and to uphold and comply with them (when they do exist); and second, assuming that we have knowingly accepted the benefits of these institutions and plan to continue to do so, and that we have encouraged and expect others to do their part, we also have an obligation to do our share when, as the arrangement requires, it comes our turn. Thus, we often have both a natural duty as well as an obligation to support just and efficient institutions, the obligation arising from our voluntary acts while the duty does not.

Now all this is perhaps obvious enough, but it does not take us very far. Any more particular conclusions depend upon the conception of justice which is the basis of a theory of political obligation. I believe that the appropriate conception, at least for an account of political obligation in a constitutional democracy, is that of the social contract theory from which so much of our political thought derives. If we are careful to interpret it in a suitably general way, I hold that this doctrine provides a satisfactory basis for political theory, indeed even for ethical theory itself, but this is beyond our present concern.[1] The interpretation I suggest is the following: that the principles to which social arrangements must conform, and in particular the principles of justice, are those which free and rational men would agree to in an original position of equal liberty; and similarly, the principles which govern men's relations to institutions and define their natural duties and obligations are the principles to which they would consent when so situated. It should be noted straightway that in this interpretation of the contract theory the principles of justice are understood as the outcome of a hypothetical agreement. They are principles which would be agreed to if the situation of the original position were to arise. There is no mention of an actual agreement nor need such an agreement ever be made. Social arrangements are just or unjust according to whether they accord with the principles for assigning and securing fundamental rights and liberties which would be chosen in the original position. This position is, to be sure, the analytic analogue of the traditional notion of the state of nature, but it must not be mistaken for a historical occasion. Rather it is a hypothetical situation which embodies the basic ideas of the contract doctrine; the description of this situation enables us to work out which principles would be adopted. I must now say something about these matters.

The contract doctrine has always supposed that the persons in the original position have equal powers and rights, that is, that they are symmetrically situated with respect to any arrangements for reaching agreement, and that coalitions and the like are excluded. But it is an essential element (which has not been sufficiently observed although

---

[1] By the social contract theory I have in mind the doctrine found in Locke, Rousseau, and Kant. I have attempted to give an interpretation of this view in: "Justice as Fairness," *Philosophical Review* (April, 1958); "Justice and Constitutional Liberty," *Nomos*, VI (1963); "The Sense of Justice," *Philosophical Review* (July 1963). [Ed. note. See also "Distributive Justice," in Peter Laslett and W. G. Runciman, eds., *Philosophy, Politics and Society* (1967).]

it is implicit in Kant's version of the theory) that there are very strong restrictions on what the contracting parties are presumed to know. In particular, I interpret the theory to hold that the parties do not know their position in society, past, present, or future; nor do they know which institutions exist. Again, they do not know their own place in the distribution of natural talents and abilities, whether they are intelligent or strong, man or woman, and so on. Finally, they do not know their own particular interests and preferences or the system of ends which they wish to advance: they do not know their conception of the good. In all these respects the parties are confronted with a veil of ignorance which prevents any one from being able to take advantage of his good fortune or particular interests or from being disadvantaged by them. What the parties do know (or assume) is that Hume's circumstances of justice obtain: namely, that the bounty of nature is not so generous as to render cooperative schemes superfluous nor so harsh as to make them impossible. Moreover, they assume that the extent of their altruism is limited and that, in general, they do not take an interest in one another's interests. Thus, given the special features of the original position, each man tries to do the best he can for himself by insisting on principles calculated to protect and advance his system of ends whatever it turns out to be.

I believe that as a consequence of the peculiar nature of the original position there would be an agreement on the following two principles for assigning rights and duties and for regulating distributive shares as these are determined by the fundamental institutions of society: first, each person is to have an equal right to the most extensive liberty compatible with a like liberty for all; second, social and economic inequalities (as defined by the institutional structure or fostered by it) are to be arranged so that they are both to everyone's advantage and attached to positions and offices open to all. In view of the content of these two principles and their application to the main institutions of society, and therefore to the social system as a whole, we may regard them as the two principles of justice. Basic social arrangements are just insofar as they conform to these principles, and we can, if we like, discuss questions of justice directly by reference to them. But a deeper understanding of the justification of civil disobedience requires, I think, an account of the derivation of these principles provided by the doctrine of the social contract. Part of our task is to show why this is so.

III. THE GROUNDS OF COMPLIANCE WITH AN UNJUST LAW

If we assume that in the original position men would agree both to the principle of doing their part when they have accepted and plan to continue to accept the benefits of just institutions (the principle of fairness), and also to the principle of not preventing the establishment of just institutions and of upholding and complying with them when they do exist, then the contract doctrine easily accounts for our having to conform to just institutions. But how does it account for the fact that we are normally required to comply with unjust laws as well? The injustice of a law is not a sufficient ground for not complying with it any more than the legal validity of legislation is always sufficient to require obedience to it. Sometimes one hears these extremes asserted, but I think that we need not take them seriously.

An answer to our question can be given by elaborating the social contract theory in the following way. I interpret it to hold that one is to envisage a series of agreements as follows: first, men are to agree upon the principles of justice in the original position. Then they are to move to a constitutional convention in which they choose a constitution that satisfies the principles of justice already chosen. Finally they assume the role of a legislative body and guided by the principles of justice enact laws subject to the constraints and procedures of the just constitution. The decisions reached in any stage are binding in all subsequent stages. Now whereas in the original position the contracting parties have no knowledge of their society or of their own position in it, in both a constitutional convention and a legislature, they do know certain general facts about their institutions, for example, the statistics regarding employment and output required for fiscal and economic policy. But no one knows particular facts about his own social class or his place in the distribution of natural assets. On each occasion the contracting parties have the knowledge required to make their agreement rational from the appropriate point of view, but not so much as to make them prejudiced. They are unable to tailor principles and legislation to take advantage of their social or natural position; a veil of ignorance prevents their knowing what this position is. With this series of agreements in mind, we can characterize just laws and policies as those which would be enacted were this whole process correctly carried out.

In choosing a constitution the aim is to find among the just constitutions the one which is most likely, given the general facts about the society in question, to lead to just and effective legislation. The principles of justice provide a criterion for the laws desired; the problem is to find a set of political procedures that will give this outcome. I shall assume that, at least under the normal conditions of a modern state, the best constitution is some form of democratic regime affirming equal political liberty and using some sort of majority (or other plurality) rule. Thus it follows that on the contract theory a constitutional democracy of some sort is required by the principles of justice. At the same time it is essential to observe that the constitutional process is always a case of what we may call imperfect procedural justice: that is, there is no feasible political procedure which guarantees that the enacted legislation is just even though we have (let us suppose) a standard for just legislation. In simple cases, such as games of fair division, there are procedures which always lead to the right outcome (assume that equal shares is fair and let the man who cuts the cake take the last piece). These situations are those of perfect procedural justice. In other cases it does not matter what the outcome is as long as the fair procedure is followed: fairness of the process is transferred to the result (fair gambling is an instance of this). These situations are those of pure procedural justice. The constitutional process, like a criminal trial, resembles neither of these; the result matters and we have a standard for it. The difficulty is that we cannot frame a procedure which guarantees that only just and effective legislation is enacted. Thus even under a just constitution unjust laws may be passed and unjust policies enforced. Some form of the majority principle is necessary but the majority may be mistaken, more or less willfully, in what it legislates. In agreeing to a democratic constitution (as an instance of imperfect procedural justice) one accepts at the same time the principle of majority rule. Assuming that the constitution is just and that we have accepted and plan to continue to accept its benefits, we then have both an obligation and a natural duty (and in any case the duty) to comply with what the majority enacts even though it may be unjust. In this way we become bound to follow unjust laws, not always, of course, but provided the injustice does not exceed certain limits. We recognize that we must run the risk of suffering from the defects of one another's sense of justice; this burden we are prepared to carry as long as it is more or less evenly distributed or does not weigh too heavily. Justice binds us to a just constitution and to the unjust laws which may be enacted under it in precisely the same way that it binds us to any other social arrangement. Once we take the sequence of stages into account, there is nothing unusual in our being required to comply with unjust laws.

It should be observed that the majority principle has a secondary place as a rule of procedure which is perhaps the most efficient one under usual circumstances for working a democratic constitution. The basis for it rests essentially upon the principles of justice and therefore we may, when conditions allow, appeal to these principles against unjust legislation. The justice of the constitution does not insure the justice of laws enacted under it; and while we often have both an obligation and a duty to comply with what the majority legislates (as long as it does not exceed certain limits), there is, of course, no corresponding obligation or duty to regard what the majority enacts as itself just. The right to make law does not guarantee that the decision is rightly made; and while the citizen submits in his conduct to the judgment of democratic authority, he does not submit his judgment to it.[2] And if in his judgment the enactments of the majority exceed certain bounds of injustice, the citizen may consider civil disobedience. For we are not required to accept the majority's acts unconditionally and to acquiesce in the denial of our and others' liberties; rather we submit our conduct to democratic authority to the extent necessary to share the burden of working a constitutional regime, distorted as it must inevitably be by men's lack of wisdom and the defects of their sense of justice.

IV. THE PLACE OF CIVIL DISOBEDIENCE IN A CONSTITUTIONAL DEMOCRACY

We are now in a position to say a few things about civil disobedience. I shall understand it to be a public, nonviolent, and conscientious act contrary to law usually done with the intent to bring about a change in the policies or laws of the government.[3] Civil disobedience is a political act in the sense that it is an act justified by moral principles which define a conception of civil society and the public good. It rests, then, on political conviction as opposed to a search for self or group interest; and in the case of a constitutional democracy, we may assume that this conviction involves the conception of justice (say that expressed by the contract doctrine) which underlies the constitution itself. That is, in a viable democratic regime there is a common conception of justice by reference to which its citizens regulate their political affairs and interpret the constitution. Civil disobedience is a public act which the dissenter believes to be justified by this conception of justice and for this reason it may be understood as addressing the sense of justice of the majority in order to urge reconsideration of the measures protested and to warn that, in the sincere opinion of the dissenters, the conditions of social cooperation are not being honored. For the principles of justice express precisely such conditions, and their persistent and deliberate violation in regard to basic liberties over any extended period of time cuts the ties of community and invites either submission or forceful resistance. By engaging in civil disobedience a minority leads the majority to consider whether it wants to have its acts

---

[2] On this point see A. E. Murphy's review of Yves Simon's *The Philosophy of Democratic Government* (1951) in the *Philosophical Review* (April, 1952).

[3] Here I follow H. A. Bedau's definition of civil disobedience. See his "On Civil Disobedience," *Journal of Philosophy* (October, 1961).

taken in this way, or whether, in view of the common sense of justice, it wishes to acknowledge the claims of the minority.

Civil disobedience is also civil in another sense. Not only is it the outcome of a sincere conviction based on principles which regulate civic life, but it is public and nonviolent, that is, it is done in a situation where arrest and punishment are expected and accepted without resistance. In this way it manifests a respect for legal procedures. Civil disobedience expresses disobedience to law within the limits of fidelity to law, and this feature of it helps to establish in the eyes of the majority that it is indeed conscientious and sincere, that it really is meant to address their sense of justice.[4] Being completely open about one's acts and being willing to accept the legal consequences of one's conduct is a bond given to make good one's sincerity, for that one's deeds are conscientious is not easy to demonstrate to another or even before oneself. No doubt it is possible to imagine a legal system in which conscientious belief that the law is unjust is accepted as a defense for noncompliance, and men of great honesty who are confident in one another might make such a system work. But as things are such a scheme would be unstable; we must pay a price in order to establish that we believe our actions have a moral basis in the convictions of the community.

The nonviolent nature of civil disobedience refers to the fact that it is intended to address the sense of justice of the majority and as such it is a form of speech, an expression of conviction. To engage in violent acts likely to injure and to hurt is incompatible with civil disobedience as a mode of address. Indeed, an interference with the basic rights of others tends to obscure the civilly disobedient quality of one's act. Civil disobedience is nonviolent in the further sense that the legal penalty for one's action is accepted and that resistance is not (at least for the moment) contemplated. Nonviolence in this sense is to be distinguished from nonviolence as a religious or pacifist principle. While those engaging in civil disobedience have often held some such principle, there is no necessary connection between it and civil disobedience. For on the interpretation suggested, civil disobedience in a democratic society is best understood as an appeal to the principles of justice, the fundamental conditions of willing social cooperation among free men, which in the view of the community as a whole are expressed in the constitution and guide its interpretation. Being an appeal to the moral basis of public life, civil disobedience is a political and not primarily a religious act. It addresses itself to the common principles of justice which men can require one another to follow and not to the aspirations of love which they cannot. Moreover by taking part in civilly dis-

---

[4] For a fuller discussion of this point to which I am indebted, see Charles Fried, "Moral Causation," *Harvard Law Review* (1964).

obedient acts one does not foreswear indefinitely the idea of forceful resistance; for if the appeal against injustice is repeatedly denied, then the majority has declared its intention to invite submission or resistance and the latter may conceivably be justified even in a democratic regime. We are not required to acquiesce in the crushing of fundamental liberties by democratic majorities which have shown themselves blind to the principles of justice upon which justification of the constitution depends.

V. THE JUSTIFICATION OF CIVIL DISOBEDIENCE

So far we have said nothing about the justification of civil disobedience, that is, the conditions under which civil disobedience may be engaged in consistent with the principles of justice that support a democratic regime. Our task is to see how the characterization of civil disobedience as addressed to the sense of justice of the majority (or to the citizens as a body) determines when such action is justified.

First of all, we may suppose that the normal political appeals to the majority have already been made in good faith and have been rejected, and that the standard means of redress have been tried. Thus, for example, existing political parties are indifferent to the claims of the minority and attempts to repeal the laws protested have been met with further repression since legal institutions are in the control of the majority. While civil disobedience should be recognized, I think, as a form of political action within the limits of fidelity to the rule of law, at the same time it is a rather desperate act just within these limits, and therefore it should, in general, be undertaken as a last resort when standard democratic processes have failed. In this sense it is not a normal political action. When it is justified there has been a serious breakdown; not only is there grave injustice in the law but a refusal more or less deliberate to correct it.

Second, since civil disobedience is a political act addressed to the sense of justice of the majority, it should usually be limited to substantial and clear violations of justice and preferably to those which, if rectified, will establish a basis for doing away with remaining injustices. For this reason there is a presumption in favor of restricting civil disobedience to violations of the first principle of justice, the principle of equal liberty, and to barriers which contravene the second principle, the principle of open offices which protects equality of opportunity. It is not, of course, always easy to tell whether these principles are satisfied. But if we think of them as guaranteeing the fundamental equal political and civil liberties (including freedom of conscience and liberty of thought) and equality of opportunity, then it is often relatively clear whether their principles are being honored. After all, the equal liberties are defined by the visible structure of social institutions; they are to be incorporated into the recognized practice, if not the letter, of social arrangements. When minorities are denied the right to vote or to hold certain political offices, when certain religious groups are repressed and others denied equality of opportunity in the economy, this is often obvious and there is no doubt that justice is not being given. However, the first part of the second principle which requires that inequalities be to everyone's advantage is a much more imprecise and controversial matter. Not only is there a problem of assigning it a determinate and precise sense, but even if we do so and agree on what it should be, there is often a wide variety of reasonable opinion as to whether the principle is satisfied. The reason for this is that the principle applies primarily to fundamental economic and social policies. The choice of these depends upon theoretical and speculative beliefs as well as upon a wealth of concrete information, and all of this mixed with judgment and plain hunch, not to mention in actual cases prejudice and self-interest. Thus unless the laws of taxation are clearly designed to attack a basic equal liberty, they should not be protested by civil disobedience; the appeal to justice is not sufficiently clear and its resolution is best left to the political process. But violations of the equal liberties that define the common status of citizenship are another matter. The deliberate denial of these more or less over any extended period of time in the face of normal political protest is, in general, an appropriate object of civil disobedience. We may think of the social system as divided roughly into two parts, one which incorporates the fundamental equal liberties (including equality of opportunity) and another which embodies social and economic policies properly aimed at promoting the advantage of everyone. As a rule civil disobedience is best limited to the former where the appeal to justice is not only more definite and precise, but where, if it is effective, it tends to correct the injustices in the latter.

Third, civil disobedience should be restricted to those cases where the dissenter is willing to affirm that everyone else similarly subjected to the same degree of injustice has the right to protest in a similar way. That is, we must be prepared to authorize others to dissent in similar situations and in the same way, and to accept the consequences of their doing so. Thus, we may hold, for example, that the widespread disposition to disobey civilly clear violations of fundamental liberties more or less deliberate over an extended period of time would raise the degree of justice throughout society and would insure men's self-esteem as well as their respect for one another. Indeed, I believe this to be true, though certainly it is partly a matter of conjecture. As the contract doctrine emphasizes, since the principles of justice are principles which we would agree to in an original position of equality when we do not know our social position and the like, the refusal to grant justice is either the denial of the other as an equal (as one in regard to whom we are prepared to constrain our actions by principles which we would consent to) or the manifestation of a willingness to take advantage of natural contingencies and social fortune at his expense. In either case, injustice invites submission or resistance; but submission arouses the contempt of the oppressor and confirms him in his intention. If straightway, after a decent period of time to make reasonable political appeals in the normal way, men were in general to dissent by civil disobedience from infractions of the fundamental equal liberties, these liberties would, I believe, be more rather than less secure. Legitimate civil disobedience properly exercised is a stabilizing device in a constitutional regime, tending to make it more firmly just.

Sometimes, however, there may be a complication in connection with this third condition. It is possible, although perhaps unlikely, that there are so many persons or groups with a sound case for resorting to civil disobedience (as judged by the foregoing criteria) that disorder would follow if they all did so. There might be serious injury to the just constitution. Or again, a group might be so large that some extra precaution is necessary in the extent to which its members organize and engage in civil disobedience. Theoretically the case is one in which a number of persons or groups are equally entitled to and all want to resort to civil disobedience, yet if they all do this, grave consequences for everyone may result. The question, then, is who among them may exercise their right, and it falls under the general problem of fairness. I cannot discuss the complexities of the matter here. Often a lottery or a rationing system can be set up to handle the case; but unfortunately the circumstances of civil disobedience rule out this solution. It suffices to note that a problem of fairness may arise and that those who contemplate civil disobedience should take it into account. They may have to reach an understanding as to who can exercise their right in the immediate situation and to recognize the need for special constraint.

The final condition, of a different nature, is the following. We have been considering when one has a right to engage in civil disobedience, and our conclusion is that one has this right should three conditions hold: when one is subject to injustice more or less deliberate over an extended period of time in the face of normal political protests; where the injustice is a clear violation of the liberties of equal citizenship; and provided that the general disposition to protest similarly in similar cases would have acceptable consequences. These conditions are not, I think, exhaustive but they seem to cover the more obvious points; yet even when they are satisfied and one has the right to engage in civil disobedience, there is still the different question of whether one should exercise this right, that is, whether by doing so one is likely to further one's ends. Having established one's right to protest one is then free to consider these tactical questions. We may be acting within our rights but still foolishly if our action only serves to provoke the harsh retaliation of the majority; and it is likely to do so if the majority lacks a sense of justice, or if the action is poorly timed or not well designed to make the appeal to the sense of justice effective. It is easy to think of instances of this sort, and in each case these practical questions have to be faced. From the standpoint of the theory of political obligation we can only say that the exercise of the right should be rational and reasonably designed to advance the protester's aims, and that weighing tactical questions presupposes that one has already established one's right, since tactical advantages in themselves do not support it.

VI. CONCLUSION: SEVERAL OBJECTIONS CONSIDERED

In a reasonably affluent democratic society justice becomes the first virtue of institutions. Social arrangements irrespective of their efficiency must be reformed if they are significantly unjust. No increase in efficiency in the form of greater advantages for many justifies the loss of liberty of a few. That we believe this is shown by the fact that in a democracy the fundamental liberties of citizenship are not understood as the outcome of political bargaining nor are they subject to the calculus of social interests. Rather these liberties are fixed points which serve to limit political transactions and which determine the scope of calculations of social advantage. It is this fundamental place of the equal liberties which makes their systematic violation over any extended period of time a proper object of civil disobedience. For to deny men these rights is to infringe the conditions of social cooperation among free and rational persons, a fact which is evident to the citizens of a constitutional regime since it follows from the principles of justice which underlie their institutions. The justification of civil disobedience rests on the priority of justice and the equal liberties which it guarantees.

It is natural to object to this view of civil disobedience that it relies too heavily upon the existence of a sense of justice. Some may hold that the feeling for justice is not a vital political force, and that what moves men are various other interests, the desire for wealth, power, prestige, and so on. Now this is a large question the answer to which is highly conjectural and each tends to have his own opinion. But there are two remarks which may clarify what I have said: first, I have assumed that there is in a constitutional regime a common sense of justice the principles of which are recognized to support the constitution and to guide its interpretation. In any given situation particular men may be tempted to violate these principles, but the collective force in their behalf is usually effective since they are seen as the necessary terms of cooperation among free men; and presumably the citizens of a democracy (or sufficiently many of them) want to see justice done. Where these assumptions fail, the justifying conditions for civil disobedience (the first three) are not affected, but the rationality of engaging in it certainly is. In this case, unless the costs of repressing civil dissent injures the economic self-interest (or whatever) of the majority, protest may simply make the position of the minority worse. No doubt as a tactical matter civil disobedience is more effective when its appeal coincides with other interests, but a constitutional regime is not viable in the long run without an attachment to the principles of justice of the sort which we have assumed.

Then, further, there may be a misapprehension about the manner in which a sense of justice manifests itself. There is a tendency to think that it is shown by professions of the relevant principles together with actions of an altruistic nature requiring a considerable degree of self-sacrifice. But these conditions are obviously too strong, for the majority's sense of justice may show itself simply in its being unable to undertake the measures required to suppress the minority and to punish as the law requires the various acts of civil disobedience. The sense of justice undermines the will to uphold unjust institutions, and so a majority despite its superior power may give way. It is unprepared to force the minority to be subject to injustice. Thus, although the majority's action is reluctant and grudging, the role of the sense of justice is nevertheless essential, for without it the majority would have been willing to enforce the law and to defend its position. Once we see the sense of justice as working in this negative way to make established injustices indefensible, then it is recognized as a central element of democratic politics.

Finally, it may be objected against this account that it does not settle the question of who is to say when the situation is such as to justify civil disobedience. And because it does not answer this question, it invites anarchy by encouraging every man to decide the matter for himself. Now the reply to this is that each man must indeed settle this question for himself, although he may, of course, decide wrongly. This is true on any theory of political duty and obligation, at least on any theory compatible with the principles of a democratic constitution. The citizen is responsible for what he does. If we usually think that we should comply with the law, this is because our political principles normally lead to this conclusion. There is a presumption in favor of compliance in the absence of good reasons to the contrary. But because each man is responsible and must decide for himself as best he can whether the circumstances justify civil disobedience, it does not follow that he may decide as he pleases. It is not by looking to our personal interests or to political allegiances narrowly construed, that we should make up our mind. The citizen must decide on the basis of the principles of justice that underlie and guide the interpretation of the constitution and in the light of his sincere conviction as to how these principles should be applied in the circumstances. If he concludes that conditions obtain which justify civil disobedience and conducts himself accordingly, he has acted conscientiously and perhaps mistakenly, but not in any case at his convenience.

In a democratic society each man must act as he thinks the principles of political right require him to. We are to follow our understanding of these principles, and we cannot do otherwise. There can be no morally binding legal interpretation of these principles, not even by a supreme court or legislature. Nor is there any infallible procedure for determining what or who is right. In our system the Supreme Court, Congress, and the President often put forward rival interpretations of the Constitution. Although the Court has the final say in settling any particular case, it is not immune from powerful political influence that may change its reading of the law of the land. The Court presents its point of view by reason and argument; its conception of the Constitution must, if it is to endure, persuade men of its soundness. The final court of appeal is not the Court, or Congress, or the President, but the electorate as a whole. The civilly disobedient appeals in effect to this body. There is no danger of anarchy as long as there is a sufficient working agreement in men's conceptions of political justice and what it requires. That men can achieve such an understanding when the essential political liberties are maintained is the assumption implicit in democratic institutions. There is no way to avoid entirely the risk of divisive strife. But if legitimate civil disobedience seems to threaten civil peace, the responsibility falls not so much on those who protest as upon those whose abuse of authority and power justifies such opposition.

THE PROBLEM OF KNOWLEDGE

VI

When Am I Justified in Claiming to Know?

39. KNOWLEDGE AS THE RIGHT TO BE SURE

A. J. Ayer

A. J. Ayer (1910–   ) is Wykeham Professor of Logic, Oxford University. At the age of 26, Ayer published Language, Truth and Logic, *which is regarded as a classic defense of logical positivism, a philosophical position with wide appeal in the 30s and 40s. Ayer, having revised his earlier views, later published* The Foundations of Empirical Knowledge *(1940),* Philosophical Essays *(1954),* The Problem of Knowledge *(1956), and* The Concept of a Person and Other Essays, *(1963).*

The first requirement [for giving a complete account of what it is to know that something is the case] is that what is known should be true, but this is not sufficient; not even if we add to it the further condition that one must be completely sure of what one knows. For it is possible to be completely sure of something which is in fact true, but yet not to know it. The circumstances may be such that one is not entitled to be sure. For instance, a superstitious person who had inadvertently walked under a ladder might be convinced as a result that he was about to suffer some misfortune; and he might in fact be right. But it would not be correct to say that he knew that this was going to be so. He arrived at his belief by a process of reasoning which would not be generally reliable; so, although his prediction came true, it was not a case of knowledge. Again, if someone were fully persuaded of a mathematical proposition by a proof which could be shown to be invalid, he would not, without further evidence, be said to know the proposition, even though it was true. But while it is not hard to find examples of true and fully confident beliefs which in some ways fail to meet the standards required for knowledge, it is not at all easy to determine exactly what these standards are.

One way of trying to discover them would be to consider what would count as satisfactory answers to the question How do you know? Thus people may be credited with knowing truths of mathematics or logic if they are able to give a valid proof of them, or even if, without themselves being able to set out such a proof, they have obtained this information from someone who can. Claims to know empirical statements may be upheld by a reference to perception, or to memory, or to testimony, or to historical records, or to scientific laws. But such backing is not always strong enough for knowledge. Whether it is so or not depends upon the circumstances of the particular case. If I were asked how I knew that a physical object of a certain sort was in such and such a place, it would, in general, be a sufficient answer for me to say that I could see it; but if my eyesight were bad and the light were dim, this answer might not be sufficient. Even though I was right, it might still be said that I did not really know that the object was there. If I have a poor memory and the event which I claim to remember is remote, my memory of it may still not amount to knowledge, even though in this instance it does not fail me. If a witness is unreliable, his unsupported evidence may not enable us to know that what he says is true, even in a case where we completely trust him and he is not in fact deceiving us. In a given instance it is possible to decide whether the backing is strong enough to justify a claim to knowledge. But to say in general how strong it has to be would require our drawing up a list of the conditions under which perception, or memory, or testimony, or other forms of evidence are reliable. And this would be a very complicated matter, if indeed it could be done at all.

Moreover, we cannot assume that, even in particular instances, an answer to the question How do you know? will always be forthcoming. There may very well be cases in which one knows that something is so without its being possible to say how one knows it. I am not so much thinking now of claims to know facts of immediate experience, statements like 'I know that I feel pain', which raise problems of their own into which we shall enter later on.[1] In cases of this sort it may be argued that the question how one knows does not arise. But even when it clearly does arise, it may not find an answer. Suppose that someone were consistently successful in predicting events of a certain kind, events, let us say, which are not ordinarily thought to be predictable, like the results of a lottery. If his run of successes were sufficiently impressive, we might very well come to say that he knew which number would win, even though he did not reach this conclusion by any rational method, or indeed by any method at all. We might say that he knew it by intuition, but this would be to assert no more than that he did know it but that we could not say how. In the same way, if someone were consistently successful in reading the minds of others without having any of the usual sort of evidence, we might say that he knew

---

[1] *Vide* ch. 2, section iv.

these things telepathically. But in default of any further explanation this would come down to saying merely that he did know them, but not by an ordinary means. Words like 'intuition' and 'telepathy' are brought in just to disguise the fact that no explanation has been found.

But if we allow this sort of knowledge to be even theoretically possible, what becomes of the distinction between knowledge and true belief? How does our man who knows what the results of the lottery will be differ from one who only makes a series of lucky guesses? The answer is that, so far as the man himself is concerned, there need not be any difference. His procedure and his state of mind, when he is said to know what will happen, may be exactly the same as when it is said that he is only guessing. The difference is that to say that he knows is to concede to him the right to be sure, while to say that he is only guessing is to withhold it. Whether we make this concession will depend upon the view which we take of his performance. Normally we do not say that people know things unless they have followed one of the accredited routes to knowledge. If someone reaches a true conclusion without appearing to have any adequate basis for it, we are likely to say that he does not really know it. But if he were repeatedly successful in a given domain, we might very well come to say that he knew the facts in question, even though we could not explain how he knew them. We should grant him the right to be sure, simply on the basis of his success. This is, indeed, a point on which people's views might be expected to differ. Not everyone would regard a successful run of predictions, however long sustained, as being by itself a sufficient backing for a claim to knowledge. And here there can be no question of proving that this attitude is mistaken. Where there are recognized criteria for deciding when one has the right to be sure, anyone who insists that their being satisfied is still not enough for knowledge may be accused, for what the charge is worth, of misusing the verb 'to know.' But it is possible to find, or at any rate to devise, examples which are not covered in this respect by any established rule of usage. Whether they are to count as instances of knowledge is then a question which we are left free to decide.

It does not, however, matter very greatly which decision we take. The main problem is to state and assess the grounds on which these claims to knowledge are made, to settle, as it were, the candidate's marks. It is a relatively unimportant question what titles we then bestow upon them. So long as we agree about the marking, it is of no great consequence where we draw the line between pass and failure, or between the different levels of distinction. If we choose to set a very high standard, we may find ourselves committed to saying that some of what ordinarily passes for knowledge ought rather to be described as probable opinion. And some critics will then take us to task for flouting ordinary usage. But the question is purely one of terminology. It is to be decided, if at all, on grounds of practical convenience.

One must not confuse this case, where the markings are agreed upon, and what is in dispute is only the bestowal of honours, with the case where it is the markings themselves that are put in question. For this second case is philosophically important, in a way in which the other is not. The sceptic who asserts that we do not know all that we think we know, or even perhaps that we do not strictly know anything at all, is not suggesting that we are mistaken when we conclude that the recognized criteria for knowing have been satisfied. Nor is he primarily concerned with getting us to revise our usage of the verb 'to know,' any more than one who challenges our standards of value is trying to make us revise our usage of the word 'good.' The disagreement is about the application of the word, rather than its meaning. What the sceptic contends is that our markings are too high; that the grounds on which we are normally ready to concede the right to be sure are worth less than we think; he may even go so far as to say that they are not worth anything at all. The attack is directed, not against the way in which we apply our standards of proof, but against these standards themselves. It has, as we shall see, to be taken seriously because of the arguments by which it is supported.

I conclude then that the necessary and sufficient conditions for knowing that something is the case are first that what one is said to know be true, secondly that one be sure of it, and thirdly that one should have the right to be sure. This right may be earned in various ways; but even if one could give a complete description of them it would be a mistake to try to build it into the definition of knowledge, just as it would be a mistake to try to incorporate our actual standards of goodness into a definition of good. And this being so, it turns out that the questions which philosophers raise about the possibility of knowledge are not all to be settled by discovering what knowledge is. For many of them reappear as questions about the legitimacy of the title to be sure. They need to be severally examined; and this is the main concern of what is called the theory of knowledge.

40. SOME PROBLEMS WITH DEFINING KNOWLEDGE AS "JUSTIFIED TRUE BELIEF"

Edmund Gettier

Edmund L. Gettier *is Professor of Philosophy at the University of Massachusetts.*

Various attempts have been made in recent years to state necessary and sufficient conditions for someone's knowing a given proposition. The attempts have often been such that they can be stated in a form similar to the following: [1]

(a) S knows that P   *IFF*   (i) P is true,
(ii) S believes that P, and
(iii) S is justified in believing that P.

For example; Chisholm has held that the following gives the necessary and sufficient conditions for knowledge: [2]

(b) S knows that P   *IFF*   (i) S accepts P,
(ii) S has adequate evidence for P, and
(iii) P is true.

Ayer has stated the necessary and sufficient conditions for knowledge as follows: [3]

(c) S knows that P   *IFF*   (i) is true,
(ii) S is sure that P is true, and
(iii) S has the right to be sure that P is true.

I shall argue that (a) is false in that the conditions stated therein do not constitute a *sufficient* condition for the truth of the proposition that S knows that P. The same argument will show that (b) and (c) fail

From Analysis, *Vol. 23 (Blackwell, 1963), pp. 121–3. Reprinted by permission of the author and the editor.*

---

[1] Plato seems to be considering some such definition at *Theaetetus* 201, and perhaps accepting one at Meno 98.
[2] Roderick M. Chisholm, *Perceiving: A Philosophical Study,* Cornell University Press (Ithaca, New York, 1957), p. 16.
[3] A. J. Ayer, *The Problem of Knowledge,* Macmillan (London, 1956), p. 34.

if 'has adequate evidence for' or 'has the right to be sure that' is sub-stituted for 'is justified in believing that' throughout.

I shall begin by noting two points. First, in that sense of 'justi-fied' in which S's being justified in believing P is a necessary condition of S's knowing that P, it is possible for a person to be justified in be-lieving a proposition that is in fact false. Secondly, for any proposition P, if S is justified in believing P, and P entails Q, and S deduces Q from P and accepts Q as a result of this deduction, then S is justified in believing Q. Keeping these two points in mind, I shall now present two cases in which the conditions stated in (a) are true for some proposi-tion, though it is at the same time false that the person in question knows that proposition.

Case I:

Suppose that Smith and Jones have applied for a certain job. And suppose that Smith has strong evidence for the following conjunc-tive proposition:

(d) Jones is the man who will get the job, and Jones has ten coins in his pocket.

Smith's evidence for (d) might be that the president of the company assured him that Jones would in the end be selected, and that he, Smith, had counted the coins in Jones's pocket ten minutes ago. Proposition (d) entails:

(e) The man who will get the job has ten coins in his pocket.
Let us suppose that Smith sees the entailment from (d) to (e), and accepts (e) on the grounds of (d), for which he has strong evidence. In this case, Smith is clearly justified in believing that (e) is true.

But imagine, further, that unknown to Smith, he himself, not Jones, will get the job. And, also, unknown to Smith, he himself has ten coins in his pocket. Proposition (e) is then true, though proposition (d), from which Smith inferred (e), is false. In our example, then, all of the following are true: *(i)* (e) is true, *(ii)* Smith believes that (e) is true, and *(iii)* Smith is justified in believing that (e) is true. But it is equally clear that Smith does not *know* that (e) is true; for (e) is true in virtue of the number of coins in Smith's pocket, while Smith does not know how many coins are in Smith's pocket, and bases his belief in (e) on a count of the coins in Jones's pocket, whom he falsely be-lieves to be the man who will get the job.

Case II:

Let us suppose that Smith has strong evidence for the following proposition:

(f) Jones owns a Ford.

Smith's evidence might be that Jones has at all times in the past within Smith's memory owned a car, and always a Ford, and that Jones has just offered Smith a ride while driving a Ford. Let us imagine, now, that Smith has another friend, Brown, of whose whereabouts he is totally ignorant. Smith selects three place-names quite at random, and constructs the following three propositions:

(g) Either Jones owns a Ford, or Brown is in Boston;
(h) Either Jones owns a Ford, or Brown is in Barcelona;
(i) Either Jones owns a Ford, or Brown is in Brest-Litovsk.

Each of these propositions is entailed by (f). Imagine that Smith realizes the entailment of each of these propositions he had constructed by (f), and proceeds to accept (g), (h), and (i) on the basis of (f). Smith has correctly inferred (g), (h), and (i) from a proposition for which he has strong evidence. Smith is therefore completely justified in believing each of these three propositions. Smith, of course, has no idea where Brown is.

But imagine now that two further conditions hold. First, Jones does *not* own a Ford, but is at present driving a rented car. And secondly, by the sheerest coincidence, and entirely unknown to Smith, the place mentioned in proposition (h) happens really to be the place where Brown is. If these two conditions hold then Smith does *not* know that (h) is true, even though *(i)* (h) *is* true, *(ii)* Smith does believe that (h) is true, and *(iii)* Smith is justified in believing that (h) is true.

These two examples show that definition (a) does not state a *sufficient* condition for someone's knowing a given proposition. The same cases, with appropriate changes, will suffice to show that neither definition (b) nor definition (c) do so either.

41. THE A PRIORI AND THE EMPIRICAL

A. C. Ewing

A. C. Ewing (1899–   ) is Reader in Moral Science at the University of Cambridge. During a long and distinguished career he has had visiting lectureships in both Great Britain and the United States. A few of his many works are Kant's Treatment of Causality (1924), Idealism, A Critical Survey (1934), The Individual, the State and World Government (1947), The Definition of the Good (1947), and The Fundamental Questions of Philosophy (1962).

MEANING OF THE DISTINCTION, 'A PRIORI' CHARACTER OF MATHEMATICS

In the theory of knowledge, the first point that confronts us is the sharp distinction between two kinds of knowledge which have been called respectively *a priori* and empirical. Most of our knowledge we obtain by observation of the external world (sense-perception) and of ourselves (introspection). This is called empirical knowledge. But some knowledge we can obtain by simply thinking. That kind of knowledge is called *a priori*. Its chief exemplifications are to be found in logic and mathematics. In order to see that $5 + 7 = 12$ we do not need to take five things and seven things, put them together, and then count the total number. We can know what the total number will be simply by thinking.

Another important difference between *a priori* and empirical knowledge is that in the case of the former we do not see merely that something, S, is in fact P, but that it must be P and why it is P. I can discover that a flower is yellow (or at least produces sensations of yellow) by looking at it, but I cannot thereby see why it is yellow or that it must be yellow. For anything I can tell it might equally well have been a red flower. But with a truth such as that $5 + 7 = 12$ I do not see merely that it is a fact but that it must be a fact. It would be quite absurd to suppose that $5 + 7$ might have been equal to 11 and just happened to be equal to 12, and I can see that the nature of 5 and 7 constitutes a fully adequate and intelligible reason why their sum should be 12 and not some other number. It is indeed conceivable that some of the things which make the two groups of 5 and 7 might, when they were put together, fuse like drops of water, or even vanish, so that there were no longer 12 things; but what is inconceivable is that there could *at the same time* be $5 + 7$ things of a certain kind at once in a certain place and yet less than 12 things of that kind in that place. Before some of the things fused or vanished they would be $5 + 7$ in number and also 12 in number, and after the fusion or disappearance they would be neither $5 + 7$ nor 12. When I say in this connection that something is inconceivable, I do not mean merely or primarily that we cannot conceive it—this is not a case of a mere psychological inability like the inability to understand higher mathematics. It is a positive insight: we definitely see it to be impossible that certain things could happen. This we do not see in the case of empirical propositions which are false: they are not true but might for anything we know have been true. It is even conceivable, so far as we can see, that the fundamental laws of motion might have been quite different from what they are, but we can see that there could not have been a world which contradicted the laws of arithmetic. This is expressed by saying that empirical propositions are *contingent*, but true a priori propositions *necessary*. What we see to be necessary is not indeed that arithmetic should apply to the universe. It is conceivable that the universe might have been constituted entirely of a homogeneous fluid, and then, since there would have been no distinction between different things, it is difficult to see how arithmetic could have applied to it. What we do see is that arithmetic must be true of whatever can be numbered at all.

We must not be misled here by the fact that in order to come to understand arithmetic we originally required examples. Once we have learnt the beginnings of arithmetic in the kindergarten with the help of examples, we do not need examples any more to grasp it, and we can see the truth of many arithmetical propositions, e.g. that $3112 + 2467 = 5579$, of which we have never had examples. We have probably never taken 3112 things and 2467 things, put them together and counted the resulting set, but we still know that this is what the result of the counting would be. If it were empirical knowledge, we could not know it without counting. The examples are needed, not to prove anything, but only in order to enable us to come to understand in the first instance what is meant by number.

In geometry we indeed stand more in need of examples than in arithmetic, though I think this is only a psychological matter. In arithmetic we only need examples at the most elementary stage, but in geometry most people need a drawn figure, or at least an image of one in their minds, to see the validity of most proofs. But we must distinguish between an illustration and the basis of a proof. If the particular figure were not merely an illustration but the basis of the theorem, the latter would have to be proved by measuring it, but a measurement with a ruler or protractor never figures in Euclid's proofs. That the proof is not really based on the figure drawn is shown by the fact that we can still follow a proof concerning the properties of right-angled triangles even if the figure used to illustrate it is so badly drawn that it is obviously not a right-angled triangle at all. Again, if geometry were empirical, it would be a very hazardous speculation from the single example before us on the blackboard to conclude that all triangles had a property. It might be an individual idiosyncracy of some triangles and not others. These considerations should be conclusive of themselves, but we might add that recent developments in geometry have had the effect of much loosening the connection between geometrical proofs and the empirical figure. It is possible to work out non-Euclidean geometries where we cannot depend on figures.

THE 'A PRIORI' IN LOGIC

Another important field for *a priori* knowledge is logic. The laws of logic must be known *a priori* or not at all. They certainly are not a matter for empirical observation, and the function of logical argument is just to give us conclusions which we have not discovered by observation. The argument would be superfluous if we had observed them already. We are able to make inferences because there is sometimes a logical connection between one or more propositions (the premise or premises) and another proposition, the conclusion, such that the latter must be true if the former is. Then, if we know the former, we can assert the latter on the strength of it, thus anticipating any experience. To take an example, there is a story that Mr. X., a man of high reputation and great social standing, had been asked to preside at a big social function. He was late in coming, and so a Roman Catholic priest was asked to make a speech to pass the time till his arrival. The priest told various anecdotes, including one which recorded his embarrassment when as confessor he had to deal with his first penitent and the latter confessed to a particularly atrocious murder. Shortly afterwards Mr. X. arrived, and in his own speech he said: 'I see Father——is here. Now, though he may not recognize me, he is an old friend of mine, in fact I was his first penitent.' It is plain that such an episode would enable one to infer that Mr. X. had committed a murder without having observed the crime. The form of inference involved: The first penitent was a murderer, Mr. X. was the first penitent, therefore Mr. X. was a murderer—is of the famous kind to which logicians have given the name of *syllogism*. The importance of syllogisms has often been exaggerated, but they are as important as any kind of inference, and we cannot deny that in many cases a syllogism has given people information of which they were not in any ordinary sense aware before they used the syllogism and which they did not acquire by observation. Inference is only possible because there are special connections between the propositions involved such that one necessarily follows from others. It is a chief function of logic to study these connections, of which that expressed in the syllogism is by no means the only one.

(A *syllogism* consists of three propositions, two forming the *premises* and the other the *conclusion*. Each proposition can be expressed by a subject and predicate connected by the verb to be, the *copula*, and if we call everything which stands as either subject or predicate a *term*, there must be three and only three terms in the syllogism. The one common to the two premises is called the *middle term*, and it is on this common element that the inference depends. The other two, having been connected by means of it, occur without it in the conclusion. Thus in the usual example of the syllogism—All men are mortal, Socrates is a man, ∴ Socrates is mortal—man is the middle term connecting Socrates with mortality so that we could, even if he had not already died, know that he was mortal.)

OTHER CASES OF THE 'A PRIORI'

A *priori* knowledge, while most prominent in mathematics and logic, is not limited to these subjects. For instance, we can see *a priori* that the same surface cannot have two different colours all over at the same time, or that a thought cannot have a shape. Philosophers have been divided into *rationalists* and *empiricists* according to whether they stressed the *a priori* or the empirical element more. The possibility of metaphysics depends on *a priori* knowledge, for our experience is quite inadequate to enable us to make on merely empirical grounds any sweeping generalizations of the kind the metaphysician desires. The term *a priori* covers both self-evident propositions, i.e. those which are seen to be true in their own right and those which are derived by inference from propositions themselves self-evident.

THE LINGUISTIC THEORY OF THE 'A PRIORI' AND THE DENIAL THAT 'A PRIORI' PROPOSITIONS OR INFERENCES CAN GIVE NEW KNOWLEDGE

At the present time even empiricist philosophers recognize the impossibility of explaining away *a priori* propositions as merely empirical generalizations, but they are inclined to the view that *a priori* propositions and *a priori* reasoning are merely concerned with language, and so cannot tell us anything new about the real world. Thus it is said that, when we make an inference, the conclusion is just part of the premises expressed in different language.[1] If so, inference would be of use merely for clarifying our language and would involve no real advance in knowledge. Some inferences are of this type, e.g. A is a father, therefore A is male. But are they all? That would be hard indeed to square with the *prima facie* novelty of many conclusions. Take, for instance, the proposition that the square on the hypotenuse of a right-angled triangle is equal to the sum of the squares on the other two sides. Such a proposition can be inferred from the axioms and postulates of Euclid, but it certainly does not seem to be included in their meaning. Otherwise we should know it as soon as we understood the axioms and postulates. The example I gave of the murder discovered by a logical argument seems to be another case of a fact not known at all beforehand by the reasoner which is discovered by his reasoning. Extreme empiricist philosophers contend that this appearance of novelty is really illusory, and that in some sense we knew the conclusion all along; but they have never succeeded in making clear in what sense we did so. It is not enough to say that the conclusion is implicit in the premises. 'Implicit' means 'implied by,' and of course a conclusion is implied by its premises, if the inference is correct at all. But this admission leaves quite open the question whether or not a proposition can follow from a different one which does not contain it as part of itself; and since we obviously can by deductive inference come to know things which we did not know before in any ordinary sense of 'know,' we must treat the empiricist's claim as unjustified till he has produced a clearly defined sense of 'implicit in' or 'contained in' which leaves room for that novelty in inference which we all cannot help really admitting. In any ordinary sense of 'know' the conclusion is not in the cases I have mentioned known prior to the inference, and since the premises are and indeed must be known before we know the conclusion, it is therefore in no ordinary sense of 'part' part of the premises.

It is indeed sometimes said that the premises include the conclusion in a confused form, but it is obvious that the beginner in geometry cannot be said to be aware of Pythagoras's theorem even in a confused form though he may know all the premises from which it can be deduced. Nor does awareness of the propositions that A was B's first penitent and that B's first penitent was a murderer include even confusedly the awareness that A was a murderer as long as the premises are not combined. When they are combined therefore something new

---

[1] This theory is not applied to *inductive* inference.

appears that was not present to consciousness before in any way; there is a new discovery. . . .

. . . Nevertheless, the view that inference cannot yield new conclusions dies hard, and so it will not be superfluous to bring further arguments. (1) 'This has shape' admittedly follows logically from 'this has size' and vice versa. If the view I am criticizing were true, 'this has size' would, therefore, have to include in its meaning 'this has shape,' and 'this has shape' would also have to include in its meaning 'this has size.' But this would only be possible if the two sentences meant exactly the same thing, which they obviously do not. (2) Take an argument such as—Montreal is to the north of New York, New York is to the north of Washington, therefore Montreal is to the north of Washington. If the view I am discussing is true, the conclusion is part of the premises. But it is not part of either premise by itself, otherwise both premises would not be needed. So the only way in which it could be part of both together would be if it were divisible into two propositions one of which was part of the first and the other part of the second. I defy anybody to divide it in this way. (3) The proposition 'Socrates was a philosopher' certainly entails the proposition 'if Socrates had measles some philosophers have had measles,' but it cannot be that the second proposition is included in the first. For the first proposition certainly does not include the notion of measles.

What is really the same view is often expressed by saying that all *a priori* propositions are 'analytic.' A distinction has commonly been drawn between *analytic* propositions, in which the predicate is in the notion of the subject already formed before the proposition is asserted, so that the proposition gives no new information, and *synthetic* propositions in which the predicate is not so contained and which are thus capable of giving new information.[2] Analytic propositions are essentially verbal, being all true by definition, e.g. all fathers are male. As an example of a synthetic proposition we could take any proposition established by experience such as 'I am cold' or 'It is snowing,' but empiricists often assert that there are no synthetic *a priori* propositions. That this view cannot be justified may be shown at once. The proposition that there are no synthetic *a priori* propositions, since it cannot be established by empirical observations, would be, if justified, itself a synthetic *a priori* proposition, and we cannot affirm it as a synthetic *a priori* proposition that there are no synthetic *a priori* propositions. We may therefore dismiss off-hand any arguments for the theory. Such arguments,

[2] This definition would have to be amended slightly to suit modern logicians who (I think, rightly) deny that all propositions are of the subject-predicate form, but this would not alter the principle though imparting a complication of detail with which we need not deal here.

whatever they were, would have to involve synthetic *a priori* propositions. Further, the view must be false if it is ever true that the conclusion of an inference is not part of its premises. For, if the proposition—S is Q—ever follows validly from—S is P, the proposition—all that is SP is SQ must be true *a priori*. But, unless the concept Q is part of the concept SP, the proposition—all that is SP is SQ—cannot be analytic. Therefore our arguments against the view that in all valid inferences the conclusion is part of the premises expressed in different language are also arguments against the view that all *a priori* propositions are analytic.

The analytic view seems plausible when we are concerned with the simplest propositions of logic and arithmetic, but we must not assume that a proposition is analytic because it is obvious. Though it may be very difficult to determine precisely where analytic propositions end and synthetic propositions begin, we cannot use this as a ground for denying the latter. It is very difficult to say precisely where blue ends and green begins, since the different shades run into each other imperceptibly, but we cannot therefore argue that all blue is really green. Taking arithmetic, even if there is a good deal of plausibility in saying that $2 + 2$ is included in the meaning of '4,' there is none in saying $95 - 91$ or $\dfrac{216}{2} - \dfrac{67 + 25}{3}$ are so included. Yet, if the analytical view were true, all the infinite numerical combinations which could be seen *a priori* to be equal to 4 would have to be included in the meaning of '4.'

Some empiricists, without committing themselves to the view that all *a priori* propositions are analytic, still say these are a matter of arbitrary choice or verbal convention. They are influenced here by a modern development in the view of geometry. It used to be held that the axioms of Euclid expressed a direct insight into the nature of physical space, but this is denied by modern scientists, and the view is taken that they are arbitrary postulates which geometricians make because they are interested in what would follow *if* they were true. Whether they are true or not is then a matter of empirical fact to be decided by science. But, even if this suggests that the premises of our *a priori* arguments may be arbitrary postulates, this does not make the subsequent steps arbitrary. From the postulates of Euclid it follows that the three angles of a triangle are equal to two right angles. If the original postulates are arbitrary, it is not certain that the conclusion is true of the real world; but it is still not an arbitrary matter that it follows from the postulates. The postulates may well be false, but there can be no doubt that *if* they were true the conclusions must be so, and it is in this hypothetical working out of the consequences of postulates which may not be true that pure geometry consists. The *a priori* necessity of pure geometry is not therefore in the least invalidated by modern developments. What is *a priori* is that the conclusions follow from the axioms and postulates, and this is not at all affected by the (empirical) discovery that not all the axioms and postulates exactly apply to the physical world. (Applied Euclidean geometry is possible in practice because it is an empirical fact that they approximately apply. The divergencies only show themselves when we consider unusually great velocities or distances.)

If not only the postulates but the successive stages in the inference were themselves arbitrary, we might just as well infer from the same premise that the angles of a triangle were equal to a million right angles or to none at all. All point in inference would be lost. Dictators may do a great deal, but they cannot alter the laws of logic and mathematics; these laws would not change even if by a system of intensive totalitarian education every human being were persuaded to fall in with a world dictator's whim in the matter and believe they were different from what they are. Nor can they change with alterations in language, though they may be expressed differently. That the truth of *a priori* propositions does not just depend on the nature of language can be easily seen when we consider that, even if we do not know any Fijian or Hottentot, we can know that also in these languages and not only in the languages we know the proposition $5 + 7 = 12$ must be true. It is of course true that by altering the meaning of the words we could make the proposition we expressed by '$5 + 7 = 12$' false, e.g. if I used '12' in a new sense to mean what other people mean by '11,' but then it would be a different proposition. I could play the same trick with empirical propositions and say truly, e.g., that 'fire does not burn' or 'there is an elephant in this room' if I used 'burn' to mean 'drown' or 'elephant' to mean 'table.' This does not in the least impair the obviousness of the contrary propositions established by experience. Finally, as we argued above that the proposition that there can be no synthetic *a priori* propositions would itself, if justified, have to be a synthetic *a priori* proposition, so we may argue that the proposition that all *a priori* propositions are a matter of arbitrary linguistic convention would, if true, have to be itself a matter of arbitrary linguistic convention. It therefore could not be vindicated by any argument and would be merely a matter of a new usage of words arbitrarily established by the persons who assert it, since it certainly does not express the usual meaning of '*a priori* propositions.' So we must reject any attempt to explain away the *a priori* as a genuine source of new knowledge. If the attempt had succeeded, we should have had to admit that philosophy in anything like its old sense was impossible, for philosophy clearly cannot be based merely on observation.

The views we have been criticizing contain the following elements of truth. (1) *A priori* propositions can be seen to be true and the conclusions of an inference seen to follow from their premises without any further observation, provided we understand the meaning of the words used. But to say that q follows from p once we understand the meaning of the words is not to say that q is part of the meaning of the words used to express p. 'Follow from' and 'be part of' are not synonyms. (2) If q follows from p you cannot assert p and deny q without contradicting yourself, but this is only to say that in that case the denial of q implies the denial of p. It is not to say that q is part of what you assert when you assert p, unless we already assume that what is implied is always part of what implies it, i.e. beg the question at issue. (3) An *a priori* proposition cannot be fully understood without being seen to be true. It may be impossible to understand something fully without understanding something else not included in it at all, so it may still be synthetic.

People have been inclined to deny synthetic *a priori* propositions because they could not see how one characteristic could necessarily involve another, but that this could not happen would be itself a synthetic *a priori* metaphysical proposition. People have also thought that it was necessary to give some sort of explanation of *a priori* knowledge, and could not see how this could be done except in terms of language. To this I should reply that there is no reason to suppose that *a priori* knowledge requires some special explanation any more than does our ability to attain knowledge empirically by observation. Why not take it as an ultimate fact? Human beings certainly cannot explain everything, whether there is ultimately an explanation for it or not. . . .

. . . The main argument of those who attack the notion of intuition is that apparent intuitions are liable to conflict with each other and there is then no means of deciding which is right. But this is a mistake: we can in fact test them in various ways. We can consider whether they are capable of any clear and internally consistent statement. We can ask whether they fit into a coherent system with the rest of our well-established beliefs. We can also ask whether intuitions of the same kind have been confirmed in the past. We can ask whether an intuition stands or falls by itself or is a presupposition of a whole number of other beliefs which we cannot help holding, as some (though confused) intuition of the occurrence of causation or the uniformity of nature seems a necessary presupposition of all inductive beliefs. We can consider the plausibility of giving an alternative explanation of the intuitive belief. The result may then be negative or positive. It may be that our apparent intuition will evaporate when we think of the explanation, and then the latter is probably a correct one at least as to why *we* held the belief. Or it may be that the intuition will persist unshaken, in which case the explanation is probably at least inadequate. We can again consider whether the intuition repeats itself when considered in different contexts and different moods or with different examples.

So when two people have conflicting intuitions we need not suppose that there is just an irreducible difference of intuitive faculty between them and that there is nothing more to be done about it. Arguments may well be available which without strictly proving either side to be wrong put a disputant into a position in which he can see better for himself whether he is right or wrong or at least partially confirm or cast doubt on the truth of his view. In general, the clearer we have made ourselves about a subject by inferential thought, by analysing the different factors involved and by clearing up our terminology, the more likely are we to have correct intuitions on the matter if such are available at all. Again, intellectual confusions may be revealed which were responsible for the truth of the belief in question. Thus a person who really sees that A is B may confuse B with C and will then think he sees intuitively that A is C. Some such conflicts may be caused simply or mainly by ambiguities of terminology or the attaching of different meanings to some word. And of course we need not deny that differences of intuition may sometimes be due on one side or even on both to 'wishful thinking' or to the kind of cause which it is the business of the psycho-analyst (or of a patient and tactful friend) to remove. These remarks are specially applicable to ethical disputes. We cannot of course settle all disputes in these ways, but neither can we in practice settle all disputes in science. The most we can say is that they are soluble in principle, though we may not have the ability to hit on the right way of solving a particular dispute. Similarly, there is no reason to believe that conflicts between rival intuitions would not all be capable of a solution if these methods were applied aright and with good will on both sides, though in fact we cannot so apply them.

42. KNOWLEDGE AS INDUBITABLE BELIEF

René Descartes

René Descartes. *(See essay number 11 for biographical note.)*

It is now some years since I detected how many were the false beliefs that I had from my earliest youth admitted as true, and how doubtful was everything I had since constructed on this basis; and from that time I was convinced that I must once for all seriously undertake to rid myself of all the opinions which I had formerly accepted, and commence to build anew from the foundation, if I wanted to establish any firm and permanent structure in the sciences. But as this enterprise appeared to be a very great one, I waited until I had attained an age so mature that I could not hope that at any later date I should be better fitted to execute my design. This reason caused me to delay so long that I should feel that I was doing wrong were I to occupy in deliberation the time that yet remains to me for action. To-day, then, since very opportunely for the plan I have in view I have delivered my mind from every care [and am happily agitated by no passions] [1] and since I have procured for myself an assured leisure in a peaceable retirement, I shall at last seriously and freely address myself to the general upheaval of all my former opinions.

Now for this object it is not necessary that I should show that all of these are false—I shall perhaps never arrive at this end. But inasmuch as reason already persuades me that I ought no less carefully to withhold my assent from matters which are not entirely certain and indubitable than from those which appear to me manifestly to be false, if I am able to find in each one some reason to doubt, this will suffice to justify my rejecting the whole. And for that end it will not be requisite that I should examine each in particular, which would be an endless undertaking; for owing to the fact that the destruction of the foundations of necessity brings with it the downfall of the rest of the edifice, I shall only in the first place attack those principles upon which all my former opinions rested.

DOUBTS ABOUT KNOWLEDGE GAINED THROUGH THE SENSES

All that up to the present time I have accepted as most true and certain I have learned either from the senses or through the senses;

From Meditations, *translated by E. S. Haldane and G. R. T. Ross,* included in The Philosophical Works of Descartes, *published by Cambridge University Press, Cambridge, 1931, and reprinted with their permission.*

[1] This translation is from the Latin version of the *Meditations*. Additional readings from the French version are inserted within brackets.—Ed.

but it is sometimes proved to me that these senses are deceptive, and it is wiser not to trust entirely to any thing by which we have once been deceived.

But it may be that although the senses sometimes deceive us concerning things which are hardly perceptible, or very far away, there are yet many others to be met with as to which we cannot reasonably have any doubt, although we recognize them by their means. For example, there is the fact that I am here, seated by the fire, attired in a dressing gown, having this paper in my hands and other similar matters. And how could I deny that these hands and this body are mine, were it not perhaps that I compare myself to certain persons, devoid of sense, whose cerebella are so troubled and clouded by the violent vapours of black bile, that they constantly assure us that they think they are kings when they are really quite poor, or that they are clothed in purple when they are really without covering, or who imagine that they have an earthenware head or are nothing but pumpkins or are made of glass. But they are mad, and I should not be any the less insane were I to follow examples so extravagant.

At the same time I must remember that I am a man, and that consequently I am in the habit of sleeping, and in my dreams representing to myself the same things or sometimes even less probable things, than do those who are insane in their waking moments. How often has it happened to me that in the night I dreamt that I found myself in this particular place, that I was dressed and seated near the fire, whilst in reality I was lying undressed in bed! At this moment it does indeed seem to me that it is with eyes awake that I am looking at this paper; that this head which I move is not asleep, that it is deliberately and of set purpose that I extend my hand and perceive it; what happens in sleep does not appear so clear nor so distinct as does all this. But in thinking over this I remind myself that on many occasions I have in sleep been deceived by similar illusions, and in dwelling carefully on this reflection I see so manifestly that there are no certain indications by which we may clearly distinguish wakefulness from sleep that I am lost in astonishment. And my astonishment is such that it is almost capable of persuading me that I now dream.

DOUBTS ABOUT MATHEMATICAL KNOWLEDGE

Now let us assume that we are asleep and that all these particulars, e.g. that we open our eyes, shake our head, extend our hands, and so on, are but false delusions; and let us reflect that possibly neither our hands nor our whole body are such as they appear to us to be. At the same time we must at least confess that the things which are represented to us in sleep are like painted representations which can only

315

have been formed as the counterparts of something real and true, and that in this way those general things at least, i.e. eyes, a head, hands, and a whole body, are not imaginary things, but things really existent. For, as a matter of fact, painters, even when they study with the greatest skill to represent sirens and satyrs by forms the most strange and extraordinary, cannot give them natures which are entirely new, but merely make a certain medley of the members of different animals; or if their imagination is extravagant enough to invent something so novel that nothing similar has ever before been seen, and that then their work represents a thing purely fictitious and absolutely false, it is certain all the same that the colours of which this is composed are necessarily real. And for the same reason, although these general things, to wit [a body], eyes, a head, hands, and such like, may be imaginary, we are bound at the same time to confess that there are at least some other objects yet more simple and more universal, which are real and true; and of these just in the same way as with certain real colours, all these images of things which dwell in our thoughts, whether true and real or false and fantastic, are formed.

To such a class of things pertains corporeal nature in general, and its extension, the figure of extended things, their quantity or magnitude and number, as also the place in which they are, the time which measures their duration, and so on.

That is possibly why our reasoning is not unjust when we conclude from this that Physics, Astronomy, Medicine and all other sciences which have as their end the consideration of composite things, are very dubious and uncertain; but that Arithmetic, Geometry and other sciences of that kind which only treat of things that are very simple and very general, without taking great trouble to ascertain whether they are actually existent or not, contain some measure of certainty and an element of the indubitable. For whether I am awake or asleep, two and three together always form five, and the square can never have more than four sides, and it does not seem possible that truths so clear and apparent can be suspected of any falsity [or uncertainty].

Nevertheless I have long had fixed in my mind the belief that an all-powerful God existed by whom I have been created such as I am. But how do I know that He has not brought it to pass that there is no earth, no heaven, no extended body, no magnitude, no place, and that nevertheless [I possess the perceptions of all these things and that] they seem to me to exist just exactly as I now see them? And, besides, as I sometimes imagine that others deceive themselves in the things which they think they know best, how do I know that I am not deceived every time that I add two and three, or count the sides of a square, or judge of things yet simpler, if anything simpler can be imagined? But possibly God has not desired that I should be thus deceived, for He is said to be supremely good. If, however, it is contrary to His goodness to have made me such that I constantly deceive myself, it would also appear to be contrary to His goodness to permit me to be sometimes deceived, and nevertheless I cannot doubt that He does permit this.

There may indeed be those who would prefer to deny the existence of a God so powerful, rather than believe that all other things are uncertain. But let us not oppose them for the present, and grant that all that is here said of a God is a fable; nevertheless in whatever way they suppose that I have arrived at the state of being that I have reached—whether they attribute it to fate or to accident, or make out that it is by a continual succession of antecedents, or by some other method—since to err and deceive oneself is a defect, it is clear that the greater will be the probability of my being so imperfect as to deceive myself ever, as is the Author to whom they assign my origin the less powerful. To these reasons I have certainly nothing to reply, but at the end I feel constrained to confess that there is nothing in all that I formerly believed to be true, of which I cannot in some measure doubt, and that not merely through want of thought or through levity, but for reasons which are very powerful and maturely considered; so that henceforth I ought not the less carefully to refrain from giving credence to these opinions than to that which is manifestly false, if I desire to arrive at any certainty [in the sciences].

But it is not sufficient to have made these remarks, we must also be careful to keep them in mind. For these ancient and commonly held opinions still revert frequently to my mind, long and familiar custom having given them the right to occupy my mind against my inclination and rendered them almost masters of my belief; nor will I ever lose the habit of deferring to them or of placing my confidence in them, so long as I consider them as they really are, i.e. opinions in some measure doubtful, as I have just shown and at the same time highly probable, so that there is much more reason to believe in than to deny them. That is why I consider that I shall not be acting amiss if, taking of set purpose a contrary belief, I allow myself to be deceived, and for a certain time pretend that all these opinions are entirely false and imaginary, until at last, having thus balanced my former prejudices with my latter [so that they cannot divert my opinions more to one side than to the other], my judgment will no longer be dominated by bad usage or turned away from the right knowledge of the truth. For I am assured that there can be neither peril nor error in this course, and that I cannot at present yield too much to distrust, since I am not considering the question of action, but only of knowledge.

I shall then suppose, not that God who is supremely good and the fountain of truth, but some evil genius not less powerful than deceitful, has employed his whole energies in deceiving me; I shall consider that the heavens, the earth, colours, figures, sound, and all other external things are nought but the illusions and dreams of which this genius has availed himself in order to lay traps for my credulity; I shall consider myself as having no hands, no eyes, no flesh, no blood, nor any senses, yet falsely believing myself to possess all these things; I shall remain obstinately attached to this idea, and if by this means it is not in my power to arrive at the knowledge of any truth, I may at least do what is in my power [i.e. suspend my judgment], and with firm purpose avoid giving credence to any false thing, or being imposed upon by this arch deceiver, however powerful and deceptive he may be. . . .

43. CAN THE PRINCIPLE OF INDUCTION BE JUSTIFIED?

Bertrand Russell

Bertrand Russell (1872–1970). *During a tempestuous and seemingly endless career, Russell managed to get himself dismissed from the faculty at Trinity College, Cambridge, sentenced to six months in prison, and be the recipient of the Order of Merit and the Nobel Prize for Literature. He also wrote about fifty books mostly in the areas of logic and theory of knowledge. But his graceful style and acid wit found targets on other topics, mainly in morality and the prominent social issues of the twentieth century.*

If we are to know of the existence of matter, of other people, of the past before our individual memory begins, or of the future, we must know general principles of some kind by means of which such inferences can be drawn. It must be known to us that the existence of some one sort of thing, A, is a sign of the existence of some other sort of thing, B, either at the same time as A or at some earlier or later time, as, for example, thunder is a sign of the earlier existence of lightning. If this were not known to us, we could never extend our knowledge

From The Problems of Philosophy, *Chapter 6, by Bertrand Russell, Copyright 1912, The Home University Library. Reprinted by permission of Oxford University Press.*

beyond the sphere of our private experience; and this sphere . . . is exceedingly limited. The question we have now to consider is whether such an extension is possible, and if so, how it is effected.

Let us take as an illustration a matter about which none of us, in fact, feel the slightest doubt. We are all convinced that the sun will rise tomorrow. Why? Is this belief a mere blind outcome of past experience, or can it be justified as a reasonable belief? It is not easy to find a test by which to judge whether a belief of this kind is reasonable or not, but we can at least ascertain what sort of general beliefs would suffice, if true, to justify the judgment that the sun will rise to-morrow, and the many other similar judgments upon which our actions are based.

It is obvious that if we are asked why we believe that the sun will rise tomorrow, we shall naturally answer, 'Because it always has risen every day.' We have a firm belief that it will rise in the future, because it has risen in the past. If we are challenged as to why we believe that it will continue to rise as heretofore, we may appeal to the laws of motion: the earth, we shall say, is a freely rotating body, and such bodies do not cease to rotate unless something interferes from outside, and there is nothing outside to interfere with the earth between now and to-morrow. Of course it might be doubted whether we are quite certain that there is nothing outside to interfere, but this is not the interesting doubt. The interesting doubt is as to whether the laws of motion will remain in operation until to-morrow. If this doubt is raised, we find ourselves in the same position as when the doubt about the sunrise was first raised.

The *only* reason for believing that the laws of motion will remain in operation is that they have operated hitherto, so far as our knowledge of the past enables us to judge. It is true that we have a greater body of evidence from the past in favour of the laws of motion than we have in favour of the sunrise, because the sunrise is merely a particular case of fulfilment of the laws of motion, and there are countless other particular cases. But the real question is: Do *any* number of cases of a law being fulfilled in the past afford evidence that it will be fulfilled in the future? If not, it becomes plain that we have no ground whatever for expecting the sun to rise to-morrow, or for expecting the bread we shall eat at our next meal not to poison us, or for any of the other scarcely conscious expectations that control our daily lives. It is to be observed that all such expectations are only *probable;* thus we have not to seek for a proof that they *must* be fulfilled, but only for some reason in favour of the view that they are *likely* to be fulfilled.

Now in dealing with this question we must, to begin with, make an important distinction, without which we should soon become involved in hopeless confusions. Experience has shown us that, hitherto, the frequent repetition of some uniform succession or coexistence has been a *cause* of our expecting the same succession or coexistence on the next occasion. Food that has a certain appearance generally has a certain taste, and it is a severe shock to our expectations when the familiar appearance is found to be associated with an unusual taste. Things which we see become associated, by habit, with certain tactile sensations which we expect if we touch them; one of the horrors of a ghost (in many ghost-stories) is that it fails to give us any sensations of touch. Uneducated people who go abroad for the first time are so surprised as to be incredulous when they find their native language not understood.

And this kind of association is not confined to men; in animals also it is very strong. A horse which has been often driven along a certain road resists the attempt to drive him in a different direction. Domestic animals expect food when they see the person who usually feeds them. We know that all these rather crude expectations of uniformity are liable to be misleading. The man who has fed the chicken every day throughout its life at last wrings its neck instead, showing that more refined views as to the uniformity of nature would have been useful to the chicken.

But in spite of the misleadingness of such expectations, they nevertheless exist. The mere fact that something has happened a certain number of times causes animals and men to expect that it will happen again. Thus our instincts certainly cause us to believe that the sun will rise to-morrow, but we may be in no better a position than the chicken which unexpectedly has its neck wrung. We have therefore to distinguish the fact that past uniformities *cause* expectations as to the future, from the question whether there is any reasonable ground for giving weight to such expectations after the question of their validity has been raised.

The problem we have to discuss is whether there is any reason for believing in what is called 'the uniformity of nature.' The belief in the uniformity of nature is the belief that everything that has happened or will happen is an instance of some general law to which there are *no* exceptions. The crude expectations which we have been considering are all subject to exceptions, and therefore liable to disappoint those who entertain them. But science habitually assumes, at least as a working hypothesis, that general rules which have exceptions can be replaced by general rules which have no exceptions. 'Unsupported bodies in air fall' is a general rule to which balloons and aeroplanes are exceptions. But the laws of motion and the law of gravitation, which account for the fact that most bodies fall, also account for the fact that balloons and aeroplanes can rise; thus the laws of motion and the law of gravitation are not subject to these exceptions.

The belief that the sun will rise to-morrow might be falsified if the earth came suddenly into contact with a large body which destroyed its rotation; but the laws of motion and the law of gravitation would not be infringed by such an event. The business of science is to find uniformities, such as the laws of motion and the law of gravitation, to which, so far as our experience extends, there are no exceptions. In this search science has been remarkably successful, and it may be conceded that such uniformities have held hitherto. This brings us back to the question: Have we any reason, assuming that they have always held in the past, to suppose that they will hold in the future?

It has been argued that we have reason to know that the future will resemble the past, because what was the future has constantly become the past, and has always been found to resemble the past, so that we really have experience of the future, namely of times which were formerly future, which we may call past futures. But such an argument really begs the very question at issue. We have experience of past futures, but not of future futures, and the question is: Will future futures resemble past futures? This question is not to be answered by an argument which starts from past futures alone. We have therefore still to seek for some principle which shall enable us to know that the future will follow the same laws as the past.

The reference to the future in this question is not essential. The same question arises when we apply the laws that work in our experience to past things of which we have no experience—as, for example, in geology, or in theories as to the origin of the Solar System. The question we really have to ask is: 'When two things have been found to be often associated, and no instance is known of the one occurring without the other, does the occurrence of one of the two, in a fresh instance, give any good ground for expecting the other?' On our answer to this question must depend the validity of the whole of our expectations as to the future, the whole of the results obtained by induction, and in fact practically all the beliefs upon which our daily life is based.

It must be conceded, to begin with, that the fact that two things have been found often together and never apart does not, by itself, suffice to *prove* demonstratively that they will be found together in the next case we examine. The most we can hope is that the oftener things are found together, the more probable it becomes that they will be found together another time, and that, if they have been found together often enough, the probability will amount *almost* to certainty. It can never quite reach certainty, because we know that in spite of frequent repetitions there sometimes is a failure at the last, as in the case of the chicken whose neck is wrung. Thus probability is all we ought to seek.

It might be urged, as against the view we are advocating, that we know all natural phenomena to be subject to the reign of law, and that sometimes on the basis of observation, we can see that only one law can possibly fit the facts of the case. Now to this view there are two answers. The first is that, even if *some* law which has no exceptions applies to our case, we can never, in pratice, be sure that we have discovered that law and not one to which there are exceptions. The second is that the reign of law would seem to be itself only probable, and that our belief that it will hold in the future, or in unexamined cases in the past, is itself based upon the very principle we are examining.

The principle we are examining may be called the *principle of induction*, and its two parts may be stated as follows:

(*a*) When a thing of a certain sort A has been found to be associated with a thing of a certain other sort B, and has never been found dissociated from a thing of the sort B, the greater the number of cases in which A and B have been associated, the greater is the probability that they will be associated in a fresh case in which one of them is known to be present;

(*b*) Under the same circumstances, a sufficient number of cases of association will make the probability of a fresh association nearly a certainty, and will make it approach certainty without limit.

As just stated, the principle applies only to the verification of our expectation in a single fresh instance. But we want also to know that there is a probability in favour of the general law that things of the sort A are *always* associated with things of the sort B, provided a sufficient number of cases of association are known, and no cases of failure of association are known. The probability of the general law is obviously less than the probability of the particular case, since if the general law is true, the particular case must also be true, whereas the particular case may be true without the general law being true. Nevertheless the probability of the general law is increased by repetitions, just as the probability of the particular case is. We may therefore repeat the two parts of our principle as regards the general law, thus:

(*a*) The greater the number of cases in which a thing of the sort A has been found associated with a thing of the sort B, the more probable it is (if no cases of failure of association are known) that A is always associated with B;

(*b*) Under the same circumstances, a sufficient number of cases of the association of A with B will make it nearly certain that A is always associated with B, and will make this general law approach certainty without limit.

It should be noted that probability is always relative to certain data. In our case, the data are merely the known cases of coexistence of A and B. There may be other data, which *might* be taken into account, which would gravely alter the probability. For example, a man who had seen a great many white swans might argue, by our principle, that on the data it was *probable* that all swans were white, and this might be a perfectly sound argument. The argument is not disproved by the fact that some swans are black, because a thing may very well happen in spite of the fact that some data render it improbable. In the case of the swans, a man might know that colour is a very variable characteristic in many species of animals, and that, therefore, an induction as to colour is peculiarly liable to error. But this knowledge would be a fresh datum, by no means proving that the probability relatively to our previous data had been wrongly estimated. The fact, therefore, that things often fail to fulfil our expectations is no evidence that our expectations will not *probably* be fulfilled in a given case or a given class of cases. Thus our inductive principle is at any rate not capable of being *disproved* by an appeal to experience.

The inductive principle, however, is equally incapable of being *proved* by an appeal to experience. Experience might conceivably confirm the inductive principle as regards the cases that have been already examined; but as regards unexamined cases, it is the inductive principle alone that can justify any inference from what has been examined to what has not been examined. All arguments which, on the basis of experience, argue as to the future or the unexperienced parts of the past or present, assume the inductive principle; hence we can never use experience to prove the inductive principle without begging the question. Thus we must either accept the inductive principle on the ground of its intrinsic evidence, or forgo all justification of our expectations about the future. If the principle is unsound, we have no reason to expect the sun to rise to-morrow, to expect bread to be more nourishing than a stone, or to expect that if we throw ourselves off the roof we shall fall. When we see what looks like our best friend approaching us, we shall have no reason to suppose that his body is not inhabited by the mind of our worst enemy or of some total stranger. All our conduct is based upon associations which have worked in the past, and which we therefore regard as likely to work in the future; and this likelihood is dependent for its validity upon the inductive principle.

The general principles of science, such as the belief in the reign of law, and the belief that every event must have a cause, are as completely dependent upon the inductive principle as are the beliefs of daily life. All such general principles are believed because mankind have found innumerable instances of their truth and no instances of their falsehood. But this affords no evidence for their truth in the future, unless the inductive principle is assumed.

Thus all knowledge which, on a basis of experience tells us something about what is not experienced, is based upon a belief which experience can neither confirm nor confute, yet which, at least in its more concrete applications, appears to be as firmly rooted in us as many of the facts of experience.

44. ATTEMPTS TO JUSTIFY INDUCTION ARE MISTAKEN

P. F. Strawson

P. F. Strawson. *(See essay number 33 for biographical note.)*

. . . 10. Let us turn from attempts to justify induction to attempts to show that the demand for a justification is mistaken. We have seen already that what lies behind such a demand is often the absurd wish that induction should be shown to be some kind of deduction—and this wish is clearly traceable in the two attempts at justification which we have examined. What other sense could we give to the demand? Sometimes it is expressed in the form of a request for proof that induction is a *reasonable* or *rational* procedure, that we have *good grounds* for placing reliance upon it. Consider the uses of the phrases 'good grounds,' 'justification,' 'reasonable,' &c. Often we say such things as 'He has *every justification* for believing that *p*'; 'I have *very good reasons* for believing it'; 'There are *good grounds* for the view that *q*'; 'There is *good evidence* that *r*.' We often talk, in such ways as these, of justification, good grounds or reasons or evidence for certain beliefs. Suppose such a belief were one expressible in the form 'Every case of *f* is a case of *g*. And suppose someone were asked what he meant by saying that he had good grounds or reasons for holding it. I think it would be felt to be a satisfactory answer if he replied: 'Well, in all my wide and varied experience I've come across innumerable cases of *f* and

From Introduction to Logical Theory, *Methuen & Co. Ltd., pp. 256–259. Reprinted by permission of the publisher, Methuen & Co. Ltd.*

never a case of f which wasn't a case of g.' In saying this, he is clearly claiming to have *inductive* support, *inductive* evidence, of a certain kind, for his belief; and he is also giving a perfectly proper answer to the question, what he meant by saying that he had ample justification, good grounds, good reasons for his belief. It is an analytic proposition that it is reasonable to have a degree of belief in a statement which is proportional to the strength of the evidence in its favour; and it is an analytic proposition, though not a proposition of mathematics, that, other things being equal, the evidence for a generalization is strong in proportion as the number of favourable instances, and the variety of circumstances in which they have been found, is great. So to ask whether it is reasonable to place reliance on inductive procedures is like asking whether it is reasonable to proportion the degree of one's convictions to the strength of the evidence. Doing this is what 'being reasonable' *means* in such a context.

As for the other form in which the doubt may be expressed, viz., 'Is induction a justified, or justifiable, procedure?', it emerges in a still less favourable light. No sense has been given to it, though it is easy to see why it seems to have a sense. For it is generally proper to inquire *of a particular belief*, whether its adoption is justified; and, in asking this, we are asking whether there is good, bad, or any, evidence for it. In applying or withholding the epithets 'justified,' 'well founded,' &c., in the case of specific beliefs, we are appealing to, and applying, inductive standards. But to what standards are we appealing when we ask whether the application of inductive standards is justified or well grounded? If we cannot answer, then no sense has been given to the question. Compare it with the question: Is the law legal? It makes perfectly good sense to inquire of a particular action, of an administrative regulation, or even, in the case of some states, of a particular enactment of the legislature, whether or not it is legal. The question is answered by an appeal to a legal system, by the application of a set of legal (or constitutional) rules or standards. But it makes no sense to inquire in general whether the law of the land, the legal system as a whole, is or is not legal. For to what legal standards are we appealing?

The only way in which a sense might be given to the question, whether induction is in general a justified or justifiable procedure, is a trivial one which we have already noticed. We might interpret it to mean 'Are all conclusions, arrived at inductively, justified?', i.e., 'Do people always have adequate evidence for the conclusions they draw?' The answer to this question is easy, but uninteresting: it is that sometimes people have adequate evidence, and sometimes they do not.

11. It seems, however, that this way of showing the request for a general justification of induction to be absurd is sometimes insufficient

to allay the worry that produces it. And to point out that 'forming rational opinions about the unobserved on the evidence available' and 'assessing the evidence by inductive standards' are phrases which describe the same thing, is more apt to produce irritation than relief. The point is felt to be 'merely a verbal' one; and though the point of this protest is itself hard to see, it is clear that something more is required. So the question must be pursued further. First, I want to point out that there is something a little odd about talking of 'the inductive method,' or even 'the inductive policy,' as if it were just one possible method among others of arguing from the observed to the unobserved, from the available evidence to the facts in question. If one asked a meteorologist what method or methods he used to forecast the weather, one would be surprised if he answered: 'Oh, just the inductive method.' If one asked a doctor by what means he diagnosed a certain disease, the answer 'By induction' would be felt as an impatient evasion, a joke, or a rebuke. The answer one hopes for is an account of the tests made, the signs taken account of, the rules and recipes and general laws applied. When such a specific method of prediction or diagnosis is in question, one can ask whether the method is justified in practice; and here again one is asking whether its employment is inductively justified, whether it commonly gives correct results. This question would normally seem an admissible one. One might be tempted to conclude that, while there are many different specific methods of prediction, diagnosis, &c., appropriate to different subjects of inquiry, all such methods could properly be called 'inductive' in the sense that their employment rested on inductive support; and that, hence, the phrase 'non-inductive method of finding out about what lies deductively beyond the evidence' was a description without meaning, a phrase to which no sense had been given; so that there could be no question of justifying our selection of one method, called 'the inductive,' of doing this.

However, someone might object: 'Surely it is possible, though it might be foolish, to use methods utterly different from accredited scientific ones. Suppose a man, whenever he wanted to form an opinion about what lay beyond his observation or the observation of available witnesses, simply shut his eyes, asked himself the appropriate question, and accepted the first answer that came into his head. Wouldn't this be a non-inductive method?' Well, let us suppose this. The man is asked: 'Do you usually get the right answer by your method?' He might answer: 'You've mentioned one of its drawbacks; I never do get the right answer; but it's an extremely easy method.' One might then be inclined to think that it was not a method of finding things out at all. But suppose he answered: 'Yes, it's usually (always) the right answer.' Then we might be willing to call it a method of finding out, though a strange one. But, then, by the very fact of its success, it would be an inductively supported method. For each application of the method would be an application of the general rule, 'The first answer that comes into my head is generally (always) the right one'; and for the truth of this generalization there would be the inductive evidence of a long run of favourable instances with no unfavourable ones (if it were 'always'), or of a sustained high proportion of successes to trials (if it were 'generally').

So every successful method or recipe for finding out about the unobserved must be one which has inductive support; for to say that a recipe is successful is to say that it has been repeatedly applied with success; and repeated successful application of a recipe constitutes just what we mean by inductive evidence in its favour. Pointing out this fact must not be confused with saying that 'the inductive method' is justified by its success, justified because it works. This is a mistake, and an important one. I am not seeking to 'justify the inductive method,' for no meaning has been given to this phrase. *A fortiori*, I am not saying that induction is justified by its success in finding out about the unobserved. I am saying, rather, that any successful method of finding out about the unobserved is necessarily justified by induction. This is an analytic proposition. The phrase 'successful method of finding things out which has no inductive support' is self-contradictory. Having, or acquiring, inductive support is a necessary condition of the success of a method.

Why point this out at all? First, it may have a certain therapeutic force, a power to reassure. Second, it may counteract the tendency to think of 'the inductive method' as something on a par with specific methods of diagnosis or prediction and therefore, like them, standing in need of (inductive) justification. . . .

45. PHYSICAL OBJECTS AS NOTHING BUT PERCEPTIONS

George Berkeley

George Berkeley (1685–1753). Although publishing only a few short works in philosophy, Berkeley's views have generated philosophical controversy and interest with every succeeding generation. After completion of his philosophical treatises while still a young man, he was made a Bishop in the Church of England

*and became increasingly occupied with ecclesiastical duties.
His works are An Essay Towards a New Theory of Vision
(1709), Three Dialogues Between Hylas and Philonous (1713),
and The Principles of Human Knowledge (1710), from which
the following excerpts are taken.*

It is evident to any one who takes a survey of the *objects* of
human knowledge, that they are either ideas actually imprinted on the
senses; or else such as are perceived by attending to the passions and
operations of the mind; or lastly, ideas formed by help of memory and
imagination—either compounding, dividing, or barely representing those
originally perceived in the aforesaid ways. By sight I have the ideas of
light and colours, with their several degrees and variations. By touch
I perceive hard and soft, heat and cold, motion and resistance, and of
all these more and less either as to quantity or degree. Smelling furnishes
me with odours; the palate with tastes; and hearing conveys sounds to
the mind in all their variety of tone and composition. And as several
of these are observed to accompany each other, they come to be marked
by one name, and so to be reputed as one thing. Thus, for example, a
certain colour, taste, smell, figure and consistence having been observed
to go together, are accounted one distinct thing, signified by the name
apple; other collections of ideas constitute a stone, a tree, a book, and
the like sensible things—which as they are pleasing or disagreeable excite the passions of love, hatred, joy, grief, and so forth.

But, besides all that endless variety of ideas or objects of knowledge, there is likewise something which knows or perceives them, and
exercises divers operations, as willing, imagining, remembering, about
them. This perceiving, active being is what I call *mind, spirit, soul,* or
myself. By which words I do not denote any one of my ideas, but a
thing entirely distinct from them, wherein, they exist, or, which is the
same thing, whereby they are perceived—for the existence of an idea
consists in being perceived.

That neither our thoughts, nor passions, nor ideas formed by the
imagination, exist without the mind, is what everybody will allow. And
it seems no less evident that the various sensations or ideas imprinted
on the sense, however blended or combined together (that is, whatever
objects they compose), cannot exist otherwise than in a mind perceiving
them—I think an intuitive knowledge may be obtained of this by any
one that shall attend to what is meant by the term *exists*, when applied
to sensible things. The table I write on I say exists, that is, I see and
feel it; and if I were out of my study I should say it existed—meaning
thereby that if I was in my study I might perceive it, or that some other

spirit actually does perceive it. There was an odour, that is, it was smelt; there was a sound, that is, it was heard; a colour or figure, and it was perceived by sight or touch. This is all that I can understand by these and the like expressions. For as to what is said of the absolute existence of unthinking things without any relation to their being perceived, that seems perfectly unintelligible. Their *esse* is *percipi*, nor is it possible they should have any existence out of the minds or thinking things which perceive them.

It is indeed an opinion, strangely prevailing amongst men, that houses, mountains, rivers, and in a word all sensible objects, have an existence, natural or real, distinct from their being perceived by the understanding. But, with how great an assurance and acquiescence soever this principle may be entertained in the world, yet whoever shall find in his heart to call it in question may, if I mistake not, perceive it to involve a manifest contradiction. For, what are the forementioned objects but the things we perceive by sense? and what do we perceive besides our own ideas or sensations? and is it not plainly repugnant that any one of these, or any combination of them, should exist unperceived? . . .

Some truths there are so near and obvious to the mind that a man need only open his eyes to see them. Such I take this important one to be, viz., that all the choir of heaven and furniture of the earth, in a word all those bodies which compose the mighty frame of the world, have not any subsistence without a mind, that their *being* is to be perceived or known; that consequently so long as they are not actually perceived by me, or do not exist in my mind or that of any other created they must either have no existence at all, or else subsist in the mind of some Eternal Spirit—it being perfectly unintelligible, and involving all the absurdity of abstraction, to attribute to any single part of them an existence independent of a spirit. To be convinced of which, the reader need only reflect, and try to separate in his own thoughts the *being* of a sensible thing from its *being perceived*.

From what has been said it follows there is not any other Substance than *Spirit*, or that which perceives. But, for the fuller proof of this point, let it be considered the sensible qualities are colour, figure, motion, smell, taste, etc., *i.e.* the ideas perceived by sense. Now, for an idea to exist in an unperceiving thing is a manifest contradiction, for to have an idea is all one has to perceive; that therefore wherein colour, figure, and the like qualities exist must perceive them; hence it is clear there can be no unthinking substance or *substratum* of those ideas.

But, say you, though the ideas themselves do not exist without the mind, yet there may be things like them, whereof they are copies or resemblances, which things exist without the mind in an unthinking substance. I answer, an idea can be like nothing but an idea; a colour or figure can be like nothing but another colour or figure. If we look but never so little into our thoughts, we shall find it impossible for us to conceive a likeness except only between our ideas. Again, I ask whether those supposed originals or external things, of which our ideas are the pictures or representations, be themselves perceivable or no? If they are, then they are ideas and we have gained our point; but if you say they are not, I appeal to any one whether it be sense to assert a colour is like something which is invisible; hard or soft, like something which is intangible; and so of the rest.

Some there are who make a distinction betwixt *primary* and *secondary* qualities. By the former they mean extension, figure, motion, rest, solidity or impenetrability, and number; by the latter they denote all other sensible qualities, as colours, sounds, tastes, and so forth. The ideas we have of these they acknowledge not to be the resemblances of anything existing without the mind, or unperceived, but they will have our ideas of the primary qualities to be patterns or images of things which exist without the mind, in an unthinking substance which they call Matter. By Matter, therefore, we are to understand an inert, senseless substance, in which extension, figure, and motion do actually subsist. But it is evident, from what we have already shown, that extension, figure, and motion are only ideas existing in the mind, and that an idea can be like nothing but another idea, and that consequently neither they nor their archetypes can exist in an unperceiving substance. Hence, it is plain that the very notion of what is called *Matter* or *corporeal substance* involves a contradiction in it.

They who assert that figure, motion, and the rest of the primary or original qualities do exist without the mind in unthinking substances, do at the same time acknowledge that colours, sounds, heat, cold, and suchlike secondary qualities, do not—which they tell us are sensations existing in the mind alone, that depend on and are occasioned by the different size, texture, and motion of the minute particles of matter. This they take for an undoubted truth, which they can demonstrate beyond all exception. Now, if it be certain that those original qualities are inseparably united with the other sensible qualities, and not, even in thought, capable of being abstracted from them, it plainly follows that they exist only in the mind. But I desire any one to reflect and try whether he can, by any abstraction of thought, conceive the extension and motion of a body without all other sensible qualities. For my own part, I see evidently that it is not in my power to frame an idea of a body extended and moving, but I must withal give it some colour or other sensible quality which is acknowledged to exist only in the mind. In short, extension, figure, and motion, abstracted from all other qualities, are inconceivable. Where therefore the other sensible qualities are, there must these be also, to wit, in the mind and nowhere else.

Again, *great* and *small, swift* and *slow,* are allowed to exist no-where without the mind, being entirely relative, and changing as the frame or position of the organs of sense varies. The extension therefore which exists without the mind is neither great nor small, the motion neither swift nor slow, that is, they are nothing at all. . . . Without extension solidity cannot be conceived; since therefore it has been shewn that extension exists not in an unthinking substance, the same must also be true of solidity. . . .

I shall farther add, that, after the same manner as modern philosophers prove certain sensible qualities to have no existence in Matter, or without the mind, the same thing may be likewise proved of all other sensible qualities whatsoever. Thus, for instance, it is said that heat and cold are affections only of the mind, and not at all patterns of real beings, existing in the corporeal substances which excite them, for that the same body which appears cold to one hand seems warm to another. Now, why may we not as well argue that figure and extension are not patterns or resemblances of qualities existing in Matter, because to the same eye at different stations, or eyes of a different texture at the same station, they appear various, and cannot therefore be the images of anything settled and determinate without the mind? Again, it is proved that sweetness is not really in the sapid thing, because the thing remaining unaltered the sweetness is changed into bitter, as in case of a fever or otherwise vitiated palate. Is it not as reasonable to say that motion is not without the mind, since if the succession of ideas in the mind becomes swifter, the motion, it is acknowledged, shall appear slower without any alteration in any external object?

In short, let any one consider those arguments which are thought manifestly to prove that colours and taste exist only in the mind, and he shall find they may with equal force be brought to prove the same thing of extension, figure, and motion. Though it must be confessed this method of arguing does not so much prove that there is no extension or colour in an outward object, as that we do not know by sense which is the true extension or colour of the object. But the arguments foregoing plainly show it to be impossible that any colour or extension at all, or other sensible quality whatsoever, should exist in an unthinking subject without the mind, or in truth, that there should be any such thing as an outward object.

But let us examine a little the received opinion. It is said ex-tension is a mode or accident of Matter, and that Matter is the *sub-stratum* that supports it. Now I desire that you would explain to me what is meant by Matter's *supporting* extension. Say you, I have no idea of Matter and therefore cannot explain it. I answer, though you have no positive, yet, if you have any meaning at all, you must at least have a relative idea of Matter; though you know not what it is, yet you must be supposed to know what relation it bears to accidents, and what is meant by its supporting them. It is evident "support" cannot here be taken in its usual or literal sense—as when we say that pillars support a building; in what sense therefore must it be taken? . . .

But, though it were possible that solid, figured, movable substances may exist without the mind, corresponding to the ideas we have of bodies, yet how is it possible for us to know this? Either we must know it by sense or by reason. As for our senses, by them we have the knowledge only of our sensations, ideas, or those things that are immediately perceived by sense, call them what you will: but they do not inform us that things exist without the mind, or unperceived, like to those which are perceived. This the materialists themselves acknowledge. It remains therefore that if we have any knowledge at all of external things, it must be by reason, inferring their existence from what is immediately perceived by sense. But what reason can induce us to believe the existence of bodies without the mind, from what we perceive, since the very patrons of Matter themselves do not pretend there is any necessary connexion betwixt them and our ideas? I say it is granted on all hands (and what happens in dreams, phrensies, and the like, puts it beyond dispute) that it is possible we might be affected with all the ideas we have now, though there were no bodies existing without resembling them. Hence, it is evident the supposition of external bodies is not necessary for the producing our ideas; since it is granted they are produced sometimes, and might possibly be produced always in the same order, we see them in at present, without their concurrence.

But, though we might possibly have all our sensations without them, yet perhaps it may be thought easier to conceive and explain the manner of their production, by supposing external bodies in their likeness rather than otherwise; and so it might be at least probable there are such things as bodies that excite their ideas in our minds. But neither can this be said; for, though we give the materialists their external bodies, they by their own confession are never the nearer knowing how our ideas are produced; since they own themselves unable to comprehend in what manner body can act upon spirit, or how it is possible it should imprint any idea in the mind. Hence it is evident the production of ideas or sensations in our minds can be no reason why we should suppose Matter or corporeal substances, since that is acknowledged to remain equally inexplicable with or without this supposition. If therefore it were possible for bodies to exist without the mind, yet to hold they do so, must needs be a very precarious opinion; since it is to suppose, without any reason at all, that God has created innumerable beings that are entirely useless and serve to no manner of purpose.

In short, if there were external bodies, it is impossible we should ever come to know it; and if there were not, we might have the very same reasons to think there were that we have now. Suppose—what no one can deny possible—an intelligence without the help of external bodies, to be affected with the same train of sensations or ideas that you are, imprinted in the same order and with like vividness in his mind. I ask whether that intelligence hath not all the reason to believe the existence of corporeal substances, represented by his ideas, and exciting them in his mind, that you can possibly have for believing the same thing? Of this there can be no question—which one consideration were enough to make any reasonable person suspect the strength of whatever arguments he may think himself to have, for the existence of bodies without the mind. . . .

But, say you, surely there is nothing easier than for me to imagine trees, for instance, in a park, or books existing in a closet, and nobody by to perceive them. I answer, you may so, there is no difficulty in it; but what is all this, I beseech you, more than framing in your mind certain ideas which you call books and trees, and the same time omitting to frame the idea of any one that may perceive them? But do not you yourself perceive or think of them all the while? This therefore is nothing to the purpose; it only shews you have the power of imagining or forming ideas in your mind: but it does not shew that you can conceive it possible the objects of your thought may exist without the mind. To make out this, it is necessary that you conceive them existing unconceived or unthought of, which is a manifest repugnancy. When we do our utmost to conceive the existence of external bodies, we are all the while only contemplating our own ideas. But the mind taking no notice of itself, is deluded to think it can and does conceive bodies existing unthought of or without the mind, though at the same time they are apprehended by or exist in itself. A little attention will discover to any one the truth and evidence of what is here said, and make it unnecessary to insist on any other proofs against the existence of *material substance*. . . .

All our ideas, sensations, notions, or the things which we perceive, by whatsoever names they may be distinguished, are visibly inactive—there is nothing of power or agency included in them. So that one idea or object of thought cannot produce or make any alteration in another. To be satisfied of the truth of this, there is nothing else requisite but a bare observation of our ideas. For, since they and every part of them exist only in the mind, it follows that there is nothing in them but what is perceived: but whoever shall attend to his ideas, whether of sense or reflection, will not perceive in them any power or activity; there is, therefore, no such thing contained in them. A little attention will discover to us that the very being of an idea implies passiveness and inertness in it, insomuch that it is impossible for an idea to do anything, or, strictly speaking, to be the cause of anything: neither can it be the resemblance or pattern of any active being. Whence it plainly follows that extension, figure, and motion cannot be the cause of our sensations. To say, therefore, that these are the effects of powers resulting from the configuration, number, motion, and size of corpuscles, must certainly be false.

We perceive a continual succession of ideas, some are anew excited, others are changed or totally disappear. There is therefore some cause of these ideas, whereon they depend, and which produces and changes them. That this cause cannot be any quality or idea or combination of ideas is clear from the preceding [paragraph]. It must therefore be a substance; but it has been shewn that there is no corporeal or material substance: it remains therefore that the cause of ideas is an incorporeal active substance or Spirit. . . .

I find I can excite ideas in my mind at pleasure, and vary and shift the scene as oft as I think fit. It is no more than willing, and straightway this or that idea arises in my fancy; and by the same power it is obliterated and makes way for another. This making and unmaking of ideas doth very properly denominate the mind active. Thus much is certain and grounded on experience but when we think of unthinking agents or of exciting ideas exclusive of volition, we only amuse ourselves with words.

But, whatever power I may have over my own thoughts, I find the ideas actually perceived by Sense have not a like dependence on my will. When in broad daylight I open my eyes, it is not in my power to choose whether I shall see or no, or to determine what particular objects shall present themselves to my view; and so likewise as to the hearing and other senses; the ideas imprinted on them are not creatures of my will. There is therefore some *other* Will or Spirit that produces them.

The ideas of Sense are more strong, lively, and distinct than those of the imagination; they have likewise a steadiness, order, and coherence, and are not excited at random, as those which are the effects of human wills often are, but in a regular train or series, the admirable connexion whereof sufficiently testifies the wisdom and benevolence of its Author. Now the set rules or established methods, wherein the Mind we depend on excites in us the ideas of sense, are called the *laws of nature;* and these we learn by experience, which teaches us that such and such ideas are attended with such and such other ideas, in the ordinary course of things.

This gives us a sort of foresight which enables us to regulate our actions for the benefit of life. And without this we should be eternally at a loss; we could not know how to act anything that might procure us the least pleasure, or remove the least pain of sense. That food nourishes, sleep refreshes, and fire warms us; that to sow in the seedtime is the way to reap in the harvest; and in general that to obtain such or such ends, such or such means are conducive—all this we know, not by discovering any necessary connexion between our ideas, but only by the observation of the settled laws of nature, without which we should be all in uncertainty and confusion, and a grown man no more know how to manage himself in the affairs of life than an infant just born.

And yet this consistent uniform working, which so evidently displays the goodness and wisdom of that Governing Spirit whose Will constitutes the laws of nature, is so far from leading our thoughts to Him, that it rather sends them wandering after second causes. For, when we perceive certain ideas of Sense constantly followed by other ideas and we know this is not of our own doing, we forthwith attribute power and agency to the ideas themselves, and make one the cause of another, than which nothing can be more absurd and unintelligible. Thus, for example, having observed that when we perceive by sight a certain round luminous figure we at the same time perceive by touch the idea or sensation called heat, we do from thence conclude the sun to be the cause of heat. And in like manner perceiving the motion and collision of bodies to be attended with sound, we are inclined to think the latter the effect of the former.

The ideas imprinted on the Senses by the Author of nature are called *real things;* and those excited in the imagination being less regular, vivid, and constant, are more properly termed *ideas,* or *images of things,* which they copy and represent. But then our sensations, be they never so vivid and distinct, are nevertheless ideas, that is, they exist in the mind, or are perceived by it, as truly as the ideas of its own framing. The ideas of Sense are allowed to have more reality in them, that is, to be more strong, orderly, and coherent than the creatures of the mind; but this is no argument that they exist without the mind. They are also less dependent on the spirit, or thinking substance which perceives them, in that they are excited by the will of another and more powerful spirit; yet still they are *ideas,* and certainly no idea, whether faint or strong, can exist otherwise than in a mind perceiving it. . . .

46. PHYSICAL OBJECTS AS NOT REDUCIBLE TO PERCEPTIONS

C. H. Whiteley

C. H. Whiteley *(1911–   ) is Lecturer in Philosophy at the University of Birmingham, England. He has written* An Introduction to Metaphysics *(1950) and numerous essays in philosophical journals.*

The problem I shall discuss is: What reason have we for believing that there are physical objects? My purpose is not either to raise or to dispel doubts as to the existence of physical objects; this doubt constitutes a medical rather than a philosophical problem. The point of asking the question is that, while there can be no reasonable difference of opinion as to whether there are physical objects, there can be and is reasonable difference of opinion as to how the notion of a physical object is to be analysed; and if we are clear as to what grounds there are for believing in physical objects, we shall also be clearer as to what sort of physical objects we have grounds for believing in. Also, it is worth while to inquire which other beliefs are logically connected with, and which are logically independent of, the belief in physical objects.

I make one important assumption at the outset: namely, that by a physical object or process we mean something that exists or occurs apart from and independently of our perceptions, and of our experiences of other kinds. The distinction between the physical or "real" world and the "subjective" or "imaginary"—illusions, hallucinations, after-images, shadows, rainbows, mental pictures, what we merely suppose, imagine or expect—is a distinction between things and events which exist or occur whether anybody is aware of them or not, and things and events which have their being only as and when somebody is aware of them. A belief in physical objects is a belief in things which are sometimes at least unobserved by the believer.

It is obvious that the existence of such things is not a question to be settled by sense-perception alone. That there is a material world cannot be established or even made plausible merely by looking, listening, touching; it is not *given* in the way in which the existence of something red and something round, of sounds, smells, aches, feelings of sad-

From Philosophy, *Vol. 34, 1959, pp. 142–149. Reprinted by permission of the author and editor.*

ness, can be given. I do not mean that the something red or round cannot be a physical object; I mean that it cannot be known to be a physical object just by looking at it or otherwise perceiving it. For I cannot, simply by perceiving something, tell whether that something continues to exist when I cease to perceive it. This logical necessity is not evaded by naïve realism, which holds that the something red or round which appears to sight is (usually at least) identical with a physical object; for though this may be so, we cannot know it just by looking. Nor is it evaded by phenomenalism; for no phenomenalist does or plausibly could analyse statements about physical objects into statements asserting the *actual* occurrence of sense-data; he must add statements about what sense-data *would* be sensed if certain conditions were fulfilled; and this fact is not given by sense-perception, but reasons for it are required. That there are physical objects is not something we observe or perceive, but something we suppose or assume (to call it a "hypothesis" or "postulate" is to suggest something rather too deliberate and self-conscious). In old-fashioned language, it is a transcendent belief; it goes beyond the evidence.

Thus there is no logical absurdity in denying or refusing to admit the existence of a material world. To say that there are no physical objects, while doubtless very foolish, does not involve a man in any logical contradiction, nor does it force him to shut his eyes to any patent and indisputable facts. An intellectually indolent percipient, whose few wants were supplied independently of his own efforts, might well abstain from supposing that there was a physical world. There is some evidence that young babies, who are more or less in this situation, do not believe that there are any material things—do not believe, for instance, that the rattle just dropped from the hand and the visitor just departed from the room are now anywhere at all.

If somebody did behave like this, in what way would he be worse off, and what other beliefs would he be debarred from entertaining? I answer—and this is my principal point—that he would be unable to make valid generalizations, or reliable forecasts of his future experience. He would have to do without the belief in an order in nature, in regular sequences of events, in causal laws. For if I confine myself to what I myself observe or am aware of, I can make no valid generalizations concerning the concomitance or sequence of types of phenomena. I find only that phenomena of one type are quite often accompanied or followed by phenomena of another type, but sometimes not. There is no type of sense-datum A of which it is true that whenever it occurs another type of sense-datum B accompanies or follows or precedes it. And this is the case however complex you make your A and your B. This point has often been overlooked. People know quite well that lightning is always accompanied by thunder, barking by the presence of dogs, that green apples are always sour, and the ground always gets dark and sticky after a heavy fall of rain; and they talk about these as though they were *phenomenal* regularities—as though the seeing of lightning always went along with the hearing of thunder, and so forth. But this is of course not the case. If, as some people have said, it was the business of science to disclose the order or regularity in phenomena, meaning by phenomena what we see and hear and feel, science would be a very unrewarding pursuit. For phenomena are disorderly and irregular, and scientists cannot make them out any different.

Many philosophers have indeed thought that natural regularities could be conceived without the postulation of actual unobserved things and events, if instead we postulate that certain phenomena would occur or would have occurred, given certain unfulfilled conditions. Instead of saying that whenever I hear barking there exists an actual dog, perceived or unperceived, I am to say that whenever I hear barking, I should perceive a dog if certain conditions were fulfilled—if my eyes were open and my sight normal, if there was an adequate amount of light, if I looked in the right direction and there was no opaque obstacle in my line of vision, etc. Such an interpretation in terms of possible phenomena would relieve us of any need to postulate another order of physical events over and above perceptual events, and would in this way be more economical. There are, however, three ways in which phenomenal generalizations of this kind cannot take the place of physical generalizations.

(1) A physical generalization associates one uniform property with another uniform property: I mean that when something is asserted to be universally true of dogs, or pieces of iron, or cases of pneumonia, or falling bodies of a weight of ten pounds, it is assumed that there is some physical property or group of properties which is common to all dogs, pieces of iron, etc. Phenomenal generalizations, however, concern associations between sets of diverse phenomena. If we wish to correlate the auditory phenomenon of barking with visual phenomena we must specify a set of canine sense-data, or views of dogs, which are not all alike in any sensory property, but form one class only in virtue of a very complex set of relations.

(2) A physical generalization applies to *all* cases of a given type, and the study of nature aims at reducing to laws all events and all features of events. But phenomenal generalizations can never apply to all cases of a given type, but only to some of them, namely to those cases in which the supplementary conditions for observation are fulfilled. The physical generalization "There's no smoke without fire" applies to all instances of smoke, whether or not either the smoke or the

fire is observed. But the corresponding phenomenal generalization brings under a uniformity-rule only those cases in which both the smoke and the fire are observed. Observed smoke can be correlated with observed fire; when I observe the smoke but not the fire, the observed smoke is correlated with nothing, and is an instance of no natural law (except in the forced and trivial sense in which a white cat with brown eyes and quick hearing is an instance of the law that all white cats with blue eyes are deaf); it forms no part of the order of nature.

(3) A phenomenal generalization must always include a reference to conditions of observation, whereas physical generalizations are independent of these. We can say without qualification "Whenever it thunders, it lightens." But we can say "Whenever thunder is heard, lightning is seen" only if we add "provided that there is an observer with adequate eyesight, facing in the appropriate direction, having his eyes open and his view not obscured by any opaque object, etc." This difference does not merely prevent the phenomenal generalization from adequately replacing the physical one. It also means that there can be no generalizations on the phenomenal level which are universally valid. For it is impossible to give in purely phenomenal terms an adequate statement of all the conditions required for perceiving lightning besides the occurrence of lightning. It is curious that the analysis of physical-objects statements in terms of sense-data and the analysis of causation in terms of regular sequence should have been so often advocated by the same philosophers. For if we restrict our attention to phenomena, we can find no instances for the regular-sequence concept of cause to apply to.

If therefore, I am to make reliable generalizations about the course of events, and reliable forecasts about my future experiences, I must suppose that there are unperceived as well as perceived events. Thus the connection between the category of substance and that of cause is, as Kant suggested, not fortuitous but necessary. We do not discover that there are (perfect) regularities in nature, that is, in the physical world, as we discover that there are (imperfect) regularities amongst phenomena. On the contrary, the regularity is essential to the concept of nature; the assumption that the physical world is orderly is inseparable from the assumption that the physical world exists. It is only to the extent that I assume it to be orderly that I have any grounds for believing that there is a physical world at all. This may help to account for our strong inclination to regard physical determinism as a necessary a priori truth.

What, then, is the sort of supposition which will make it possible to believe in regular sequences and concomitances in the world, and to regulate our expectations accordingly? A simple and comprehensive answer cannot be given to this question. The precise character of the suppositions we make about physical objects and processes is subject to variation for different kinds of case, and to modification with the improvement of our knowledge. One can, however, indicate the general line which must be followed.

There are, amongst the events which we are aware of, certain associations of characteristics which, while not invariable, are very common: for example, the association between the sound of barking and the sight of dogs, between this visual appearance of oranges and their characteristic flavour, between the brightness of sunshine and felt warmth, between the kinaesthetic sensations of speech and the sound of my own voice, between the visible immersion of a lump of sugar in a cup of tea and its gradual disappearance, between the various members of the visible sequence black-coal . . . flame . . . red-coal . . . ashes, between the patter of raindrops, the sight of rain falling, the feeling of dampness on exposed parts of the body, and the darkening of the soil or pavement. (These are, of course, examples of several different kinds of association.)

The supposition required has two parts: (1) That to these imperfect phenomenal regularities there corresponds in each case a perfect physical regularity, that is, in each case in which there is a frequent association between phenomenal characteristics there are some corresponding physical characteristics which are invariably associated. Whereas the sound of barking is often but not always accompanied by the sight of a dog, there is some type of event, physical barking, which is always accompanied by the presence of some one type of physical object, a dog. Whereas the visual brightness of sunshine is only sometimes accompanied by a feeling of warmth, there is a physical entity, sunlight, and a physical entity, heat, which always goes with it. Whereas a person may be seen setting off from A and arriving at B without being seen at intermediate places at intermediate times, physical passage from A to B involves the temporally continuous traversing of a spatially continuous path. In general, whenever there is an imperfect but frequent association between a phenomenal characteristic A and a phenomenal characteristic B, there is a thing or process having a characteristic corresponding to A which is invariably associated with a thing or process having a characteristic corresponding to B. Thus whenever I hear barking, there exists a physical dog, whether or not there also occurs the experience of my seeing him.

(2) The existence of the corresponding physical thing, or the occurrence of the corresponding physical process, is a necessary but not a sufficient condition for the awareness of the phenomenal characteristic. There can be no hearing of barks without their being (physical) barks; but there can be barks without the hearing of barks. The

further conditions, other than the existence of the dog or the occurrence of the bark, which are required if I am to have the corresponding perception of the dog or the bark, may be called the observation-conditions. Some of these conditions are pretty easy to discover. For instance, if I am to see anything at all, there must be a certain amount of light (but not enough to dazzle), and my vision must not be blocked by any obstacle. Other observation-conditions can only be discovered by much experimental research: for instance, the need for air or some other transmitting medium in the case of hearing, the need for integrity of the optic nerves in the case of sight. The occurrence of the appropriate sense experience is determined jointly by the corresponding physical process and the relevant observation-conditions. (These conditions, of course, concern the properties of other physical things and processes, so that we cannot say just what they are without knowing something about physical things other than the one to be perceived. Learning about the properties of dogs, and learning about the properties of light and the human sense-organs, go hand in hand.) Thus the assumption of a physical world involves two supposed sets of regularities: an association between one physical characteristic and another, and an association between physical processes together with observation-conditions on the one hand and sense-experiences on the other.

So far, the physical world has been presented as a set of processes which occur independently of perceptions, which are related by laws of sequence and concomitance to other processes, and which together with the relevant observation-conditions determine specific sense-experiences of ours. These are purely relational properties; and nothing has been said so far about any other properties that physical objects may possess. On the view here advocated, namely that the justification of a belief in a physical world is that it makes possible the formulation of laws of nature, the only positive reason for attributing a property to physical objects would be that by assuming physical objects to possess this property we can account for the character of our perceptions, and explain how we come to perceive this rather than that, now rather than then. One way of accounting for the character of our perceptions would be to suppose that the sensory qualities which are present in them (the particular colours, sounds, tastes, etc.) are properties of physical objects, and persist unperceived just as they appear when perceived. This is naïve realism. A completely naïve-realist theory would hold that all sensory qualities are properties of physical objects, and exist independently of perception; other theories are naïvely realistic to the extent that they identify the properties of physical things with those properties which are present in sense-experience.

Now the investigation of the properties of physical things is the business of the science of physics. And contemporary physics is not naïvely realistic in any degree. The properties which it attributes to physical objects are not sensory properties, but hypothetical properties defined by their relations to one another and to certain kinds of perceptions. The reason for this is often misunderstood. Philosophical criticism of naïve realism is apt to concentrate on the "argument from illusion," that is, on the *deceptiveness* of sense-perception. This is the wrong sort of criticism. Our perceptions can sometimes mislead us (that is, lead us to form false expectations about other perceptions to come) only because they also, and more often, lead us to form true expectations; perception could not be systematically misleading. But the question whether our perceptions induce in us true or false expectations is quite independent of the question whether they show us the permanent characteristics of material things. The damaging criticisms of naïve realism rest on this principle: given that the physical object corresponding to a given sense-datum is something which, in conjunction with the relevant observation-conditions, determines the characteristics of that sense-datum, then if a given characteristic can be shown to be determined by the observation-conditions, there can be no reason for attributing it to the corresponding physical object. The successive modifications in our concept of the physical world arise from our increasing knowledge of the dependence of sensory properties upon observation-conditions. The challenge to naïve realism with respect to colours comes from optics. The challenge to naïve realism with respect to space and time comes from relativity-theory. The challenge to naïve realism with respect to beauty and ugliness comes from our understanding of the dependence of aesthetic delight and disgust upon the dispositions and past experiences of the subject.

In abandoning naïve realism, scientific theory only carries further a process which pre-scientific common sense has already begun. The common-sense view of the physical world is by no means a purely naïve-realist view. When I look at an object from different angles and in different lights successively, the sensory properties which appear to me are many and various. Common sense does not hold that all these various sensory properties belong to the physical object and exist apart from my perception. Were that so, there would have to be either a multitude of physical objects or a constantly changing object to possess all these different properties. Common sense holds, on the contrary, that there is but one object with one shape, size, colour etc., which is unchanging throughout my changing perceptions. This postulation of a single set of physical properties corresponding to a multiplicity of sensory properties is the first and fundamental step away from naïve realism. A Berkeleian analysis, which reverses this step, is a greater affront to common sense and provokes more resistance from it than a Lockean analysis which takes a step or two further in the same direction.

It is a belief of common sense that at least some sensory properties are not properties of physical objects, but are due to conditions of observation (quantity and quality of light, distance, defects of vision, etc.). As to whether *any* sensory properties are also physical properties, I am not convinced that common sense has any clear and consistent view. Of course we say that grass is green and roses are red. But does this mean more than if we look at them under suitable conditions green and red are the colour we shall see? It is not clear to me that common sense is committed to the belief that objects have any colours when unperceived. (Examining the way we talk about the matter is of no help. Given that a certain piece of cloth looks bluish in artificial light and greyish in daylight, are we to presume that its colour changes with changes in the light, and say "It *is* blue in artificial light and grey in daylight," or are we to presume that it has a colour independently of the light, and say "It is really grey, but it looks blue in artificial light?" Ordinary idiom allows us to say either of these things indifferently.) By contrast, there are some properties which common sense does attribute to physical objects apart from perception—size and weight, for instance. When I conclude that this brick must have made that hole in the window, though nobody saw it do so, I credit the brick with having a size and weight at a time when it was not being perceived. But size and weight are not sensory properties. Blueness is a way things look; but heaviness is not a way things look or feel. A thing can, of course, look or feel heavy; but its *being* heavy is something different—it is heavy if it will hold down or make dents in other objects, if you can't lift it with one hand, and so on; and these causal characteristics are no ways of looking or feeling. Properties like size and weight, which common sense does attribute to unperceived objects, bear the same sort of relation to sense-experience as the concepts of modern physics. Thus it seems to me that one can abandon naïve realism in all its forms without abandoning any belief to which common sense is committed.

To sum up. That there are physical objects is a supposition, not a datum. The use of the supposition is to account for the regularities in sensory phenomena, to enable the course of events to be set in a framework of regular sequences and concomitances. It is confirmed by the success we achieve in ordering our experiences by its aid, in making our generalizations continually more extensive and more exact. Being a supposition, and not an inevitable and invariable category of thought, it is subject to modification as we learn more about the conditions under which perception takes place. Scientific concepts are related to sense-experience in a remoter and more complex fashion than common-sense concepts of physical objects. But they are not of an entirely different order. The common-sense concept of "table" is not, like "blue" or "bang" or "stench," a merely phenomenal concept; it is explanatory and theoretical.

47. THE OBJECTS OF PERCEPTION ARE NOT SENSE-DATA

J. L. Austin

J. L. Austin (1911–1960) was White's Professor of Moral Philosophy at Oxford and Fellow of Corpus Christi College. Through his lectures and discussions, he contributed immensely to the development of the type of analytic philosophy usually called "ordinary language analysis." Austin's lectures, which were edited posthumously and published in 1962, are entitled How to Do Things with Words *and* Sense and Sensibilia. *His* Philosophical Papers *appeared in 1961.*

The primary purpose of the argument from illusion is to induce people to accept 'sense-data' as the proper and correct answer to the question what they perceive on certain *abnormal, exceptional* occasions; but in fact it is usually followed up with another bit of argument intended to establish that they *always* perceive sense-data. Well, what is the argument?

In Ayer's statement [1] it runs as follows. It is 'based on the fact that material things may present different appearances to different observers, or to the same observer in different conditions, and that the character of these appearances is to some extent causally determined by the state of the conditions and the observer.' As illustrations of this alleged fact Ayer proceeds to cite perspective ('a coin which looks circular from one point of view may look elliptical from another'); refraction ('a stick which normally appears straight looks bent when it is seen in water'); changes in colour-vision produced by drugs ('such as

From Sense and Sensibilia, *1962, Clarendon Press, Oxford, pp. 20–32. Reprinted by permission of the publisher, Clarendon Press, Oxford.*

[1] Ayer, *The Foundations of Empirical Knowledge*, pp. 3–5.

mescal'); mirror-images; double vision; hallucination; apparent variations in tastes; variations in felt warmth ('according as the hand that is
feeling it is itself hot or cold'); variations in felt bulk ('a coin seems
larger when it is placed on the tongue than when it is held in the palm
of the hand'); and the oft-cited fact that 'people who have had limbs
amputated may still continue to feel pain in them.'

He then selects three of these instances for detailed treatment.
First, refraction—the stick which normally 'appears straight' but 'looks
bent' when seen in water. He makes the 'assumptions' (*a*) that the
stick does not *really change its shape* when it is placed in water, and
(*b*) that it *cannot be* both crooked and straight.[2] He then concludes
('it follows') that 'at least one of the *visual appearances* of the stick is
delusive.' Nevertheless, even when 'what we see is not the *real quality*
of a *material thing*, it is supposed that we are still seeing something'—
and this something is to be called a 'sense-datum.' A sense-datum is to
be 'the object of which we are *directly* aware, in perception, if it is not
part of any *materail thing.*' (The italics are mine throughout this and
the next two paragraphs.)

Next, mirages. A man who sees a mirage, he says, is 'not perceiving any material thing; for the oasis which he thinks he is perceiving
does not exist.' But 'his *experience* is not an experience of nothing'; thus
'it is said that he is experiencing sense-data, which are similar in character to what he would be experiencing if he were seeing a real oasis,
but are delusive in the sense that *the material thing which they appear
to present* is not *really there.*'

Lastly, reflections. When I look at myself in a mirror 'my body
appears to be some distance behind the glass'; but it cannot actually
be in two places at once; thus, my perceptions in this case 'cannot all be
veridical.' But I do see *something;* and if 'there really is no such material
thing as my body in the place where it appears to be, what is it that I am
seeing?' Answer—a sense-datum. Ayer adds that 'the same conclusion
may be reached by taking any other of my examples.'

Now I want to call attention, first of all, to the name of this
argument—the 'argument from *illusion,*' and to the fact that it is produced as establishing the conclusion that some at least of our 'perceptions' are *delusive.* For in this there are two clear implications—(*a*) that
all the cases cited in the argument are cases of *illusions;* and (*b*) that
illusion and *delusion* are the same thing. But both of these implications,
of course, are quite wrong; and it is by no means unimportant to point

---

[2] It is not only strange, but also important, that Ayer calls these
'assumptions.' Later on he is going to take seriously the notion of denying at
least one of them, which he could hardly do if he had recognized them here
as the plain and incontestable facts that they are.

this out, for, as we shall see, the argument trades on confusion at just this point.

What, then, would be some genuine examples of illusion? (The fact is that hardly any of the cases cited by Ayer is, at any rate without stretching things, a case of illusion at all.) Well, first, there are some quite clear cases of *optical* illusion—for instance the case we mentioned earlier in which, of two lines of equal length, one is made to look longer than the other. Then again there are illusions produced by professional 'illusionists,' conjurors—for instance the Headless Woman on the stage, who is made to look headless, or the ventriloquist's dummy which is made to appear to be talking. Rather different—not (usually) produced on purpose—is the case where wheels rotating rapidly enough in one direction may look as if they were rotating quite slowly in the opposite direction. Delusions, on the other hand, are something altogether different from this. Typical cases would be delusions of persecution, delusions of grandeur. These are primarily a matter of grossly disordered beliefs (and so, probably, behaviour) and may well have nothing in particular to do with perception.[3] But I think we might also say that the patient who sees pink rats has (suffers from) delusions—particularly, no doubt, if, as would probably be the case, he is not clearly aware that his pink rats aren't real rats.[4]

The most important differences here are that the term 'an illusion' (in a perceptual context) does not suggest that something totally unreal is *conjured up*—on the contrary, there just is the arrangement of lines and arrows on the page, the woman on the stage with her head in a black bag, the rotating wheels; whereas the term 'delusion' *does* suggest something totally unreal, not really there at all. (The convictions of the man who has delusions of persecution can be *completely* without foundation.) For this reason delusions are a much more serious matter—something is really wrong, and what's more, wrong *with* the person who has them. But when I see an optical illusion, however well it comes off, there is nothing wrong with me personally, the illusion is not a little (or a large) peculiarity or idiosyncrasy of my own; it is quite public, anyone can see it, and in many cases standard procedures can be laid down for producing it. Furthermore, if we are not actually to be taken in, we need to be *on our guard;* but it is no use to tell the sufferer from delusions to be on his guard. He needs to be cured.

Why is it that we tend—if we do—to confuse illusions with delusions? Well, partly, no doubt the terms are often used loosely. But

---

[3] The latter point holds, of course, for *some* uses of 'illusion' too; there are the illusions which some people (are said to) lose as they grow older and wiser.

[4] Cp. the white rabbit in the play called *Harvey.*

there is also the point that people may have, without making this explicit, different views or theories about the facts of some cases. Take the case of seeing a ghost, for example. It is not generally known, or agreed, what seeing ghosts *is*. Some people think of seeing ghosts as a case of something being conjured up, perhaps by the disordered nervous system of the victim; so in their view seeing ghosts is a case of delusion. But other people have the idea that what is called seeing ghosts is a case of being taken in by shadows, perhaps, or reflections, or a trick of the light— that is, they assimilate the case in their minds to illusion. In this way, seeing ghosts, for example, may come to be labelled sometimes as 'delusion,' sometimes as 'illusion'; and it may not be noticed that it makes a difference which label we use. Rather, similarly, there seem to be different doctrines in the field as to what mirages are. Some seem to take a mirage to be a vision conjured up by the crazed brain of the thirsty and exhausted traveller (delusion), while in other accounts it is a case of atmospheric refraction, whereby something below the horizon is made to appear above it (illusion). (Ayer, you may remember, takes the delusion view, although he cites it along with the rest as a case of illusion. He says not that the oasis appears to be where it is not, but roundly that 'it does not exist.')

The way in which the 'argument from illusion' positively trades on not distinguishing illusions from delusions is, I think, this. So long as it is being suggested that the cases paraded for our attention are cases of *illusion*, there is the implication (from the ordinary use of the word) that there really is something there that we perceive. But then, when these cases begin to be quietly called delusive, there comes in the very different suggestion of something being conjured up, something unreal or at any rate 'immaterial.' These two implications taken together may then subtly insinuate that in the cases cited there really is something that we are perceiving, but that this is an immaterial something; and this insinuation, even if not conclusive by itself, is certainly well calculated to edge us a little closer towards just the position where the sense-datum theorist wants to have us.

So much, then—though certainly there could be a good deal more—about the differences between illusions and delusions and the reasons for not obscuring them. Now let us look briefly at some of the other cases Ayer lists. Reflections, for instance. No doubt you *can* produce illusions with mirrors, suitably disposed. But is just *any* case of seeing something in a mirror an illusion, as he implies? Quite obviously not. For seeing things in mirrors is a perfectly *normal* occurrence, completely familiar, and there is usually no question of anyone being taken in. No doubt, if you're an infant or an aborigine and have never come across a mirror before, you may be pretty baffled, and even visibly perturbed, when you do. But is that a reason why the rest of us should speak of illusion here? And just the same goes for the phenomena of perspective—again, one *can* play tricks with perspective, but in the ordinary case there is no question of illusion. That a round coin should 'look elliptical' (in one sense) from some points of view is exactly what we expect and what we normally find; indeed, we should be badly put out if we ever found this not to be so. Refraction again—the stick that looks bent in water—is far too familiar a case to be properly called a case of illusion. We may perhaps be prepared to agree that the stick looks bent; but then we can see that it's partly submerged in water, so that is exactly how we should expect it to look.

It is important to realize here how familiarity, so to speak, takes the edge off illusion. Is the cinema a case of illusion? Well, just possibly the first man who ever saw moving pictures may have felt inclined to say that here was a case of illusion. But in fact it's pretty unlikely that even he, even momentarily, was actually taken in; and by now the whole thing is so ordinary a part of our lives that it never occurs to us even to raise the question. One might as well ask whether producing a photograph is producing an illusion—which would plainly be just silly.

Then we must not overlook, in all this talk about illusions and delusions, that there are plenty of more or less unusual cases, not yet mentioned, which certainly aren't either. Suppose that a proof-reader makes a mistake—he fails to notice that what ought to be 'causal' is printed as 'casual'; does he have a delusion? Or is there an illusion before him? Neither, of course; he simply *misreads*. Seeing after-images, too, though not a particularly frequent occurrence and not just an ordinary case of seeing, is neither seeing illusions nor having delusions. And what about dreams? Does the dreamer see illusions? Does he have delusions? Neither; dreams are *dreams*.

Let us turn for a moment to what Price has to say about illusions. He produces,[5] by way of saying 'what the term "illusion" means,' the following 'provisional definition': 'An illusory sense-datum of sight or touch is a sense-datum which is such that we tend to take it to be part of the surface of a material object, but if we take it so we are wrong.' It is by no means clear, of course, what this dictum itself means; but still, it seems fairly clear that the definition doesn't actually fit all the cases of illusion. Consider the two lines again. Is there anything here which we tend to take, wrongly, to be part of the surface of a material object? It doesn't seem so. We just see the two lines, We don't think or even tend to think that we see anything else, we aren't even raising the question whether anything is or isn't 'part of the surface' of—what, anyway? the lines? the page?—the trouble is just that one line looks longer

---

[5] *Perception,* p. 27.

than the other, though it isn't. Nor surely, in the case of the Headless Woman, is it a question whether anything is or isn't part of her surface; the trouble is just that she looks as if she had no head.

It is noteworthy, of course, that, before he even begins to consider the 'argument from illusion,' Price has already incorporated in this 'definition' the idea that in such cases there is something to be seen *in addition to* the ordinary things—which is part of what the argument is commonly used, and not uncommonly taken, to *prove*. But this idea surely has no place in an attempt to say what 'illusion' *means*. It comes in again, improperly I think, in his account of perspective (which incidentally he also cites as a species of illusion)—'a distant hillside which is full of protuberances, and slopes upwards at quite a gentle angle, will appear flat and vertical. . . . This means that the sense-datum, the colour-expanse which we sense, actually *is* flat and vertical.' But why should we accept this account of the matter? Why should we say that there is *anything* we see which *is* flat and vertical, though not 'part of the surface' of any material object? To speak thus is to assimilate all such cases to cases of delusion, where there *is* something not 'part of any material thing.' But we have already discussed the undesirability of this assimilation.

Next, let us have a look at the account Ayer himself gives of some at least of the cases he cites. (In fairness we must remember here that Ayer has a number of quite substantial reservations of his own about the merits and efficacy of the argument from illusion, so that it is not easy to tell just how seriously he intends his exposition of it to be taken; but this is a point we shall come back to.)

First, then, the familiar case of the stick in water. Of this case Ayer says (*a*) that since the stick looks bent but is straight, 'at least one of the visual appearances of the stick is *delusive*'; and (*b*) that 'what we see [directly anyway] is not the real quality of [a few lines later, not part of] a material thing.' Well now: does the stick 'look bent' to begin with? I think we can agree that it does, we have no better way of describing it. But of course it does *not* look *exactly* like a bent stick, a bent stick out of water—at most, it may be said to look rather like a bent stick partly immersed *in* water. After all, we can't help seeing the water the stick is partly immersed in. So exactly what in this case is supposed to be *delusive?* What is wrong, what is even faintly surprising, in the idea of a stick's being straight but looking bent sometimes? Does anyone suppose that if something is straight, then it jolly well has to *look* straight at all times and in all circumstances? Obviously no one seriously supposes this. So what mess are we supposed to get into here, what is the difficulty? For of course it has to be suggested that there *is* a difficulty—a difficulty, furthermore, which calls for a pretty radical solution, the introduction of sense-data. But what is the problem we are invited to solve in this way?

Well, we are told, in this case you are seeing *something;* and what is this something 'if it is not part of any material thing'? But this question is, really, completely mad. The straight part of the stick, the bit not under water, is presumably part of a material thing; don't we see that? And what about the bit *under* water?—we can see that too. We can see, come to that, the water itself. In fact what we see is *a stick partly immersed in water;* and it is particularly extraordinary that this should appear to be called in question—that a question should be raised about *what* we are seeing—since this, after all, is simply the description of the situation with which we started. It was, that is to say, agreed at the start that we were looking at a stick, 'a material thing,' part of which was under water. If, to take a rather different case, a church were cunningly camouflaged so that it looked like a barn, how could any serious question be raised about what we see when we look at it? We see, of course, *a church* that now *looks like a barn.* We do *not* see an immaterial barn, an immaterial church, or an immaterial anything else. And what in this case could seriously tempt us to say that we do?

Notice, incidentally, that in Ayer's description of the stick-in-water case, which is supposed to be prior to the drawing of any philosophical conclusions, there has already crept in the unheralded but important expression 'visual appearances'—it is, of course, ultimately to be suggested that all we *ever* get when we see is a visual appearance (whatever that may be).

Consider next the case of my reflection in a mirror. My body, Ayer says, 'appears to be some distance behind the glass'; but as it's in front, it can't really be behind the glass. So what am I seeing? A sense-datum. What about this? Well, once again, although there is no objection to saying that my body 'appears to be some distance behind the glass,' in saying this we must remember what sort of situation we are dealing with. It does not 'appear to be' there in a way which might tempt me (though it might tempt a baby or a savage) to go round the back and look for it, and be astonished when this enterprise proved a failure. (To say that A is *in* B doesn't always mean that if you open B you will find A, just as to say that A is *on* B doesn't always mean that you could pick it off—consider 'I saw my face in the mirror,' 'There's a pain in my toe,' 'I heard him on the radio,' 'I saw the image on the screen,' &c. Seeing something in a mirror is not like seeing a bun in a shop-window.) But does it follow that, since my body is not actually located behind the mirror, I am not seeing a material thing? Plainly not. For one thing, I can see the mirror (nearly always anyway).

I can see my own body 'indirectly,' *sc*. in the mirror. I can also see the reflection of my own body or, as some would say, a mirror-image. And a mirror-image (if we choose this answer) is not a 'sense-datum'; it can be photographed, seen by any number of people, and so on. (Of course there is no question here of either illusion or delusion.) And if the question is pressed, what actually *is* some distance, five feet say, behind the mirror, the answer is, not a sense-datum, but some region of the adjoining room.

The mirage case—at least if we take the view, as Ayer does, that the oasis the traveller thinks he can see 'does not exist'—is significantly more amenable to the treatment it is given. For here we are supposing the man to be genuinely deluded, he is *not* 'seeing a material thing.'[6] We don't actually have to say, however, even here that he is 'experiencing sense-data'; for though, as Ayer says above, 'it is convenient to give a name' to what he is experiencing, the fact is that it already has a name— a *mirage*. Again, we should be wise not to accept too readily the statement that what he is experiencing is *'similar in character* to what he would be experiencing if he were seeing a real oasis.' For is it at all likely, really, to be very similar? And, looking ahead, if we were to concede this point we should find the concession being used against us at a later stage—namely, at the stage where we shall be invited to agree that we see sense-data always, in normal cases too.

SUGGESTIONS FOR FURTHER READING

(The following list of works is highly selective; it includes only those books which a beginner in philosophy should find fairly comprehensible and illuminating.)

GENERAL INTRODUCTIONS

Beardsley, E. L., and Beardsley, M. C., *Philosophical Thinking*. New York: Harcourt Brace Jovanovich, 1965.

Cornman, J. W., and Lehrer, K., *Philosophical Problems and Arguments: An Introduction*. New York: The Macmillan Company, 1968.

Hospers, John, *An Introduction to Philosophical Analysis*. Englewood Cliffs, N.J.: Prentice-Hall, Inc., 1953.

Nielsen, Kai, *Reason and Practice*. New York: Harper & Row, Publishers, 1971.

Westphal, Fred, *The Activity of Philosophy: A Concise Introduction*. Englewood Cliffs, N.J.: Prentice-Hall, Inc., 1969.

---

[6] Not even 'indirectly,' no such thing is 'presented.' Doesn't this seem to make the case, though more amenable, a good deal less useful to the philosopher? It's hard to see how normal cases could be said to *very like* this.

The Art of Philosophy

PART ONE: WHAT IS PHILOSOPHY?

Britton, Karl, *Philosophy and the Meaning of Life*. Cambridge University Press, 1970.

Dewey, John, *Reconstruction in Philosophy*. Boston: Beacon Press, 1957.

Johnstone, H. W., Jr. (ed.), *What is Philosophy?* New York: The Macmillan Company, 1965.

Passmore, John, "Philosophy," in *The Encyclopedia of Philosophy*, Vol. 6, edited by Paul Edwards. New York: The Macmillan Company, 1967.

PART TWO: THE PROBLEM OF GOD

Blackstone, William T., *The Problem of Religious Knowledge*. Englewood Cliffs, N.J.: Prentice-Hall, Inc., 1963.

Flew, Antony, *God and Philosophy*. Delta Books, 1966.

Hick, John (ed.), *The Existence of God*. New York: The Macmillan Company, 1964.

Hick, John, *Philosophy of Religion*. Englewood Cliffs, N.J.: Prentice-Hall, Inc., 1963.

Pike, Nelson (ed.), *God and Evil*. Englewood Cliffs, N.J.: Prentice-Hall, Inc., 1964.

PART THREE: THE PROBLEM OF MIND AND IMMORTALITY

Campbell, Keith, *Body and Mind*. Garden City, N.Y.: Doubleday & Company, Inc., 1970.

Shaffer, Jerome, *Philosophy of Mind*. Englewood Cliffs, N.J.: Prentice-Hall, Inc., 1968.

Vesey, G. N. A. (ed.), *Body and Mind*. New York: Humanities Press, Inc., 1964.

White, Alan R., *The Philosophy of Mind*. New York: Random House, Inc., 1967.

PART FOUR: THE PROBLEM OF FREE ACTION

Berofsky, B. (ed.), *Free Will and Determinism*. New York: Harper & Row, Publishers, 1966.

Langford, Glenn, *Human Action*. Garden City, N.Y.: Doubleday & Company, Inc., 1971.

O'Connor, D. J., *Free Will*. Garden City, N.Y.: Doubleday & Company, Inc., 1971.

Pears, D. F. (ed.), *Freedom and the Will*. New York: St. Martin's Press, Inc., 1963.

PART FIVE: THE PROBLEM OF MORALITY

Baier, Kurt, *The Moral Point of View*. New York: Random House, Inc., 1965.
Bayles, M. D. (ed.), *Contemporary Utilitarianism*. Anchor, 1968.
Frankena, William, *Ethics*. Englewood Cliffs, N.J.: Prentice-Hall, Inc., 1963.
Hare, R. M., *Freedom and Reason*. Oxford University Press, 1965.
Moore, G. E., *Ethics*. Oxford University Press, 1912.
Nowell-Smith, P. H., *Ethics*. Baltimore: Penguin Books, Inc., 1954.
Oldenquist, A. (ed.), *Readings in Moral Philosophy*. Boston: Houghton Mifflin Company, 1965.
Rachels, J. (ed.), *Moral Problems*. New York: Harcourt Brace Jovanovich, 1971.
Wasserstrom, R. A., (ed.), *Morality and the Law*. Belmont, Calif.: Wadsworth Publishing Company, Inc., 1971.
——, *War and Morality*. Belmont, Calif.: Wadsworth Publishing Company, Inc., 1970.

PART SIX: THE PROBLEM OF KNOWLEDGE

Ayer, A. J., *The Problem of Knowledge*. Baltimore: Penguin Books, Inc., 1956.
Chisholm, R. M., *Theory of Knowledge*. Englewood Cliffs, N.J.: Prentice-Hall, Inc., 1966.
Pears, D. F., *What is Knowledge?* New York: Harper & Row, Publishers, 1971.
Scheffler, Israel, *Conditions of Knowledge*. Glenwood, Ill.: Scott, Foresman & Company, 1965.
Woozley, A. D., *Theory of Knowledge: An Introduction*. Hutchinson, 1960.